WAR IN THE BALKANS, 1991-2002

U.S. Interests in the Balkans ...

- implications for future of NATO
- future of EU-NATO relations
- Reputation (finishing the job in the region)
- Regional stability (control criminal trafficking, heading off state failure, etc.)
- Reinforcing US-EU relations

R. Craig Nation

August 2003

*****

Comments pertaining to this report are invited and should be forwarded to: Director, Strategic Studies Institute, U.S. Army War College, 122 Forbes Ave., Carlisle, PA 17013-5244. Copies of this report may be obtained from the Publications Office by calling (717) 245-4133, FAX (717) 245-3820, or be e-mail at *Rita.Rummel@carlisle.army.mil*

*****

Most 1993, 1994, and all later Strategic Studies Institute (SSI) monographs are available on the SSI Homepage for electronic dissemination. SSI's Homepage address is: *http://www.carlisle.army.mil/ssi/*

*****

The Strategic Studies Institute publishes a monthly e-mail newsletter to update the national security community on the research of our analysts, recent and forthcoming publications, and upcoming conferences sponsored by the Institute. Each newsletter also provides a strategic commentary by one of our research analysts. If you are interested in receiving this newsletter, please let us know by e-mail at *outreach@carlisle.army.mil* or by calling (717) 245-3133.

ISBN 1-58487-134-2

CONTENTS

FOREWORD

This book, by Dr. R. Craig Nation, was written to address the need for a comprehensive history of the Balkan wars provoked by the collapse of the Yugoslav Federation in 1991. These wars, and the instability that they have provoked, became preoccupations for international security management through the 1990s. After an initial phase of distancing and hesitation, Balkan conflict drew the United States and its most important European allies into an open-ended commitment to peace enforcement, conflict management, and peace-building in the region, importantly supported by the U.S. Army. These efforts are still underway, and significant tensions and potential flashpoints remain in place within former Yugoslavia and the entire Southeastern European area. The lessons learned from the new Balkan wars, and the successes and failures of U.S. and international engagement, provide a significant foundation for future efforts to manage intractable regional conflict.

Dr. Nation's work has been supported by a research grant provided by the U.S. Army War College, and is published under the auspices of the Strategic Studies Institute. The Army War College's primary mission is to prepare new generations of strategic leaders to assume positions of responsibility within the U.S. armed forces and civilian arms of the national security system. That mission includes a serious confrontation with the most pressing security issues of our time, to include the nature of contemporary armed conflict and the changing nature of war itself. The Balkan conflict of the 1990s, as a case study in state failure and medium intensity warfare, international conflict management and intervention, and U.S. military engagement, provides an excellent framework for asking basic questions about the dynamic of international security at the dawn of a new millennium. *War in the Balkans, 1991-2002* is intended to provide a foundation for addressing such questions by surveying events in both contemporary and larger historical perspectives and posing preliminary conclusions concerning their larger meaning.

There will, regretfully, be other situations comparable in broad outline to the violent decline and fall of socialist Yugoslavia. The policies of the international community in the Yugoslav imbroglio have been criticized widely as ineffective. However, in the end, after years of futility, the conflict could be contained only by a significant international military intervention spearheaded by the United

States, and a long-term, multilateral commitment to post-conflict peace-building. Few would wish to pose the outcome as a model to be emulated, but it should be a case from which we can learn.

DOUGLAS C. LOVELACE, JR.
Director
Strategic Studies Institute

PREFACE

Armed conflict on the territory of the former Yugoslavia between 1991 and 2001 claimed over 200,000 lives, gave rise to atrocities unseen in Europe since the Second World War, and left behind a terrible legacy of physical ruin and psychological devastation. Unfolding against the background of the end of cold war bipolarity, the new Balkan wars sounded a discordant counterpoint to efforts to construct a more harmonious European order, were a major embarrassment for the international institutions deemed responsible for conflict management, and became a preoccupation for the powers concerned with restoring regional stability. After more than a decade of intermittent hostilities the conflict has been contained, but only as a result of significant external interventions and the establishment of a series of de facto international protectorates, patrolled by UN, NATO, and EU sponsored peacekeepers with open-ended mandates.

The 1990s saw numerous regional conflicts—Haiti, Colombia, Tajikistan, the Caucasus, Chechnya, Afghanistan, Nepal, Sri Lanka, the Middle East, Somalia, Sudan, Rwanda, Sierre Leone, Congo—that were comparable to or, in some cases, more destructive than the Balkan war. Few of these contests have received anything like the intense scrutiny devoted to the Balkans, for reasons good and bad. The Balkans is a part of Europe, and therefore more accessible to scrutiny by the international media, and engagement by external powers, than conflicts waged in less developed and approachable regions. The atrocities committed in the Balkans were no more or less lamentable than those carried out in parallel conflicts in Africa, Latin America, or Asia, but they were prominently displayed and extensively discussed on televised news reports. The resulting impact on elite and public opinion made the Balkan conflict politically compelling—it was a war that could not be ignored. The Balkans has been an object of international political competition for centuries, and many of the great European and Eurasian powers have long-standing interests in the region. Once the stasis of the cold war system was broken, traditional perceptions of interest were quick to reemerge, perhaps to the surprise of the contending parties themselves. From the outset, therefore, the Balkan war was shaped by great power intervention—whether in support of local allies,

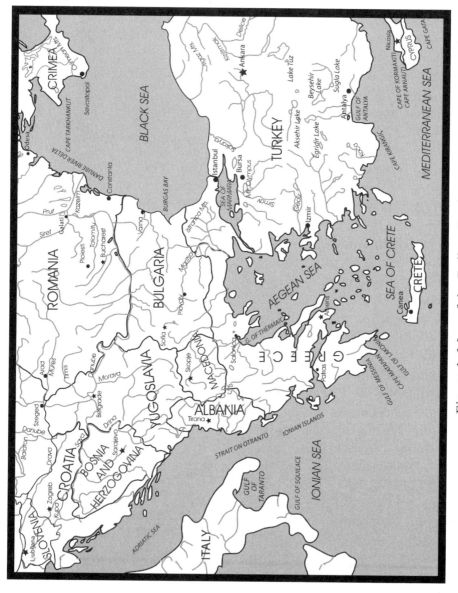

Figure 1. Map of the Balkan Region.

in the name of conflict resolution, or with an eye to the long-term benefits to be derived from geopolitical realignment in what was still regarded as a strategically relevant world region. The Balkan conflict was a part of the generic phenomenon of post-communist transition in Central and Eastern Europe as a whole, a dynamic with major implications for international relations.[1] It has likewise, and correctly, been perceived as a kind of testing ground for international conflict management efforts in the post-cold war era.

The Balkan war also posed world order concerns. The root cause of the conflict was the destruction of the multinational Yugoslav federation as a result of the rise of an intolerant and exclusionary nationalism among its constituent nations. How can the explosive demands of a politics of identity be contained in a world where the ideal of the ethnically pure nation-state is largely a myth, and agendas for self-determination retain a tremendous destructive potential? The collapse of Yugoslavia gave rise to political violence that local actors proved incapable of managing. What, if anything, is the responsibility of the international community faced with the chaos engendered by failed states and regional instability, and what international institutions are best adapted to confront such responsibilities?[2] The Balkan conflict provided familiar examples of the ethical challenges posed by modern war—lack of restraint in poorly controlled civil conflicts with a powerful ethnic or civilizational component, systematic violence against non-combatants elevated to the status of a strategy for waging war, and the moral and legal dilemmas of effective intervention in cases where the great powers are not in accord and clear cut choices between "good guys and bad guys" are simply not available. Does the premise of humanitarian intervention justify preemptive action in such cases, even without a mandate from valid international instances? Has international humanitarian law evolved to the point where standards of conduct can effectively be enforced by vested supranational authorities, and should such standards be imposed upon intervening parties as well? The economic consequences of armed conflict in the impoverished Balkans, for the belligerents themselves and for their immediate neighbors, have been particularly heavy. How can an agenda for peace building, including reconciliation and economic recovery, be forwarded in historically marginalized areas that confront a large and widening developmental gap? Such questions are not unique to the region under consideration, but the ways in which they are addressed in the Balkan case will set precedents with global reverberations.

The Balkan conflict has become the subject of a small library of journalistic reflection and scholarly analysis. The present study is nonetheless one of only a few recent interpretations that seek to look at the war as a whole.[3] It rests upon several basic assumptions about the nature of the conflict and the way in which it should be interpreted.

First, the war is considered as a single, protracted contest with a consistent strategic logic — the redistribution of peoples and terrain within the collapsing Yugoslav federation. Though it was always a contested country, Yugoslavia had for many years served as a source of stability in the Balkans by providing a framework for positive cohabitation between diverse ethnic groups and an alternative to self-destructive nationalism.[4] From the prelude in Slovenia in 1991, through the more destructive conflicts in Croatia, Bosnia-Herzegovina, and Kosovo between 1992 and 1999, to the epilogue in Macedonia in 2000-2001, what I prefer to call the War of Yugoslav Succession has been about efforts to assert sovereignty over territory in the absence of any kind of agreement concerning how the collapsing federation might have been reorganized, or disassembled, short of a resort to force. Slobodan Milošević has been singled out for special censure for his blatant manipulation of Serbian nationalism in order to secure a hold on power, and willingness to resort to blood and iron in order to carve a greater Serbia from the body of former Yugoslavia, but Milošević was only one of a generation of post-Tito leaders who opted to play the nationalist card in their respective republics in despite of the interests of the peoples of Yugoslavia as a whole. Though waged in the name of competing sovereignties, the War of Yugoslav Succession was essentially a civil war, with fellow citizens set at one another's throats at the behest of ruthless and unprincipled leaders engaged in a struggle for power and dominion. It has truly been a war without victors.

Second, although fighting was contained within the territory of the former Yugoslav federation, the impact of the conflict was not. The war had a significant regional dimension, both within the southeastern European region of which Yugoslavia was for so long an integral part, and in Europe as a whole. The War of Yugoslav Succession created a crisis of regional order, and gave rise to what might be described as a new Eastern Question, with the Balkans once again transformed into a zone of chronic instability. It was also a crisis of European order, the first major armed conflict on the continent since 1945 including abuses that most believed would "never again" be allowed to occur, and a challenge for which institutional Europe was painfully unprepared. America's belated involvement was in many ways a product of residual cold war dynamics that institutionalized European dependency upon U.S. leadership, as well as Europe's own chronic division and ineffectiveness as an international actor. At the present juncture precipitous U.S. disengagement would not be a positive option, but in the long-term the Balkan crisis will only be resolved when the American role is reduced, and a more self-confident and unified Europe embraces the region, and its problems, as its own.[5] This study makes frequent reference to European perspectives on the conflict, which is portrayed as in essence a European dilemma demanding European solutions.

Third, the international dimension of the war is considered to be essential. The end of the cold war system from 1989 onward seemed to open up new prospects for great power activism, and the Yugoslav disaster provided a convenient opportunity to test long dormant mechanisms for international crisis management. From the first days of combat operations in Slovenia, the activist role of the international community contributed importantly to shaping outcomes. Even had a will to intervene not been so clearly manifest, the dynamic of the conflict itself made some degree of international engagement an imperative. The option to "let them fight it out among themselves" was never quite as attractive in practice as some have perceived it to be in retrospect. The incapacity of local actors to resolve their differences short of a resort to arms was revealed early on, and the conflict posed numerous issues with larger significance, including the integrity of Europe, the future of the UN and UN-sponsored peacekeeping operations, the viability of NATO, relations with the new Russian Federation, the role of militant Islam and relations between the West and the Islamic world, and the post-cold war responsibilities of the American superpower. Much was at stake, and the elevation during the conflict of provincial backwaters such as Vukovar, Knin, Srebrenica, or Račak to the status of focal points for international diplomacy was not incongruous. This study examines the dynamic of international conflict management, analyzes the international community's successes and failures, and attempts to specify lessons learned.

Finally, although the present work is not intended as a military history, considerable attention is directed toward the specifically military and strategic dimensions of the conflict.[6] The particular complexity of strategic rivalry within former Yugoslavia, with its overlapping nationalities, historically conditioned ethnic rivalries, and multiple adversaries, has led analysts towards an unavoidable concentration upon sorting out ethnographic detail. But the War of Yugoslav Succession was also an armed conflict of a specific type, perhaps best characterized by General Wesley Clark with the ambiguous designation "modern war."[7]

The ideologically charged division that defined so many of the regional conflicts of the 1970s and 1980s, driven forward by guerrilla organizations with varying kinds of Marxist-Leninist inspiration, and therefore neatly subsumable within the global logic of the Cold War, had by 1989 become a thing of the past. Whether the War of Yugoslav Succession is best characterized as an "ethnic" conflict generated by intolerant nationalism, or as a campaign inspired by unprincipled opportunists for a division of spoils in the wake of state failure, it posed entirely new kinds of challenges.[8] As a medium intensity conflict, fought out in an economically troubled and politically marginalized area, between belligerents whose military capacity did not allow them to become strategically significant actors, the issues at stake were no longer self-evidently vital from a great power standpoint. In theater, the incapacity of hastily assembled, sometimes ill-disciplined, often poorly motivated, and nearly always inadequately equipped local forces to impose strategic decision was a recipe for military stalemate. Traditional UN peacekeeping proved inadequate to the demands of a conflict where only robust peace enforcement measures promised results, but the motivation (in the case of the U.S.) and the means (in the case of Europe) for decisive intervention was lacking. Though some degree of great power involvement was inevitable, the extent of engagement that was appropriate, and specifically the relevance of military intervention, quickly became hotly contested issues, and have remained so. For the United States, as the only world power with truly global power projection capacity, and for the NATO alliance, Europe's only militarily competent security forum, the strategic dilemma posed by the Balkan conflict was considerable. NATO could not simply ignore the Balkans, but like other European and Euro-Atlantic institutions it was "woefully unprepared" for post-cold war problems, and its tentative engagement and preference for partial or symbolic measures designed to contain the fighting at low risk proved no more effective than UN peacekeeping.[9] In the end, it was only when the international community's inability to bring an end to the conflict came to be seen as politically damaging in Washington that an agenda for decisive military action was prepared. The issues posed by these events are significant, and they are by no means limited to the case of former Yugoslavia. Employing military means to manage regional conflict in the chaotic circumstances of the 21st century is likely to be a recurrent security problem for some time to come.

The Balkans is often described as a grim backwater, a "no man's land of world politics" in the words of a post-World War II study "foredoomed to conflict springing from heterogeneity."[10] The stereotype is false, but it has been distressingly influential in shaping perceptions of the Balkan conflict and its origin. By encouraging pessimism about prospects for recovery, it may also make it more difficult to sustain commitments to post conflict peace building. This book seeks to refute simplistic "ancient hatreds" explanations by looking carefully at the sources and dynamics of the Balkan conflict in all of its dimensions. Chapter One attempts to define the Balkans as a region and specify the kinds of historical trends that led to its marginalization in the modern period. Chapter Two looks at the evolution of the region during Eric Hobsbawm's short twentieth century, with special emphasis upon the strengths and weaknesses of the Yugoslav idea and post-World War II projects for an enlarged Balkan federation. Chapter Three turns to the long crisis of Yugoslav federalism following the death of Josip Broz Tito in 1980, culminating with the wars of secession in Slovenia and Croatia. Chapters Four and Five analyze the conflicts in Bosnia-Herzegovina and Kosovo with an eye to the problematic nature of the resolutions imposed by international intervention. The sixth chapter steps outside the confines of former Yugoslavia to focus on Greek-Turkish relations and the Cyprus question, regarded as particularly significant pieces of the Balkan regional puzzle, and as critical issues in any long-term program for recasting regional order. In Chapter Seven the aftermath of the conflicts of the 1990s is examined, with an analysis of the flare up of ethnic violence in Macedonia during 2000-2001 added to the mix. Though this is essentially a political history arranged as a chronological narrative, I attempt to place the conflict in the broadest possible context, with attention drawn to historical, cultural, political, and strategic variables. This is, I would assert, the most appropriate way to come to terms with the war's specific character and historical weight.

The Research and Publications Board of the U.S. Army War College provided a generous Temporal Research Grant allowing time off from teaching responsibilities in order for me to concentrate on the research and writing that made this work possible. I particularly thank the former Commandant of the College, General Robert Scales, and Director of the Department of National Security and Strategy, Colonel Joseph Cerami, for their support for scholarship as an integral part of senior military education and the discipline of strategic studies. The Institute for National Security Studies of the U.S. Air Force offered additional support for fieldwork in the region. I am indebted to Stefano Bianchini and my colleagues in the Europe and the Balkans International Network and Center for East Central European and Balkan Studies at the University of Bologna, with whom I struggled to understand Balkan issues during the entire duration of the war, and from whose insights I have benefited immeasurably whether or not I have agreed with them. Special thanks are due to my colleagues Colonels Alan Stolberg and Raymond Millen, for their careful and expert commentary on an earlier version of the manuscript. The conclusions offered in the book do not necessarily reflect the positions or policies of the Department of the Army, Department of Defense, or the U.S. Government. They represent a personal attempt to make sense of a great contemporary tragedy.

ENDNOTES

1. The interesting work by Marina Glamočak, *La transition guerrière yougoslave*, Paris: L'Harmattan, 2002, is one of the few studies that looks at this aspect of the Yugoslav problem systematically.

2. Mary Kaldor usefully characterizes such conflicts as post-communist "new wars" occasioned by the dynamic of globalization, which "occur in situations in which state revenues decline because of the decline of the economy as well as the spread of criminality, corruption, and inefficiency, violence is increasingly privatized both as a result of growing organized crime and the emergence of paramilitary groups, and political legitimacy is disappearing." Mary Kaldor, *New and Old Wars: Organized Violence in a Global Era*, Stanford: Stanford University Press, 1999, p. 5.

3. See Alessandro Marzo Magno, ed., *La Guerra dei dieci anni. Jugoslavia 1991-200: I fatti, i personaggi, le ragioni dei conflitti*, Milan: il Saggiatore, 2001 and Hannes Hofbauer, *Balkan Krieg: Zehn Jahre Zerstörung Jugoslawiens*, Vienna: ProMedia, 2001

4. The phrase "contested country" is from Aleksa Djilas, *The Contested Country: Yugoslav Unity and Communist Revolution, 1919-1953*, Cambridge, MA.: Harvard University Press, 1991.

5. See Edward C. Meyer, "America, too, Needs Balkan Stability," *The International Herald Tribune*, 12 December 2002.

6. Central Intelligence Agency analysts have produced a detailed military history of the conflicts in Slovenia, Croatia, and Bosnia-Herzegovina. Central Intelligence Agency, Office of Russian and European Analysis, *Balkan Battlegrounds: A Military History of the Yugoslav Conflict, 1990-1995*, 2 vols., Washington, D.C.: Central Intelligence Agency, May 2002. On the Kosovo conflict see Benjamin S. Lambeth, *NATO's Air War for Kosovo: A Strategic and Operational Assessment*, Santa Monica: RAND, 2001 and Bruce R. Nardulli, Walter L. Perry, Bruce Pirnie, John Gordon IV, and John G. McGinn, *Disjointed War: Military Operations in Kosovo, 1999*, Santa Monica: Rand, 2002.

7. Wesley K. Clark, *Waging Modern War: Bosnia, Kosovo, and the Future of Combat*, New York: Public Affairs, 2001, p. 419.

8. For the distinction between "greed and grievance" as sources of ethnic war see Mats Berdal and David M. Malone, eds., *Greed and Grievance: Economic Agendas in Civil Wars*, Boulder: Lynne Rienner, 2000, and Alex J. Bellamy, "Grievance and Greed," *The World Today*, April 2001, pp. 10-12.

9. Joyce P. Kaufman, *NATO and the Former Yugoslavia: Crisis, Conflict, and the Atlantic Alliance*, Lanham, MD: Rowman & Littlefield Publishers, Inc., 2002, p. 2.

10. Joseph S. Roucek, *Balkan Politics: International Relations in No Man's Land*, Stanford: Stanford University Press, 1948, p. 4.

CHAPTER 1

THE BALKAN REGION IN WORLD POLITICS

On Board the Orient Express.

It has become common to use the term Balkan as a synonym for backwardness and bigotry. The most widely read and influential account of the region written during the 1990s portrays it as a repository of sadism and violence, haunted by the "ghosts" of implacable enmity.[1] A prominent European diplomat, embittered by the failure of peacemaking efforts in Bosnia-Herzegovina, speaks with disdain of the subject of his mediation as "a culture of violence within a crossroads civilization."[2] Even the Turkish novelist Nedim Gürsel, a friend of the region whose family originates from Ottoman Üsküb (Skopje), laments that hatred between peoples condemned to coexist has become "the destiny of the Balkans."[3]

Such atavisms could be dismissed as Orientalist fantasies were it not for two inconvenient facts.[4] First, the perception of the Balkans as a region torn by violence and ethnic strife has an objective foundation. From the emergence of the first national liberation movements among the Christian subjects of the Ottoman Empire in the early 19th century, Southeastern Europe has been a chronically unstable European sub-region.[5] Clashes with the Ottomans culminated in the Balkan wars of 1912-1913, and in both 20th century world wars the Balkans was a significant theater of operations. A phase of equilibrium during the Cold War could not be sustained after the collapse of communism, and the new Balkan war of the 1990s has been the only major European armed conflict since 1945 (with the partial exception of the Greek civil war of 1945-1947, really a continuation of struggles born during the Second World War). Second, even when they are exaggerated or inaccurate, perceptions matter. The fact that the Balkans is widely viewed as an area of ancient hatreds, irrespective of whatever real merit the argument may have, has shaped, and continues to shape, the international community's approach toward the region and its problems.

What is the Balkans? The term itself, derived from Persian through Turkish, originally referred to a high house or mountain. It was incorporated into the phrase "Balkan Peninsula" by the

German geographer Johann August Zeune in 1808 to call attention to the area's mountainous terrain, but did not come into common use until the mid-19th century. The pejorative connotation that the designation Balkan has taken on has led to resistance to its use, and in some ways the more neutral term "Southeastern Europe" is a preferable alternative.[6] The Balkans, however, is more than just a peninsular extension of greater Europe. It is also a distinctive physical and cultural zone possessed of what Maria Todorova calls "historical and geographic concreteness."[7]

Most histories of the modern Balkans begin with a definition of the region based upon its physical characteristics. The Balkans is constituted as a peninsula, bounded by the Adriatic and Ionian Seas in the West, the Aegean Sea in the South, and the Black Sea in the East, and its ports of call have been a focus for commercial interaction since classical antiquity. Coastal areas and outlying island groups, with a more cosmopolitan background and milder Mediterranean climate, may be distinguished from inland regions, which are predominantly mountainous, relatively isolated, and subject to more severe continental weather patterns. Mountain barriers paralleling the coastline and an absence of navigable rivers cut the Balkan interior off from the sea. Unlike the Iberian and Italian Peninsulas, divided from the European heartland by the Pyrenees and the Alps, the Balkans opens to central Europe through the valley of the Danube and across the Pannonian plain. Internally, the region is fragmented by a series of mountain chains—the Julien Alps in the north, the Dinaric and Pindus mountains stretching dorsally along the peninsula's western flank, the Carpathians in the northeast, the Balkan mountains (the Haemus range of classical antiquity) running east-west through the heart of Bulgaria, and the Rhodope mountains paralleling them in the south beyond the valley of the Maritsa River and falling away toward the Aegean. The lack of well irrigated lowlands suitable for intensive agriculture has been an impediment to population growth. Mountainous terrain has encouraged cultural differentiation, and contributed to the failure of attempts at integration.[8]

As an exposed and strategically important area without a tradition of independent statehood, the Balkan Peninsula has served as a shatterbelt and point of confrontation between neighboring power complexes—one source, externally imposed, of the propensity toward violence purported to be an indigenous trait.[9] Sea, river, and overland lines of communication running adjacent to and across the region traverse a handful of critical chokepoints, which have been contested through the centuries. The route following the valley of the Danube from Central Europe to Belgrade, and continuing via the valley of the Morava to Niš, has always been a commercial and military artery of fundamental importance. From Niš one may proceed southward across the watershed into the valley of the Vardar (Axios) leading to the Aegean port of Thessalonica, southwestward across the pass of Thermopylae into Attica, or southeastward across the Dragoman Pass to Sofia, into the valley of the Maritsa to Plovdiv and Edirne, and beyond across the Thracian plain to Istanbul. There is no natural corridor attaching the Adriatic to the Balkan interior, though an east-west highway traversing the southern Balkans was constructed by the Romans beginning in 146A.D. This *Via Egnatia* was an extension, beyond the Adriatic, of the great Roman *Via Appia* linking Rome to Brindisi. It wound from what is today the Albanian port of Durrës across mountainous terrain through Elbassan, past Lake Okhrid and Bitola, and on to Thessalonica. Contemporary development projects feature efforts to recreate the Roman corridor as a modern highway net. Both north-south and east-west arteries cross the same critical strategic juncture in today's Republic of Macedonia.

Sea lines of communication through the Turkish Straits and the Strait of Otranto, paralleling the Anatolian coastline including the Dodecanese island group, and along the Albanian and Greek coasts, have been a focus for strategic rivalry into modern times, and the scene of a long list of famous naval encounters.[10] Istanbul possesses a fine natural harbor, and the Greek ports of Thessalonica and Piraeus are friendly rivals as commercial ports in the eastern Mediterranean. The northern Adriatic includes serviceable harbors in Trieste, Koper, Rijeka, and Split, which have to some extent entered into competition for commercial traffic linking the Adriatic with the central European capitals of Vienna and Budapest. Further to the south, the port of Kotor (on the Gulf of Kotor in Montenegro) is modern Serbia's only outlet to the sea. Albania possesses several suitable anchorages which are however woefully inadequate in terms of infrastructure. The breakup of modern Yugoslavia has made access to the Adriatic an especially important issue for land-locked Serbia, Macedonia, and Bosnia-Herzegovina.

The Balkans geographic situation has made it an obligatory point of passage for migrants and invaders moving between Asia Minor and Europe. Centuries of ebb and flow have left the region one of the most diverse in the world, with distinct ethnic, linguistic, and confessional groups often living intermingled or in close proximity. The classic example of Balkan inter-culturality was once Bosnia-Herzegovina, where prior to the outbreak of war in 1992 only two towns could claim a "pure" ethnic composition with a single community representing more than 90 percent of the inhabitants, none of the twenty-five largest districts possessed a dominant community representing more than 50 percent of the population, and the rate of intermarriage among communities exceeded 25 percent (40 percent in urban areas). Despite the ravages of "ethnic cleansing" during the 1990s, the Balkans remains a repository of distinctive cultures coexisting in close proximity. Managing and organizing the region's diverse human geography is a basic strategic challenge.[11]

Accounts of national origin are controversial in the Balkans, because they are often used to justify territorial claims. Several Balkan peoples claim descent from the region's earliest known inhabitants, though the assertions are sometimes disputed on scientific grounds, or by rival nationalities seeking to prove that "we were here first." The Albanians speak a distinctive Indo-European language and may be the ancestors of the ancient Illyrians, an Iron Age tribal community with roots in the area between the Morava river valley and the Adriatic. The Illyrians shared the peninsula with the Thracians, an Indo-European group that is believed to have established an organized community north of the Danube in the 5th century B.C. and may be the distant ancestors of today's Vlachs, a pastoral people scattered through Yugoslavia, Albanian, and Greece, speaking a Latin dialect close to Romanian. The Romanians themselves argue descent from the Dacians, a branch of the Thracian tribe that was conquered for Rome by the Emperor Trajan in 106 A.D. and thereafter, according to Romanian national interpretations, transformed by intermarriage into a "Romano-Dacian" amalgam. The modern Greeks claim the heritage of the Hellenes of classical antiquity.[12] Slavic tribes began to migrate into the Balkans in the 6th century, but centuries were required before modern distinctions between various branches of the South Slavic family (Slovenian, Croatian, Serbian, Macedonian, and Bulgarian) would evolve. The Proto-Bulgarians who arrived in the southern Balkans in the seventh century were Turkic tribespeople that would eventually be assimilated by the local Slavic majority. According to some accounts the original Serbs and Croats may also have been marauding tribes of Iranian origins who were gradually assimilated. Today's Slavic Muslim communities (the Muslims of Bosnia-Herzegovina, the Pomaks of Bulgaria and Greece, the Torbeši and Čtaci of Macedonia, the Goranci of Kosovo, and other groups) are the product of conversion during the medieval period.[13] These groups are also sometimes characterized as national communities, though they are distinguished from their neighbors by confessional orientation rather than ethnicity or national origin.[14]

Modern ethnic communities are often fragmented by conflicting national or sub-regional affiliations. Montenegrins have usually been regarded as a branch of the Serb family, but there is considerable local support for an independent identity. Albanians are split along the line of the Shkumbi River into a Tosk community in the south and a Gheg community in the north, distinguished by differences in dialect and socio-economic structures. Slavic Macedonians live within Macedonia proper, the Pirin Macedonia region of Bulgaria, and northern Greece. Moldovans are virtual Romanians, but with an independent state tradition and national identity. Numerous minority communities with distinctive local identities also occupy regional niches. The most widely dispersed is the Roma (Gypsy) community, whose roots spread through the entire Balkan region. The Balkan Roma have historically been targets for discrimination, and their situation has in many ways disintegrated in the post-communist period.[15]

The Balkans is commonly described as a point of intersection between the world's major monotheistic religions—Roman Catholic and Eastern Orthodox branches of the Christian faith, Islam, and the remnants of what were once significant Jewish communities in urban centers such as Istanbul, Sarajevo, and Thessalonica. Slovenes and Croats are predominantly Catholic, though Slovenia also contains a Protestant minority, prominently represented by current president Milan Kučan. In Serbia, Macedonia, Greece, Romania, and Bulgaria autocephalous branches of Eastern Orthodoxy predominate. Turkey is a secular state, but the overwhelming majority of its citizens (over 95 percent) profess Islam. Approximately 80 percent of the Albanian population of the Balkans is Islamic, but there is also a Catholic minority in the mountainous north of Albania proper, and an Orthodox minority in the south and central areas. The Muslims of Bosnia-Herzegovina represent the area's largest Slavic Muslim community, and were granted the status of constituent nation by Titoist Yugoslavia in 1961. Small Turkic communities are also scattered throughout the southern Balkans.

Confessional division has been an important component of the fighting that has traumatized former Yugoslavia since 1991. Some analysts have attempted to interpret the conflict on the basis of Samuel Huntington's "clash of civilizations" thesis, according to which strategic rivalry beyond cold war bipolarity will be focused along the "faultlines" dividing distinctive civilizational zones essentially defined by confessional orientation.[16] Huntington's thesis has been widely criticized, both for its tendency to transform differences between civilizations into absolute and unbridgeable barriers, and for a proclivity to impose fixed and arbitrary geographical contours onto what are actually complex patterns of cultural interaction. In the Balkans, organized religion has been one factor among many promoting conflict, but it has also served as a force for empathy and mutual understanding. In any case, religious diversity is an important part of the region's cultural specificity.[17]

The extent of the differences that define Balkan inter-culturality should not be exaggerated. The South Slavic peoples speak closely related and mutually comprehensible languages—more closely related than the variety of Latin dialects spoken along the length of the Italian Peninsula. The Croat, Serb, and Bosnian Muslim communities are distinguished by little more than an inherited or elected confessional orientation and patterns of subjective self-identification.[18] Catholic, Orthodox, and Islamic affiliation cuts across boundaries and provides space for the emergence of larger, trans-national communities inspired by what are, or should be, profoundly humane belief systems. Outside the region's Slavic areas, Greeks, Turks, Romanians, and (perhaps to a lesser extent) Albanians have established state traditions. Managing diversity in the region must be considered a challenge, but it is certainly not an impossible one. From the perspective of political geography the Balkans may be defined as an integral part of greater Europe, but also as a relatively autonomous sub-region with a clear geographical outline, a distinct historical background, and a specific cultural ambience. The conflicts of the past decade have focused attention on the region's many problems. Its accomplishments and potential are also worthy of note.

Traditional accounts emphasize the strategic importance of the Balkans as a land-bridge between the European, Asian, and African continents, and as an apple of discord within the European balance of power system. In classic geostrategic terms, many of the region's assets have declined in salience. Modern means of communication make a capacity to transit the region less vital than once was the case. Critical strategic resources are not at stake. The region's national economies are weak, and their attraction as potential markets is limited. No local power, with the exception of Turkey, is in a position to generate strategically relevant military forces, and engagement in the region by external actors no longer threatens to disrupt continental or global balances. The Balkans remains strategically relevant nonetheless. As a part of Europe, instability in the region will inevitably affect great power relations. The Turkish straits and entire eastern Mediterranean region have gained new relevance as the terminus for potential east-west pipeline routes carrying oil and natural gas resources from the Caspian oil hub onto international markets.[19] The fallout that could result from open-ended civilizational rivalry along Balkan fault lines is potentially quite great. And the sixty mile wide Strait of Otranto between Albania and Puglia has become sensitive as a conduit for criminal trafficking and boat people seeking a point of entry into the European Union.

The famous Orient Express train line, inaugurated in the latter decades of the 19th century to link western European capitals with Istanbul, was christened with reference both to its terminus and itinerary. Since the term Balkan came into common usage, the region has been viewed as a transition zone spanning "an accepted fundamental difference between Orient and Occident."[20] The distinctiveness of the Balkans as a European sub-region is without a doubt a product of cultural affiliations and social norms derived from involvement in both the central European and Ottoman experiences. But East and West are not mutually exclusive categories. Real historical interaction along the so-called faultlines that traverse the region has been at least as much defined by reciprocal influence and convergence as it has by confrontation and hostility.[21] Moreover, such perceptions risk undervaluing the extent to which the Balkans represents an entity in its own right, "a unity embedded in European civilization, quite different from the culture of central Europe or that of the west of the continent, but a unity characterized by a homogenous civilization despite the rifts occasioned by cultural, religious, historical, or political differences."[22] Efforts to deconstruct the Balkans on the basis of false and offensive civilizational distinctions, or to co-opt it as a peripheral extension of the "real" Europe, have been at the foundation of the violence of the past decade. Effective conflict management and post-conflict peace building must eventually return to projects for regional integration based upon shared affinities and a common legacy.

The World of Light.

In Homer's account of the Phoenician origins of Europe, Zeus, disguised as a swimming bull, abducts Europa, the daughter of the King of Tyre, and carries her off to the island of Crete where she bears him a son, King Minos.[23] The legend calls attention to the Asian sources of Greek civilization of the classical age, for which the eastern Mediterranean provided the setting. Indo-European peoples, some of whom were speaking a variant of the Greek language, are believed to have migrated into the area at the end of the third millennium B.C. From the beginning of the second millennium, the Minoan and Mycenaean civilizations of Crete and the Greek mainland initiated a civilizational tradition that was distinct from those that had preceded it in the Fertile Crescent and Egypt.[24] Doric colonization in the northern Aegean and Adriatic areas began in the 8th and 7th centuries B.C., leading to the cultural flowering of the classical Greek *polis* (city-state) in 5th century Athens. These are the foundations of what has come to be called Western Civilization.

In 336-323 B.C. Alexander of Macedon ("the Great") swept aside the remnants of the Greek city-state system and used the Balkans as a base for a campaign of conquest that penetrated into the heart of Asia. In the course of the 2nd century Macedon fell in turn to the expanding power of Rome, which gradually transformed the Balkans into a series of Roman provinces. The Romans subjugated the Greek world strategically, absorbed it politically, and derived great economic advantage from control of the trade routes leading eastward to the Black Sea. They also adopted the region's indigenous culture, the Hellenistic civilization of the Greek East. Hellenism, grounded in the social and political legacy of classical Greek civilization but also a living tradition that absorbed new influences and continued

8

to evolve over centuries, became an early source of differentiation between East and West.[25]

The Hellenistic world was gradually absorbed into the Eastern Roman Empire, focused on the city of Constantinople, with its unparalleled strategic situation on a promontory at the confluence of the Bosphorus and the Sea of Marmara. Constantinople was inaugurated on 11 May 330, on the site of the ancient fortress town of Byzantion, and christened in honor of the emperor Constantine as "New Rome which is Constantinople." The formal division of the Roman Empire into western and eastern branches occurred at the conclusion of the reign of Emperor Theodosius Flavius in 395. After the sack of the Eternal City and the abdication of Romulus Augustulus in 476, the title of emperor in the West was allowed to lapse. For nearly a thousand years, however, to the arrival of the conquering Ottomans in 1453, a succession of Roman emperors exercised autocratic power in the Byzantine polity that would carry the legacy of Roman law and civilization through the European Middle Ages. Greek in language, Roman in administration, Christian in spirit, influenced by significant borrowings from the Orient, the Eastern Empire became increasingly self-aware and self-contained as Roman power in the west ebbed away.

For centuries the northern frontier of the Byzantine Empire was approximately drawn at the line of the Danube. The northern Balkan region was a frontier zone, where indigenous tribal communities sometimes managed to assert independence from Byzantine authority, but more often accepted various degrees of dependency and subordination.[26] The empire assimilated these communities culturally. As a consequence the Byzantine experience became a foundation for modern Balkan identity.

Politically, the empire was a theocracy whose ruler, the *Basileus*, also stood at the head of the Eastern Church. It bequeathed a tradition of autocratic governance and of *Cæseropapism*, a union of secular and spiritual authority that would encourage the definition of national identity on the basis of confessional orientation. Greek became the language of commerce, administration, and culture, but the empire was a vast complex that included a wide range of ethnic and linguistic communities. Its citizens called themselves Romans (*Rômaioi*), and were defined by allegiance to an ideal of civilization, to the concept of the empire as an ecumenical whole beyond whose boundaries stretched the world of barbarism. These flattering self-

9

images were not entirely false—up to the capture of Constantinople by the marauding knights of the Fourth Crusade in 1204 the city was the undisputed center of European civilization. Strategically, the empire served as a defensive bastion for the idea of Europe against invasion from the south and east. "Had the Saracens captured Constantinople in the seventh century rather than the fifteenth," writes John Norwich, somewhat provocatively, "all Europe—and America—might be Muslim today."[27] Economically, Byzantium was a commercial civilization whose gold-based currency unit was the basis for trade in the eastern Mediterranean for centuries.

Political autonomy, material prosperity, and strategic unity became the foundation for cultural specificity, reflected above all in the dominant role of the Eastern Orthodox Church. The empire pursued a missionary vocation—the brothers Cyril and Methodius, who set out from Thessalonica in the 9th century to bring a written language and the message of the gospel to the Slavic tribes of Central Europe and the Balkans, were dispatched as representatives of the Emperor—and under its aegis Eastern Christianity became the faith of a vast region stretching from the Balkans into the Russian plain and the Caucasus. A formal schism between Eastern and Western Churches occurred in 1054, but it was only a step along the way in a long process of growing apart. Many of the differences between the two communities were superficial. But the Eastern Church refused to acknowledge the spiritual hegemony of the Papacy, and adhered to the ideal of a Christian community governed by its bishops in the tradition of the seven Ecumenical Councils of the early Church. Orthodox spirituality, grounded in the unique beauty of the Eastern liturgy and a vision of mystic union with the Holy Spirit, evolved in a manner distinct from that of the Western Church.

Byzantium would eventually decline and fall, but the political traditions of the empire, its contributions to social and cultural development, and the integrative role of the Orthodox Church left powerful legacies. Contemporary perceptions of the Balkans as peripheral and backward must at least be conditioned by an awareness of the tradition of which it is the heir. Steven Runciman's panegyric to Byzantine Constantinople as "the centre of the world of light" against the foil of the European Dark Ages is exaggerated, but not altogether devoid of sense.[28]

The mass migration of Slavic tribes into the Balkans during the 6th and 7th centuries corresponded to a phase of Byzantine weakness and loss of control. The Basileus Nicephoros I died in battle against the proto-Bulgarian ruler Khan Krum in 811, establishing the First Bulgarian Empire as a strategic rival on the empire's northern marches. The medieval Bulgarian state reached its high point under tsar Simeon the Great (893-927), whose armies briefly threatened Constantinople.[29] But the tide turned, and with the defeat of the Bulgars at the hands of Emperor Basil II (dubbed *Bulgaroctonos*, "the Bulgar Slayer") in 1018, the entire Balkan Peninsula was brought under the direct control of Constantinople. George Ostrogorsky's classic *History of the Byzantine State* posits the reign of Basil II as the empire's apogee, "followed by a period of decline in which in its foreign policy Byzantium lived on the prestige won in the previous age and at home gave play to all the forces making for disintegration."[30]

One source of decline was intensified strategic pressure. By 1071 the Normans had conquered Bari, the last bastion of Byzantine power in Italy, and in the same year the Selçuk Sultan Alparslan defeated the Byzantine army of Romanus Diogenes at the Battle of Manzikert, opening a route westward into Anatolia. In 1082 the merchant city of Venice, still technically a subject of the empire, established de facto independence by negotiating a Charter of Privileges. Henceforward *La Serennissima* would be a dangerous commercial and strategic rival. On 18 November 1094 at the Council of Clermont, Pope Urban II opened the era of the Crusades, and the First Crusade passed through the imperial outpost of Belgrade in 1096.[31] In the following centuries a series of campaigns promoted by the Western Church would undermine the empire commercially by opening up alternative trade routes between the Arabic world and the West, and bring a series of Frankish armies into the heartland of the Byzantine realm. In 1204, urged on by the Doge of Venice, the knights of the 4th Crusade seized Constantinople, vandalizing the city's artistic treasures and establishing a short-lived Latin Kingdom of Constantinople from 1204-1261.

In the Balkan area external pressure and strategic overextension allowed space for the rise of autonomous feudal principalities. The Croatian kingdom of kings Tomislav (910-929), Krešimir IV (1058-1074), and Zvonimir (1075-1089) converted to Western Christianity and secured limited autonomy by accepting a *Pacta Conventa* with Hungary in 1102, subjugating Croatia to the crown of St. Stephen in exchange for a degree of self-government under an indigenous prince or *ban*. In 1185 a local rebellion established Turnovo as the capital of a second Bulgarian empire, which at the end of the 13th century briefly accepted the suzerainty of the expanding Tatar empire of Batu Khan. In 1219 Stefan Nemanja (Saint Sava) obtained autocephaly for the Serbian Orthodox Church, and laid the foundation for the great Nemanja dynasty that would control much of the southern Balkans at its culmination in the reign of Stefan Dušan (1331-1355). In Wallachia and Moldavia independent Romanian principalities emerged as the result of the merger of smaller units under the princes Basarab (1310-1352) and Bogdan I (1359-1365). A large Bosnian kingdom also saw the light during the 14th century, reaching its high water mark under Roman Tvrtko (1353-1391), crowned in 1377 as the "king of the Serbs, Bosnians, and Croats." Despite the best efforts of twentieth century nationalists to rewrite the past in service of the present by asserting a glorious and unbroken national tradition stretching back into the Middle Ages, these were medieval dynasties, not modern national states in any sense of the term, bound together by allegiance to a ruling family rather than ethnic, cultural, or linguistic affinity.[32] The rise of such kingdoms became a reflection of Byzantium's decline. By 1425 the population of Constantinople had shrunk to barely more than 50,000, and its effective area of control been reduced to the Thracian hinterland and several Aegean islands.

Under the Yoke.

The power that would eventually replace the failing empire originated as one of the several Turkish tribes that had migrated into Anatolia in the preceding centuries. There is a store of surviving coins stamped with the name of the ruler Osman dating from the 1280s, about the time at which the Osmali Turks, or Ottomans, moved into western Anatolia to escape subordination to the Mongols descendents of Genghis Khan. By 1354 the Ottomans had crossed the Straits into the Balkans and launched a campaign of expansion inspired by the ideology of *gazavat*, or holy war. Without the defensive barrier provided in earlier centuries by a potent Byzantium, the feudal principalities of the late medieval Balkans were in no position to hold out. In 1371 predominantly Slavic armies were defeated by the Ottomans on the Maritsa, and in 1389 fought to a standstill at the famous Battle of Kosovo Field outside modern

Priština.[33] The Kosovo battle was not the decisive and irreversible defeat that Serbian legend would eventually make it out to be—it was part of a process of advance and retreat that would, however, lead inexorably toward the subordination of the Balkan region to Ottoman rule.[34] The process was already well advanced when Sultan Mehmed *Fatih* ("the Conqueror"), after a seven-week siege, finally breached the famous walls of Constantinople and subdued the city on 24 May 1453.[35] For most of the five subsequent centuries, up to the collapse of Ottoman rule in Europe in the Balkan Wars of 1912-1913, the Balkans was ruled from the renamed capital of Istanbul as an integral part of the Ottoman Empire.[36]

The Ottoman legacy is another pillar of modern Balkan identity. In architecture, music, language, cuisine, and social mores commonalities derived from the Ottoman centuries continue to provide the elements of a distinctive cultural ambience that is unmistakable, albeit not easily defined. The historical substance of the Ottoman experience, and its significance for the peoples of the Balkans themselves, however, are bitterly contested.[37]

For the varied Christian communities of the peninsula, the judgment has always been clear—subordination to the Sublime Porte meant centuries "under the yoke" (*Under the Yoke* is the title of Bulgaria's national novel by Ivan Vazov, recounting the story of the 1876 uprising against Ottoman rule). As a direct result of imposed foreign domination, it is argued, the flourishing late medieval kingdoms of the peninsula were swept away and the historical momentum of a normal state and nation building process set backwards. The indigenous relationship with a greater Europe that had characterized the medieval centuries was broken, and replaced with alien cultural norms that would henceforward impose separation. Ottoman hegemony is defined as consistently exploitative, and as the source of a widening developmental gap. "The Turk," wrote the Bosnian novelist and Nobel Prize winner Ivo Andrić in a passage fairly reflective of regional attitudes, "could bring no cultural content or sense of higher historic mission, even to those South Slavs who accepted Islam; for their Christian subjects, their hegemony brutalized custom and meant a step to the rear in every respect."[38]

Such judgments were an inevitable response to perceptions of imperial domination. They do little justice to the sophistication of Ottoman institutions, or to the empire's substantial achievements.

Under Mehmet II (1451-1481) the empire had already emerged as the dominant power in the eastern Mediterranean, with a political, administrative, cultural, and socio-economic order well adapted to the ethnic and religious diversity of Anatolia and the Balkans. The Ottoman dynasty presided over an autocratic, patrimonial tributary state with all power concentrated in the hands of the sultan and a small group of advisors surrounding him. Islam was the religion of state, but no effort was made to suppress the cosmopolitan character of the empire's population. Rather, the Ottomans adopted the so-called *millet* system, which granted the monotheistic Christian (Armenian, Gregorian, Catholic, and Orthodox) and Jewish subjects of the sultan, organized as self-governing confessional communities, substantial religious freedom. In an age of religious intolerance in the West, Mehmet II hosted the Orthodox Patriarchate in his capital, conducted a formal correspondence with the Catholic Pope, and invited the Sephardic Jews expelled from Spain and Portugal after 1492 to resettle within the boundaries of his empire. Confessional groups remained separate and distinct, but relations between communities were generally respectful. Under Süleyman the Magnificent (1520-1566) the empire created a sophisticated legal code, maintained a splendid court, completed the conquest of Hungary, and in 1526 briefly laid siege to Vienna, transforming itself into an actor in the emerging European balance of power system. At its height, the empire was an imposing reality and a force for cohesion throughout the eastern Mediterranean. Dorothea Gräfin Razumovsky, writing in the wake of the carnage of the 1990s, speaks fairly of the "astonishing achievement of Ottoman statecraft, which succeeded in maintaining peace and preserving the unity of the conquered Balkan region, with its many national traditions, languages, sects, and religions, over many centuries."[39]

The reign of Süleyman the Magnificent was the empire's high point. Thereafter it entered into the long decline that would eventually earn it the title, coined by tsar Nicholas I of Russia, of "the sick person of Europe." The Treaty of Zsitva-Torok, concluded with the Habsburgs in 1606, brought an end to territorial acquisitions in Europe. The second Ottoman siege of Vienna in 1683 was history repeated as farce. The Peace of Westphalia in 1648 had freed the hands of the Habsburgs, who in 1683 swept aside the armies of Kara Mustafa on the Kahlenberg and launched a campaign to roll back Ottoman conquests. Led by famed commanders such as the

Markgraf Wilhelm I of Baden (the "Türkenlouis") and Prince Eugen of Savoy, the Habsburgs pushed their boundary with the Ottoman Empire southward, taking Ofen (modern Buda) in 1686, Belgrade in 1687, and Niš in 1689. In the first decades of the 18th century the Venetians seized control of the Peloponnesus and part of Attica (in the process occasioning the destruction of the Athenian Parthenon, which had survived from classical antiquity nearly intact). The most dangerous long-term rival of the Sublime Porte would however be the rising Russian Empire, which under Peter the Great (1682-1725) pressed south toward the Black Sea, initiating a series of Russo-Turkish military encounters that would extend up to the First World War. In the Treaty of Küçük Kaynarca in 1774, the Treaty of Iaşi of 1792, and the Treaty of Bucharest of 1812 Russia took control of all Ottoman lands along the northern littoral of the Black Sea including the Crimea, shattering the Ottoman trade monopoly in the region and earning formal recognition as the protector of the Orthodox Christian subjects of the Porte.

The disintegrative effect of external pressure upon the integrity of the Sublime Porte was accompanied by increasing domestic instability. The Ottoman Empire had been maintained for centuries with the help of a statist economic order that was strongly resistant to change, strict autocratic governance that crushed individual autonomy, and military expenditure that imposed a massive burden on state finances. As the 19th century dawned the empire had not succeeded in moving from a traditional agrarian economic base toward manufacturing and industry. It remained in the grips of a parochial and conservative state bureaucracy dedicated to the preservation of privilege at all costs. It had not managed to redefine the relationship between subject and ruler in such a way as to allow for the consolidation of a modern nation-state on what was becoming the western European model. Internationally and domestically, the Ottoman Empire had entered into a spiral of retreat and disintegration that it would not be able to reverse.

Ottoman decline was paralleled by western Europe's "takeoff" in the 16th and 17th centuries, including the gradual disappearance of feudal patterns of natural economy, a revival of commerce, the emergence of the early modern dynastic state, and the associated cultural aspirations of Renaissance humanism. By the 17th century an economically progressive European core had come into being, cutting across the western edge of the continent from England to northern Italy. Beyond these dynamic regions stretched peripheral areas that came to include much of eastern and Balkan Europe as well as the Mediterranean and far northern littorals. The process of differentiation between east and west in Europe had come full circle, with the Mediterranean world that had once been the focus of classical civilization now pressed to the margin of a dynamic capitalist heartland covering the continent's northwestern tier.

Differentiation had many facets. Economically, the east and south was reduced to a position of dependency and underdevelopment, reflected by the persistence of inefficient primary production and the absence of dynamic urban complexes.[40] Politically, the early modern dynastic state was not able to strike roots in regions that continued to be dominated by vast, centralized multinational empires.[41] Culturally, the Byzantine and Ottoman experiences came to be seen as manifestations of a significant civilizational divide.[42] The marginalization of Eastern Europe from the 17th century onward encouraged the emergence of a perceptual gap, based upon a prevalent Western image of the East as a constituting other. The few enterprising travelers that penetrated these distant regions brought back colorful accounts of "rude and barbarous kingdoms" that reinforced a sense of apartness.[43] Armed confrontations with the Ottomans strengthened that perception by encouraging the propagation of a vulgarized image of the "terrible Turk" as an external threat.[44] The result was an essentially stereotypical, but widespread and compelling, representation of the East as the domain of the baleful and bizarre — of vampires, boyars, brigands, beyler-beys and bashi-bazouks. A line between East and West was drawn between Europe and the Balkans, and touted as a divide between two sharply contrasting civilizational zones. "The Danube," remarks the British travel writer Sachervell Sitwell in a passage reflecting these perceptions, "passes out of civilization into nothingness, towards the Tatar steppe."[45]

In the early Ottoman centuries, the empire maintained a kind of prideful isolation that limited interaction with the external world. When more intensive contact became unavoidable, the empire was already well along the path of decline. The consignment of Europe's wild east to the periphery of the "real" Europe was in part a function of that decline. Nonetheless, at the end of the Ottoman experience the economic gap between Southeastern Europe and the most developed western European states was considerably smaller than it is today. For the Balkans, the Ottoman experience was in many ways a positive one. Islam would become an essential component of the region's identity. The policy of limited tolerance embodied in the *millet* system allowed Muslim, Christian, and Jewish peoples to cohabit without sacrificing communal identity. In 1910, on the eve of the Balkan wars, only about half of the sultan's subjects were Muslims, with 41 percent representing various Orthodox Christian communities, 6 percent Roman Catholic, and another 3 percent composed of Nestorian, Druse, and Jewish minorities.[46] These were in large measure disaffected communities, however, which by the dawn of the twentieth century had become committed to an ideology of liberation that perceived the empire as a feudal remnant, a zone of economic exploitation and backwardness, and a barrier to independent national development. The new national movements set out from a position of weakness, but they were eventually to triumph.

The Eastern Question.

Ottoman weakness was the foundation for what would become known in European diplomatic history as "the Eastern Question."[47] Posed as a question, this asked whom among the European great powers would benefit from Ottoman vulnerability. Levron Stavrianos identifies three related dimensions of the problem: (1) The failure of reform movements to arrest and reverse the empire's long historical decline; (2) The rise of national consciousness and national liberation movements among the Christian subjects of the Sublime Porte; and (3) The repeated intervention of the European great powers, concerned with the implications of Ottoman weakness for the continental balance of power.[48] The third point is of particular importance—though rooted in a crisis of Ottoman institutions, the Eastern Question was essentially a problem of international order.

Between the Congress of Vienna in 1815 and the outbreak of the First World War in 1914, the European state system experienced something like a long peace, only partially disrupted by the Crimean War in 1854-55 and the wars of German unification between 1866-1871. Through the mechanisms of the "Congress System" and the principle of elite consensus upon which it rested, the five acknowledged great powers (Great Britain, France, Austria/Austria-Hungary, Prussia/Germany, and Russia) maintained a stable international order that was successful in warding off hegemonic warfare on the scale of the Napoleonic period.[49] Interstate rivalry was not eliminated, however—it was pushed onto the periphery, as colonial rivalry further abroad, and as a struggle for influence in the neighboring Balkans.

Each of the great powers had some kind of stake in the Balkan Peninsula. Russia was in the midst of a phase of imperial expansion and was particularly interested in access to the Turkish Straits, through which an increasing amount of its commercial traffic was routed. It sought to pose as the protector of the Orthodox Christian subjects of the Porte, partly as a calculated search for influence, but also because the ideology of the "Third Rome" (which identified Russia as the heir of Byzantium) had become an important component of its international identity.[50] Austria was determined to resist Russian encroachment, and concerned lest restiveness among the South Slav subjects of the Porte affect its own disgruntled Slavic population (over 50 percent of the population of the Habsburg empire at the time of its dissolution in 1918 were Slavs). Britain was determined to maintain naval supremacy in the Mediterranean, and concerned with Russian imperial pretensions. Throughout most of the century France played the role of a non-status quo power, seeking to redefine a system of European order originally conceived to keep her hemmed in, and instability in the Balkans provided more than enough opportunity to pursue that end. Of all the great powers, Prussia (after 1871 Germany) was the least directly engaged (it was the German Chancellor Otto von Bismarck who in 1878 made the famous remark that "For me all the Balkans are not worth the healthy bones of a single Pomeranian grenadier") but it had no choice but to monitor the machinations of its rivals.[51]

Ottoman weakness was in part a product of institutional stagnation. The early warrior sultans soon gave way to reclusive monarchs cut off from affairs of state. The famed elite units of the Ottoman army, the Janissaries, had by the end of the 18th century become a parasitic hereditary caste attached to the imperial palace, where they repeatedly intervened to destroy sultans whose policies did not suit them. Sultan Mahmed II suppressed the Janissaries in 1826, but at this point military decline was far advanced. Ottoman governance had always been light-handed. Most subject peoples administered their own local affairs and had only occasional interaction with representatives of the central authority. Eventually, however, the sultan became dependent upon administrative agents as tax gatherers, and increasingly incapable of controlling them. The successful revolt of the empire's Egyptian provinces in the first decades of the 19th century, led by the Albanian warlord Mehmet Ali, and the simultaneous assertions of local autonomy by Osman Pasvanoğlu in Vidin and Ali Pasha in Janina, were only particularly dramatic examples of the inability of the empire to resist centrifugal forces.[52] External pressure was a constant, and as time went on the empire was increasingly incapable of defending its far-flung frontiers. The French Revolution, with its subversive messages of nationalism and liberty, also reached out to the East with the conquest of Egypt by Napoleon in 1798, the French occupation of the Ionian Islands from 1807-1814, and the creation of the French-sponsored Illyrian Provinces in Dalmatia from 1809-1814.

The most important source of instability within the empire was the increasing restiveness of its Christian subjects. This restiveness had many sources. Growing financial strain combined with aggressive local tax gatherers imposed an ever-harsher burden on the *raya* (the "flock," or common people). The *millet* system did not eliminate all forms of discrimination and attendant resentment. Christians and Jews were not permitted to testify against Muslims in court or to bear arms, marriage with Muslims was banned, and in lieu of military service a heavy tax (the *haradj*) was imposed. Throughout the region local tradition glorified resistance to the Ottoman authorities, often by propagating a virtual cult of brigandage such as that carried on by the Greek *klefts* or south Slavic *hajduks*. These bands of marauders preyed off the inability of the empire to maintain law and order, but they also took on the aura of primitive rebels and became "a symbol of resistance to political and social oppression."[53] By the later part of the 18th century an indigenous Balkan entrepreneurial caste had also begun to make its appearance, better educated and with wider horizons than their peasant forebears. The radical fringe of this new mercantile elite would stand at the head of the varied national liberation movements that were about to erupt.[54]

National uprisings in 1804 and 1815 in Serbia and 1821 in Greece inaugurated an era of revolutionary nationalism that would continue through most of the following century. Although the varied national liberation movements bore the traces of their specific local and regional situations, they also shared many common traits. All were influenced by the romantic nationalism of the early 19th century, with its faith in Johann von Herder's cultural nation and belief in the unspoiled wellspring of popular culture. The imagined communities that became the subject of nationalist passion were established on mythic foundations, usually including the legends of a lost golden age of national greatness, followed by centuries of martyrdom under the yoke of oppression, Ottoman or otherwise.[55] The Serbian Kosovo cycle, an epic poem that laments the martyrdom of the Serbian nation after its defeat at Kosovo Field, is a particularly sophisticated rendition of this kind of myth, but it is by no means unique.[56] Independence movements were usually the product of revolutionary conspiracies that sought to provoke popular uprisings and use them as vehicles to generate indigenous armed resistance and great power intervention. The tactic was effective, but neat breaks were seldom achieved. In most cases a struggle for independence was waged over decades, producing harvests of martyrs, massacres, and betrayals that would poison the air for generations to come.

The states that emerged from these confrontations were usually the product of compromise negotiated above the heads of the new national leaders by the European powers. Great power concern for the hoary diplomatic premises of compensation and balance almost guaranteed that all parties to the dispute would be unsatisfied – the Porte frustrated by its inability to hold on to territories that it had ruled for centuries, new national leaders determined to extend their area of control, and the powers wary of the possibility for the division of spoils to work to their disadvantage. The social structure of the new states juxtaposed small administrative elites with vast peasant populations living in the pre-modern environment of small villages and towns. Politically, they were crafted on what was perceived as the western European model, with a centralized state structure housed in an expanding "modern" capital, and with nationalism as an integrating (but also exclusionary) ruling ideology. Comparisons with the 20th century experience of de-colonization are not exact, but they are apt. The peoples of the region were judged to be too immature for self-governance, and were usually provided with monarchs drawn from the ruling families of the West, incongruously parachuted in from Bavaria or the Rhineland to preside over the heirs of Agamemnon and King Priam. These rulers were quick to adopt the frustrated nationalism of their new compatriots. The Balkan's cultural complexity did not permit the creation of ethnically pure national states, and the new regimes usually contained only a small part of the larger community that they aspired to represent. As a result the agenda of independence was expressed as a host of revisionist demands aimed at territorial expansion that would set the new states at one another's throats. The ideology of national liberation is another of the pillars upon which modern Balkan identity rests, but its impact has been almost uniformly negative. The problems that have emerged from the attempt to impose modernization from above through the instrument of a centralized state bureaucracy inspired by an ideology of exclusionary nationalism, overseen by the powers in a complex and poorly understood inter-cultural environment, continue to plague the region to this day.

The Powder Keg.

The Eastern Question was also a font of war. The dynamic of decline inside the Ottoman Empire occasioned increasing concern in Vienna.[57] All of the great powers were to some extent put off by aggressive Russian support for national liberation movements among the Orthodox Christian subjects of the Porte. Given the mix of economic, cultural, and military interests that bound it to the region, Russian engagement was inevitable, but in strategic terms it was destabilizing. Consequent tensions would become an essential cause of the First World War.[58]

As the 19th century dawned, Russia's relations with the Orthodox peoples of the Balkans were still undeveloped—only the Greeks were meaningful economic partners, and St. Petersburg's interests in the region focused mainly on the Danubian principalities and the Straits.[59] Catherine the Great's "Greek Project," which envisioned the expulsion of the Ottomans from Europe and the creation of a new Byzantium under Russian protection with Constantinople as its capital, never advanced beyond the status of a visionary ideal.[60] When, after the rebellion of 1804, a Serbian delegation journeyed to St. Petersburg for an audience with the tsar, the two nations had to build their relationship from scratch. "We are setting forth down the quiet Danube to find Russia," wrote the legate of the Serbian leader Karadjordje during the voyage, "about which we know nothing, not even where she lies."[61] Mutual incomprehension would soon dissolve, however, as Russia set out to use cultural affinity with the Balkan Slavs to advance its own strategic agenda.

Russian-Serbian relations during the first Serbian uprising

assumed what would become a familiar pattern of mutual sympathy tempered by calculations of vested self-interest. Russia expressed support for Serbian autonomy in a formal agreement with the rebels, but assistance was limited by the desire to block a diplomatic alignment between the Porte and Napoleonic France. This constraint was removed after the Austerlitz campaign, when Sultan Selim III opted for a rapprochement with Paris. In March 1806 Russian forces occupied Kotor, and by the end of the year, the tsar and the sultan were at war for the fifth time since 1711. During the war the Serbian rebels fought as allies of Russia, but confronted by the threat of a direct French invasion, St. Petersburg chose to negotiate a compromise peace. The Treaty of Bucharest of May 1812 placed the Russian-Ottoman border at the Prut River and engaged the Porte to grant full autonomy to Serbia. But Russia's withdrawal to confront Napoleon's *Grand Armée* left the Serbs exposed, and in July 1813 Karadjordje's uprising was put down by force.[62]

Russia's disengagement from the Balkans in 1812 was the product of compelling circumstances, and with Napoleon in retreat a forward posture in the region was resumed. Pressure on the Porte to make good upon its commitments under the terms of the Treaty of Bucharest became a leitmotif of policy from 1813 onward. The second Serbian uprising of 1815, and the Greek uprising of 1821, once again posed the problem of how to relate to insurrectionary movements among the Orthodox subjects of the Porte. In Serbia, after some initial military success and with Russian support, the new national leader Miloš Obrenović concluded a compromise peace in exchange for local autonomy. But the Greek insurrection sputtered on and remained a source of tension in Russian-Ottoman relations. In October 1826 Russia imposed the Akkerman Convention upon a weakened Porte, obtaining an effective protectorate over Serbia and the Danubian principalities Moldavia and Wallachia, reconfirming Serbia's autonomy, and securing a promise to restore to Serbia six districts that had been confiscated in 1813 (the districts increased Serbia's area by over 30 percent). As negotiations over the implementation of the agreement proceeded, however, in October 1827 the Ottoman fleet was destroyed at the Battle of Navarino by a combined Russian, British, and French fleet. A nationalist reaction led the Porte to denounce the Convention of Akkerman and declare a "Holy War" against Russia, with hostilities commencing in April 1828.

Russia took the initiative once the contest was joined, pushing its armies southward into the Danubian principalities. Warned against excessive ambition by its great power allies, St. Petersburg limited its war aims to the reassertion of the Akkerman Convention. In the Treaty of Adrianople of September 1829 the terms of the Convention were dutifully confirmed, and the Treaty of London of February 1830 proceeded to establish the first independent Greek state of the modern era, in a constricted territory including only about a quarter of the Greek peoples of the Balkans, and with the seventeen year old Prince Otto of Bavaria as the head of an imposed ruling dynasty. Russia's position was strengthened further by the revolt of Mehmet Ali in the Ottoman Empire's Middle Eastern provinces. In July 1833 the Porte accepted the Treaty of Unkiar Skelessi, a mutual assistance pact with St. Petersburg that included a secret protocol in which the Ottomans pledged to keep the Straits closed to foreign warships. In the *Hatt-i Sherif* of November 1833, the Porte also acknowledged Serbia in its borders of 1812 as a hereditary principality with full internal autonomy.[63] Greece was now independent, Serbia formally autonomous, the Danubian principalities under Russian protection, and tiny Montenegro effectively outside of Ottoman control within its mountain fastness. The process of disintegration that would eventually destroy the empire was well advanced, and Russia appeared to be its principle beneficiary.

In fact, the tsar's regime had no intention of exploiting Ottoman weakness provocatively. In 1829 a special commission appointed by tsar Nicholas I recommended that Russia's Balkan policy seek to preserve a weak Ottoman Empire as the best means for achieving its goals in the region without alienating the powers and risking isolation.[64] Britain nonetheless viewed Russia's position as threatening, and was determined to reverse the trend toward increasing Russian assertion. The opportunity came in the Crimean War of 1853-1856, a conflict with obscure origins in a dispute between St. Petersburg and Paris over access to holy sites in Jerusalem, but with the underlying logic of braking Russian expansion in the south.[65] In July 1853 Russian forces reoccupied the Danubian principalities as a means to place pressure on the Porte, but St. Petersburg immediately found itself isolated. Austria refused to guarantee Russian forces safe passage in the event of hostilities, while Britain and France openly sided with the Porte, which declared war against Russia on 4 October 1853. In August 1854 Russian forces withdrew from the principalities, but in September 1854 a British-French-Ottoman expeditionary force landed on Russian territory on the Crimean Peninsula. Denied naval access and lacking sufficient infrastructure to mass forces in a distant southern theater of operations, Russia was never able to dislodge them, despite months of fighting under appalling conditions (the Crimean conflict claimed over 500,000 victims, about two-thirds of whom died as a result of epidemic disease). The Peace of Paris on 30 March 1856 made clear the balance of power considerations that had motivated the fighting. Russia was forced to renounce special rights in the Danubian principalities, which became autonomous under Ottoman suzerainty (this was the effective birth of modern Romania). Navigation on the Danube was placed under the control of a European commission. The Black Sea was neutralized, which obligated Russia to dismantle all military facilities along the littoral, and all parties agreed to respect the territorial integrity of the Ottoman Empire. The outcome created a state of affairs that St. Petersburg was determined to reverse.

In 1860 Mihailo Obrenović assumed the Serbian throne. Inspired by the nationalist ideologies of Giuseppe Mazzini and Lajos Kossuth, and urged on by the Serbian foreign minister Ilija Garašanin and the Russian ambassador to the Porte Nikolai Ignat'ev, the new monarch affiliated with an agenda for territorial expansion and national liberation.[66] In 1866-1867 a Balkan League was assembled around Serbia (including military pacts with Montenegro and Greece, a friendship pact with the Danubian Principalities, and informal contacts with Bulgarian and Croatian nationalists) with active Russian financial and military assistance. The goal was a war of liberation waged against the Porte, but a change of heart by Obrenović in the autumn of 1867 led to the fall of Garašanin, and in June 1868 Mihailo himself was assassinated. The idea of a Balkan pact inspired by Russia and committed to expelling the Ottomans from Europe was set aside, but not abandoned. Meanwhile, St. Petersburg continued to advance its pawns in other directions. The creation in 1870, with Russian backing, of a Bulgarian exarchate as an autocephalous national branch of the Orthodox community, offered St. Petersburg an alternative base of support among the South Slavs. Russia's rapprochement with Austria-Hungary in the Schönbrunn Convention of June 1873 created a new range of options, permitting a sphere of influence arrangement that seemed to put the Eastern Question on hold. The convention did not address the underlying sources of strategic rivalry, however, and the resulting rapprochement proved to be nothing more than the calm before the storm.

Popular uprisings against exploitative local administrators in Bosnia-Herzegovina and Bulgaria in 1875-1876 once again exposed the critical weakness of the tottering edifice of Ottoman governance. International outrage over the atrocities committed by Ottoman irregulars in Bulgaria, which left over 12,000 dead, left the Porte isolated internationally, and provoked declarations of war by Serbia and Montenegro. Despite the better judgment of its diplomats, Russia was pushed to join the fray by a wave of public sympathy for the South Slavs. The Russo-Turkish War of 1877-78, writes M. A. Anderson, "represented the fullest practical expression ever given in Russian foreign policy to the Panslav ideal."[67] On 28 April 1876 the Russian Panslav general M. G. Cherniaev arrived in Belgrade together with some 5000 Russian volunteers to take command of the Serbian army. His catastrophic defeat in the field at the hands of the Ottomans virtually compelled Russia to opt for war. A major Russian offensive was launched through the Principalities in the summer of 1876, but it was temporarily halted in the Balkan mountain passes at the famous siege of Plevna.[68] The Russians regrouped and overran Ottoman resistance, but at high cost both in lives and to the tempo of the campaign. By February 1878 Russian forces had reached the village of San Stefano, some ten kilometers from Istanbul.[69] On the third of March the aggressive Panslav envoy Ignat'ev negotiated the Treaty of San Stefano, which created an independent greater Bulgaria, stretching from the Straits to the Adriatic and the Danube to the Aegean, beholden to Aleksandr II the "Tsar Liberator" and capable of serving as a basis for Russian leverage in the Balkans.

Russia had recovered from its defeat in the Crimea only too well. The terms of San Stefano were quickly reversed by the powers, fearful that a dependent greater Bulgaria would become an agent of preponderant Russian influence. With her armies exposed south of the Danube, an unreliable Austria blocking their line of retreat and a British fleet in the Sea of Marmara threatening bombardment should they move to occupy the Ottoman capital, Russia was not in a strong strategic position despite its military exploits, and was virtually forced to accept revisions. They were affected by the Congress of Berlin, convened in June 1878 under the direction of Otto von Bismarck in the capital of united Germany, which dismantled the edifice of San Stefano and balanced Russia's more limited gains by applying the premise of diplomatic compensation. Austria-Hungary was permitted to occupy Bosnia-Herzegovina (a majority of whose population were Serbs at this date) and place military garrisons in the Ottoman province known as the Sanjak of Novi Pazar, thus positioning its armed forces between landlocked Serbia and its outlet to the sea in Montenegro. Britain was rewarded with the island of Cyprus. Vardar Macedonia, which had been an integral part of the greater Bulgaria of San Stefano, was returned to the Porte. Russia obtained Bessarabia and additional territories in the Transcaucasus, recognition of full independence for Serbia, Montenegro, and Romania (the latter was granted the Dobrudja in exchange for the surrender of Bessarabia to Russia), autonomy for a rump Bulgaria (divided into two parts, dubbed Bulgaria and Eastern Rumelia, with varying degrees of subordination to the Porte), and the pledge of a heavy war indemnity. It had nonetheless been humiliated by the powers and forced to surrender the essential gains of a war in which over 200,000 of its soldiers had given their lives. The result, for B. H. Sumner, was "the temporary extinction of Russia's panslav dream and the nadir of Russian influence in the peninsula."[70]

No single event has contributed more to the structure of regional order in the modern Balkans than the Congress of Berlin. The positive premise that inspired the congress was the assumption that the Eastern Question was a problem for the Concert of Europe as a whole that could only be resolved by consensus. But that premise sat uncomfortably alongside an increasingly vicious strategic rivalry that was driving Europe toward a general war. The terms of settlement were satisfactory to no one. The Porte, which lost a third of its territory and over 20 percent of its population, was permanently destabilized by the outcome.[71] Russia had triumphed in the field, but its political aspirations were blocked. Austria-Hungary remained paralyzed by fear of Slavic irredentism, of which the occupation of Bosnia-Herzegovina was more of a symptom than a cure. Serbia was upset by the loss of Bosnia and by denial of access to the sea. Bulgaria was preoccupied by the vision of San Stefano and determined to assert full independence. By consigning Macedonia to the Porte the diplomats at Berlin had created the modern Macedonian Question, as well as stimulating yet another terrorist campaign of national liberation.[72] All of the newly independent Balkan national states were unhappy with their borders and divided by territorial disputes. In 1885, when Bulgaria moved unilaterally to unify with Eastern Rumelia, a brief war with Serbia was the result, in which Bulgarian forces achieved a surprising and devastating victory. Even the consignment of tiny Cyprus, with its peacefully coexisting Greek and Turkish communities, to the great empire upon which the sun never set would eventually prove to be the source of endless problems.

The Congress of Berlin made no progress at all toward resolving the core problems that would eventually transform the Eastern Question into the root of the First World War. These were: (1) The frustrated nationalism of the emerging Balkan national states; (2) The critical weakness of the Porte; (3) Vienna's concern for the subversive effect of Slavic nationalism, judged a mortal threat to its national integrity; (4) Russian ambitions in the Balkan region and Austrian determination to thwart them; and (5) Austria's close ties to Germany as a pillar of the European balance of power. This volatile mix was temporarily defused by the rapprochement negotiated by Milan Obrenović with Austria-Hungary in January 1881, marking a victory of the Austrophile faction in Belgrade, and by the decline of Panslav enthusiasm in Russia, occasioned in part by St. Petersburg's disillusionment with its would be Balkan allies.[73] But once again a phase of rapprochement would prove to be short-lived. The brutal assassination of the last Obrenović monarch in June 1903 brought the Russophile Peter Karadjordjević to the throne in Belgrade. Coupled with the political ascendancy of the Serbian Radical Party of Nikola Pašić, the change of dynasties meant that Belgrade would once again commit to a policy of expansion under Russian protection.[74] Vienna's annexation of Bosnia-Herzegovina in 1908, bitterly resented by Serb national opinion, undermined any possibility of renewed collaboration with the Habsburgs.[75]

From the autumn of 1909 the Russian envoy to Belgrade N. G. Hartvig, "a Panslav of the old type" according to Andrew Rossos, played a role in mobilizing the South Slavs comparable to that of Ignat'ev during 1876-78.[76] By 1912, with active Russian sponsorship, a new Balkan League had been assembled uniting Serbia, Bulgaria, Greece, and Montenegro with the goal of liberating the peninsula from all remaining Ottoman control. After careful preparation, the First Balkan War was launched preemptively in October 1912 with a Montenegrin attack against Kotor. In political turmoil since the triumph of the Young Turk movement in 1909, the failing Ottoman

Empire was in no position to resist. After a series of defeats, the Porte accepted the Treaty of London of May 1913, which pressed Ottoman boundaries back across the Straits for the first time since the 14th century. The Balkan national states had apparently triumphed across the line, but the regional order that was emerging on the peninsula remained hostage both to the whims of the great powers and to deep-rooted local division. Vienna insisted on reinforcing its position in Bosnia-Herzegovina. To block Serbian access to the Adriatic, and with German and Italian support, it sponsored the creation of an independent Albanian state (minus the predominantly Albanian Serbian province of Kosovo). Greece was granted *enosis* (union) with the island of Crete, but other predominantly Greek islands and territories in the Aegean and Asia Minor remained outside its grasp. Russia, which had played a key role in the genesis of the conflict, proved incapable of constraining the ambitions of its allies. Within a month of the Treaty of Bucharest, on 13 June 1913, Bulgaria launched a surprise attack against Serbia to enforce its demands concerning territorial allocations in Macedonia. Romania, Greece, and the Porte, with shameless opportunism, quickly joined forces with Belgrade. The Second Balkan War lasted less than a month and ended with Bulgaria's abject defeat. The result was confirmed by the Treaty of Bucharest of August 1913, which returned Edirne (Adrianople) to the Ottomans, gave Romania control over the southern Dobrudja, and incorporated most of Macedonia into Serbia—all at Sofia's expense.[77]

The winners of the Balkan wars were scarcely more content than the losers. All emerged from the fighting with unfulfilled national objectives. The atrocities associated with these confrontations, where the burning of villages and the systematic expulsion of entire populations from contested areas became models for what would later come to be known as ethnic cleansing, created a legacy of enmity that would be difficult to eradicate.[78] The Eastern Question had not been laid to rest, only transformed into a new context where rivalry among new national states took precedence over resistance to the Porte. A certain kind of future for Europe's troubled southeastern marches had been unveiled, which future events would do more to confirm than to deny.

Conclusion: The Balkans on the Eve.

The European great powers had never come to terms over what their preferred answer to the Eastern Question should be. Western European perceptions of the region tended to swing between the extremes of Phil Hellenic romanticism (notes of which reappeared in William Gladstone's famed pamphlet following the Bulgarian massacres of 1876) and condescension for the benighted subjects of "Turkey in Europe." The essence of the Eastern Question, according to one all too typical Victorian era account, was "the determination of Europe to impose its civilization on uncivilized and half-civilized nations."[79] Such attitudes did not promote a considered approach to the long-term challenge of regional order (nor do they do so today). The Balkan wars confirmed Ottoman decline, but did little to shape a positive foundation for a new southeastern European state system.

Despite their grandiose pretensions, the new Balkan national states were extremely fragile — "tiny, insecure polities, pale shadows of the grand visions of resurrected empires whose prospect animated Balkan revolutionaries."[80] All were relatively impoverished and in consequence politically unstable. All were tormented by frustrated national designs, by variants of the Greek *megali idea* (Great Idea) seeking to unite all co-nationals within the borders of a single state inspired by an ideology of integral nationalism. All were dependent upon great power sponsorship to facilitate pursuit of their national goals. The powers were anxious to manipulate dependency to their own advantage, but overly sanguine about their ability to control regional turmoil. Sensitive observers were well aware of the risks. "The Balkan war has not only destroyed the old frontiers in the Balkans," wrote Leon Trotsky as a war correspondent on the Balkan front in March 1913, "it has also lastingly disturbed the equilibrium between the capitalist states of Europe."[81]

The assassination of the Habsburg Archduke Franz Ferdinand during a state visit to Sarajevo by the Bosnian Serb nationalist Gavrilo Princip on 28 June 1914 was the product of a frightful combination of arrogance and incompetence. Ferdinand's choice of *Vidovdan* (St. Vitus' Day), the anniversary of the Serbian defeat at Kosovo Field and a sacred day for Serb nationalists, to review the Habsburg soldiery in the contested city, was an unabashed provocation. The decision to proceed, in the company of his wife Sofia, with a motorcade through the heart of the Bosnian capital, in the face of woefully (if not criminally) inadequate security procedures, permitted a desperate and amateurish assassination plot, carried out by what Misha Glenny describes as "one of the most disorganized and inexperienced squadrons of assassins ever assembled," to succeed beyond all imaginable expectations.[82] European chancelleries originally regarded the assassination as a domestic affair in a far-away province. Vienna's decision to use the event as the pretext for an admonitory punishment of Serbia, which became the prelude to a general war, was made with most of the continent's leading diplomats away on vacation. The incapacity to grasp the Eastern Question as an essential, rather than marginal challenge, contributed importantly to the catastrophic outcome.

World War I began as a Third Balkan War, with an Austrian declaration of war against Serbia and an artillery barrage across the Sava into Belgrade. In this case, however, unlike the experience of 1912-1913, great power equilibriums were perceived to be at stake. The Austrian aggression set off a chain reaction that within a matter of days had brought all of the European great powers into the fray. At the end of August, following the early successes of his offensive against France through Belgium and Lorraine, the German commander in chief Helmuth von Moltke bravely claimed "in six weeks this will all be over."[83] Never had a commander been more mistaken. During the second week of September French and British armies stopped the German advance on the Marne. In a matter of weeks, a series of defensive lines had been extended from the Jura Mountains to the English Channel, against which the mass armies of the belligerent coalitions ground to a halt. The Western Front had been born — the embodiment of a military stalemate that would continue for four long years.

Throughout the long and bloody conflict the Balkan front remained a significant theater of operations. Austria's initial "punishment" of Serbia soon degenerated into a travesty. After capturing Belgrade, the Austrians were driven back by a Serbian counterattack, and expelled beyond the Sava. In February and March 1915, a British-French expedition launched against Ottoman positions on the Gallipoli Peninsula, with the intent of driving on Istanbul and forcing the Turks from the war, turned into an embarrassing failure. The demoralized survivors of the expedition were eventually evacuated to Thessalonica, where a neutral but politically divided Greece was pressured to accept them. Encouraged by the setback, and lured by promises of territorial gains, Bulgaria intervened on behalf of the Central Powers during October. This intervention was the final straw for the Serbian army, already weakened by the price of its victories and ravaged by typhus, which now broke down under combined pressure from north and south. Its disorganized remnant, accompanied by the old King Peter traveling in an oxcart, withdrew across the Albanian mountains to the sea, suffering cruelly at the hands of the elements and of Albanian irregulars. A force of 40,000 Serb survivors was moved from the coast to the French-controlled island of Corfu, and eventually to a newly constituted Thessalonica front. Allied troubles in the theater were not yet at an end, however. On 27 August 1916, attracted by secret treaty provisions promising control over disputed territories and reassured by recent Russian advances in Galicia, Romania joined the Entente. The gesture was premature, and in December a German army led by the "Death's Head" General August von Mackenson marched into Bucharest. The allied armies on the Thessalonica front remained intact, but they were only called to action in the war's final months. Against the background of Germany's impending collapse, and spearheaded by Serbian units anxious to participate in the liberation of their homeland, in September 1918 they began to fight their way north, and in November occupied Belgrade.[84]

Interstate relations in the Balkan context during the Great War mirrored the pre-war period, with the great powers seeking to bend local actors to support their strategic aims, and the smaller Balkan states opportunistically exploiting perceived windows of opportunity to what they hoped would be their own advantage. The Ottoman Empire, whose military hierarchy had close ties to imperial Germany, allied with Berlin in September 1914. One month later it was at war with the Russian Empire for one final time. Albania, Bulgaria, Romania, and Greece originally declared neutrality, but their desires to remain above the fray were not respected. In the secret Pact of London negotiated by the entente powers on 26 April 1915 it was agreed that in the event that Greece and Italy joined the Entente, Albanian territories would be partitioned between them, leaving only a small central zone as an autonomous Albanian province. Greece was divided between a pro-German faction led by King Constantine and a pro-Entente lobby led by the liberal politician Elefthérios Venizélos, but in the spring of 1917 Constantine was forced into exile by allied pressure. Russia and Serbia remained closely aligned up to the collapse of the tsarist regime in February 1917. In the first phase of the conflict Russia provided considerable financial aid to Belgrade. Faced with the collapse of Serbian resistance in the autumn of 1915, it urged, in vain, a policy of emergency assistance upon the allies.[85] The Russian representative to Belgrade Grigorii Trubetskoi was the only representative of the international community to march with the Serbian army during its withdrawal in 1916, and St. Petersburg thereafter became a strong supporter for rebuilding the Serbian army on Corfu and reopening a Balkan front.[86]

Wartime alignments also effected the postwar settlement. The Russian, Habsburg, and Ottoman Empires were all swept away by the tidal wave of defeat. At the Versailles peace conference the Allies accepted a diluted version of Woodrow Wilson's premise of self-determination by sanctioning the creation of new national states, but the weight of the commitment was diluted by the contrasting assumption that to the victors belonged the spoils. Romania, Greece, and Serbia (now the core of the new Kingdom of Serbs, Croats, and Slovenes) emerged from the contest with their gains of the Balkan wars confirmed or extended. Bulgaria, Albania, and the Turkish heir of the Ottoman state inherited truncated territories and considerable national frustration. Greece's defeat at the hands of the new Turkish Republic of Mustafa Kemal (Atatürk) in the war of 1919-1923 reversed these fortunes in one theater, but did not alter the overall picture.

The Great War had a decisive impact upon the political structure of the Balkan Peninsula, but it did not transform the status of the region as a whole in the larger spectrum of European or world politics. The Balkans emerged from the Ottoman centuries as a culturally distinct, economically and socially underdeveloped, politically immature, and crisis prone European sub-region, with structural affinities with much of the colonial world. The legacy of frustrated nationalism that was a product of the lengthy and incomplete process of disentanglement from Ottoman domination left the new Balkan national states weak, subordinate, and strategically dependent. Failure to resolve the Eastern Question consensually had transformed the region into the famous "powder keg" that set off the First World War. None of these underlying issues was resolved during the course of the war, and they were only aggravated by the contested work of the Versailles peacemakers. The Ottomans and the Habsburgs were gone, but the Eastern Question had not disappeared along with them. Nearly a century later, its legacy is still being felt.

ENDNOTES - CHAPTER 1

1. Robert D. Kaplan, *Balkan Ghosts: A Journey through History*, New York: St. Martin's Press, 1992.

2. David Owen, *Balkan Odyssey*, New York: Harcourt, Brace & Company, 1995, p. 3.

3. Nedim Gürsel, *Retour dans les Balkans: Récit*, Ottignies: Quarnum, 1997, p. 70. Gürsel puts it this way: "De toute façon, bien que tous soient contraints de vivre ensemble, les Macédoniens détestent les Bulgares, les Bulgares les Turcs, les Turcs les Albanais, les Albanais les Serbes, les Serbes les Bosniaques, les Bosniaques les Croates, les Croates les Valaques, les Valaques les Tziganes et les Tziganes les détestent tous. Dans un sens, on peut dire que c'est le destin des Balkans."

4. Orientalism refers to an imputed, but false opposition between East and West, used to assert the uniqueness and superiority of Western civilization. The concept is developed by Edward W. Said, *Orientalism*, New York: Pantheon Books, 1978.

5. Misha Glenny *The Balkans: Nationalism, War and the Great Powers 1804-1999*, New York: Viking, 2000, p. 2, asserts that the Serbian uprising of 1804 "marked the beginning of modern history in the Balkan peninsula." Glenny portrays national discord and endemic violence as a consequence of external manipulation.

6. See Elena Zamfirescu, "The 'Flight From the Balkans'," *Südosteuropa*, Nos. 1-2, 1995, pp. 51-62.

7. Maria Todorova, *Imagining the Balkans*, Oxford: Oxford University Press, 1997, p. 11.

8. Ferdinand Shevill, *The History of the Balkan Peninsula: From the Earliest Times to the Present Day*, New York: Harcourt, Brace and Company, 1922, p. 13.

9. Shatterbelt is a term of art in geopolitical analysis used to refer to a politically fragmented and ethnically divided zone that serves as a field of competition between neighboring powers. See Philip Kelly, "Escalation of Regional Conflict: Testing the Shatterbelt Concept," *Political Science Quarterly*, Vol. 5, No. 2, 1986, pp. 161-180.

10. Fernand Braudel, *The Mediterranean and the Mediterranean World in the Age of Philip II*, 2 vols., New York: Harper & Row, 1972, Vol. I, pp. 103-167.

11. Hugh Poulton, *The Balkans: Minorities and States in Conflict*, London: Minority

Rights Publications, 1993, provides a guide to Balkan national communities.

12. Challenges to this assertion by the 19th century Austrian historian Jakob Fallmerayer, whose work sought to deny an organic link between the modern Greeks and their classical predecessors, have been a source of continuing resentment. See Richard Clogg, *A Concise History of Greece*, Cambridge: Cambridge University Press, 1992, p. 2; and Jakob Philipp Fallmerayer, *Byzanz und das Abendland: Ausgewälte Schriften*, Vienna: W. Andermann, 1943.

13. The reason for the conversion of Balkan Christian communities to Islam remains a subject of debate. Desire to maintain social status by adopting the faith of the conqueror, resistance to the repression of the local *Bogomil* tradition (a Manichaean religious movement denounced as heresy by the established church), the conversion of child-levy (*devşirme*) military recruits and slaves promised freedom, and imposed conversion at the behest of Muslim landlords have all been cited. It should also be noted that there were conversions in all directions, not just from Christian to Muslim. See John V. A. Fine Jr., *The Bosnian Church, A New Interpretation: A Study of the Bosnian Church and its Place in State and Society from the 13th to the 15th Centuries*, New York: Columbia University Press, 1975.

14. The most important of the Balkan Slavic Muslim communities, the Muslims of Bosnia-Herzegovina (referred to as *Muslimani* in Titoist Yugoslavia), officially adopted the name Bosniac (*Bošnjak*) in 1993. A regional variant of the Serbo-Croat language (including numerous Turkish loan words) was also designated as the Bosnian (*Bosanski*) language. See Senahid Halilović, *Bosanski jezik*, Sarajevo: Biblioteka Ključanin, 1991. Bosnian Muslim nationalist movements, hoping to buttress their case for an independent national identity, had urged these changes for several decades, but they did not win significant popular support until the violent breakup of Yugoslavia. Francine Friedman, *The Bosnian Muslims: Denial of a Nation*, Boulder: Westview Press, 1996, p. 192.

15. The size of Roma communities in the region is difficult to determine, due in part to resistance within the community to census gathering. An approximate breakdown would be 800,000 in Bulgaria, 800,000 in Hungary, 60,000 in Macedonia, 2 million in Romania (according to some estimates as many as 3.5 million), 60,000 in Albania, 7000 each in Slovenia and Montenegro, 18,000 in Croatia, and 500,000 in Serbia. See André Liebich, "Minorities in Eastern Europe: Obstacles to a Reliable Count," *RFE/RE Research Report*, Vol. 1, No. 1, May 20, 1992. Portraits of the situation of the Roma in the contemporary Balkans appear in Zoltan Barany, "Living on the Edge: The East European Roma in Postcommunist Politics and Society," *Slavic Review*, No. 2, Summer 1994; Zoltan Barany, "Orphans of Transition: Gypsies in Eastern Europe," *Journal of Democracy*, Vol. 9, No. 3, July 1998, pp. 142-155; and David M. Crowe, *A History of the Gypsies of Eastern Europe and Russia*, New York: St. Martin's Press, 1994.

16. Huntington asserts that "religion is a central defining characteristic

of civilizations," and cites Christopher Dawson's observation that "the great religions are the foundation on which the great civilizations rest." Samuel P. Huntington, *The Clash of Civilizations and the Remaking of World Order*, New York: Simon & Schuster, 1996, p. 47.

17. See the essay "Ex-Yougoslavie: une fausse guerre de religion," in Paul Garde, *Fin de Siècle dans les Balkans 1992-2000: Analyses et chroniques*, Paris: Editions Odile Jacob, 2001, pp. 17-33.

18. Thus the Nobel Prize winning novelist Ivo Andrić, born of Croatian parents, baptized a Roman Catholic, and raised and educated in Bosnia, could claim Serbian nationality as an adult. The Bosnian novelist Meša Selimović, author of the great Yugoslav novel *Death and the Dervish*, raised a Bosnian Muslim but a professed communist and atheist, also asserted Serbian nationality in his later years.

19. Bulent Gokay, "Oil, War and Geopolitics from Kosovo to Afghanistan," *Journal of Southern Europe and the Balkans*, Vol. 4, No. 1, May 2002, pp. 5-14.

20. Todorova, *Imagining the Balkans*, p. 59. Todorova suggests that the series of stereotypes she designates as balkanism is more than just a "subspecies" of Orientalism because of the region's close but ambivalent relationship with both East and West. "Unlike Orientalism, which is a discourse about an imputed opposition, balkanism is a discourse about an imputed ambiguity." (*Ibid.*, p. 17).

21. Mark Mazower, *The Balkans: A Short History*, New York: The Modern Library, 2000, p. 62.

22. Jean-Arnault Dérens, *Balkans: la Crise*, Paris: Éditions Gallimard, 2000, p. 12.

23. Herodotus describes the episode in a somewhat more scientific light: "Persian historians put the responsibility for the quarrel on the Phoenicians. These people came originally from the coasts of the Indian Ocean . . . in Argos they displayed their wares . . . the king's daughter Io and some others were caught and bundled aboard the ships . . . Later on some Greeks . . . probably Cretans—put into the Phoenician port of Tyre and carried off the king's daughter Europa, thus giving them tit for tat . . . Some forty of fifty years afterward Paris, the son of Priam, was inspired by these stories to steal a wife for himself out of Greece . . . And that was how he came to carry off Helen." Herodotus, *The Histories*, trans. Aubrey de Selincourt, Baltimore: Penguin Books, 1969, pp. 13-14.

24. Michael Grant, *The Rise of the Greeks*, London: Phoenix Books, 2001.

25. In his classic account, Arnold Toynbee equates Hellenism with the entire Greek civilization of the classical age and beyond. He defines it as "a civilization

which came into existence towards the end of the second millennium B.C. and preserved its identity from then onwards until the seventh century of the Christian era." Arnold J. Toynbee, *Hellenism: The History of a Civilization*, New York and London: Oxford University Press, 1959, p. 3.

26. For a discussion of Constantinople's role in the northern frontier regions see Paul Stephenson, *Byzantium's Balkan Frontier: A Political Study of the Northern Balkans, 900-1204*, Cambridge: Cambridge University Press, 2000.

27. John Julius Norwich, *A Short History of Byzantium*, New York: Knopf, 1997, p. 101.

28. Steven Runciman, *Byzantine Civilization*, New York: Meridian Books, 1956, p. 240. Runciman's evocation of the city's fall to the Ottomans, said to be destined to transform it into "the seat of brutal force, of ignorance, of magnificent tastefulness," sheds unfortunate light on the cultural bias that informs this conclusion. *Ibid.*

29. John V. A. Fine, Jr., *The Early Medieval Balkans: A Critical Survey from the Sixth to the Late Twelfth Century*, Ann Arbor: The University of Michigan Press, 1983, pp. 94-158. Fine's work is the best introduction to the period.

30. George Ostrogorsky, *History of the Byzantine State*, New Brunswick: Rutgers University Press, 1957, p. 283.

31. The misgivings that the arrival of the Crusaders provoked among the Byzantine hierarchy are described in Anna Comnena's *Alexiad*, perhaps the greatest surviving monument of Byzantine literature. See *The Alexiad of Anna Comnena*, trans. E. R. A. Sewter, Baltimore: Penguin Books, 1969, books ten and eleven,

32. John V. Fine Jr., *The Late Medieval Balkans: A Critical Survey from the Late Twelfth Century to the Ottoman Conquest*, Ann Arbor: University of Michigan Press, 1987.

33. Noel Malcolm, *Kosovo: A Short History*, New York: New York University Press, 1998, pp. 58-80, gives a good account of the battle and its place in historical memory.

34. See Paul Wittek, *The Rise of the Ottoman Empire*, London: Royal Asiatic Society, 1938; and Fuat Köprülü, *Les Origines de l'Empire Ottoman*, Paris: E. de Boccard, 1935.

35. One of the best biographies of Mehmed remains Franz Babinger, *Mehmed the Conqueror and his Time*, Princeton: Princeton University Press, 1953.

36. Philip Mansel, *Constantinople: City of the World's Desire, 1453-1924*, New York: St. Martin's Press, 1995, offers a portrait of the city as imperial capital.

37. Maria Todorova, "The Ottoman Legacy in the Balkans," in L. Carl Brown, ed., *The Ottoman Imprint on the Balkans and the Middle East*, New York: Columbia University Press, 1996, pp. 45-77; and Peter Sugar, *Southeastern Europe Under Ottoman Rule, 1354-1804*, Seattle: University of Washington Press, 1977.

38. Ivo Andrić, *The Development of Spiritual Life in Bosnia Under the Influence of Turkish Rule*, Durham, NC: Duke University Press, 1990, p. 38. This is the text of Andrić's doctoral dissertation, written in 1924 for the University of Graz.

39. Dorothea Gräfin Razumovsky, *Der Balkan: Geschichte und Politik seit Alexander der Grossen*, Munich: Piper, 1999, p. 203. Razumovsky goes on to note with "astonishment" that this achievement has been no more respected than Marshall Tito's comparable accomplishment in promoting peace and unity several centuries later.

40. Peter Gunst, "Agrarian Systems of Central and Eastern Europe," in Daniel Chirot, ed., *The Origins of Backwardness in Eastern Europe: Economics and Politics from the Middle Ages Until the Early Twentieth Century*, Berkeley: University of California Press, 1989, pp. 53-91.

41. George Schöpflin, "The Political Traditions of Eastern Europe," *Daedalus*, Vol. 119, No. 1, Winter 1990. pp. 55-90.

42. The theme of cultural differentiation is developed at length in Michael W. Weithmann, *Balkan-Chronik: 2000 Jahre zwischen Orient und Okzident*, Regensburg: Verlag Friedrich Pustet, 1995.

43. See the collection by Lloyd E. Berry and Robert O. Crummey, eds., *Rude and Barbarous Kingdom: Russia in the Accounts of Sixteenth-Century English Voyagers*, Madison: University of Wisconsin Press, 1968; and especially the colorful account by the Protestant radical Adam Olearius in Samuel H. Baron, ed., *The Travels of Olearius in Seventeenth-Century Russia*, Stanford: Stanford University Press, 1967.

44. Norman Daniel, *Islam, Europe and Empire*, Edinburgh: The University Press, 1966; and Franco Cardini, *Europa e Islam: Storia di un malintesa*, Rome: Editori Laterza, 1999.

45. Sacherwell Sitwell, *Romanian Journey*, Oxford: Oxford University Press, 1992, p. 63.

46. Razumovsky, *Der Balkan*, p. 204. Figures are cited from the 1910 edition of the Encyclopedia Britannica.

47. M. S. Anderson, *The Eastern Question, 1774-1923: A Study in International Relations*, London: Macmillan, 1966.

48. L. S. Stavrianos, *The Balkans 1815-1914*, New York: Holt, Rinehart and Winston, 1963, pp. 16-19.

49. See Paul W. Schroeder, *The Transformation of European Politics 1763-1848*, Oxford: Clarendon Press, 1994.

50. The doctrine of the Third Rome was coined in the reign of Ivan III (1462-1515). It argued that after the fall of Rome and Constantinople, Moscow inherited the mantle of the true Christian faith.

51. Bismarck cited from Weithmann, *Balkan-Chronik*, p. 297.

52. K. E. Fleming, *The Muslim Bonaparte: Diplomacy and Orientalism in Ali Pasha's Greece*, Princeton: Princeton University Press, 1999.

53. Barbara Jelavich, *History of the Balkans: Vol. I: Eighteenth and Nineteenth Centuries*, Cambridge: Cambridge University Press, 1983, p. 61. The classic study of the primitive rebel phenomenon is Eric Hobsbawm, *Bandits*, 2nd ed., Harmondsworth: Penguin Books, 1985.

54. L. S. Stavrianos, *The Balkans since 1453*, New York: New York University Press, 2000, pp. 215-229.

55. See Benedict Anderson, *Imagined Communities: Reflections on the Origin and Spread of Nationalism*, London: Verso, 1983.

56. See Wayne S. Vucinovich and Thomas A. Emmert, eds., *Kosovo: Legacy of a Medieval Battle*, Minneapolis: Minnesota Mediterranean and East European Monographs, 1991.

57. R. W. Seton-Watson, *The Southern Slav Question and the Habsburg Monarchy*, New York: Howard Fertig, 1969.

58. The best survey of Russian engagement in the Balkans during the 19th century is Barbara Jelavich, *Russia's Balkan Entanglements, 1806-1914*, Cambridge: Cambridge University Press, 1991.

59. The terms of the Treaty of Küçük Kaynarca of 1774, which did not permit the passage of Russian warships into the Mediterranean, were not satisfactory to St. Petersburg, and became a source of constant revisionist demands. See E. I. Druzhinina, *Kiuchuk Kainardzhiiskii mir 1774 goda: Ego podgotovka i zakliuchenie*, Moscow: Izdatel'stvo Akademii Nauk SSSR, 1955, p. 334.

60. I. S. Dostian, *Rossiia i balkanskii vopros: Iz istorii russko-balkanskikh politicheskikh sviazei v pervoi treti XIX v.*, Moscow: Nauka, 1972, pp. 36-42. Peter the Great had called upon Balkan Christians to rise against the Porte as early as 1711, but this was a rhetorical gesture that was not attached to any kind of substantial policy.

61. Cited in Frank Fadner, *Seventy Years of Pan-Slavism in Russia: Karamzin to Danilevskii, 1800-1870*, Washington, DC: Georgetown University Press, 1962, p. 30.

62. Article VIII of the treaty of Bucharest pledged the Porte to grant a general amnesty to Serbian rebels and limited internal autonomy. It required the Serbs to destroy fortresses constructed during the rebellion, accept the re-establishment of Ottoman military garrisons in place in 1804, and pay an annual tribute. The treaty was negotiated between St. Petersburg and the Porte, without the Serbian side being consulted. Georges Castellan, *Histoire des Balkans (xive-xxe siècle)*, Paris: Fayard, 1991, p. 252.

63. On these events, see E. P. Kudriavtseva, *Rossiia i obrazovanie avtomnogo Serbskogo gosudarstva (1812-1833 gg.)*, Moscow: Institut rossiiskoi istorii RAN, 1992. Serbia was finally able to seize control of the six districts that it claimed from the Ottomans in the summer of 1833, thanks to the presence of Russian troops in Moldavia and a Russian naval squadron in the Straits. As a result, Serbia's territory was expanded by one-third.

64. William C. Fuller, *Strategy and Power in Russia 1600-1914*, New York: Free Press, 1992, p. 222.

65. John Shelton Curtiss, *Russia's Crimean War*, Durham, NC: Duke University Press, 1975.

66. Garašanin was the author of the 1844 *Načertanije* (Guideline) that argued for the creation of a greater Serbia under Russian sponsorship. P. N. Helm, "The Origins of Modern Pan-Serbism: The 1844 Načertanije of Ilija Garašanin: An Analysis and Translation," *East European Quarterly*, No. 2, 1975: pp. 158-169; Wolf Dietrich Behschnitt, *Nationalismus bei Serben und Kroaten 1830-1914: Analyse und Typologie der nationalen Ideologie*, Munich: Oldenbourg, 1980, pp. 54-65; and Vaša Čubrilović, *Istorija političke misli Srbiji XIX veka*, 2nd ed., Belgrade: Narodna knjiga, 1982, pp. 165-193. The text is often referenced as an inspiration for the conflicts of the 1990s.

67. Anderson, *The Eastern Question*, p. 203. On the role of public pressure for war in Russia, see David MacKenzie, *The Serbs and Russian Pan-Slavism 1875-1878*, Ithaca, N.Y.: Cornell University Press, 1967, pp. 73-77.

68. I. I. Rostunov, *Russko-turetskaia voina, 1877-1878*, Moscow: Voenizdat, 1977,

pp. 113-168.

69. See the excellent accounts in Bruce W. Menning, *Bayonets Before Bullets: The Imperial Russian Army, 1861-1914*, Bloomington: Indiana University Press, 1992, pp. 51-86; and A. A. Kersnovskii, *Istoriia russkoi armii*, 4 vols., Moscow: Golos, 1993, Vol. 3, pp. 202-247.

70. B. H. Sumner, *Russia and the Balkans, 1870-1880*, Oxford: The Clarendon Press, 1937, p. 571.

71. Erik J. Zürcher, *Turkey – A Modern History*, London: Taurus, 1993, p. 85.

72. Duncan M. Perry, *The Politics of Terror: The Macedonian Liberation Movements 1893-1903*, Durham, NC: Duke University Press, 1988.

73. Charles Jelavich, *Tsarist Russia and Balkan Nationalism: Russian Influence in the Internal Affairs of Bulgaria and Serbia, 1879-1886*, Berkeley: University of California Press, 1958.

74. Pašić was strongly influenced by Russian Panslav thinking, particularly Nikolai I. Danilevskii's *Russia and Europe*. For a contemporary evaluation see "Srbi i Rusi," *Vreme*, February 28, 1994, pp. 34-38.

75. The Russian and Austrian foreign ministers Izvolskii and Alios Baron von Lexa Aehrenthal met in Buchlau in 1907 and agreed informally to a compensation agreement in which Austria would be permitted to absorb Bosnia in exchange for an agreement granting Russia free access to the Straits. In the end Austria cashed in on Bosnia, but gave no ground on the Straits.

76. Andrew Rossos, *Russia and the Balkans: Inter-Balkan Rivalries and Russian Foreign Policy 1908-1914*, Toronto: University of Toronto Press, 1976, p. 27.

77. Ernst Christian Helmreich, *The Diplomacy of the Balkan Wars, 1912-1913*, Cambridge, MA: Harvard University Press, 1938; and Katrin Boekh, *Von den Balkankriegen zum Ersten Welt Krieg: Kleinstaaten Politik und etnische Selbstbestimmung auf dem Balkan*, Munich: Oldenbourg Verlag, 1996.

78. The original Carnegie Endowment report documenting atrocities perpetrated during the Balkan Wars was reprinted, as a form of tragic commentary, during the new Balkan war of the 1990s. *The Other Balkan Wars: A 1913 Carnegie Endowment Inquiry in Retrospect*, Washington, DC. Carnegie Endowment Book, 1993.

79. Sir Charles Eliot, *Turkey in Europe*, London: Frank Cass & Co., 1965, p. 3. The original edition dates from 1900.

80. Mazower, *The Balkans*, p. 88.

81. Leon Trotsky, *The Balkan Wars 1912-13*, New York: Monad Press, 1980, p. 314.

82. Glenny, *The Balkans*, p. 304. See Vladimir Dedijer, *The Road to Sarajevo*, London: MacGibbon & Kee, 1967, for an engaging account of the plot.

83. Cited in Pierre Miquel, *La grande guerre*, Allear: Marabout, 1988, p. 139.

84. Alan Palmer, *The Gardeners of Salonika*, London: Deutsh, 1965, provides a colorful account.

85. Iu. A. Pisarev, *Tainy pervoi mirovoi voiny: Rossiia i Serbiia v 1914-1915 gg.*, Moscow: Nauka, 1990, pp. 147-153, 187-194.

86. Russia pushed these arguments in the face of strong opposition from its British and French allies. Iu. A. Pisarev, *Serbiia na golgofe i politika velikikh derzhav 1916 g.*, Moscow: Nauka, 1993, pp. 40-41.

CHAPTER 2

THE BALKANS IN THE SHORT 20th CENTURY

The Cordon Sanitaire.

The southeastern European regional order that emerged from the First World War was highly unstable. All of the new nation states carved from the wreckage of empire by the Versailles peacemakers were required to deal with the challenges of weak institutions, economic backwardness, unassimilated minorities and ethnic tensions, and strategic exposure. The impact of the world depression was particularly severe in an area whose economies remained primarily agrarian. Political polarization and the rise of extremist movements, including communist parties on the left and nationalist parties on the right, was an inevitable consequence. In every country in the region the resultant tensions would eventually be resolved by some variant of royal or military dictatorship.

A brief phase of democratic governance in postwar Albania was brought to an end by the Gheg tribal chieftain Ahmed Zogu, who overthrew the parliamentary regime of Fan Noli in 1924 and was crowned King Zog I in 1928.[1] In the new Kingdom of Serbs, Croats, and Slovenes, the mortal wounding, on the floor of the national parliament, of the leader of the Croatian Peasant Party Stjepan Radić by the Serb nationalist Puniša Račić in June 1928 prompted King Aleksandar to declare a royal dictatorship on January 6, 1929.[2] Bulgaria experienced failed Agrarian and Communist insurrections during 1918 and 1923, and in 1935, following a short-lived military coup, King Boris III proclaimed personal rule.[3] The Versailles Treaty of Trianon nearly doubled Romania's territory, but a troubled interwar experience led through the rise of the fascistic Iron Guard and its leader Cornelia Codreanu to the promulgation of a new authoritarian constitution by King Carol II in 1938.[4] In 1936 General Ioannis Metaxas dissolved the Greek parliament and established himself as dictator under the restored monarch of Giorgios II.[5] Mustafa Kemal and his Republican People's Party ruled Turkey as an authoritarian one party state up to Kemal's death in 1938, when the presidency moved to his hand picked successor İsmet İnönü.[6] The varied national experiences were not identical, but the political consequences of interwar development—failed democratization, sharp social differentiation, ethnic tension, and an authoritarian *dérive*—were remarkably similar.[7]

The region also confronted international challenges. From 1919 the Communist International (Comintern) adopted an assertive Balkan policy linked to the great power aspirations of the Soviet regime. After the war of 1919-1923, Greece and Turkey crafted a rapprochement and shifted priorities to domestic transformation, but relations with their Balkan neighbors remained tense. Bulgaria maintained a revisionist orientation toward the existing regional order, eventually leading Sofia toward closer relations with Mussolini's Italy. Once installed in power, Albania's King Zog chose to subordinate his country to the Mussolini regime almost completely. With irredentist claims in Istria and Dalmatia, Italy posed a constant threat to the territorial integrity of Yugoslavia. Hungary and Austria also adopted revisionist postures, and in March 1921 Karl of Habsburg launched an abortive putsch in Budapest in hopes to restore his thrown.

France and Britain took on the role of guarantors of the status quo, and France in particular sought to contain the perceived threats of Bolshevik subversion and German revanchism by constructing a central European *cordon sanitaire* from Versailles' new national states.[8] After 1921 the Quay d'Orsay became the most important international sponsor of the so-called Little Entente, a mutual assistance pact called into being at Czechoslovak initiative in 1920, uniting Yugoslavia, Czechoslovakia, and Romania around an anti-communist and anti-revisionist agenda. The Little Entente was complemented in Central Europe by a Polish-Romanian mutual assistance pact, but Polish-Czechoslovak friction prevented its extension to cover the entire Central European corridor between Germany and the USSR.[9] In February 1934, following Hitler's rise to power, a new Balkan Entente brought Yugoslavia, Romania, Greece and Turkey together in an agreement to guarantee existing frontiers, encouraged by the Soviet Union and with French sponsorship.[10] But the assassination of Yugoslavia's King Aleksandar during a state visit to Marseilles in 1934 weakened Belgrade's commitment to regional cooperation, and the Balkan Entente never evolved into an initiative with teeth. When Romania and Yugoslavia stood aside in 1938 as Czechoslovakia was surrendered to Hitler, the death knell of the Little Entente, and of Balkan cooperation under the aegis of the Western democracies, had sounded. The Balkan states would be swept into war after 1939 as they had been after 1914 — unprepared militarily and divided amongst themselves, the willing or unwilling accomplices of great power initiatives that they were powerless to resist. "We are part of the general European mess," as it was stoically explained to the Slovene-American writer Louis Adamic during a visit to Sarajevo in 1933, "we do not have the complete and final decision as to our destiny. We are caught in the dynamics of the international politics of the great powers."[11]

The Yugoslav Idea.

The most innovative aspect of the postwar settlement in the Balkans was the creation of the Kingdom of Serbs, Croats, and Slovenes as a Balkan federation spanning the former Habsburg and Ottoman empires. In 1929 the new state was re-christened Yugoslavia (Land of the South Slavs). Despite a rocky initiation marked by inter-ethnic friction, Yugoslavia survived the traumas of depression and royal dictatorship, and in 1939 managed to initiate a hopeful institutional reform.

The first Yugoslavia represented a long standing ideal of assembling south Slavic nationalities in some kind of federative association. During the 1830s the Croatian Ljudevit Gaj created the Illyrian Movement as a forum to promote unity, using the classical name Illyrian as a common denominator to connote the shared origin and essential unity of the South Slavs.[12] The movement flourished in Croatia, and in 1850 Croat writers inspired by Gaj's ideas joined with Serb counterparts (including the famous linguist and humanist Vuk Karadžić) in Vienna to produce a "Literary Agreement" that attempted to define a single literary language common to both Serb and Croat dialects on the basis of the assumption that "one people should have one language." After 1850 the Catholic Bishop of Djakovo, Josip Juraj Strossmayer, carried Gaj's project forward, introducing the term Yugoslavism (jugoslavenstvo) to express the common aspirations of all South Slavs. The road ahead would not be easy, however. There was no consensus in place over the forms that political cooperation might take, Serbia's stature as an independent state gave it options that the Croatian and Slovenian national movements inside the Dual Monarchy did not possess, and Yugoslavism remained an elite phenomenon without popular roots. Contacts between Serb and Croat supporters of Illyrianism nonetheless continued through the second half of the century, and from 1906-1918 a Croat-Serb coalition supportive of the Yugoslav idea held a majority in the Croatian Diet (*sabor*).[13] It required the crisis of order provoked by the First World War, however, before purposeful movement toward the creation of a south Slavic federation became possible.

A Yugoslav Committee in exile inspired by the Yugoslav idea was established in Paris on April 30, 1915, with a leadership dominated by Croats and Slovenes, including Frano Supilo (who would later resign in principled opposition to any agreement surrendering Croat autonomy), Ante Trumbić, and the sculpture Ivan Meštrović.[14] Supilo was aware of the terms of the secret Treaty of London of 1915 and feared eventual collusion between Serbian Radical Party leader Nikola Pašić and the Entente at the Croats' and Slovenes' expense. The Croats and Slovenes looked to association as a means to strengthen their claim to independence from the Habsburg regime, to resist irredentist claims on the part of Italy and other neighbors, and to dilute potential Serbian overreaching. In the wartime environment, beleaguered Serbia was ready to reciprocate. In the so-called Niš Declaration of December 7, 1914, the Serbs included the goal of a united Yugoslav state among their war aims.[15] The Versailles peacemakers eventually sanctioned the Yugoslav idea, but its genesis was a consequence of initiatives undertaken by the south Slavic peoples themselves.

In a manifesto of May 1915, the Yugoslav Committee asserted "the Jugoslavs form a single nation, alike by their identity of language, by the unanswerable laws of geography and by their national consciousness."[16] These were noble words, but they offered little guidance concerning what kind of state a union of South Slavs should become, and despite protestations of unity differences between the three nationalities engaged in the effort to create a common national framework remained strong. During the summer of 1917 members of the Serbian government met with leaders of the Yugoslav Committee on Corfu and agreed to the creation of a common state. Most discussion at Corfu revolved around a disagreement between the Serbian side, represented by the patriarchal Pašić, which insisted upon the creation of a unitary state under the Karadjordjević dynasty, and the Slovene and Croatian side represented by Trumbić, which favored a looser federation that would allow for substantial cultural and political autonomy. At Corfu a declaration favoring the Serbian position was adopted asserting "that Serbs, Croats, and Slovenes are one people and must form one monarchical state under the Karadjordjević dynasty."[17] After the Habsburg defeat a National Council of Serbs, Croats, and Slovenes representing the south Slavic populations of the Habsburg empire attempted to backtrack by requesting a looser, federative association, but to no avail. The Kingdom of Serbs, Croats, and Slovenes declared into being on November 24, 1918 was a unitary state under the Serbian royal dynasty, with Belgrade as its capital.

Serbian dominance would quickly become the Achilles Heel of the south Slavic union. In retrospect, however, no alternative seems to have been practicable. At the end of the war Slovenia and Croatia were still attempting to extract themselves from the failing Dual Monarchy. Slovene and Croat soldiers had fought with the armies of the Central Powers from 1914-1918. Slovenia had no history of independent statehood, and the Croats had to look back to the Middle Ages to find something approximating full sovereignty. Both confronted territorial challenges from neighboring Italy and Austria that they were not in a position to resist left to their own devices. Serbia, by way of contrast, was an established state with an indigenous monarchy and a powerful army that could point to its war record as a mark of special distinction. Given Serbia's status as a victorious belligerent, the only alternative to association would have been the creation of a greater Serbia including significant non-Serb minorities, bounded by weak and exposed Slovene and Croat mini-states.[18]

The violent disintegration of Yugoslavia during the Second World War, and again during the 1990s, has led many to conclude that the Yugoslav idea was flawed from the start, an artificial attempt to impose unity upon diverse peoples for whom the prerequisites for statehood were lacking.[19] Whatever merit the argument may have, there was a powerful logic to association in 1918 that remains in some measure valid to this day. No less than twenty distinct national communities lived within what would become the Yugoslav space, often inextricably intermingled. Under these circumstances shaping "ethnically pure" nation states was not a realistic option. The Greek-Turkish population transfer agreed to in the Treaty of Lausanne in 1923 (on the basis of which over 1.5 million people were forced to leave their homes) is sometimes cited as a model for separation, but it was the product of a catastrophic war, was extraordinarily traumatic in personal terms, and in the long term has not contributed to stable Greek-Turkish relations. Association among the major south Slavic nations addressed the dilemma of inter-culturality positively by allowing for cohabitation in a multinational framework. It was assumed that cultural affinity between Slovenes, Croats, and Serbs was sufficiently strong to serve as a basis for nationhood, and during the 1920s and 1930s sincere efforts were undertaken to promote cultural unity.[20] Federation also addressed the Serbian Question by allowing the Serb population of the central Balkans to live together within a common state. There was concern among the peacemakers at Versailles that Balkan mini-states without a sufficient material base would become pawns in the hands of rival powers, rekindling the kind of strategic friction that had made the Eastern Question so volatile in the pre-war years. A Yugoslav association provided a more substantial foundation for regional order, as a barrier to revisionist agendas and a component of a sustainable European balance of power.

The Yugoslav ideal did not become a reality. An enlarged regional market failed to generate prosperity—between 1918 and 1941 Yugoslavia's anemic annual growth rate of 2 percent failed to keep pace with demographic increases. During the 1930s Yugoslavs were subjected to depression conditions, and the gap between the new state and the more developed economies of the western European core widened. Economic frustration became a foundation for political discontent, often manifested as ethnic mobilization. Politically, the Serb dominated monarchical regime that emerged from the process of unification was formalized by the Saint Vitus Day Constitution of 28 June 1921. From the outset, it confronted serious domestic challenges. The most serious was that posed by Croatian nationalism, primarily represented during the 1920s by Radić's Croatian Republican Peasant Party, which pressed for Croatian autonomy inside a loose Yugoslav or expanded Balkan confederation. Another source was the international communist movement. From its founding in Belgrade in April 1919 the Community Party of Yugoslavia (KPJ) assumed the Moscow line denouncing Yugoslavia as a pawn in the hands of the Versailles powers, and urging the creation of a Soviet republic. Between 1926 and 1935, the party's left wing championed the line of the Comintern's 6th world congress in 1928, condemning Yugoslavia as a "prison house of peoples."[21]

Branches of the Internal Macedonian Revolutionary Organization (VMRO) in the Vardar Macedonia region also proclaimed a policy of armed struggle against the Yugoslav state. After 1929 the KPJ focused its attention on the Macedonian question (the Comintern's 1924 Vienna Manifesto was ground-breaking in recognizing a distinct Macedonian nationality), conspiring with VMRO activists who would eventually be involved, together with the Croatian fascists of Ante Pavelić's *Ustaša* movement, in the assassination of King Aleksandar.[22]

The Radić assassination opened the door for royal dictatorship, but no underlying problems were resolved. King Aleksandar reconfirmed a commitment to the unitary state, dividing the country into nine administrative regions (*banovine*) named after local rivers (the Drava, Sava, Drina, Vrbas, Primorje, Zeta, Dunav, Morava, and Vardar regions) with intentional disregard for ethnic boundaries. Following the King's assassination the young crown prince Petar came to the thrown under the regency of Prince Pavle, but political contestation only intensified. A concerted effort to resolve Serb-Croat frictions resulted in the *Sporazum* (Agreement) of April 27, 1939, signed by Radić's successor Vladko Maček and Prime Minister Dragiša Cvetković, which came toward Croat national sensitivities by creating a new *banovina* of Croatia, combining the old Sava and Primorje districts plus the city and region of Dubrovnik, with greatly expanded autonomy. The *Sporazum* was a step toward Serb-Croat co-administration that resembled the Habsburg *Ausgleich* of 1867, but it was contested politically and never fully implemented. The agreement did not take into account the national complexity of the entire Yugoslav space and was resented by Yugoslav nationalities other than Serbs and Croats. It was nonetheless a step away from uncontested Serbian hegemony that could have provided a context for addressing the Yugoslav national question given time to evolve. But no time was provided. The cumulative experience of the interwar decades created considerable disillusionment with Yugoslavia, and helped prepare the ground for the destructive ethnic mobilizations that followed.

Upon the outbreak of war in Europe in September 1939, Belgrade declared neutrality. But the Balkan region as a whole, and Yugoslavia in particular, were too important to remain outside the fray. Nonferrous minerals derived from Yugoslavia were considered critical to the German war effort, air corridors reaching to the

German expeditionary force in northern Africa crossed the region, and Berlin sought to maintain access to Thessalonica and the oil resources of Romania and the Black Sea, and to protect them from British bombing raids. With plans for an invasion of the Soviet Union maturing in Berlin, Hitler was particularly concerned that the Balkan region should remain outside the reach of potential enemies.[23]

Mussolini, who had long expressed the desire to transform the Balkan region into an Italian sphere of influence, precipitated events by launching an invasion of Greece on October 28, 1940. Had the assault gone well Hitler would have been pleased, but it did not. The Greek dictator Metaxas earned enduring fame by responding to Rome's demands for capitulation with the laconic response "no" (okhi). The Greeks went on to reverse the Italian advance, and in late 1940 the first British units were disembarked in southern Greece to bolster resistance.[24]

In view of the Italians' frustration, Hitler determined to subdue the region once and for all as a prelude to his assault upon the USSR. In a matter of weeks Hungary and Romania were pressed to join the Tripartite Pact (constituted when Italy joined the Germany-Japan axis in September 1940) and to permit German occupation of their territory. On March 1, 1941, threatened by a German offensive and lured by promises of control over Macedonia, Bulgaria granted German forces right of passage and joined the Pact as well. Yugoslavia was pressured to follow suit, and on 25 March the Maček-Cvetković government agreed to accede to the Pact in exchange for a secret pledge of control over Thessalonica (which Berlin, inconveniently, had already secretly promised to Bulgaria). A contemporary historian interprets this capitulation as "a diplomatic triumph" for Belgrade insofar as it promised to preserve Yugoslav neutrality at minimal cost (the granting of a right of transport for war materials, but not troops, through Yugoslav territory) — a retrospective evaluation that displays touching regard for Hitler's good will.[25] It was not considered a triumph at the time by the Western democracies struggling to block German expansion, or by the citizens of Yugoslavia contemplating the prospect of collusion with fascist aggression. Within days of the arrangement, the Maček-Cvetković government was overthrown on behalf of the new monarch King Petar II by popular mobilizations in the streets of Belgrade, with demonstrators famously chanting bolje rat nego pakt (better war than the pact) and bolje grob nego rob (better grave than slave).

The Belgrade putsch was noble, but it was also a spontaneous and confused response to a desperate situation. Yugoslavia was unprepared for war, and Hitler's immediate reaction was to order an all out assault. On April 6 Belgrade signed a treaty of friendship with the USSR, but with Stalin engaged in his own desperate effort to appease Berlin, and with Romania and Bulgaria pledging to block any attempted Soviet incursion, no real help could be expected from that quarter. At dawn on April 6 Belgrade was subjected to a massive air attack leaving nearly 3000 dead in its wake. By April 10 German forces had occupied Zagreb, on April 12, propelled by simultaneous attacks from Bulgaria, Romania, and Austria, they entered Belgrade, and by April 17 Yugoslavia had capitulated. With organized resistance temporarily crushed the Italians went on to strengthen their control over Albania and northern Epirus, while the German *Operation Maritsa* pressed southward through the Greek mainland and on to the island of Crete. The Balkans had been conquered at a stroke, and the *Wehrmacht* given a free hand to launch *Operation Barbarossa*, its fateful assault against the USSR.

Yugoslav resistance was unsuccessful, but it is unlikely that appeasement would have spared the country the horrors of war any more than it spared any other of Hitler's sacrificial lambs. Despite its manifold problems, and unlike so many other victims of German aggression, Yugoslavia had marshaled the will to resist an ultimatum from the *Führer*. The first Yugoslavia was not undermined from within, as a result of uncontainable ethnic tension. It was subjugated from without, by foreign invasion and occupation. It was only after the country had been dismantled, its leadership dispersed, its armed forces disbanded, and power placed in the hands of quislings, that the descent to civil war could begin.

The Killing Fields.

During the Second World War the Balkans was a secondary theater of operations. At the moment of Germany's attack upon the Soviet Union on June 22, 1941, the region appeared to be safely under the control of the Axis. Turkey clung to a precarious neutrality. Organized resistance in Greece was broken and the country suborned to a combined German, Italian, and Bulgarian occupation.[26] Albania was an Italian protectorate. Bulgaria, under the calculating rule of

King Boris III, and Romania, subjected to the dictatorship of General Ion Antonescu, had allied with Germany. Yugoslavia was gone, replaced by a number of dependent statelets held under the thumb of Rome and Berlin. Eventually, the catastrophic impact of foreign occupation would provoke the rise of resistance, but this would not become a strategic factor until the Axis war effort had stumbled elsewhere.

Foreign occupation was accompanied by an aggressive redrawing of frontiers. Bulgaria, which had already received the southern Dobrudja as a "gift" from Romania under German auspices in September 1940, now took control of western Thrace, Macedonia up to Lake Ohrid, and small parts of Kosovo and eastern Serbia. In addition to ceding the southern Dobrudja, Romania was forced to surrender Bessarabia and northern Bucovina to the Soviet Union in June 1940, and northern Transylvania to Hungary on the basis of the so-called *Vienna Diktat* of August 30. A greater Albania was assembled under Italian occupation including most of Kosovo and parts of Montenegro and western Macedonia. Rump Montenegro was transformed into an Italian protectorate. The major part of Yugoslav territory was annexed by neighboring states allied with Berlin. What remained was placed under collaborationist administrations watched over by occupation forces. Germany, Italy, Hungary, Bulgaria, and Albania all benefited by territorial acquisitions. Parts of Slovenia were absorbed by Germany and Italy, with the remainder constituted as a dependent Province of Ljubljana. A rump Serbia, within boundaries that predated the Balkan wars, was subjected to a German military command working through the quisling regime of General Milan Nedić. Most ominously, a so-called Independent State of Croatia including Croatia proper, Slavonia, Srem, a small part of Dalmatia, and all of Bosnia-Herzegovina, was placed in the hands of Ante Pavelić and his *Ustaša* movement. The Ustaša leadership had survived politically during the prior decade as protégés of Mussolini, who maintained them as virtual prisoners in guarded residences in Italy. They were now parachuted into Zagreb with an unrepentant agenda for cultural assimilation and ethnic cleansing.[27]

The territorial revisions engineered by the Axis lacked any kind of principled foundation. Collaborators were purchased, allies rewarded, and opponents punished on the basis of short term expediency, with complete disregard for the consequences.

Pavelić's Independent State of Croatia, for example, encompassed a population that was barely 50 percent Croat (30 percent of the population were Serbs and 20 percent Bosnian Muslims). Berlin's goals were to prevent the region's utilization as a theater for hostile military operations, and to maintain access to strategic resources such as those derived from Romania's Ploesti oil fields. It had no interest in exerting effort to create a sustainable regional order. Balkan dependencies mortgaged their future by subordinating themselves to great power strategic ends in exchange for territorial acquisitions, a wager for which the notes would soon come due. The German New Order in the Balkans was a house of cards defended by force. When the power equation shifted, it was bound to collapse.

The leading force behind organized resistance in the Balkans, and elsewhere in occupied Europe, was the pro-Soviet communist movement. With their traditions of militancy, discipline, and underground activity, communist parties were well prepared for the demands of armed struggle. They drew inspiration from the Soviet Union's fight against the *Wehrmacht* on the Eastern Front, and operated on the basis of a coherent strategy for sustaining resistance, and seizing and maintaining power at the moment of Germany's defeat. The Greek and Yugoslav Communist parties, in particular, succeeded in mobilizing large-scale partisan resistance and placing real military pressure on occupation forces. The outcomes of their respective struggles, however, were strikingly diverse.

The Greek Communist Party (KKE) created a National Liberation Front (EAM) in September 1941. By 1943 its armed wing, the Greek National Liberation Army (ELAS), commanded over 60,000 fighters. In 1944, however, encouraged by Moscow for whom positive relations with its wartime allies remained all important, the leaders of ELAS opted to subordinate their movement to British command. When the Germans withdrew from Greece in November 1944, the British were able to occupy Athens and establish an interim administration. Accord quickly broke down, but in street fighting between ELAS and British occupation forces during December (known as the "Second Round" of the Greek civil war) the communists failed to press home their advantage. Instead the KKE accepted the Varzika Agreement of February 9, 1945, calling for the disarming of ELAS. The outcome allowed a revival of right wing nationalist forces shielded by the British occupation. Civil war between the KKE and nationalists erupted in 1947, but by then Greek communism had lost any hope of affecting a quick march to power. The wild cards that decided the outcome were the loyalty of the Greek communist leadership to Stalin's direction, the Soviet decision to prioritize ties to its wartime allies, and the timely arrival of the British expeditionary force in Athens, inspired by a commitment to maintain Greece as a British sphere of influence in the eastern Mediterranean.[28]

In Yugoslavia, events moved in a different direction. Immediately after its proclamation in April 1941 the Independent State of Croatia and its *Poglavnik* (Supreme Leader) Pavelić launched a campaign of genocide directed against non-Croat minorities including Serbs, Jews, and Roma. On June 22, speaking in the town of Gospić, Pavelić's Minister of Education Mile Budak publicly declared that one-third of Croatia's nearly two million Serbs were to be deported, one-third forced to convert to Roman Catholicism, and one-third killed.[29] The incidence of killing was particularly severe in the ethnically mixed regions of the old military frontier zone (*Vojna Krajina*) that had divided the Habsburg and Ottoman empires, and in Bosnia-Herzegovina, where wooden platforms were constructed in the squares of occupied villages to which adult males were led, while their families looked on, to have their throats cut. The Croat and Bosnian Jewish community of about 36,000 was almost totally destroyed. Over 200,000 Serbs were subjected to forced conversion to Catholicism, justified on the specious ground that the Serbs of Croatia were actually ethnic Croats who had been forcefully converted to Orthodoxy in centuries past. The Bosnian Muslims were declared to be "Croats of the Muslim Faith," and thereby spared extermination, but there were plenty of victims to go around. The crimes of the Ustaša were colored by anti-Serb resentment cultivated during the interwar decades, but their real source was the fanatic desire to create an ethnically pure Croatia informed by the pathological racial doctrine of European fascism. Genocidal violence directed against the Jewish and Roma communities had nothing to do with Serb-Croat rivalry. Indeed, Josip Frank, one of the most outspoken Croat nationalists of the *fin de siècle* and father-in-law of Ustaša leader Slavko Kvaternik, was a Jew.

The impact of these assaults upon future prospects for civilized inter-communal relations in Yugoslavia and the Balkans was disastrous.[30] The Ustaša came to power in Croatia at the behest of foreign occupiers without a significant popular base — less that 5 percent of the population affiliated with the movement prior to the war. But the crimes of the movement, and the patterns of resistance that these crimes provoked, sowed the seeds of enduring inter-communal resentment.

Unadulterated terror drove all Yugoslav citizens of good will into the arms of the opposition.[31] Remnants of the defeated Royal Yugoslav Army withdrew into isolated mountainous areas and rallied around the leadership of Colonel Draža Mihailović to form the Chetnik movement (the name derives from the term *četa*, an armed band) with a greater Serbia nationalist ideology and ties to the Yugoslav government in exile in London.[32] Immediately upon the fall of the state the KPJ and its leader Josip Broz (Tito) also declared a strategy of armed resistance, based upon an ideology of national liberation that sought to unite all of the Yugoslav peoples in opposition to occupation. Over time the rivalry between Tito's Partisans and Mihailović's Chetniks evolved into open civil war, waged simultaneously with the struggle against occupation forces. The barbarity of the Pavelić regime, the ideologically charged contest between Serbian nationalism and communist internationalism within the resistance, and the harshness of the German occupation all contributed to making Yugoslavia one of the greatest victims, calculating in war-related losses per capita, among the nations engaged in the Second World War.

The Partisans' victory was the result of many variables. Unlike the Ustaša and the Chetniks, whose political appeal was limited to Croats and Serbs respectively, the Titoists reached out to all Yugoslav nationalities. The resort to genocide discredited Pavelić's movement, which in the end remained dependent upon the fortunes of its German and Italian masters. Mihailović's Chetniks were tainted by the tactical choice of occasional collaboration with German occupation forces, whether to defend Serb communities from reprisals, or as a result of antipathy toward the Communists. The Partisans were no angels, but they were disciplined and determined, their forces sought to root themselves in local communities, and the decision for resistance *à outrance* placed them on the side of history. The class line associated with the communist movement appealed to the impoverished young peasants who made up the bulk of recruits (75 percent of the Partisan army was 23 or younger), and provided a source of political affiliation capable of transcending narrow nationalism. Success in the field won Tito's movement international recognition, and by the end of 1943, after the arrival of Fitzroy

Maclean in Tito's headquarters as a British military liaison officer in September, London shifted its support from the Chetnik movement to the Titoists, who in Churchill's words "were killing Germans." Not least, ideological affinity with Stalin and Soviet communism tied the Partisans to what would become the dominant force shaping political outcomes in the post-war Balkans — the Soviet Red Army. Troops drawn from the Soviet Third Ukrainian Front participated alongside of Partisan units in the liberation of Belgrade in October 1944. Even more importantly, after having helped to secure the Yugoslav capital Soviet forces passed on into Central Europe, leaving Tito's Partisans in control, a gesture of confidence from which other occupied Balkan states were not able to benefit. From the outset, Tito had aspired not only to win the war, but also to initiate a revolution. With a triumphant Soviet Union in his corner the cause appeared to be assured.

A Balkan Federation?

The defeat of the Axis meant the collapse of quisling and occupation regimes, leaving a political vacuum which pro-Soviet communist parties and pro-Western democratic forces both aspired to fill. The Yalta bargain that established the contours of cold war order in Europe was prefigured in the Balkans by an informal arrangement concluded between Stalin and Churchill during a meeting in Moscow in October 1944. The British Prime Minister presented Stalin with a scheme for allocating influence according to crude percentages. In Greece, the United States and Britain would assume 90 percent "predominance," leaving 10 percent influence for the USSR. In Romania, the percentages were reversed. Hungary and Yugoslavia were to be split 50-50, and Bulgaria 75-25 percent to Soviet advantage. Stalin is reported to have approved the curious agreement by checking the paper Churchill had sketched it on with a blue pencil.[33] The accord was a sphere of influence arrangement according to which Churchill staked out a British claim to control in Greece, while the Soviets were granted predominance in their sensitive border areas. Once again the fate of the Balkan peoples was being decided by collusion between the powers conducted behind their backs.

Despite the intrusive role of their Soviet sponsor, the victorious Balkan communist parties also sought to have their say. The discrediting of the pre-war establishments provided an opportunity to recast regional order to promote development and reduce the impact of self-destructive nationalism. During and immediately after the war, this effort took the form of a Yugoslav-led campaign to create a Balkan federation that would extend well beyond the boundaries of Yugoslavia. The project was one of the most ambitious attempts to recast the Balkans of the modern period. Had it been even partially successful, many of today's most intractable regional dilemmas could have been considerably muted, if not altogether eliminated.

The idea of a Balkan federation extends back for at least two centuries. In the 19th century it became a goal of Balkan socialist movements, and after 1919 was adopted by the Comintern, which briefly sponsored a Communist Balkan Federation with its seat in Moscow.[34] During the first phase of World War II the Greek and Yugoslav governments-in-exile, with British support, revived the concept as a context for a postwar settlement. Little emerged from their initiative, however, which in the understanding of the sponsors was intended to create "a powerful guarantee against an eventual Bolshevik danger from the Northeast," and which was rejected by the Soviet Union at the foreign ministers conference in Moscow during October 1943.[35]

During 1943 and 1944 similar projects began to emerge from the communist-led resistance movements. Paul Shoup speculates that in approving a degree of autonomy for the Macedonian provincial committee of the resistance in the autumn of 1942, Tito may already have had in mind the goal of a broadened Yugoslav federation including an enlarged Macedonia.[36] In February 1943 Svetozar Vukmanović-Tempo arrived in Macedonia as Tito's prefect, where he inspired the founding of an autonomous Macedonian Communist Party and pushed for the creation of a Balkan General Staff to link the region's resistance movements. Tempo engineered a June 20, 1943, agreement, signed by representatives of the Yugoslav, Greek, and Albanian Communist parties, pledging cooperation. A meeting of July 12, 1943, on Greek territory committed to build a permanent headquarters of the People's Liberation Army of the Balkans as "the military embryo of a future confederation."[37] At a session on October 16-18, 1943, the Politburo of the KPJ made the goal of a "South Slavic Federation" a programmatic slogan, and in his report to the session Milovan Djilas evoked a "federative union of the South Slavic peoples from Trieste to the Black Sea."[38] These ends would be pursued in the months to come in formal and informal discussions between the Yugoslav, Albanian, and Bulgarian Communist movements.

The issue of relations with the Albanians was sharpened by Italy's capitulation in October 1943. In a dispatch sent by the Central Committee of the KPJ to the Second Corps headquarters of the People's Liberation Army of Albania in late January 1944, an option for association based upon the Yugoslav model was outlined. The dispatch urged the Albanians to "further popularize the possibility of other Balkan peoples joining this federation, and the creation of a strong and large Balkan state of equal peoples which would be a major factor in Europe."[39] The status of Kosovo, however, remained a point of dissension. The fourth congress of the KPJ in Dresden in 1928, in line with what was then the official line of the Comintern supporting the dismemberment of Yugoslavia, had agreed to cede Kosovo to Albania. The call for dismemberment was officially abandoned with the shift to a popular front strategy in 1935, however, and Tito made clear that in a postwar settlement any territorial revisions at Yugoslavia's expense would be out of the question. At Jajce in November 1943 the Partisans supported a federal Yugoslavia with the right of self-determination for constituent nations, but that status was not accorded to the Albanian population, which was described as a national minority. A conference of December 31, 1943-January 2, 1944, at Bujana in Albanian territory, bringing together representatives of the national liberation movements of Kosovo, Sanjak, and Montenegro, contradicted these premises by asserting a will to unite with Albania. The gesture was supported by Albanian communist leader Enver Hoxha in a pamphlet, but rejected by Djilas as "a politics of *fait accompli*."[40] The issue of association had been posed, but the conditions for the kind of compromises necessary to bring the project to fruition were not in place. The only hope for a positive solution seemed to lie in some kind of federal arrangement associating Kosovo with Albania inside an enlarged Yugoslavia.[41]

In September 1944 the Soviet Army entered Bulgaria and a communist dominated regime under the so-called Fatherland Front came to power. In the second week of September the Bulgarian communist leader Georgi Dimitrov, from his wartime base in Moscow, sent several radiograms to Tito urging cooperation between the Yugoslav Partisans and the "new" Bulgarian army (which up to a week before had been an army of occupation in

Vardar Macedonia).[42] From September 21-28, Tito was in Moscow, where together with Dimitrov and upon Stalin's urging he approved a military cooperation agreement.[43] During the return journey, on a stopover in the Romanian city of Craiova, Tito met with Bulgarian officials and signed a pledge to pursue a common struggle against Germany.[44]

In early November 1944 the Yugoslavs brought dialogue with the Bulgarians to a higher level by sending a project for federation to Sofia by special courier. Between November and January an intense discussion was pursued, in the course of which a number of variants for association were exchanged.[45] The Yugoslav side was in general more avid, posing the goal of a "unitary federal state" and suggesting the creation of a joint military command with Tito as commander in chief. The intention was to unite the Bulgarian and Yugoslav Macedonian regions (Pirin and Vardar Macedonia) as a single federal entity, with the remainder of Bulgaria joining the federation as a seventh republic, a "6+1" approach to federation building (the Titoists having already decided to recast the new Yugoslavia as a federation of six republics—Slovenia, Croatia, Serbia, Montenegro, Bosnia-Herzegovina, and Macedonia) that would advantage the Yugoslavs and reduce Bulgaria by separating it from Pirin Macedonia. The Bulgarian proposal emphasized the need for gradualism, refused to consider a transfer of Pirin Macedonia, and suggested a "1+1" approach in which Bulgaria and Yugoslavia would federate as equal partners.[46] Despite intensive negotiations, these basic differences could not be resolved.

In discussions in Moscow with the Yugoslav leaders Edvard Kardelj and Ivan Šubašić on November 22, 1944, Stalin approved the Yugoslav variant, though he also proposed waiting before any decisive action was taken in order to assess possible British and American reactions.[47] During talks with Dimitrov during December, the Soviet dictator moved toward the Bulgarian approach, recommending "a two-sided Government on a basis of equality, something analogous to Austria-Hungary."[48] This inconsistency can be explained in several ways. Stalin does not seem to have been particularly committed to either variation of the project at this point, and may simply have sought to cater to the interests of his interlocutor of the moment. More likely, his concern with the Yugoslav driven agenda for association was beginning to grow as the implications of the project became clearer. For the time being, he preferred to hedge his bets.

On September 11-19, 1944, Roosevelt and Churchill met in Quebec, where the British Prime Minister urged that greater priority be given to military operations in the Balkans to block growing Soviet influence. In October, Churchill's "Percentage Pact" arrangement with Stalin combined a strong play for dominance in Greece with the curious designation of a 50/50 division of influence in Yugoslavia. The Russian scholar L. Ia. Gibianskii interprets the British proposal as an attempt to promote a political balance between Tito's Partisans and the pro-Western Yugoslav government-in-exile—and Stalin's willingness to acquiesce as another indication of the Soviet leader's eagerness to maintain privileged relations with his Big Three partners, if need be at the expense of communist resistance movements.[49] London sought to resist Soviet incursion in the region, including ambitious plans for union between emerging pro-Soviet communist regimes. On December 4 a memorandum from British Foreign Minister Anthony Eden conveyed London's objection to any kind of union between Yugoslavia and Bulgaria to both Moscow and Sofia. Fitzroy Maclean expressed similar reservations to the Titoists in Belgrade.[50]

British intransigence placed Soviet great power interests at stake. As a consequence the Kremlin backed away from aggressive support for any kind of Balkan federation. During the April 11, 1945, signing of a Soviet-Yugoslav Treaty of Friendship, Cooperation, and Mutual Assistance, Stalin threw cold water on the project, asserting that further initiatives would have to wait for the end of hostilities.[51] Formal dialogue between the Yugoslavs and the Bulgarians, which had been the real motor of progress, was now broken off. Albania had also been considered a candidate for association, but the Land of the Eagles, with its long Adriatic coastline, was of considerable strategic value, and Moscow may already have come to look askance at the prospect of its absorption by a federative entity under effective Yugoslav control.

The case of Greece was particularly complex. The KKE had struggled to organize a movement of armed resistance without guidelines from Moscow during most of the war.[52] By the time that contacts were reestablished, Moscow's first priority had become to defend its status within the wartime Grand Coalition. The Soviet military mission that arrived at the headquarters of ELAS at the end of June 1944 demanded respect for the Lebanon Charter of May 1944,

60

calling for the creation of a unified government that the Communists would not be in a position to control. During the fighting in Athens of December 1944 Moscow remained passive, and Stalin subsequently urged acceptance of the Varzika Agreement. Peter Stavrakis asserts that Stalin clung to the hope of using the KKE as "a potential source of political leverage in post-war Greece," but agrees that in 1944-1945 the Kremlin sought to tame the KKE in accordance with its sphere of influence bargain with London.[53] All things considered the issue was of secondary importance in the larger sweep of Soviet diplomacy. C. M. Woodhouse describes Moscow's policies as "indifferent to Greece and ill-informed about the Balkans during most of the occupation."[54]

The Yugoslav Partisans had the strongest interest in federative options. Association with Communist Albania would help to secure the allegiance of the Albanian populations of Kosovo, Montenegro, and Macedonia. The unification of the Macedonian Slavs within a common state could set a precedent for Yugoslav territorial revindication in the north, where a call for the unification of the Slovenes implied territorial demands against Austria and Italy. But the Titoists were possessed by a swelling sense of self-confidence, and determined that issues such as the Macedonian Question could only be resolved on Yugoslav terms. What Branco Petranović calls Tito's "megalomaniac" conception of federation became a barrier in its own right.[55] The combination of Western opposition and Soviet reticence was decisive, however. In the end Stalin opted to discourage a dynamic of association, direct the Yugoslav-Bulgarian dialogue toward the minimal goal of a friendship treaty, and accept the KKE's defeat in Athens and the logic of the Varzika Agreement. The Yalta conference of February 1945, which devoted very little attention to the Balkan region, brought a first round of discussion concerning federative options to an end.

The last word concerning Balkan union had not yet been spoken. Between 1945 and 1947 the onset of the Cold War gave new impetus to cooperation among the emerging Communist party states. The Yugoslav-Bulgarian relationship once again became a key source of dynamism. Collaboration during the final phase of the war, Yugoslav material assistance to Bulgaria, pledges of diplomatic support in postwar peace negotiations, and joint aid to the Greek partisans after the outbreak of the "Third Round" of fighting in the Greek civil war in the spring of 1946 all provided a foundation for cooperation. The culmination of these trends came with the visit of a Bulgarian state delegation to Yugoslavia on July 27-August 3, 1947. Discussions conducted at the Slovenian resort of Lake Bled resulted in a Treaty of Friendship, Cooperation and Mutual Assistance of "unlimited" duration, and three accords covering economic cooperation, reduction of customs barriers, and open borders.[56] Although the goal of federation was not mentioned, alarm bells rang in Western capitals, as well as in Ankara and Athens. From the spring of 1946, the Communist partisans were on the offensive in Greece. To many observers, federation had now become a logical step in a drive for Communist hegemony in the Balkans.[57]

Relations between the Balkan parties were more troubled than those concerned for the spread of "monolithic" world communism presumed. Yugoslavia and Bulgaria had made no progress toward resolving their dispute over the Macedonian Question.[58] The KKE was fighting for its life in the mountains of northern Greece. And Stalin remained ambivalent at best about association between his Balkan understudies. Moscow's public response to the Lake Bled accords was a telling silence. Behind the scenes the Soviet leadership reacted strongly to what it perceived to be an independent initiative undertaken without consultation. In a telegram to Tito and Dimitrov immediately after the Lake Bled sessions Stalin criticized the results. In discussions with Hoxha in Moscow during July 1947 he expressed "dissatisfaction" with Yugoslavia's overbearing role in Albania, and during Dimitrov's sojourn in Moscow for a health cure between August and mid-November 1947 evoked "negative signals" from the West concerning Yugoslav-Bulgarian cooperation.[59]

These concerns were aggravated by developments in Yugoslav-Albanian relations. In the autumn of 1947 the head of the Albanian State Planning Commission, Nako Spiru, committed suicide after his expulsion from the Communist Party for protesting Tirana's concessions to Belgrade.[60] With the situation within the Albanian party unstable, and, in Djilas's words, increasingly nervous that "the Russians would get the jump on us and 'grab' Albania," Tito began to press for federative association. In January 1948, reacting to what it portrayed as a possibility of Greek aggression, Belgrade announced the intention of moving two Yugoslav divisions onto Albanian territory. Informed by Tirana, Soviet Foreign Minister Viacheslav Molotov fired off several critical telegrams to Tito and Kardelj, in response to which the Yugoslavs opted to back down.[61]

At the end of December 1946 Djilas, accompanied by a military delegation, was called to Moscow for consultations with Stalin. The military leaders emerged from the talks deeply disillusioned with Soviet comportment.[62] In his discussions with Djilas Stalin prodded the Yugoslavs, claiming; "we have no special interest in Albania. We agree that Yugoslavia should swallow Albania."[63] These cynical remarks, probably calculated to draw out and expose an idealistic communist militant, were being directly contradicted by Soviet actions.

After his return from Moscow to Sofia in mid-November, Dimitrov temporarily abandoned any public references to a federative option. A dynamic of association nonetheless remained alive. During his address upon the signing of the Yugoslav-Bulgarian friendship treaty on November 27, 1947, Tito urged the creation of a full customs union.[64] Between November 1947 and January 1948, Yugoslavia negotiated bilateral friendship treaties with Hungary and Romania, and on his travels through Eastern Europe Tito was greeted as a popular hero.[65] On January 16 Bulgaria also concluded a bilateral treaty with Romania that foresaw the creation of a customs union. On January 18, 1948, at an impromptu press conference conducted on a special train returning from Romania after the signing ceremony, an expansive Dimitrov outlined the goal of an Eastern European federation to include "Romania, Bulgaria, Yugoslavia, Albania, Czechoslovakia, Poland, Hungary, and Greece." The interview appeared in the Bulgarian Communist journal *Rabotnichesko Delo* on January 20, and immediately provoked a wave of critical responses in the Western press.

On January 23 *Pravda* published a resume of the Dimitrov interview without commentary. One day later, Stalin sent a telegram to both Dimitrov and Tito that condemned the idea of federation unambiguously.[66] A *Pravda* editorial of January 28 brought the dissonance into the open, insisting that the Soviet Union was not opposed to federation in principle, but asserting that for the moment such a goal was premature. The Yugoslav leadership offered no official rejoinder. In deference to the Soviet criticism, a Bulgarian Press Agency statement of January 29 repudiated both the Lake Bled declaration and Dimitrov's interview, pretending that "neither the Prime Minister [Dimitrov] nor any other member of the Government has thought or will be thinking about the formation of an eastern bloc in any form whatsoever."[67] Despite the disclaimer, on 1 February

Moscow summoned both the Bulgarian and the Yugoslav leadership to the Kremlin for a settling of accounts.[68]

In retrospect it is clear that the ensuing summit, conducted on the evening of February 10, 1948, marked a full stop for federative projects in the Balkans in the postwar period.[69] Molotov opened the session with an attack on the independent comportment of Belgrade and Sofia, and both he and Stalin blamed their "fraternal allies" for complicating relations with the West, reiterating the "unacceptable" character of international initiatives undertaken without prior consultation with Moscow. Stalin was particularly annoyed by the Dimitrov press conference, and addressed the Bulgarian leader with shocking rudeness, likening his comportment to that of "an old woman in the street who says to everyone whatever comes into her head."[70] The Soviet leader rejected the kind of broad Balkan federation that Dimitrov had evoked, and casually dismissed the Communist cause in the Greek civil war as irretrievably lost. Enigmatic to the end, Stalin nonetheless concluded by supporting a Yugoslav-Bulgarian union, to which he noted that Albanian might eventually be attached.

Immediately following the session of February 10 the Bulgarian and Yugoslav representatives dutifully assembled to discuss association, but the goal of a Balkan union was a lost cause. Both parties agreed to a text drawn up by Molotov on February 11 obligating consultation in reaching foreign policy decisions. The Yugoslavs were now wary of Soviet intentions, however, and concerned with the potential for Bulgaria to play the role of a "Trojan Horse" on behalf of Soviet priorities inside an enlarged south Slavic union. A special session of the KPJ Politburo on March 1 followed Tito in interpreting Stalin's suggestion for union with Bulgaria as a form of pressure on Yugoslavia, and agreed that under the circumstances federation was no longer appropriate.[71] Thoroughly intimidated by Soviet resistance, the Bulgarians bowed to the priorities of their sponsors in Moscow. Revelatory of the Soviets' real intentions, the Soviet-Bulgarian peace treaty signed on March 18 was accompanied by a private pledge by Sofia to refuse a south Slavic federation with Yugoslavia.[72]

Soviet comportment during the session of February 10 exposed the imperial mentality that dominated the ruling circle in the Kremlin. Stalin's bullying treatment of Dimitrov was shameless. His dismissive reference to the "naked illusion" of a Greek Communist victory, though not unrealistic, was cruel. Nor was consistency a virtue. While accusing his Balkan lieutenants of provoking the West with loose talk of association, Stalin had already launched a series of provocations of his own. The creation of the Communist Information Bureau (Cominform) in September 1947, and the confrontational tone of Andrei Zhdanov's keynote address, put the West on warning. Within 10 days of the session of February 10, the coalition government of Edvard Beneš in Prague was subverted with Soviet connivance. In June 1948 the Berlin blockade was initiated. A Soviet dominated regional sub-system was being created in Central and Southeastern Europe whose essential logic was the reinforcement of Soviet control. Ambitious agendas for regional association, such as the project for a Balkan union as it had unfolded between 1943 and 1948, conflicted with rather than reinforced that logic.

The new communist leaders of several Balkan states had pursued a serious dialogue about the prospect of union. John Lampe's characterization of the Balkan federation project as a "phony issue" and "the Macedonian question in disguise" captures the frustrations that plagued the project, but trivializes its intent.[73] Wartime dislocations had created the possibility for change, and local leaders were committed to pursuing new directions. Though they did not succeed in coming to terms, discussions were substantial and the differences aired were not unbridgeable. In the end the project was shattered less by regional disaccord than by the intervention of the great powers. Britain and the Western allies were opposed to any federative project with the potential to extend Soviet leverage in Southeastern Europe and the eastern Mediterranean. Stalin may have been intrigued by the possibility of Balkan union at an early stage, but he moved away from the idea as the weight of Western objections became clear. In 1944-45, rather than argue the point at the expense of Soviet relations with its wartime allies, Stalin acquiesced to London's demand for a dominant role in Greece, and embraced a regional sphere of influence arrangement with Churchill that precluded association. By the time that the federative project had revived in 1947, Tito's Yugoslavia had emerged as a new source of concern. Tito's aspirations called into question the sovereignty of Albania, considered by Moscow to be a useful strategic ally. Belgrade's support for the KKE in the third round of the Greek civil war threatened to create "international complications" at a moment when Moscow's main priority had become to draw together a disciplined bloc as a defensive glacis against the West. And Tito himself was a wild card, independent minded and with considerable popular support. Meanwhile, Western policy was oriented toward integrating Greece and Turkey into a consolidating security community with an anti-Soviet orientation. Though Soviet intervention was decisive in reversing the momentum of dialogue, the fate of postwar projects for Balkan federation was sealed by the triumph of the cold war system in Europe as a whole. In the decades to come the dilemmas of regional order would be addressed in a context of competitive bipolarity.

The Cold War in Miniature.

Following their clash over Balkan union, Tito and Stalin moved rapidly toward a public break. Stalin took the initiative, convinced, according to Nikita Khrushchev, that he had only to "shake his little finger and Tito would disappear."[74] On March 18, 1948, all Soviet military and civilian advisors to Yugoslavia were withdrawn, aid programs were frozen, and a campaign to rally pro-Soviet sentiment inside the KPJ against Tito was initiated. A special session of the Yugoslav Central Committee on April 2 responded defiantly, initiating a mass arrest of suspected pro-Soviet "Cominformists."[75] On June 28, 1949 (*Vidovdan* once again), the new Communist Information Bureau issued a resolution that denounced Yugoslav "deviationism," and in July the 5th Congress of the KPJ consummated the rift by organizing an impressive display of public defiance.[76] This was the first open split within the Soviet led international communist movement, and a blow to the USSR's international position that the West was anxious to support. The Titoists were communists, but they had become anti-Soviet communists. In the years to come, non-aligned Yugoslavia would be the beneficiary of a de facto strategic guarantee from NATO as well as liberal U.S. and Western economic assistance.

The break with Tito sparked a series of Soviet-style purge trials elsewhere in Eastern Europe, designed to root out national communists with the potential to follow in Tito's footsteps, and to reinforce Soviet control. The purges contributed to the consolidation of the Soviet bloc, eventually to be institutionalized as an economic union in the Council for Mutual Economic Assistance (CMEA) in 1949, and as a military pact in the Warsaw Treaty Organization in

1955.[77] Yugoslavia stood apart, an independent national communist regime governed in an authoritarian manner but not subordinated to Soviet direction. The ruling parties of Albania, Bulgaria, and Romania, which had earlier contemplated association with Yugoslavia in a Balkan federation, were coerced into the Soviet glacis. Albania became the site of a Soviet naval facility, but during the 1960s its maverick leader Enver Hoxha joined Communist China in criticizing Soviet direction. In 1969, following the Soviet occupation of Czechoslovakia, Tirana announced its withdrawal from the Warsaw Pact.[78] Greece and Turkey, which had been prime subjects of the 1947 Truman Doctrine, emerged from the war closely aligned with the West, and in 1952 joined the NATO alliance.[79] The result was a Balkan regional sub-system that reproduced the Cold War in miniature, with Greece and Turkey representing NATO, Bulgaria and Romania the Warsaw Pact, and Yugoslavia and Albania positioned as maverick national communist regimes whose non-alignment helped preserve an approximate regional balance.

Although it was externally imposed and essentially artificial, the mature cold war system provided for the longest unbroken period of stable development in the modern history of the Balkan Peninsula. The kind of external threats that had drawn the Balkans into the twentieth century world wars receded. Territorial claims with implications for East-West rivalry were muted, and chronic sources of regional tension, such as the Macedonian and Kosovo issues, were relegated to the back burner. With the threat index on low, Balkan communist states had the luxury of developing relatively autonomous international policies. Yugoslav non-alignment, Albanian isolationism, and Romanian attempts to achieve greater autonomy by developing a territorial defense policy independent of the Warsaw Pact from the mid-1960s onward are diverse examples of what might be called a regional trend. Greek-Turkish relations soured with the rise of nationalist agitation on the island of Cyprus beginning in the mid-1950s, but this was now a problem of Alliance management that did not threaten to spill over into the region as a whole. During the 1980s, a momentum of regional dialogue was created that sought to define premises for cooperation across the fault lines of the Cold War, culminating in the convening of foreign ministers' conferences bringing together representatives of all six Balkan states in Belgrade during 1988 and Tirana during 1990.[80] The results of these consultations were modest — commercial interaction and cultural orientation remained dominated by the logic of bloc affiliation. But they represented a step in the direction of closer regional cooperation.

Such initiatives were sorely needed. The Balkan states that emerged from the Second World War remained overwhelmingly rural in character. Modernization was a basic challenge on both sides of the region's "Iron Curtain," and a dynamic of economic cooperation and commercial exchange could have worked to the advantage of all. Unfortunately, prior to the 1980s cold war structures posed significant barriers to all but relatively superficial forms of interaction.

The Western-oriented countries of the region benefited dramatically from the rapid expansion of the capitalist world economy during the postwar decades. At the end of the civil war in 1949, approximately half the population of Greece still lived in traditional rural communities. By the 1990s the proportion had fallen to less than a third. Over 12 percent of the population left the country in search of work opportunities in the decade of the 1970s alone, but by the dawn of the 21st century, Greece was confronting a wave of labor immigration (particularly from the former Soviet Union and Albania). These trends were reflective of a fundamental transformation that was bringing the country closer to the standards of developed Europe. Similar changes occurred in Turkey, where in 1950 only 18 percent of the population lived in towns with over 10,000 residents. Sixty-seven percent of Yugoslavia's population worked the land in 1948, over 40 percent had no formal schooling, and an additional 46 percent had completed only a basic four-year curriculum. Buoyed by international largesse, flexible public policy, and open borders that allowed labor migration as an economic safety valve and encouraged hard currency remittances, Yugoslav growth rates in the 1950s and 1960s were among the highest in the world. By 1980, only 20 percent of the population worked the land, and the illiteracy rate had dropped below 10 percent.

Comparable, but less impressive trends were visible within the Soviet-oriented states of the region. Bulgaria and Romania were approximately 80 percent rural at the beginning of the Second World War. Social norms were defined by traditional patriarchy, and technological standards were low—only a small fraction of villages had access to electricity. The Soviet extensive growth model was a useful devise for development under the circumstances, and a process of industrialization and urbanization continued into the 1980s. The bizarre preoccupation with self-reliance that characterized the long rule of Enver Hoxha made Albania the exception to every rule, but even here education and broadened horizons made inroads into traditional clan structures and social mores. It is doubtless true, as the case of Greece seems to indicate, that modernization and development would have proceeded more effectively absent the authoritarian structures of communism—but in the postwar decades these structures were firmly in place. Communism was the context within which the shift away from patriarchal, semi-feudal, and dependent patterns of social and economic organization occurred in large parts of the Balkans, a fact that would make the transition away from communist norms after 1989 particularly challenging.

In Turkey and Greece, traditions of authoritarian governance were softened, but not altogether overcome. The Greek polity remained polarized after the conclusion of the civil war in 1949. In 1967 the probable victory of a left-wing coalition in scheduled elections was preempted by a military coup led by a group of junior officers including Colonels Georgios Papadopoulos and Nikolaos Makarezos. The colonels' regime remained in power until 1974, but its ineffectiveness only served to discredit the resort to authoritarianism. The junta collapsed in 1974 against the background of the Cyprus crisis, and Greece has since sustained a stable democratic order. Turkey moved away from the Kemalist tradition of one party rule after 1945, but chronic political instability provoked periods of military rule in 1960, 1971, and 1980, as well as a "silent coup" to reverse the rise of political Islam in 1997. Turkey can boast of democratic institutions and real political pluralism, but the disproportionate role of the military in its political system, the dilemma of political Islam in a self-styled secular state, and the incapacity to integrate the large Kurdish minority remain barriers to the realization of democratic norms.[81]

In the communist party states, the authoritarian legacy was reinforced by the perpetuation of single party regimes under the guidance of all-powerful despots.[82] Tito exercised absolute power in Yugoslavia from 1945 until his death in 1980, and became the subject of an elaborate cult of personality.[83] Enver Hoxha shifted from being Tito's protégé in the immediate postwar years, to a loyal Stalinist in the 1950s, to an ally of Maoist China in the 1960s, but remained Albania's unchallengeable strongman throughout.[84] Todor Zhivkov inherited power in Bulgaria from his predecessor Vŭlko Chervenkov under the impetus of Khrushchev's reforms in 1956, and clung to office until forced to resign as the communist order crashed down around his shoulders in 1990.[85] In Romania, after the death of the Stalinist leader Gheorghe Gheorgiu-Dej in 1965, power passed into the hands of the young Nicolae Ceauşescu. After a brief flirtation with reformism, Ceauşescu retreated into what may have been the most oppressive of all the eastern European communist regimes, brought to a violent end with his arrest and summary execution in December 1989.[86]

Communist authoritarianism in the Balkans was not seriously challenged from within. Economic growth and modernization, the intimidation of dissent, and relative international stability allowed the repressive regimes in power to achieve at least the passive allegiance of a critical mass of citizens. Nationalism was also used and manipulated by all of the ruling satraps as a means for cementing support. Tito reacted to popular disaffection in the late 1960s and early 1970s by granting greater autonomy to Yugoslavia's constituent nations. Hoxha justified his radical isolationism as a means for preserving Albania's unique national essence. Ceauşescu distanced Romania from Soviet direction in the foreign policy sphere during the 1960s as a sop to national feeling, and the imposition of draconian austerity measures during the 1980s in an effort to eliminate Romania's foreign debt had the goal of reinforcing autonomy. Zhivkov's campaign of forced assimilation directed against Bulgaria's Turkish minority during the 1980s was likewise a demagogic effort to identify the regime with nationalist opinion. Such measures were distasteful, but not altogether ineffective. The cycles of popular mobilization and Soviet-led repression that unfolded in Hungary, Czechoslovakia, and Poland had no equivalent in Southeastern Europe. Balkan backwardness left more room for extensive growth models to satisfy citizen demands, authoritarian traditions had deeper roots, civil society remained less developed, and frustrated nationalism was a wild card available for manipulation when all else failed. Despite real achievements in promoting economic growth and social equity, the authoritarian regimes of the cold war Balkans would leave a heavy legacy once the death knell of European communism had sounded.

Yugoslavia Redux.

The most distinctive of the cold war communist regimes was unquestionably Titoist Yugoslavia. The Yugoslav communists had emerged triumphant from the civil war of 1941-45 in large measure due to their commitment to represent all of the Yugoslav peoples, and from the outset Tito's government sought to avoid the errors of the interwar regime by promoting a true multinational federation. Tito's wartime record gave him domestic legitimacy, and his defiance of Stalin won widespread international admiration. With its central location, impressive diversity, ideological affinities with Soviet-style communist regimes, and close economic and strategic relations with the West, Yugoslavia was a vital cold war actor.

Over time, the Yugoslav system became a close reflection of the personal priorities of its leader. Although Tito was an eminently practical ruler who left no significant theoretical legacy, it is possible to speak of "Titoism" to characterize the unique qualities of Yugoslavia's socialist model.[87] This was not a static model, but it did present elements of continuity.[88] In comparison with the unredeemed or barely inflected Stalism of the Soviet bloc states, or of neighboring Albania, Yugoslav communism was remarkably liberal and open. As a model for sustainable social and economic development it was nonetheless badly flawed. Was it fatally flawed? Many analysts have placed the "wages of communism" alongside of "ancient hatreds" as a means of explaining Yugoslavia's anarchic disintegration in the 1990s—the anti-democratic essence of Titoism, it is argued, made it impossible for the regime to develop defense mechanisms that could sustain it once the protective shield of the party state and supreme leader was withdrawn.[89] There is obviously some truth to such arguments, but it is a partial truth. Post-communist development within a Yugoslav framework could have occurred had the right choices been made. The fact that those choices were not made was not preordained, either by the poisoned harvest of ethnic rivalry or by the foibles of communist state systems.[90] There was nothing inexorable about Yugoslavia's demise—it was an "avoidable catastrophe."[91]

From the outset, Titoism rested upon an unambiguous commitment to the Yugoslav idea, embodied in the omnipresent slogan "Brotherhood and Unity" (*bratstvo i jedinstvo*). Through the

1950s, the 19th century aspiration to create a common Yugoslav identity was favored. Thereafter, consociational relations between Yugoslavia's varied nations and national minorities received greater emphasis. In retrospect, by opening the door to a stronger affirmation of ethnic nationalism, the shift in direction may well have been fatal.

The basis for Titoist national policy was the Soviet system of titular nationalities, according to which officially recognized national communities were granted a degree of autonomy within their "own" territorial units, though subordinated to national institutions on the federal level. A basic distinction was made between constituent nations with the republican status and a formal right of secession, and national minorities, defined as communities that were already represented by a neighboring state, and therefore denied republican status and a right to secede (the Magyars of Vojvodina and the Kosovar Albanians were cases in point).[92] Bosnia-Herzegovina was an exception to the rule, insofar as it did not contain a single dominant constituent nation or titular nationality. Though the Bosnian Muslims were recognized as a constituent nation in 1961, they did not represent a majority of the republic's population. In the case of Macedonia, a concerted effort was made to formalize a Macedonian literary language that was distinct from Bulgarian (the two languages are nearly identical), and to bolster a distinctive Macedonian Slavic identity. The borders between republics were in many cases identical to historical boundaries. In other cases, such as the boundary between Serbia and Croatia in Slavonia, lines were drawn according to approximate ethnic and geographical divisions. Yugoslavia's internal borders would become objects of contestation during the 1990s, but they were established as a matter of convenience, with the intent to unite rather than to divide.

The Serbs, representing 40 percent of the total Yugoslav population and with a wide geographic distribution inside the country, posed a special problem. Great Serbian chauvinism had damaged the Yugoslav idea during the inter-war decades, and an unspoken premise of Titoism was "a weak Serbia means a strong Yugoslavia." From the outset, Montenegro was set apart from Serbia as a full-fledged republic. Serbia was also the only Yugoslav republic to be internally sub-divided. In the north, a Vojvodina Autonomous Province with its capital in the Danubian city of Novi Sad was created to represent an area of great ethnic complexity including a large Magyar minority. In the south, a Kosovo Autonomous Province was constituted to administer an historically disputed area that included many of Serbia's most important cultural shrines, but also a population that was at least 80 percent Albanian. It was further decided to deny the Serb populated areas in Croatia's Krajina and Slavonia regions a status analogous to that of the autonomous provinces established inside Serbia. Diluting the critical mass of the Serb population inside the Yugoslav federation was the unspoken goal.

Even the most refined manipulation could not put feuding among Yugoslav nationalities to rest. Prior to the crisis of the Yugoslav state at the end of the 1980s, however, ethnic rivalry was a muted theme in national life. The era of international political contestation of the late 1960s and early 1970s gave rise to manifestations of ethnic nationalism, but they focused on reform of Yugoslav institutions rather than challenges to the Yugoslav idea, and were eventually co-opted by a combination of repression and concession. Albanian demonstrations in Kosovo and western Macedonia in November 1968, prompted by a sense of socio-economic discrimination and focused on demands for special status were put down by force, and public opinion was calmed by limited concessions—Kosovo was granted the status of an autonomous province, display of the Albanian flag with its red background and black double headed Eagle was permitted as a national symbol, and a bi-lingual (Serbo-Croatian and Albanian) University of Priština was chartered.[93] A dispute over funding and routing for inter-republican highways led to a brief flare up of friction between Slovenia and the federal government in 1969, revealing of emerging inter-republic rivalries but not a threat in its own right.[94] Most dramatically, cultural and social issues propelled a reformist coalition to power in Zagreb in the late 1960s and sparked a "mass movement" (*masovni pokret*, usually abbreviated as *maspok*) demanding expanded cultural autonomy that some Western observers dubbed the Croatian Spring. Anti-Yugoslav elements were associated with the movement at the margin, but, like the Prague Spring phenomenon in Alexander Dubček's Czechoslovakia, it was essentially a reformist current spearheaded by the leadership of the Croatian League of Communists. The movement was suppressed after Tito's personal intervention in the course of 1971, leaving a legacy of alienation.[95] These incidents were important, but they were exceptions to the rule. Yugoslavia's commitment to the ethic of *bratstvo i jedinstvo* was profound, and appreciated by a clear majority of citizens.

In the aftermath of victory in 1945, Tito and his lieutenants set out to impose a mirror image of the Soviet system that they had learned to admire as militants in the service of the Comintern. After the break with Stalin in 1948, it became necessary to differentiate Yugoslavia from a Soviet Union that had suddenly become a menacing rival. From 1948 onward Titoism emerged as a variant of national communism, aggressively patriotic and insistent that a strategy for social change must be crafted in light of local circumstances. In the context of the Cold War, many of Tito's initiatives appeared innovative, but they were often frustrated by the authoritarian context within which Yugoslav experimentation was forced to unfold. From 1950 onward, under the direction of Kardelj, a commitment to the concept of workers' self-management became a pillar of a new economic strategy intended to impose direction "from the bottom up" and bring to life the old socialist ideals of workers' control and grass roots democracy.[96] Yugoslav self-management evolved constantly, but though self-management committees soon became a fixture in every public enterprise, the system never came close to achieving its more ambitious aspirations. Direction at the point of production was never seriously forwarded as an alternative to the pervasive role of the ruling party (after 1952 renamed the Yugoslav League of Communists). The public challenge launched by Milovan Djilas from 1954 onward, warning of the eventual consequences of a communist monopoly of power and urging movement towards broader political pluralism, was greeted with political ostracism and a series of jail sentences.[97] The liberal tendencies that coalesced around the Croatian *maspok* in the early 1970s were squelched, and in 1972 Tito moved to oust a liberal faction arguing for democratization within the Serbian League of Communists—a fateful gesture from which many of the disasters of the 1990s would eventually spring.[98] The cult of Tito was less foreboding than the Stalin cult in the USSR, but no less totalitarian in its implications. And the logic of economic liberalization was not followed consistently. Buoyed by generous economic assistance from the United States in the 1950s, and the World Bank and other international development funds thereafter, Yugoslavia was able to maintain high rates of growth, a substantial military sector, and aspirations to European living standards without confronting the need for fundamental economic redirection.

When it did turn to a more comprehensive reform program in 1966 implementation was piecemeal and half-hearted — through the 1970s growth rates and living standards were maintained artificially by borrowing. Even with all its flaws, however, the Yugoslav economic model remained more attuned to the exigencies of the world market than the economic systems of its communist neighbors, and more sensitive to real citizen demands.

Internationally, Titoism rested upon a commitment to non-alignment as an alternative for developing states against the backdrop of cold war bipolarity. Tito himself became one of the founders and most outspoken champions of the nonaligned movement, for which Yugoslavia was the only European affiliate. He reveled in the role of a leading international personality, and used his personal stature to give Yugoslavia a visibility and influence in world affairs that was incommensurate with its real strategic weight. For critics, the aspiration to stand at the head of the Third World regimes affiliated with the non-aligned movement represented a form of overreaching that only served to obscure Yugoslavia's inevitable European vocation. But international prestige helped the regime sustain itself in the face of domestic critics, and was a source of national pride. It also mirrored Yugoslavia's careful balancing act, following a partial rapprochement with Nikita Khrushchev's USSR from 1955 onward, between Western sponsors and the Soviet superpower.

Tito's Yugoslavia was successful in promoting economic growth, re-creating a shared political space after the terrible bloodletting of the war years, and sustaining international independence and prestige in the polarized climate of cold war Europe. The new Yugoslavia continued to fulfill many of the functions for which the Yugoslav idea had originally been conceived — to provide an alternative to political fragmentation and conflict over territory in a region marked by strong inter-culturality, promote development by maintaining an integrated economic space, and prevent the manipulation of local rivalries by external powers. It remained a fragile state nonetheless, with a sharp developmental divide between north and south that the best efforts of the regime could not succeed in closing, festering ethnic tensions that were contained but not eliminated, and a democratic deficit embodied by the dominating role of Tito himself. In the wake of the suppression of political agitation in Croatia and Serbia during 1971-72, Tito shifted back toward a policy of concession by promulgating the new federalist constitution of 1974.

This document, one of the longest constitutions in world history and correspondingly complex, attempted to address the Yugoslav national dilemma by delegating authority to the republic level, a potentially dangerous devolution that presumed tight oversight on the part of a League of Communists that was itself increasingly fragmented along republic lines. Broadened autonomy for the republics and autonomous provinces proved to be viable so long as Tito himself was on hand to play the role of arbiter. In his absence, it would prove to be a recipe for disaster.

Tito's death in May 1980, after a protracted illness, initiated a long crisis that would culminate a decade later with the state's anarchic collapse. The crisis had distinct and overlapping dimensions. By the late 1970s the economic boom that had been so important a source of stability had turned to bust. Endemic inefficiencies, the cumulative burden of politically motivated concentration on heavy industry, and adverse world market trends created shortfalls that were increasingly met by borrowing. By 1980, external debt approached $20 billion, or 5 percent of Gross Domestic Product, and debt service had become a permanent drain on state revenues.

During the ensuing decade a sequence of ineffective plans for "stabilization" failed to reverse a sharp and continuous economic decline. In 1989 Yugoslav foreign debt remained near $17 billion, and in December of that year the dinar (the national currency unit) fell prey to hyperinflation.[99] Tito's 1974 constitution, with its exaggerated federalism, also created a crisis of leadership. Tito himself, who had served as president for life, was replaced by a collective presidency with eight members representing each of Yugoslavia's federal entities (the six republics plus Vojvodina and Kosovo) rotating annually in the position of chair. The arrangement was a good example of the exaggerated sensitivity to ethnic balance that characterized the 1974 constitutional order, and a recipe for ineffectiveness — it is no surprise that in the post-Tito years no national leader was able to emerge with an agenda for positive change. In fact, the 1974 constitution created a general crisis of federal institutions by concentrating power inside the individual republics and provinces and creating a situation of "republican autarky" that made the crafting of consensual national policy virtually impossible. Yugoslavia also moved slowly toward a crisis of legitimacy. From 1985 onward Mikhail Gorbachev was working to promote détente between the Soviet Union and the West. In the process he softened competitive bipolarity and undermined non-alignment as a third way alternative. Revival of the project for European unification with the promulgation of the Single European Act in 1987 raised concerns that Yugoslavism, with its undemocratic essence, third world orientation, and assumptions of national exceptionalism, would eventually become a barrier to integration with Europe.

Not least, the crisis of European communism from 1989 directly affected what had always been the most essential foundation of Titoism—its affiliation with the international communist movement's world historical project for social transformation. Despite its independence and individuality, Tito's Yugoslavia was first and foremost a personal dictatorship and a communist party state built upon a rigid ideological foundation. Without Tito, and the red star that lit his way, very little would remain to bind the constituent parts of Aleksa Djilas' "contested country" together.[100]

The Short 20th Century.

Eric Hobsbawm's "short 20th century" begins with the assassination of Franz Ferdinand in Sarajevo on June 28, 1914, and ends with the destruction of the Berlin Wall on the night of November 10-11, 1989. For Hobsbawm, the defining event of the century was the First World War, which shattered traditional sources of cohesion, and gave birth to international communism as an anti-systemic movement aimed at the subversion of the liberal world order.[101] The communist challenge eventually became embodied in the interstate rivalry between the United States and the USSR that we have come to call the Cold War. The collapse of international communism, culminated by the implosion of the Soviet Union at the end of 1991, brought a phase of world history to an end.

Past may be prologue, but more than a decade after the end of the Cold War the nature of the new world order that is taking its place remains unclear. The cold war system was competitive and militarized, but it included shared assumptions about the nature of strategic interaction and a significant cooperative dimension.[102] The widespread perception of a "post-cold war disorder," for which the Balkan crisis of the 1990s may serve as an appropriate model, emerges from the absence of such assumptions, and of the constraint once imposed by competitive bipolarity. For sub-regional complexes such as the Balkans, the Cold War offered a relatively stable strategic context, a sense of direction defined by international alignments, the possibility for development under great power sponsorship, and a framework for identity with ideological underpinnings that looked beyond the narrow confines of blood and soil. For Greece and Turkey, association with the Euro-Atlantic community became a stimulus for development, and helped contain bilateral tensions. Inside the Warsaw Pact, communism provided a functional context for modernization, and imposed a kind of *pax sovietica* in areas still divided by disputes over territory and identity. Yugoslavia was respected and admired, and its flaws downplayed or overlooked, precisely because it seemed to represent a viable third way that avoided subservience to either of the antagonistic blocs. Though often harsh and dictatorial, the cold war system in the Balkans supplied a predictable context for domestic development, interstate relations, and great power engagement.

The Balkan communist regime that would be most severely affected by the end of the short twentieth century was Yugoslavia, ironically the most liberal of them all. In retrospect this is not as surprising as it might appear at first glance. Yugoslav communism was an indigenous phenomenon, not imposed by an external aggressor, and therefore more integral to the state's identity and cohesion, and less easily discarded, than was the case in neighboring regimes. The relative success of Titoism made the collapse of the Yugoslav development model that occurred during the 1980s all the harder to bear. Given the challenges of ethnic complexity and a recent history of inter-communal bloodletting, the Yugoslav experiment was inherently at risk. And the strong international sponsorship that had helped Tito to defy Stalin was no longer forthcoming. During the cold war decades a violent disintegration of the Yugoslav federation such as occurred during the 1990s would not have been allowed. The superpowers had too much at stake to permit an eruption of anarchic warfare in a critical theater, and they possessed the will to prevent it. After 1989, with the Warsaw Pact in tatters, Tito's fragile federation lost much of its salience as a strategic buffer, and as a positive example for neighboring regimes still subject to Soviet control.

As the 1990s dawned the only realistic option for the post-communist Balkan states seemed to be association with a triumphant West. But the euphoria of the "end of history" was short-lived.[103] The European powers, unprepared for the collapse of cold war structures, preoccupied with other issues, and unconvinced that the game was worth the candle, were reluctant to engage the new democratic states of the region unambiguously. Meanwhile, the collapse of Yugoslavia, promoted by primitive nationalisms that seemed to be very much rooted in history indeed, gave rise to a series of local wars that plunged the entire region into a spiral of decline, and left the international community at a loss to make sense of the chaos. Against a backdrop of burning villages and ethnic violence, long dormant images of the Balkans as a land beyond the pale of civilization sprang back to life, the great powers struggled to define their priorities in a secondary theater where vital interests did not appear to be at stake, and the premises of a viable regional order became more and more difficult to define.

Part of the reason for the difficulty was the implosion of the instrument forged by the history of the 20th century to serve as the keystone for political order in the multicultural Balkans—a south Slavic federation. For all its flaws, Yugoslavia permitted civilized cohabitation between its diverse peoples and allowed unresolved national questions to be managed according to something other than zero sum criteria. If the federation was a lost cause, and there are grounds for arguing that in view of the new dynamics created by the end of the Cold War it had at a minimum become dysfunctional, it was urgently necessary to define alternative patterns of regional order capable of addressing the dilemmas traditionally managed by voluntary association. Easily stated in retrospect, the complex circumstances surrounding Yugoslavia's decline made this a difficult conclusion to grasp and act upon when it counted. Faced with dramatically altered circumstances and hosts of unknowns, Yugoslavia's citizenry and the international community should have striven to preserve the federation at all costs as the only instrument capable of providing a stable framework for transition toward new patterns of interaction. Whether through neglect, disorientation, or active support for new political forces bent upon sowing the wind of nationalism, they did not do so, and would reap the whirlwind of war.

ENDNOTES - CHAPTER 2

1. Miranda Vickers, *The Albanians: A Modern History*, London: I. B. Taurus, 1995, pp. 117-140.

2. The Radić assassination was deeply resented in Croatia, where it became a source of enduring bitterness. See Dušan Bilandžić, *Hrvatska moderna povijest*, Zagreb: Golden Marketing, 1999, pp. 80-90, and Zvonimir Kulundžić, *Attentat na Stjepana Radića*, Zagreb: Stvarnost, 1967.

3. Richard J. Crampton, *A Concise History of Modern Bulgaria*, Cambridge: Cambridge University Press, 1997, pp. 148-171.

4. Vlad Georgescu, *The Romanians: A History*, Columbus: Ohio State University Press, 1991, pp. 189-222; and Ewald Hibbeln, *Codreanu und die Eiserne Garde*, Siegen: J. G. Herder-Bibliothek Siegerland e. V., 1984.

5. C. M. Woodhouse, *Modern Greece: A Short History*, London: Faber & Faber, 1968, pp. 212-237.

6. Feroz Ahmad, *The Making of Modern Turkey*, London: Routledge, 1993, pp. 52-71.

7. The best overview remains Joseph Rothschild, *East Central Europe between the Two World Wars*, Seattle: University of Washington Press, 1974, pp. 201-366.

8. See Renata Bournazel, *Rapallo: Naissance d'un mythe: La politique de la peur dans la France du bloc national*, Paris: Fondation nationale des sciences politiques, 1974.

9. Magda Adam, *The Little Entente and Europe, 1920-1929*, Budapest: Akademiai Kiadó, 1993.

10. E. H. Carr, *International Relations Between the Two World Wars, 1919-1939*, New York: Harper Torchback, 1947, pp. 213-214. The Balkan Entente was focused on the German menace but it had the effect of creating new barriers to regional cooperation. Bulgaria originally refused to join if it meant accepting the legitimacy of its postwar borders, and Albania was not invited to participate. Plamen Tsvetkov, *Evropeiskite sili, balkanite i kolektivnata sigurnost 1933-1935*, Sofia: Izdatelstvo na Bŭlgarskata Akademiia na Naukite, 1990, pp. 78-84. See also Robert Joseph Kerner and Harry Nicholas Howard, *The Balkan Conference and the Balkan Entente, 1930-1935: A Study in the Recent History of the Balkan and Near Eastern Peoples*, Berkeley: University of California Press, 1936; and Theodore I. Geshkoff, *Balkan Union: A Road to Peace in Southeastern Europe*, New York: Columbia University Press, 1940, pp. 203-231.

11. Louis Adamic, *The Native's Return*, New York: Harper & Brothers, 1934, p. 188. John R. Lampe, *Yugoslavia as History: Twice There was a Country*, 2nd ed., Cambridge: Cambridge University Press, 2000, p. 164, describes inter-war Yugoslavia as "trapped in the wings of a wider international stage."

12. Elinor Murray Despatalović, *Ljudevit Gaj and the Illyrian Movement*, New York: Columbia University Press, 1975.

13. Mirjana Gross, *Vladavina Hrvatske-Srpske Koalicije 1906-1917*, Belgrade: Jugoslavenski Istorijski Institut, 1960.

14. See Gale Stokes, "The Role of the Yugoslav Committee in the Formation of Yugoslavia," in Dimitrije Djordjevic, ed., *The Creation of Yugoslavia 1914-1918*, Santa Barbara, CA: Clio Books, 1980, pp. 51-72.

15. Milorad Ekmečić, "Serbian War Aims," in Djordjević, *The Creation Of Yugoslavia*, pp. 19-36; and Dragoslav Janković, "Niška deklaracija," *Istorija XX veka*, No. 10, 1969, pp. 7-11. Lampe, *Yugoslavia as History*, p. 102, proposes that the declaration "is best seen as a defensive document intended to attract wartime support from Habsburg South Slavs."

16. Cited in Marcus Tanner, *Croatia: A Nation Forged in War*, New Haven: Yale University Press, 1997, p. 115.

17. Cited in Paul Garde, *Vie et mort de la Yougoslavie*, Paris: Fayard, 1992, p. 50.

18. The Chetnik Stevan Moljević, associated with the Serbian national movement of Draža Mihailović, proposed an arrangement along these lines at the outset of the Second World War. Lampe, *Yugoslavia as History*, p. 206.

19. See the influential study by Ivo Banac, *The National Question in Yugoslavia: Origins, History, Politics*, Ithaca, NY: Cornell University Press, 1984. In the words of Philippe Boulanger, *La Bosnie-Herzégovine: Une géopolitique de la déchirure*, Paris: Éditions Karthala, 2002, p. 32: "the first Yugoslvia did nothing more than to impose, from above, a common structure upon peoples with histories, cultures, and collective memories that were radically different. The Yugoslav idea may be viewed as an ill-considered attempt to found a small empire in the face of great empires, and to counter, to the extent possible, the influence of pan-Germanism in the Balkans."

20. Andrew Baruch Wachtel, *Making a Nation, Breaking a Nation: Literature and Cultural Politics in Yugoslavia*, Stanford: Stanford University Press, 1998, pp. 67-127, details efforts to foster a common south Slavic identity in inter-war Yugoslavia.

21. Branko Dzhordzhevich, *Kominternŭt i iugoslavskata komunisticheska partiia 1919-1929*, Sofia: Izdatelstvo na Bŭlgarskata Akademiia na Naukite, 1987.

22. Stephen Palmer and Robert King, *Yugoslav Communism and the Macedonian Question*, Hamden, CT: Archon Books, 1971, pp. 31-46; and Kostadin Paleshutski,

Iugoslavskata komunisticheska partiia i makedonskiit vŭpros 1919-1945, Sofia: Izdatelstvo na Bŭlgarskata Akademiia na Naukite, 1985.

23. Martin L. Van Crefeld, *Hitler's Strategy 1940-1941: The Balkan Clue*, Cambridge: Cambridge University Press, 1973.

24. Mario Cervi, *The Hollow Legions: Mussolini's Blunder in Greece 1940-1941*, Garden City, NY: Doubleday, 1971.

25. Misha Glenny, *The Balkans: Nationalism, War and the Great Powers, 1804-1999*, New York: Viking, 2000, p. 473.

26. Mark Mazower, *Inside Hitler's Greece: The Experience of Occupation, 1941-1944*, New Haven: Yale University Press, 1993.

27. Bilandžić, *Hrvatska Moderna Povijest*, pp. 120-125.

28. On these events, see David H. Close, *The Origins of the Greek Civil War*, London: Longman, 1995; and C. M. Woodhouse, *The Struggle for Greece 1941-1949*, London: Hart-Davis, MacGibbon, 1976.

29. On the Pavelić regime, see Ladislav Hory, *Der kroatische Ustasha Staat, 1941-1945*, Stuttgart: Deutsche Verlags-Anstalt, 1964; and Fikreta Jelić-Butić, *Ustaše i Nezavisna Država Hrvatska, 1941-1945*, Zagreb: Školska Knjiga, 1977. Budak, a literary figure of some significance, signed the Pavelić regime's 1941 racial law, which identified a "Jewish Problem" in Croatia and Bosnia-Herzegovina. During the 1990s a number of Croatian cities, including Split, renamed streets in his honor.

30. The extent of the Ustaša genocide became a subject of ideologically charged (and highly distasteful) debate in the postwar decades. Franjo Tudjman helped recreate himself politically as a Croatian nationalist by publicly arguing for a radical reduction in the number of victims officially expounded in Titoist Yugoslavia (the official figures were 1.7 million total victims including 700,000 killed in the Jasenovac death camp). Balanced and credible studies prepared in Yugoslavia during the 1980s reduced the total number of victims to about one million, including 500,000 Serbs. See Bogoljub Kočović, *Žrtve drugog svjetskog rata u Jugoslaviji*, London: Naše Delo, 1985 and Vladimir Žerjavić, *Gubici stanovništva Jugoslavije u drugom svjetskom ratu*, Zagreb: Jugoslovensko viktimološko društvo, 1990. This did not prevent the manipulation of the issue for political purposes during the phase of Yugoslavia's disintegration. The Serb nationalist leader Vuk Drašković, *Odgovori*, Belgrade: Stilos, 1993, p. 84, argued a total of 1.5 million Serb victims alone. Garde, *Vie et Mort de la Yougoslavie*, pp. 75-85, usefully summarizes the debate and its implications.

31. Milovan Djilas, *Wartime: With Tito and the Partisans*, New York: Harcourt

Brace Jovanovich, 1977, gives a portrait of the process of mobilization at work.

32. Walter R. Roberts, *Tito, Mihailović, and the Allies, 1941-1945*, New Brunswick, NJ: Rutgers University Press, 1973; and Jozo Tomasevich, *The Chetniks*, Stanford: Stanford University Press, 1975.

33. This remarkable interaction is described in Winston Churchill, *Triumph and Tragedy*, Boston: Houghton Mifflin, 1953, pp. 194-195.

34. The classic study is L.S. Stavrianos, *Balkan Federation: A History of the Movement toward Balkan Unity in Modern Times*, Hamden, CT: Archon Books, 1964. On the Communist Balkan Federation, see Joseph Rothschild, *The Communist Party of Bulgaria: Origin and Development*, New York: Columbia University Press, 1959, pp. 223-254.

35. Cited in Branko Petranović, *Balkanska federacija 1943-1948*, Belgrade: Edicija Svedočanstvo, 1991, pp. 34-37.

36. Paul Shoup, *Communism and the Yugoslav National Question*, New York: Columbia University Press, 1968, pp. 84-85.

37. Petranović, *Balkanska federacija*, p. 60; and *Dokumenti o spoljnoj političi Socijalističke Federativne Republike Jugoslavije 1943*, Belgrade: Jugoslovenski pregled, 1985, pp. 224, 228.

38. Support for the goal of a Bulgarian-Yugoslav federation was articulated at the session by the Bulgarian communist emissary Shteria Atanasov (alias Viktor), a message presumably approved by Bulgarian communist leader Georgi Dimitrov in Moscow. Petranović, *Balkanska federacija*, p. 73.

39. Cited in Branko Petranović, "Kosovo in Yugoslav-Albanian Relations and the Project of a Balkan Federation," reprinted from *Serbs and Albanians in the 20th Century*, Academic Conference of the Serbian Academy of Sciences and Arts, Vol. LXI, Department of Historical Sciences, No. 20, Belgrade, 1991, p. 348.

40. Petranović, *Balkanska federacija*, pp. 90-93.

41. Djilas recalls that during his visit to Albania in May 1945 "there was unofficial talk of their joining Yugoslavia as one unit in a future Balkan federation," and notes that during 1945-1946 "we all assumed we were heading toward economic and political unity." Milovan Djilas, *Rise and Fall*, San Diego: Harcourt Brace Jovanovich, 1985, pp. 110, 113.

42. Milcho Lalkov, *Ot nadezhda kum razocharovanie: Ideiata za federatsiiata v balkanskiia iugoiztok (1944-1948 g.)*, Sofia: Natsionalniia Tsentŭr na Knigata, 1993, pp. 101-105. On negotiations between military commands see Svetozar

Vukmanović-Tempo, *Revolucija koja teče: Memoari*, 2 vols., Belgrade: Kommunist, 1971, Vol. I, pp. 413-426.

43. According to the memoirs of the Slovenian communist leader Edvard Kardelj, Stalin encouraged Tito to consider the option of a Balkan federation during these sessions. "The idea of that federation," writes Kardelj, "was given to Tito by Stalin himself in the autumn of 1944, when Tito met him for the first time." Edvard Kardelj, *Borba za priznanje i nezavisnost nove Jugoslavije, 1944-1957, Sečanja*, Belgrade: Radnička stampa, 1980, p. 103.

44. Lalkov, *Ot nadezhda kum razocharovanie*, pp. 76-100. Dobrin Michev, *Makedonskiiat vŭpros i bŭlgaro-iugoslavskite otnosheniia, 9 septemvri 1944-1949*, Sofia: Universitetsko izdatelstvo "Sv. Kliment Okhridski," 1994, pp. 57-76, offers a Bulgarian nationalist perspective on these interactions that accuses the Bulgarian communist leadership of "national nihilism" in regard to the Macedonian Question.

45. The texts of these variants are assembled in Ž. Abramovski, "Devet projekata ugovora o jugoslovensko-bugarskom savezu i federaciji (1944-1947)," *Istorija XX veka*, No. 2, 1983, pp. 91-124.

46. These negotiations are analyzed in Lalkov, *Ot nadezhda kum razocharovanie*, pp. 158-163. See also G. Daskalov, "Problemŭt za federatsiiata v bŭlgaro-iugoslavskite otnosheniia (noemvri 1944-april 1945)," *Izvestiia na Instituta po Istoriia na BKP*, No. 62, 1988, pp. 5-53; and Petranović, *Balkanska federacija*, pp. 121-130.

47. Lalkov, *Ot nadezhda kum razocharovanie*, pp. 164-165.

48. In his diary Josip Smodlaka, who represented the Yugoslavs during many of the talks, claims that on December 19, 1944, Tito showed him a draft treaty defining a permanent political, military, and customs union between Yugoslavia and Bulgaria, and states that a similar draft treaty with Albania was being prepared. Josip Smodlaka, *Partizanski dnevnik*, Belgrade: Nolit, 1972, p. 224.

49. L. Ia. Gibianskii, *Sovetskii soiuz i novaia Iugoslaviia 1941-1947 gg.*, Moscow: Nauka, 1987, pp. 122-124.

50. Elizabeth Barker, *British Policy in South-East Europe in the Second World War*, New York: Barnes & Noble, 1976, pp. 200-201.

51. Tito nonetheless continued to speak enthusiastically about prospects for association. See, for example, his remarks of June 13, 1945, to the Bulgarian First Army in *Dokumenti o spoljnoj političi Socijalističke Federativne Republike Jugoslavije 1945*, Belgrade: Jugoslovenski pregled, 1984, p. 91.

52. Between 1939 and early 1944 the Greek communist movement received no

official communications from either the Soviet Union or the Comintern, and the KKE was not listed among the parties officially informed of the dissolution of the Comintern in May 1943. Giorgio Vaccarino, *La Grecia tra resistenza e guerra civile 1940-1949*, Milan: F. Angeli, 1988, p. 63.

53. Peter J. Stavrakis, *Moscow and Greek Communism, 1944-1949*, Ithaca, NY: Cornell University Press, 1989, p. 29.

54. Woodhouse, *The Struggle for Greece*, p. 23.

55. Petranović, "Kosovo in Yugoslav-Albanian Relations," p. 348, and *Balkanska federacija*, p. 138.

56. See Slobodan Nešović, *Bledski sporazumi: Tito-Dimitrov 1947*, Zagreb: Globus, 1979. The minutes of the proceedings and documents appear in *Dokumenti o spoljnoj političi Socijalističke Federativne Republike Jugoslavije 1947*, Vol. 2, Belgrade: Jugoslovenski pregled, 1986, pp. 84-100.

57. Stefano Bianchini suggests that at this point Stalin saw in the goal of federation "the possibility of affirming his own hegemony, ideological and political, over the Balkan Communist parties." Stefano Bianchini, *Sarajevo, le radici dell'odio: Identità e destino dei popoli balcanici*, Rome, 1993, p. 214.

58. Lalkov, *Ot nadezhda kum razocharovanie*, pp. 246-249.

59. During his first state visit to Belgrade in June 1946, Hoxha had discussed the option of federation with Tito, judged retrospectively as "in principle the right way" but a concept "which still needed a lot of work." Enver Hoxha, *The Titoists: Historical Notes*, Tirana: 8 Nëntori, 1982, p. 328. On Stalin's talks with Hoxha in Moscow, see D. S. Chubakhin, "S diplomaticheskoi missiei v Albanii," *Otechestvennaia istoriia*, No. 1, 1995, pp. 121-122. The text of the telegram is given in Iu. S. Girenko, *Stalin – Tito*, Moscow: Izdatel'stvo politicheskoi literatury, 1991, pp. 325-326. See also Nedelcho Ganchovski, *Dnite na Dimitrov, kakto gi vidakh i zapisakh*, 2 vols., Sofia: Partizdat, 1975, Vol. I, pp. 494-495.

60. Hoxha, *The Titoists*, pp. 316-359; and the postscript to Chubakhin, "S diplomaticheskoi missiei," pp. 131-140.

61. Texts in "Konflikt, kotorogo ne dolzhno bylo byt' (iz istorii sovetsko-iugoslovenskikh otnoshenii)," *Vestnik ministerstva inostrannykh del SSSR*, No. 6, Vol. 64, March 31, 1990, pp. 57, 59. See also Girenko, *Stalin-Tito*, pp. 336-338.

62. The best account is in Vukmanović-Tempo, *Revolucija koja teče*, Vol. 2, pp. 44-59. The Soviet side was equally displeased with its Yugoslav guests. Note the telegram of January 7, 1948, from the Soviet Ambassador in Belgrade A. I. Lavrent'ev to Molotov in "Konflikt, kotorogo ne dolzhno bylo byt'," p. 5.

63. Milovan Djilas, *Conversations with Stalin*, New York: Harcourt Brace & World, 1962, p. 143. Djilas claims to have responded that unification was at issue, not "swallowing," to which Stalin is alleged to have answered "Yes, yes, swallowing, here we are in agreement. You must swallow Albania, the sooner the better."

64. In this address Tito also made positive reference to the display of signs along the route of his motorcade through Bulgaria reading "we want federation." *Dokumenti o spoljnoj političi 1947*, Vol. 2, p. 372-373.

65. V. Zelenin, "Stalin protiv Tito: Istoki i peripeti konflikta 1948 goda," *Nauka i zhizn'*, No. 6, 1990, pp. 80-81.

66. L. Ia. Gibianskii, "K istorii sovetsko-iugoslovenskogo konflikta 1948-1953 gg.; Sekretnaia sovetsko-bulgarskaia vstrecha v Moskve 10 fevralia 1948 goda," *Sovetskoe slavianovedenie*, No. 3, 1991, p. 15; and Girenko, *Stalin – Tito*, p. 333.

67. Gibianskii, "K istorii," No. 3, 1991, p. 17. In an address to the second congress of the Fatherland Front on February 2, 1948, Dimitrov reiterated these comments, claiming that "we are far from the thought of creating any kind of Eastern bloc in any form whatsoever." *Ibid.*, p. 18.

68. The summons cited the emergence of "serious differences on foreign policy issues." "Konflikt, kotorogo ne dolzhno bylo byt'," p. 60.

69. The best description and analysis of the session is the series of articles by L. Ia. Gibianskii, "K istorii sovetsko-iugoslavskogo konflikta," *Sovetskoe slavianovedenie*, No. 3, 1991, pp. 12-23; No. 4, 1991, pp. 27-36; No. 1, 1992, pp. 42-56; and *Slavianovedenie*, No. 3, 1992, pp. 35-51. See also the participant accounts in Djilas, *Rise and Fall*, pp. 150-151; and Kardelj, *Borba za priznanje*, pp. 111-120.

70. Kardelj, *Borba za priznanje*, p. 113.

71. Vukmanović-Tempo, *Revolucija koja teče*, Vol. 2, pp. 60-62.

72. Lalkov, *Ot nadezhda kum razocharovanie*, p. 284.

73. Lampe, *Yugoslavia as History*, p. 245.

74. This remark is mentioned in the famous "Secret Speech" that Khrushchev delivered to a closed session of the Soviet Communist Party at its 20th Party Congress during 1956. See "O kul'te lichnosti," *Izvestiia TsK KPSS*, No. 1, 1989, p. 154.

75. Ivo Banac, *With Stalin Against Tito: Cominformist Splits in Yugoslav*

Communism, Ithaca, NY: Cornell University Press, 1988.

76. See Adam Ulam, *Titoism and the Cominform*, Cambridge, MA: Harvard University Press, 1952, and the insider perspective by Vladimir Dedijer, *The Battle Stalin Lost: Memoirs of Yugoslavia, 1948-1953*, New York: Gossett, 1971.

77. François Fejtö, *Histoire des démocraties populaires*, 2 vols., Paris: Éditions du Seuil, 1969, Vol. I, p. 256.

78. Elez Biberaj, *Albania: A Socialist Maverick*, Boulder: Westview Press, 1990, pp. 24-26.

79. The text of Truman's March 12, 1947, address to Congress outlining the doctrine, which committed the United States to resist communist expansion in the Near East, appears in Bruce Robellet Kuniholm, *The Origins of the Cold War in the Near East: Great Power Conflict in Iran, Turkey, and Greece*, Princeton: Princeton University Press, 1980, pp. 434-439.

80. Stefano Bianchini, "Conflitti e cooperazione regionale nei Balcani," in Roberto Spanò, ed., *Jugoslavia e Balcani: Una bomba in Europa*, Rome: FrancoAngeli, 1992, pp. 12-15; and Stefano Bianchini, "I Balcani tra rinnovamento e destabilizzazione," in L. Guazzone, ed., *L'Europa degli anni Novanta: La Geopolitica del cambiamento*, Milan: Angeli Editore, 1991, pp. 216-224.

81. Heinz Kramer, *A Changing Turkey: The Challenge to Europe and the United States*, Washington, DC: The Brookings Institution Press, 2000, pp. 1-92.

82. In an influential study published legally on the eve of the fall of the Todor Zhivkov regime, future Bulgarian President Zheliu Zhelev subtly, and not altogether unfairly, compared the character of communist totalitarianism and the cult of the leader to that of wartime fascism and nationalist-authoritarian regimes. Zheliu Zhelev, *Fashismŭt (Totalitarnata dŭrzhava)*, Sofia: Izdatelstvo na BZNS, 1990, pp., 307-327.

83. For many years the standard, admiring biography of Tito was Phyllis Auty, *Tito: A Biography*, New York: McGraw Hill, 1970. A critical reappraisal is offered by Richard West, *Tito and the Rise and Fall of Yugoslavia*, New York: Carroll Graf Publishers, Inc., 1994.

84. Vickers, *The Albanians*, pp. 185-209.

85. Crampton, *A Concise History of Modern Bulgaria*, pp. 164-215.

86. Stephen Fischer-Galati, *20th Century Romania*, 2nd ed., New York: Columbia University Press, 1991, pp. 159-206.

87. Fred Warner Neal, *Titoism in Action: The Reforms in Yugoslavia After 1948*, Berkeley: University of California Press, 1958, is an early effort in this direction that perceives the Yugoslav example as "a devastating criticism of Soviet theory and practice" (p. 33).

88. In the new discipline of comparative communist studies, a branch of comparative politics that developed inside Western academia from the 1960s onward, the Yugoslav model was nearly always singled out as a unique and exceptional variant. This was even more the case for Yugoslav scholarship, which went to great lengths to demonstrate the distinctiveness of Yugoslav socialism. Gary K. Bertsch and Thomas W. Ganschow, *Comparative Communism: The Soviet, Chinese, and Yugoslav Models*, San Francisco: W. H. Freeman, 1976; and Branko Pribićević, *Socijalizam: Uspon i pad*, Belgrade: Naučna knjiga, 1991, pp. 169-173.

89. Ivan Vejvoda, "Yugoslavia 1945-91: From Decentralization Without Democracy to Dissolution," in David A. Dyker and Ivan Vejvoda, eds., *Yugoslavia and After*, London: Longman, 1996, pp. 9-27.

90. "Although it is possible in hindsight to see why the Yugoslav experiment did not succeed," writes Andrew Wachtel, "it would be an error to think that its failure was inevitable. Specific choices made by groups and individuals destroyed it, but different choices could have been made." Wachtel, *Making a Nation, Breaking a Nation*, p. 228.

91. As described by Dennison Rusinow, "The Avoidable Tragedy," in Sabrina Petra Ramet and Ljubiša Adamović, eds., *Beyond Yugoslavia: Politics, Economics, and Culture in a Shattered Community*, Boulder: Westview Press, 1995, pp. 13-38.

92. The linguistic distinction, adapted from Soviet national policy, was that between the nation (*narod*), with a presumed right to sovereignty, and the nationality (*narodnost*) or national minority.

93. Vickers, *The Albanians*, 191-207.

94. Steven Burg, *Conflict and Cohesion in Socialist Yugoslavia*, Princeton: Princeton University Press, 1983, pp. 88-99.

95. Dennison Rusinow, *The Yugoslav Experiment 1948-1974*, Berkeley: University of California Press, 1977, pp. 287-307.

96. Stefano Bianchini, ed., *L'Autogestione jugoslava*, Milan: F. Angeli, 1982.

97. The best summary of Djilas' viewpoint, written under incarceration and an influential text in and outside of Yugoslavia in the years to come, is his *The New Class: An Analysis of the Communist System*, New York: Praeger, 1955.

98. Rusinow, *The Yugoslav Experiment*, pp. 318-326; and Slavoljub Djukić, *Slom srpskih liberala*, Belgrade: Filip Višnjić, 1990.

99. For perspectives on the economic decline of the 1980s, see David A. Dyker, *Yugoslavia: Socialism, Development, and Debt*, London: Routledge, 1996; Harold Lydall, *Yugoslavia in Crisis*, Oxford: Clarendon Press, 1989; and Susan L. Woodward, *Socialist Unemployment: The Political Economy of Yugoslavia, 1945-90*, Princeton: Princeton University Press, 1995.

100. Aleksa Djilas, *The Contested Country: Yugoslav Unity and Communist Revolution, 1919-53*, Cambridge, MA: Harvard University Press, 1991.

101. Eric Hobsbawm, *The Age of Extremes: The Short Twentieth Century, 1914-91*, London: Abacus, 1995.

102. Roger E. Kanet and Edward A. Kolodziej, eds., *The Cold War as Cooperation*, Baltimore: The Johns Hopkins University Press, 1991.

103. See the argument in Francis Fukuyama, *The End of History and the Last Man*, New York: The Free Press, 1992.

CHAPTER 3

THE STATE OF WAR:
SLOVENIA AND CROATIA, 1991-92

Battles and Quarrels.

Yugoslavia's decline during the 1980s was transformed into collapse due to the rise of opportunistic leaders in the republics, who found in nationalism a new source of legitimization and were willing to resort to ruthless measures to perpetuate power. The prototype of this new breed of "ethnocrat" was Serbia's Slobodan Milošević.[1]

Milošević was born in 1946 in the southern Serbian town of Požarevac. His parents were Montenegrin by origin, father Svetozar an Orthodox priest excommunicated by the Church for collaboration with the communist authorities after the war, and mother Stanislava a school director and party activist. Both parents would eventually take their own lives, but Stanislava's work with the League of Communists seems to have oriented her children toward political careers. Slobodan's older brother Borislav rose to become Yugoslav ambassador to Algeria, and his influence would prove useful in forwarding his sibling's ascent.[2]

Milošević's marriage while a law student at the University of Belgrade in the early 1960s to childhood sweetheart Mirjana (Mira) Marković, brought him closer to the Yugoslav political elite. Mira Marković's mother was associated with the communist underground in Belgrade during the war. In 1942, in a murky affair whose details remain unclear, she was executed by the partisans after being accused of revealing the names of comrades to the occupation authorities under torture. Mira was raised by her grandparents, while her estranged father went on to become the party chief of Serbia. It is insistently rumored that her mother was Tito's mistress, and that Mira was his illegitimate daughter.[3] Slobodan used such associations to help launch a career of his own. He early on became the protégé of the friend of his student years Ivan Stambulić, succeeding him during the 1970s as director of the Technogaz conglomerate, chief of cabinet for the mayor of Belgrade, and director of the Bank of Belgrade. When Stambulić moved to the head of the League of Communists of Serbia in 1984, Milošević was selected to occupy his vacated post as leader of the Belgrade League of Communists. Up to this point there was nothing particular remarkable in the story of a young man from the provinces made good--native talent, political connections, and sponsorship by a well-placed member of the power elite were typical roads to advancement for aspiring Yugoslav leaders.[4]

Milošević made his way to the top as a loyal servant of Stambolić, a flamboyant bureaucrat who was nonetheless devoted to the Yugoslav idea. His career took a turn in 1986, at a point when the crisis of post-Tito Yugoslavia was well advanced and "the preconditions of a revolutionary situation" were apparent.[5] One manifestation of the crisis was the rise of nationalist currents in Yugoslavia's republics. In both Slovenia and Croatia cultural leaders emphasized their Catholic and Central European heritage and precarious situation "on the edge of the Orthodox and Muslim abyss."[6] In Slovenia, the "New Cultural Movements" of the 1980s challenged stale dogmas with a provocative modernism that only partially disguised an emerging sense of cultural superiority. Croatian nationalism was squelched by the repression that followed the *maspok* of the early 1970s, but during the 1980s it revived with support from the anti-Yugoslav Croat Diaspora in Europe and North America. Franjo Tudjman, a former Titoist general and party historian who had associated with the Croatian national movement in the 1960s, was expelled from the Yugoslav League of Communists in 1967, and eventually served several terms in prison, was in touch with representatives of the émigré community from the mid-1980s onward.[7] In 1989 he founded the Croatian Democratic Community (*Hrvatska Demokratska Zajednica* — HDZ) as a forum for nationalist politics.[8] Most ominously, due to the critical mass and wide dispersion of the Serb population inside Yugoslavia, where about three million of the eight million plus Serbs in the federation lived outside of Serbia proper, a Serbian national revival began to articulate resentments that under Tito were strictly taboo.

A key event in the genesis of the new Serb nationalism was the partial publication in 1986 of a Memorandum drawn up by the Serbian Academy of Sciences describing a variety of grievances concerning the lot of the Serbs inside Yugoslavia. The gray eminence whose ideas inspired the document was the writer Dobrica Ćosić, a former partisan expelled from the League of Communists in 1968 for nationalist deviations, author of a series of novels tracing the course of modern Serbian history through the trials and tribulations of the fictional Katić family, firmly convinced, in the words of his hero Vukašin Katić, that the Yugoslav idea had been "the most costly and tragic illusion ever pursued by the Serbian people."[9] The Memorandum included the assertions that Serbia had consistently sacrificed its own interests on behalf of ungrateful neighbors, and was the victim of systematic discrimination, particularly due to the loss of control over Vojvodina and Kosovo imposed by the 1974 constitution. The document made the explosive claim that the ongoing exodus of the Serb minority from Kosovo was the result of "genocide" in progress propelled by a "physical, moral, and psychological reign of terror" that the federation was either unable or unwilling to prevent. Extracts from the text were published in the mass circulation Yugoslav daily *Večernje Novosti* in September 1986, probably in an attempt to discredit the argument by exposing it to public scrutiny, and were widely discussed.[10] Milošević publicly rebuked the Memorandum as late as June 1987, describing it as an expression of "the darkest nationalism."[11] In fact, the ill-stared initiative, subsequently characterized by Ivan Stambolić as a "requiem for Yugoslavia," offered precisely the kind of political platform that he needed to catapult to power.[12]

The cathartic event in Milošević's rise occurred on April 24, 1987, when, during a visit to Kosovo on behalf of Stambolić, who at the last moment sent his protégé in his stead, he stepped before a crowd of angry Serbs protesting mistreatment at the hands of the local Albanian police and intoned that "no one should dare to beat you" (*niko ne sme da vas bije*).The apparently spontaneous admonition was accompanied by an aggressive speech, in which the functionary from Belgrade, while admonishing that "we must preserve brotherhood and unity as the apple of our eye," also evoked the "injustice and humiliation" suffered by the Krajina Serbs.[13] Widely publicized, the remarks brought Milošević considerable popularity inside Serbia, as well as opprobrium in the non-Serb republics. It is still unclear at what point Milošević made a conscious decision to play the nationalist card. Up to this date he had always presented himself as an opponent of nationalist provocations, and may have been sincerely surprised, as well as flattered and fascinated, by the swell of public feeling that accompanied his initiative.[14] In the event, with this magical incantation the incongruous Sorcerer's Apprentice released the genie of Serb nationalism from the bottle where Tito had kept it enclosed for several generations.

The cameo appearance at Kosovo Polje won Milošević the support of a critical mass of Serb public opinion, and he ruthlessly pushed home his advantage, using nationalism to consolidate a political base inside Serbia and then to expand it. The first step was a consummate act of betrayal. Between June and December 1987, Milošević engineered the ouster of his friend and sponsor Stambolić, and took his place at the head of the League of Communists of Serbia. Serbian nationalism was not yet a battle cry — Stambolić was isolated and defeated politically in the back stabbing manner typical of the old style communist cadre.[15] But nationalism would become the be all and end all in the months to come, as the new master of Belgrade set out to ride the Serb wave to power in all of Yugoslavia.

The use of nationalism as a foundation for political legitimacy required the cultivation of popular support. During the summer of 1988 the preferred tactic for mobilization became a series of "meetings of truth," designed in the manner of religious revivals to "restore dignity" to the purportedly downtrodden Serbs. Encouraged by media support trumpeting the theme of national renaissance, millions of citizens flocked to such meetings conducted the length and breadth of Serbia. Nationalist agitation soon began to have a political impact. On October 5, 1988, crowds gathered in Novi Sad forced the resignation of the leadership of the Vojvodina Autonomous Province, which was immediately replaced with Milošević loyalists.[16] On November 17 the leadership of the Kosovo Autonomous Province was replaced after a similar protest.[17] Two days later, while strikers in Kosovo's Trepča mining complex vainly protested against the affront to provincial autonomy, over a million supporters arrived for the "meeting of meetings" in Belgrade, where Milošević boasted of Kosovo's eternal attachment to the Serbian motherland. In January 1989, again under the pressure of popular mobilization, the leadership of the Republic of Montenegro was forced to give way to Milošević supporters. These pretentiously termed "anti-bureaucratic revolutions" (a Tito-era concept originally intended to describe assaults against vested privilege) had, with shocking suddenness, brought four of the eight positions on the Yugoslav Federal Presidency under the control of one man, creating a "Serb Bloc" that shattered Titoist equilibriums. Between 1987 and 1989 these initiatives were lent a gothic coloration with the unprecedented public display, in a series of Orthodox monasteries, of an open coffin containing the bones of the 14th century Kosovo martyr Prince Lazar. The culmination of this phase of ethnic mobilization came with the great demonstration of Serb nationalism convoked on Kosovo Field on Vidovdan, June 28, 1989, the 600th anniversary of the legendary defeat. "Six centuries later," intoned Milošević to an adoring crowd from a high platform constructed on the Gazimestan battle site, "again we are in battles and quarrels. They are not yet armed battles, though such things should still not be excluded."[18]

Milošević had made himself the most powerful figure in the country, "the first Yugoslav leader to realize that Tito was dead," as a contemporary witticism had it. What did he aspire to accomplish? A May 1988 report published by the "Milošević Commission" argued for a renewed Yugoslav federation that would centralize authority, reestablish a national economic space, and promote efficiency through the mechanism of the free market. The agenda was respectable, but the coercive tactics that had brought Milošević to power went far toward discrediting the Yugoslav idea altogether, and his subsequent exercise of power demonstrated little allegiance to the values that the Milošević Commission sought to represent. Vidosav Stevanović characterizes Milošević's ideology as "Stalinism impregnated by Slavophilism and Orthodoxy," an apparent contradiction in terms that captures the confusion that still reigns concerning the Serbian strong man's long-term intentions.[19] Unlike his Croatian counterpart Tudjman, an exalted authoritarian nationalist, or Slovenian president Milan Kučan, a convinced nationalist liberal, Milošević was not a man of principle, but a political opportunist swept forward by a populist current unleashed in the void created by the collapse of Titoist norms.[20] Milošević was more than happy to ride with the tide, but as events would prove, his attempt to manipulate Serb nationalism amounted to seizing a tiger by the tail.

The absence of liberal resistance was a striking feature of Milošević's ascendancy. Inside of Serbia, Tito's purge of the Serbian League of Communists in the early 1970s had destroyed the careers of the most talented partisans of democratic reform, and the wave of nationalism unleashed after 1989 temporarily precluded effective opposition. On the federal level, the Bosnian Croat Ante Marković, who replaced Branko Mikulić as federal prime minister in December 1988, was the only major figure to step forward with a Yugoslav alternative to a politics of ethnic mobilization. Unfortunately, it was an alternative that could only offer a distraught citizenry, traumatized by economic decline, even more blood, sweat, and tears. In December 1989 the "Marković Plan" was initiated. Its first goal was to stabilize the Yugoslav national currency (the *dinar*), in the throes of hyperinflation, through the latest in a sequence of International Monetary Fund (IMF) austerity programs. Marković hoped to use a strong dinar to encourage private initiative as a motor of growth.[21] In the course of 1990s he managed to achieve some progress in bolstering the currency and improving investor confidence.[22] But the Marković Plan brought little short-term relief to the public, which was now being lured by the sirens of nationalism promising that outside the federation all would be well. Years of neglect had led Yugoslavia toward a crisis for which IMF-inspired structural adjustment offered no solution.[23]

As an aspiring national figure with a primary allegiance to the Yugoslav idea, Marković was an exception to the rule. Since at least 1974 the real power brokers inside the Yugoslav hierarchy were regional leaders whose political associations lay almost exclusively within their republic of origin. Serbia's power play frightened republic-level elites and weakened popular confidence in Yugoslavia, creating an objective foundation for a resort to nationalist demagoguery. It also created a window of opportunity for nationalist extremists, brought back onto the political scene due to the weakening of federal institutions and the crisis of European communism from 1989 onward.

The Marković program might have had some chance to take off in a Yugoslav context if it had been supported by a unified League of Communists, promulgated by a strong state, and legitimized in a national election. Such an outcome was within reach--opinion polls suggest that well into 1990 a majority of Yugoslav citizens maintained an allegiance to the federation. But the emerging nationalist leaders of the feuding Yugoslav republics did not will it to be so. Led by Serbia, the individual republics reacted to economic austerity with a series of protectionist gestures and inflationary raids on the national bank, undermining reform efforts and giving rise to what one analyst describes as "a full fledged economic war."[24] At the Fourteenth, and final Congress of the League of Communists of Yugoslavia at Belgrade's Sava Center in January 1990 the Slovenian delegation, followed by its Croatian counterpart, walked out in protest against purported Serbian hegemonism. For all intents and purposes, the ruling party that had presided over the fortunes of communist Yugoslavia since the origins of the state had ceased to exist. With it disappeared any realistic chance for coordinating a process of transition on the federal level. Paralyzed by republic-level opposition and without the leadership of the League, the Yugoslav federal government was not able to pass a single piece of legislation in a span of eighteen months from late 1989 through 1991.

Yugoslavia's fate was sealed by the inability of the federal power structure to impose national elections as a first step toward political pluralism. In lieu of a federal contest, targeted for December 1990 but in fact never held, between April and December 1990 the individual Yugoslav republics scheduled separate elections that in almost every case confirmed nationalist leaderships committed to a break with the past.

The Slovenian election of April 1990 pitted the Democratic United Opposition of Slovenia (DEMOS), a united front bringing together six disparate parties (the Christian Democrats, Peasants' Union, Democratic Alliance, Social Democrats, Liberal Democrats, and Greens) around an anti-communist agenda, against Kučan's post-communist Party of Democratic Renewal. In a split decision, DEMOS secured 55 percent support in parliamentary elections, while Kučan, until recently a loyal communist apparatchik, won the presidency by a 59-42 percent margin against the DEMOS candidate Jože Pucnik. All parties to the contest rallied behind the slogan "Europe, Now" and called for a restructuring of Yugoslavia as a loose confederation of sovereign states. Subsequently, on July 2, 1990, Slovenia declared sovereignty within the federation. Through the 1980s Slovenia had been a subversive force within Yugoslavia, pressing consistently for anti-federal solutions on behalf of its own, republican and nationalist priorities. The election of 1990 brought this trend to a head.

One week later, elections in Croatia conducted according to a double ballot that favored stronger parties in the first round, gave Tudjman's HDZ 205 of 356 parliamentary seats, an outcome disproportionate to its real margin of popular votes (41.5 percent), and more than sufficient to assert control of the republic's political future. The HDZ was in the process of consolidation, and Croatia was not yet ready to pursue an agenda for separation, but Tudjman made no secret of his allegiance to the "thousand year dream" of national independence. He was also inspired by less edifying sentiments. On February 24, 1990, at the HDZ's first public rally, Tudjman stepped toward a rehabilitation of the genocidal regime of Ante Pavelić, calling it "an expression of the historical aspirations of the Croatian people."[25] At an electoral rally in Dubrava on March 17, 1990, the HDZ leader offered an astonishing personal observation: "Thanks to God that my wife is neither a Jew nor a Serb."[26] Between May and July 1990, his party revived many of the symbols of the Ustaša period including the historical Croatian shield with its red and white checkerboard (the *šahovnica*), promoted a bogus historical revisionism that sought to downplay the crimes of the Ustaša, instituted obligatory loyalty oaths for ethnic Serbs in public positions, discouraged use of the Serbian Cyrillic alphabet and made the Latin script obligatory in official documents and proceedings, purged members of Croatia's Serb minority (17 percent of the population) from positions in state administration and local police forces, and rewrote the Croatian constitution in such a way as to demote Croatian Serbs from the status of a constituent nation to that of a national minority.[27]

The measures emanating from Zagreb were bound to provoke a reaction. By the spring of 1990 the Serb populations of Croatia in the old Habsburg Military Frontier region amidst the arid karst lands around the provincial center and rail junction of Knin (the *Kninska Krajina*), organized locally but with the support of Belgrade, had initiated a revolt against what was perceived as the prospect of separation from Yugoslavia, establishing an *ad hoc* association of Serb municipalities in May and beginning the construction of self-defense militias.[28] Hundreds of years of cohabitation had made the Serbs of Krajina indistinguishable from their Croat neighbors in dialect, appearance, and way of life. But they were Orthodox Christians for whom the memory of the World War II massacres was still alive. During July and August, in the aftermath of the Croatian Assembly's decision to refuse official status to the Cyrillic alphabet, a hastily organized Serb referendum produced a nearly unanimous outcome for loyalty to Yugoslavia, and a " Serb Autonomous Province (later Republic) of Krajina" (*Srpska Autonomna Oblast Krajina*-SAOK) was declared into being under the political leadership of former dentist Milan Babić, and military direction of the police inspector Milan Martić. Only about a third of the 600,000 Croatian Serbs actually resided inside Croatia's former military frontier districts (Lika, Slunj, Banija, and Kordun), which apart from their significance as a transportation corridor were of marginal economic importance. But the political weight of the Krajina Serbs' challenge to the new regime in Zagreb, and to the legitimacy of inter-republican borders, was substantial. Within months of Yugoslavia's first-ever democratic elections, a process of fragmentation had been launched that would eventually consume the country as a whole.

It was not until July 29, 1990, in his native Bosnia-Herzegovina, that Ante Marković announced the creation of an all-national political party, dubbed the Alliance of Reform Forces of Yugoslavia (*Savez Reformskih Snaga Jugoslavije*), committed to contesting republican elections beneath a Yugoslav banner. At this point the process of ethnic mobilization had gone too far to reverse. During November and December 1990 elections in Bosnia-Herzegovina, Macedonia, and Serbia-Montenegro all produced strong results for nationalist factions, while Marković's movement was marginalized.

In Bosnia-Herzegovina Alija Izetbegović's Muslim Party of Democratic Action (*Stranka Demokratska Akcija* — SDA) won 34 percent of the vote, the Serbian Democratic Party (*Srpska Demokratska Stranka* — SDS) 30 percent, and the Bosnian branch of the Croatian HDZ 18 percent. These parties were products of ethnic mobilization, with mandates to represent the communal interests of national communities. Marković's Alliance of Reform Forces, tragically in view of polling data that indicates that in June 1990 nearly 70 percent of Bosnians continued to support preservation of the Yugoslav federation, received only 5.4 percent of the vote.[29] The vote distribution tallied with the proportionate weight of national communities within Bosnia-Herzegovina as a whole, leading some critics to describe the result as something closer to a census than an electoral outcome.[30] Both the SDS and the HDZ were for all intents and purposes extensions of their mother parties inside Serbia and Croatia proper. Izetbegović had authored a controversial *Islamic Declaration* in the 1960s that posed the goal of attaching Bosnia-Herzegovina to a larger pan-Islamic political community, and had been sentenced to several jail terms as a Muslim nationalist and separatist.[31] His SDA was challenged internally in September 1990 by the émigré businessman Adil Zulfikarpašić out of concern for the movement's implied Islamism, but Zulfikarpašić and his supporters were expelled by an extraordinary SDA assembly by a 272-11 vote, and the new Muslim Bosniak Organization which they created in response did not rally meaningful support.[32] Steven Burg and Paul

Shoup underline the SDA's "overtly Islamic and Muslim nationalist orientation."[33]

In the Macedonian elections the nationalist Internal Macedonian Revolutionary Organization--Democratic Party for Macedonian National Unity (IMRO--DPMNU) under Ljubčo Georgievski, which took its name from the terrorist organization of the late Ottoman and interwar period, won a plurality of 32 percent of the popular vote, but ceded power to a moderate coalition led by the former Titoist Kiro Gligorov. Aware of his republic's fragility, Gligorov strove to assemble a broad based coalition including representatives of the large Albanian minority (23 percent of the population according to the census of 1994). Macedonian nationalism remained an important source of cohesion in the new Macedonia, however, and would soon become a source of contention with neighboring states including Greece, which feared the revival of territorial claims dating to the era of the Balkan Wars. Milošević prepared the ground for Serbian elections by promulgating a new constitution in July 1990 that eliminated Vojvodina and Kosovo autonomy. On the basis of a full-blown demagogic populism, in December 1990 the Serbian Socialist Party that Milošević had established on the ruins of the League of Communists won 77 percent of the tally for the Serbian parliament, while Milošević himself took the presidency with 66 percent of the vote.[34]

With nationalist mobilizations proceeding apace and the League of Communists *hors de combat*, only the Federal Presidency was in a position to build a new basis for national unity. Reduced to a platform for the articulation of conflicting agendas by republican leaderships committed to go their own way, it failed miserably. When in May 1991 the Croat Stjepan (Stipe) Mesić came due to succeed Borisav Jović as chair according to the annual rotation established by Tito, opposition by the Serb bloc, justified by the assertion that Mesić had publicly expressed his opposition to Yugoslavia, prevented him from assuming his seat.[35] On October 4, 1990, Slovenia and Croatia released a plan, inspired by the recommendations of EC councilors, to recast Yugoslavia along confederal lines, as a union of sovereign states united by a customs union, a common market, and perhaps a common currency, with some coordination in the areas of foreign policy and diplomacy.[36] The project was appealing, but insincere—its real purpose was to win time while an agenda for secession matured. From the spring of 1990 onward both of the western republics were illegally importing arms, and using what were still nationally controlled media establishments to encourage support for independence. A Slovenian referendum on independence conducted in December 1990 won overwhelming support, and a Croatian counterpart, held in May 1991 after fighting had already erupted in Krajina and Slavonia, carried by more than 90 percent. On March 8, 1991, the Slovenian parliament attempted an unadulterated assertion of sovereignty by moving that military service in the Yugoslav People's Army (*Jugoslovenska Narodna Armija*--JNA) would no longer be mandatory for Slovene citizens, and refusing to proceed with the republic's annual call-up.[37] In the spring and summer of 1991, Macedonian president Gligorov and his Bosnian counterpart Izetbegović, representing weak and ethnically divided republics for whom the breakup of the Yugoslav federation represented a dire threat, reintroduced a version of the Croat-Slovene program calling for "asymmetrical federation" that would allow individual republics to define their own degree of association with national institutions.[38] Tudjman and Milošević approved the proposal, but in the certainty that it would never be implemented--Burg and Shoup describe the entire episode as "political theater."[39] The terms of the proposal remained imprecise, and it was rapidly overtaken by events, precipitated above all by Slovenia's rush to burn its bridges and break irrevocably with the Yugoslav union.

If it had received the consistent support of republican leaders and been unambiguously promulgated by the international community, the project to reconfigure Yugoslavia as a loose or asymmetric confederation could possibly have succeeded in preventing war. Even allowing the separation of Slovenia and Croatia, some arrangement for holding together the remaining four republics in a rump Yugoslavia might have prevented the worst of the violence that would follow. During 1990-1991, however, neither a will for peace among republican leaders nor a serious commitment to preventive diplomacy or conflict management among key international actors was in place. The international community remained disengaged, and the leaders of Yugoslavia's six republics could not arrive at a consensual position regarding their country's future because they did not want to.

Milošević, joined by his protégé Momir Bulatović of Montenegro, was increasingly committed to support for the emerging Serb entities inside Croatia and Bosnia-Herzegovina. This decision to prioritize the creation of a "greater Serbia" would eventually be singled out as the root cause of the entire Yugoslav tragedy, though in fact the unambiguous orientation of the western republics toward secession left the Serbian leadership with little choice but to see to its own interests. On March 16, 1991, as the crisis of federal institutions climaxed, Milošević remarked on Belgrade television that "Yugoslavia has entered into the final phase of its agony." In an address to Serb mayors on the same day he asserted that Belgrade's task was now "to defend the interests of our republic, as well as the interests of the Serb people outside Serbia," and opined that "frontiers and states are in play, and it is always the strong, never the weak, who determine borders."[40] Such statements outlined a program, to accept the dismantlement of Yugoslavia and use force to assemble an enlarged Serbia from the ruins. Ljubljana and Zagreb viewed confederation as a kind of halfway house that would buy them time to prepare for independence, and the Slovenes in particular pushed hard to provoke a break as soon as possible. Sarajevo and Skopje feared the breakup of Yugoslavia, but they were not willing to accept incorporation in a rump state where the western republics were not on hand to balance Serbia.[41] All parties pursued their goals through collusive bargaining, on the basis of confidences that would sometimes be respected and sometimes betrayed. In a memoir, the Slovene Janez Drnovšek notes that already in August 1990, at a moment when he was serving as chair of the Yugoslav Federal Presidency, Milošević and Borisav Jović informed him that Slovenia would be allowed to depart the federation peacefully on the basis of a referendum.[42] Milošević reiterated the message to Kučan during a private meeting on January 24, 1991, with the clarification that Serbia would not attempt to prevent Slovenian separation (Slovenia contained a negligible Serb minority) in order to concentrate on reassembling the Serb populations of Croatia and Bosnia-Herzegovina.[43] In March 1991, following the suppression of student demonstrations in Belgrade, Milošević met with Tudjman in Tito's (and before him King Aleksandar's) isolated hunting preserve Karadjordjevo, midway between their respective capitals, and agreed to support the dissolution of Yugoslavia and a partition of Bosnia-Herzegovina.[44] The only thing that the former communist henchmen could not agree upon was the territorial status of an independent Croatia. Milošević was willing to grant Zagreb the right to secede, but insisted that the Serb-dominated areas inside Croatia be granted a similar right. Serbian and Croatian delegations conducted three secret sessions during April 1991 in a vain attempt to resolve these differences.[45]

As for the international community, on the rare occasions when it turned its attention to the Yugoslav crisis it failed to speak with one voice. The United States and the European Community (EC) publicly reiterated support for Yugoslav unity, and the EC offered support for economic reform and promised fast track accession for a reformed federation committed to maintain unity, but the message was neither compelling nor consistent. During March 1991 the United States went on record in opposition to secession and insisted that border alterations should only result from "peaceful consensual means." [46] Unfortunately, preoccupied with the conduct and aftermath of the Gulf War and the impending dissolution of the USSR, and convinced that vital interests were not really at stake, Washington did little to give its admonitions the sense of urgency that was required. Several European states (Germany, Austria, Denmark, Hungary, and the Holy See among others) openly promoted secession, sometimes pledging diplomatic support and arranging for illegal arms transfers to prepare the way for independence. The "ambiguity and mixed messages" emanating from international actors did nothing to constrain the self-destructive egoism of Yugoslavia's ethnocrats, or to block a resort to arms.[47]

The way for Yugoslavia's anarchic collapse was prepared by a crisis of federal institutions, the nationalist *dérive* in key republics, and tacit support for a policy of secession by influential international actors. Collapse was precipitated by a sequence of local clashes that provided a spur to the militarization of the contending republics. Between May and September 1990 the Serb revolt in Krajina established the precedent of de facto armed secession as a response to ethnic mobilization, with local militia eventually reconstituted as the SAOK-Territorial Defense Forces. In November 1990 Slovenia and Croatia assumed control over the remnants (after federal efforts to confiscate weapons stores in the spring of the year) of their republican Territorial Defense Forces, and escalated illegal arms transfers in order to build up combat readiness. In February 1991 the JNA received an order from the Federal Presidency to disarm militias, but made do with an ineffective compromise that failed to block Slovene arms transfers and allowed Croatia to continue a force build up under its special police battalions and reconstituted National Guard Corps

(*Zbor narodne garde*). March 1991 also saw the deployment of JNA forces in Belgrade to repress student led demonstrations protesting against the policies of the Milošević regime — the first of many cases where popular resistance to ethno-national mobilization would be beaten down by force. Neglected by the international community, without a ruling party, without a functioning executive, and with an army in crisis incapable of responding to the defiant militarization of secessionist republics, Yugoslavia was moving closer to Thomas Hobbes' depiction of anarchy, "the state of warre, and such a warre as of every man against every manne."[48]

The war of all against all began in April 1990 as the Krajina Serbs took to constructing barricades to cut off access to Serb majority areas or areas with significant Serb populations, and initiated a campaign of harassment against Croat residents in the regions under their control. The Serb revolt, romanticized as the *balvan revolucjia* (Tree Trunk Revolution, after the tree limbs used to construct barricades), was in part a spontaneous reaction to the provocations of the Tudjman regime. It had an anachronistic and folkloric character, led by local militias dressed in patriotic uniforms that evoked Chetnik resistance during World War II. From the outset, however, it was supported and manipulated by Belgrade in order to forward an agenda for the extension of Serb-controlled territories outside of Serbia proper. In the first months of the rebellion organized resistance was concentrated within six communes in the vicinity of Knin populated by consistent Serb majorities. In the months to come it would expand, across southern Croatia through Kordun, Banija, and Posavina, where Serb and Croat populations were in something closer to a balance, and into the plains of Slavonia and Baranja on the Hungarian border, where the Serbs were a clear minority. The essence of the revolt was the attempt to assert control over terrain, affected by the construction of roadblocks and barriers, defiance of local authorities, or the dynamiting of symbols of sovereignty as well as the homes of undesired "outsiders."

A major escalation began in February 1991 when Serb militia attempted to broaden their area of control by seizing a police station and municipal building in the small town of Pakrac in western Slavonia. This action was followed in late March by an attempt to take control of the Plitvice national park complex, after the HDZ had established a new police station with an all-Croatian staff in the local town of Titova Korenica, provoking a firefight with the

Croatian National Guard that resulted in the first combat fatalities of Yugoslavia's ethnic wars. The victims were Josip Jović, a 20-year old Croatian policeman, and Rajko Vukadinović, a Serb butcher from Titova Korenica who had joined the local militia — the first of tens of thousands of normal citizens to be swept away in the battles to come. The Krajina Serbs were not always the initiators in these encounters. Extremists within the HDZ sought out confrontations as a means to up the ante and make secession inevitable. In April, future Croatian defense minister Gojko Šušak organized and participated in an attack on the ethnically mixed but Serb controlled Slavonian village of Borovo Selo, firing three shoulder-launched Armbrust missiles into the town in an attempt to fan the flames of war.[49] On May 1 a spontaneous effort by Croat policemen, undertaken during the festivities attending a national holiday, to replace the Yugoslav flag on display at the town hall with the *šahovnica* resulted in a firefight wounding two, and on the next day a busload of Croatian policemen seeking to reassert control ran headlong into an ambush, leaving 15 dead (12 Croats and 3 Serbs) and over 20 wounded. The mutilation of the bodies of the Croat victims in a manner evocative of the atrocities of World War II (ears and eyes cut out) made the incident particularly provocative. In each case a stand off between local forces was broken by the intervention of the JNA, which prevented Croatia from reasserting control over disputed terrain by inter-positioning forces, including heavy artillery, between the belligerents — a pattern that would repeat itself frequently in the months to come. The Yugoslav conflict had begun as a war of villages, and more than 400 people would lose their lives in local incidents prior to the outbreak of full-scale combat operations.

In this environment, pushed forward by Ljubljana's inflexible timetable, and indifferent to the implications of their actions for the peoples of Yugoslavia as a whole, on 24 July 1991 Zagreb and Slovenia announced their "disassociation" (*razdruživanje*) from the Yugoslav federation.[50] The term disassociation was preferred to secession in order to make the point that from its origins the Yugoslavia federation had been a voluntary union of peoples, but the harshness and irrevocability of the gesture was hardly disguised. On June 21, an 11th-hour visit to Belgrade by U.S. Secretary of State James Baker, including eleven meetings with the entire spectrum of Yugoslav leaders conducted in the space of a single day, sought to ward off the fatal step. But Baker had arrived too late, and with too little of substance to offer, to make a difference. With Milošević committed to an agenda for breaking the federation, nationalist elites in the secessionist republics pressing for independence, and the international community unwilling to weigh in, the break up of Yugoslavia, and the tragic consequences that would come in its train, although in principle avoidable, had become inevitable. For many of the same reasons, a serious effort to guarantee that a process of disassociation would go forward peacefully was never undertaken. With the secession of Slovenia and Croatia, Yugoslavia's war of villages would become a war of states.

The Slovene Drôle de Guerre.

Belgrade reacted to the Slovenian declaration of disassociation and seizure of border crossings (including the erection of barriers between Slovenia and Croatia) with what seems to have been intended as a symbolic show of force. On June 26-27, 1991, units of the Federal Army deployed from posts within Slovenia to reassert control over the state border. They were in fact walking into a trap.

Aided by sympathizers inside the federal decision making structure, Slovene leaders were fully aware of the Federal Army's contingency plans. Their strategy aimed to provoke a military response in the conviction that it could be neutralized, and that public reactions to the repression launched by federal forces would reinforce the legitimacy of a declaration of independence. In this regard, the seizure of border posts and dismantling of symbolic representations of Yugoslav sovereignty were considered to be vital--Slovenian Defense Minister Janez Janša called it a "key step across the Rubicon."[51] Between May 1990 and July 1991, Janša had built up an independently commanded national militia with over 30,000 effectives.[52] The prospect of standing up to a limited JNA disciplinary action with these forces in hand was good. Moreover, Ljubljana was being assured by friends inside the EC that in the event of a military confrontation, European intervention in support of separation would result.[53] This scenario played out without a hitch.

First attempts to reassert control of the state border using units drawn from JNA posts within Slovenia were thwarted by carefully planned resistance. On June 27 federal forces began to move toward contested border crossings, but immediately encountered blocking positions and harassing attacks. When helicopters operating from the military airport at Cerklje were put in service to ferry federal forces to border posts, the Slovenes upped the ante by shooting down two unarmed JNA Gazelle helicopters over Ljubljana, the first of which had a Slovene pilot and carried a shipment of bread for beleaguered JNA barracks. James Gow and Cathie Carmichael assert that the incident "defined the whole conflict," timed as it was at the moment when "images of destroyed helicopters could be beamed across Europe in main evening news broadcasts."[54] Ljubljana's integrated military-media strategy, typical of modern war, was a striking success. Despite initial setbacks, by the evening of June 27 federal forces, backed up by a small number of tanks supported by tactical aviation, succeeded in regaining control of the disputed border crossings, but also provided the international media with images that could be pressed into the familiar mold of communist brute force crushing gallant national resistance.[55]

By June 28, fighting had escalated across the republic, as battles for border posts swayed to and fro, and Slovene defense forces challenged federal units moving onto their territory and surrounded and besieged federal garrisons. The JNA reacted with ineffective air strikes. In the critical first days of the operation, the large majority of the more than 25,000 federal soldiers deployed in the republic remained on their posts, surrounded and held under fire by the Slovene National Guard. From June 29 onward, ceasefire negotiations slowed the momentum of conflict, but did little to aid federal forces cut off from their command structure, lacking access to supplies, and without any apparent game plan for proceeding once control of state border crossings was reestablished. In the entire course of the conflict, the JNA did not deploy more than 3,000 soldiers into combat, against a Slovene militia force that outnumbered them ten to one.

The measures undertaken by the JNA were well within the prerogatives of a sovereign state. In the absence of Mesić, who had not been able to assume the chair of the Federal Presidency due to the opposition of the Serb bloc, responsibility devolved upon federal Prime Minister Marković, who formally approved a military incursion. Marković would subsequently backtrack, arguing that the extent of military actions exceeded his instructions, but it should be obvious that, in seeking to counter secession and secure control of the state border, federal armed forces were acting within their mandate. What proved decisive was the refusal of

Yugoslav political authorities, true to the spirit of Milošević's January bargain with Kučan, to make preservation of Yugoslavia's integrity a priority. The JNA had a contingency plan to mobilize its entire Fifth Military District against the Slovenes, a force that Ljubljana would have been unable to resist.[56] But the rump Federal Presidency, dominated by the Milošević faction, refused to sanction the army's plea for action.[57] Milošević himself instructed Yugoslav Defense Minister Veljiko Kadijević on June 27 that the army's job was not to defend the Yugoslav border, but rather "the borders of a future state."[58] By July 2, when Slovene attacks against contested border posts resumed in force, most mobile JNA units had already initiated a process of withdrawal, under fire, from Slovene territory. Abandoned, the defenders of most of the contested border posts negotiated surrenders. Belgrade's strong man had kept his faith with the Slovenes, though to no good end. Simultaneously, Croatia's Tudjman refused to honor an agreement to aid Slovenia in the event that it should come under attack on the pretext, in the event quite accurate, that Croatia was not prepared. The bizarre patterns of betrayal that would become characteristic of the Yugoslav conflict were already being manifested.

The confused fighting in Slovenia was cut short by international mediation, inspired by a great deal of sympathy for the Slovene national cause. The last combat operations, ambushes carried out by Slovene forces against JNA units attempting to withdraw, were conducted on July 4. Slovenia's war of national liberation was over in the space of 10 days. It took the modest toll, according to official statistics, of thirteen Slovenes killed (eight military or police and five civilians), eight international civilians (truck drivers who refused to abandon their vehicles which had been commandeered by the Slovenes to serve as barricades, and which were subsequently attacked by Yugoslav aviation), and 44 JNA killed and 187 wounded.[59] Over 1,700 JNA soldiers were also taken prisoner. The JNA victims were mostly teenage conscripts killed in ambushes, who probably never understood what it was that they had been asked to die for. A rapid ceasefire was possible because neither party to the conflict (Ljubljana and the Serb bloc that controlled the policies of the federal government) really objected to the facts on the ground that Slovene defiance had created.

The shock of armed conflict in Slovenia was particularly acute for neighboring states, and both Italy and Austria immediately appealed for explanations through the Conference on Security and Cooperation in Europe (CSCE).[60] Simultaneously, and in line with its larger strategy of provoking intervention, the Slovenian government requested diplomatic mediation on the part of the EC and CSCE. The request was picked up by the European Council, in the midst of a summit in Luxembourg as the crisis unfolded. The Council, with CSCE approval, dispatched the EC's "Troika" of foreign ministers (the foreign ministers of the states holding the past, present, and future presidency of the European Council), at the moment composed of the Netherlands, Luxembourg, and Italy, as mediators. The Troika arrived in Belgrade within days of the outbreak of hostilities, and proceeded to craft a ceasefire agreement that was nailed down, with the endorsement of all six Yugoslav republics and the impotent Yugoslav Federal Presidency, on the Adriatic island of Brioni on July 7.[61]

The Brioni agreement granted Slovenia control over its border crossings and customs revenues — the symbolic issue over which the conflict had technically been waged. JNA units in Slovenia and Croatia were required to withdraw into their garrisons, and Yugoslavia was threatened by EC sanctions should hostilities be resumed. In exchange, the Slovenian blockade of federal army bases was to be lifted, Slovenian territorial defense forces deactivated, and captured JNA equipment returned (a pledge that the Slovenes never honored). Both of the separatist republics were required to suspend their declarations of disassociation for 3 months and to accept the presence on their territory of an unarmed international observer mission organized by the EC on behalf of the CSCE. The authority of the Yugoslav Federal Presidency was reaffirmed, and on July 1 Mesić was finally confirmed as acting president.[62] In the midst of the negotiations the flamboyant Italian Foreign Minister Gianni De Michaelis spoke incautiously of the EC's success in "blocking the spiral of conflict."[63] Regretfully, the European reaction that De Michaelis encouraged, which as promised awarded Slovenia's provocations by underwriting its independence, ensured that the spiral of conflict would continue to widen.

Although the EC had to threaten Ljubljana with economic penalties in order to win its approval, the Brioni agreement granted Slovenia an essential element of sovereignty by awarding it control of state borders and the right to collect customs revenues. It neutralized the JNA, which was the only force capable of reversing a declaration of independence, by confining it to garrison under threat of sanctions. Brioni held the door open for a reconfirmation of disassociation after a brief 3-month interval, and both Slovenia and Croatia punctually affirmed their original declarations on October 8. Bent to the will of Milošević, with Mesić casting the only opposing vote out of fear of the consequences for Croatia, on July 18 the Yugoslav Federal Presidency agreed to withdraw its military forces from the republic, a process that was concluded by October 26. At this point Slovenia had become an independent state in all but name.

These events established a destructive precedent. Yugoslavia had been shattered without any arrangements in place for resolving the manifold issues that its disappearance as a unified state was bound to create. The instrumentality of violence as a means to affect secession was confirmed. An attempt to shape international attitudes toward the conflict by using stereotypes to manipulate the media proved remarkably successful. The conniving satraps that had inherited power in the Yugoslav republics were embraced as international statesmen and essential interlocutors. A false distinction between the "good Europeans and democrats" of predominantly Catholic Slovenia and the "evil Byzantines and communists" of predominately Orthodox Serbia was adopted as an organizing premise for approaching Balkan affairs. Not least, the ability of secessionist forces to use an appeal to the international community as a mechanism for neutralizing the superior military forces of their adversaries was clearly demonstrated. Given its high degree of ethnic homogeneity, relative prosperity, and more developed civil society, Slovenia was able to break free from the Yugoslav federation with a minimum of domestic trauma.[64] The same would not be the case when the ethnically more complex, economically more troubled, and politically less mature populations of Croatia and Bosnia-Herzegovina set out to follow the Slovene example.

Za Dom Spremni: The War in Croatia.

The contract between Milošević and Kučan that had allowed Slovenia's secession to succeed could not be reproduced in the case of Croatia. According to Milošević's agenda, the geographically concentrated Serb population inside Croatia had a right to secession in order to retain its affiliation with the remainder of Yugoslavia. "I

110

am in contact with our brothers in Knin and Bosnia," he articulated in the programmatic statement of March 16, "and they are under enormous pressure. We will not at any price abandon our formula--a popular referendum and application of the right of self-determination. This is the only solution, the alternative is violence."[65] According to the logic of Tudjman's HDZ, defined within the tradition of Croatian state rights, the Croatian national sanctuary was one and indivisible. These were irreconcilable positions, and in the end they would be regulated by force. In contrast to the brief armed confrontation in Slovenia, where a resort to violence was limited by governments that remained in contact and shared a mutual understanding about the preferred outcome, fighting in Croatia expanded from the ground up, driven forward by heightened passions and ill-controlled paramilitary factions. The actions of Martić's militia, the *Martićevci*, (which together with other territorial defense forces would be redesignated at the Serb Army of the Krajina [*Srpska Vojska Krajine*] on March 19, 1992), aided by volunteer paramilitary units arrived from Serbia proper, included systematic efforts to conquer territory by driving out the indigenous Croat population, a process of *čišćenje terena* ("purging of the terrain," later known as ethnic cleansing) that would soon become sadly familiar. Croatian forces responded in kind, terrorizing the Serb minority, forcing thousands from their homes as refugees or displaced persons, and eventually presiding over massacres. Vile hate propaganda using the centrally controlled mass medias of the communist era dredged up the worst atrocities of the Second World War and created an atmosphere of paranoia that was grist to the mill of extremists.[66]

The area controlled by the Krajina Serbs expanded rapidly into the summer of 1991. The ability of Serb militias to seize and hold territory was reinforced by the interventions of the JNA, aimed in principle at imposing an end to hostilities by inter-positioning between warring factions, but objectively supportive of the facts on the ground created by local aggression. Despite the progressive loss of control over strategically vital regions, Tudjman warded off calls originally posed by Defense Minister Martin Špegelj (who resigned at the end of June 1991 in protest against Zagreb's refusal to move against federal garrisons with the JNA engaged in Slovenia), and by other hardliners in his entourage, for an assault on the JNA and all out war. Concerned about Croatian unpreparedness, and convinced that international sympathy was a key to success, he continued to hope that the expanding Croatian National Guard could contain the Serb insurgency without resort to an attack upon federal forces. In the spring of 1991 Croatia briefly attempted a blockade of JNA garrisons in protest against the army's pro-Serb bias, but in May the Yugoslav Federal Presidency condemned and reversed the initiative. Following the check in Slovenia during July 1991, however, columns of JNA forces moved directly from the breakaway republic into threatening positions in Croatia and Bosnia-Herzegovina. Defense Minister Špegelj's eventual replacement by the hardline former émigré and leader of the "Herzegovinian faction" in Tudjman's entourage Gojko Šušak did nothing to reinforce negotiated options. In August, confronting territorial losses and a swelling casualty count, Zagreb presented the JNA with an ultimatum--either disarm the Serb militias in Croatia immediately or face attack as an army of occupation. With international assistance from Germany, Hungary, and other sources, efforts to transform the Croatian National Guard Corps and special units of the Ministry of the Interior into a national army were accelerated, and on September 14 a campaign of encirclement, including blockage of food and water supply, was initiated against over 100 federal army garrisons on Croatian territory. The action did not roll back the gains of the Krajina Serbs, but it secured Croatia certain advantages, including a stock of confiscated arms and valuable combat experience. The Central Intelligence Agency's military history of the conflict describes the "battle of the barracks" as "one of the decisive actions of the Croatian war."[67] The blockade also sparked fighting along a broad front stretching the length of Croatia from the Adriatic port of Dubrovnik in southern Dalmatia to Vukovar on the Danube in the heart of Slavonia, as the JNA, supported by Serb paramilitary units, instituted a plan to relieve the barracks by defeating Croatia in detail. Zagreb responded in late September by creating a general staff to control combat operations, under the command of former Yugoslav Air Force General Anton Tus. The fighting in Croatia had escalated in a matter of months from small-scale encounters between local militias to a full-scale war.

The role of the JNA in the genesis of the Yugoslav conflict remains contested. Analysts sympathetic to Slovene and Croatian national aspirations, or committed to a pattern of explanation that identifies the unique source of the Yugoslav problem as Milošević's agenda to construct a greater Serbia, tend to portray the army as a consistent source of support for Serb imperialism.[68] These arguments cannot be dismissed out of hand. The Milošević regime encouraged Serb separatist movements in both Croatia and Bosnia-Herzegovina. Collusion with the federal army was critical to the ability of local militias to arm and prepare for battle, and the JNA made no effort to restrain the depredations of paramilitary forces such as those sponsored by the colorful mercenary from the Serb Australian Diaspora "Kapetan Dragan" in Krajina, or the "Chetniks" and "White Eagles" of the ultra-nationalist leader of the Serbian Radical Party Vojislav Šešelj and "Tigers" of the gangster warlord Željko Ražnatović (Arkan) in Slavonia.[69] Unlike the case in Slovenia, Milošević pushed the JNA into action in Croatia without a mandate from Yugoslav federal instances, and used it under the guise of peacekeeping to reinforce the autonomy of Serb controlled regions.[70]

It is nonetheless incorrect to conflate the JNA leadership of the spring of 1991 with what it would be become 1 year later, after a series of purges, including the ouster of 170 generals, had transformed it, root and branch, into a Serbian national force. The high command at the outset of the conflict was what several generations of indoctrination in Titoist Yugoslavia had prepared it to be, a professionally competent and ethnically diverse group of officers committed to the preservation of the Yugoslav idea. Tito had repeatedly referred to the Yugoslav armed forces as the ultimate guarantor of national unity, and in the confused circumstances of 1990-91 the JNA would have been acting within its prerogative had it seized the initiative, declared a state of emergency as a pretext for dismissing nationalist leaders in Ljubljana, Zagreb, and Belgrade, and imposed federal elections and association between republics on a new foundation.[71] Pretexts for intervention were not lacking. On January 25, 1991, a secretly filmed video was shown on national television documenting the illegal arming of Croatian paramilitaries in Slavonia. The video featured defense minister Špegelj, his back to a hidden camera, instructing fellow officers on techniques for murdering their Serb colleagues in the context of a national rising. The "Špegelj Affair" created a sensation, but a majority of the Federal Presidency refused to sanction a military response, and the army balked at acting without a political mandate.[72] Following the May 6, 1991, demonstrations protesting efforts to disarm the Croatian territorial militia outside the Yugoslav naval headquarters in Split, during which a young Macedonian conscript was killed, Yugoslav Defense Minister Kadijević spoke publicly of a "state of civil war," but his rhetoric was not backed up by action.[73] The decision by Milošević's Serb bloc to veto the accession of Mesić as chair of the Federal Presidency in May 1991 has also been represented as a possible occasion for the declaration of a state of emergency and military crackdown, which was not exploited for lack of political support.[74]

The refusal of federal instances to use decisive force to defend Yugoslavia's integrity made possible the anarchic breakdown that followed. Why did the JNA not intervene in defense of the Yugoslav idea? Part of the answer is pure confusion. By the spring of 1991, with the federation in the first stage of its death agony, a military command whose entire worldview had been shaped inside the federal context was challenged to find fixed points of orientation. Divided council also played a role--as events progressed the JNA high command was increasingly split between senior leaders with a Yugoslav orientation and ambitious young officers, such as Colonel Ratko Mladić, Chief of Staff of the JNA's 9th (Knin) Corps during 1990, affiliated with a Serb nationalist agenda. Kadijević made several visits to Moscow in the first months of 1991 that are sometimes represented as attempts to plot a military putsch with Soviet support. Whether or not this was the case, any hopes for help from Soviet hardliners were removed after the failure of the abortive August 1991 coup in Moscow. Declining capacity played a potentially decisive role. Like all federal institutions, the JNA had by 1991 entered into a phase of dissolution, revealed by inadequate responses to mobilization, poor discipline, and friction within the leadership. International pressure may also have contributed. On January 17, U.S. Ambassador William Zimmermann instructed Milošević confidant Jović that although America supported Yugoslav unity, it would not tolerate the use of force by the federal army in Slovenia and Croatia.[75] The EC offered the same contradictory council--simultaneous opposition to secession and to the only effective means to combat secession--in June 1991 on the eve of the Slovenian and Croatian declarations of disassociation.[76]

The key factor, however, was probably the JNA's essential character, not only as a Yugoslav but also as a communist military organization. Commanders weaned on a doctrine of strict subordination to party leadership, and not willing to desert to secessionist national guards, could only look at Belgrade as the embodiment of a national command authority. At the critical juncture, between January and August 1991, Milošević was able to establish credibility with some leadership figures as the only Yugoslav politician rhetorically committed to preserving national unity, and the privileges of the old Titoist establishment, by opposing "fascist" national movements and liberal agitation in general.[77] The deployment of JNA tanks on the streets of Belgrade in March 1991 to intimidate anti-Milošević demonstrators was telling in this regard. This misreading of circumstances made the JNA the unwitting agent of a political project that was not its own, but only briefly. Yugoslav army officers suffered high casualties in the fighting in Croatia during 1991. In January 1992, following the downing by Yugoslav aviation of a UN observer mission helicopter in which four Italian and one French crew members were killed, Kadijević tendered his resignation, and during the next 2 months, 59 JNA generals were cashiered. In April 1992, simultaneous with the declaration of a new Federal Republic of Yugoslavia as the successor state of the Titoist federation, the JNA, which had already surrendered most of its communist symbols and heritage, was formally renamed the Yugoslav Armed Forces (*Vojska Jugoslavije* − VJ). By May, the officer corps had been purged of its remaining cadre of Yugoslav orientation, meaningful continuity with the JNA was broken, and the army that traced its origins to Tito's partisans, and that had been committed throughout its history to the ethic of Brotherhood and Unity, was transformed into an instrument for the hegemonic policies of Belgrade.[78]

Kadijević has argued that the original intent of the forces under his command in Croatia was to isolate the republic, defeat secessionist forces in detail, move against Zagreb, and restore the federation's territorial integrity.[79] These plans were abandoned due to the ongoing disintegration of the national armed forces (draft resistance, desertions, and operational shortcomings all playing a role), the refusal of Belgrade to act upon Kadijević's call for general mobilization, unexpectedly stiff Croatian resistance, and the disguised war aims of the Milošević clique. Through August and early September the JNA continued to provide de facto support to Croatia's Serb militia in its effort to seize territory and force out the Croat population. From mid-September onward essential military tasks included the extraction of personnel and heavy weapons from encircled garrisons and the attempt to carve a geographically unified Serb area from the body of Croatia. These campaigns possessed a rough strategic logic focused on securing control of areas with significant Serb populations and regions allowing access to critical choke points and transportation corridors. Key targets included eastern and western Slavonia with their sizable Serb minorities and openings onto the Danube, access to the Sava River paralleling the now ironically named "Brotherhood and Unity" highway linking Zagreb and Belgrade, and the Dalmatian littoral, including Zadar and Split as well as the Prevlaka Peninsula south of the port of Dubrovnik guarding the Serb outlet to the sea on the Gulf of Kotor in Montenegro. Such regions were to be the bastions of what Kadijević would call "a new Yugoslavia made up of the peoples who desired to live together inside it," an appropriate description of the much-referenced rump Yugoslavia (*krnja Jugoslavija*) already rejected as unacceptable by Sarajevo and Skopje.[80]

Croatian defense forces included the emerging national army (National Guard Corps and Interior Ministry units) as well as volunteer militia formations such as the ultra-nationalist Croatian Defense Forces (*Hrvatske Odbrambene Snage – HOS*) led by Dobroslav Paraga, the military wing of a reconstituted Croatian Party of Right in the Ustaša tradition, with its *Sieg Heil* salute and uniforms emblazoned with the slogan "*Za Dom Spremni*" (Ready for the Homeland). By January 1992 the emerging Croatian Army (*Hrvatska Vojska*-HV) numbered over 200,000, assisted by about 40,000 Interior Ministry and police forces, but was still basically a light infantry force, with a rudimentary organization and without access to significant heavy weaponry.[81] The HV and associated militia were able to slow down the advance of the federals and extract a high price in casualties, but not to reverse the momentum of a better-equipped and trained rival. By November 1991 federal forces had established a naval blockade of Croatian ports, cleared the majority of encircled garrisons, seized the Dalmatian hinterland around Dubrovnik, and battled their way into Slavonia after ending the siege of the Danubian town of Vukovar (which lasted from August 26 through November 19) by reducing most of the baroque city center to rubble with a protracted air, naval, and artillery barrage.

In retrospect the battle of Vukovar appears to have been the critical turning point of the campaign. The JNA's original intention, after relieving the local barracks from encirclement, was to bypass the city and move on toward Zagreb. Dogged resistance soon made the city itself a symbol of Croat resolve, however, that in the opinion of the JNA leadership had to be reduced at all costs. The costs would be considerable. The Croat General Mile Dedaković (known as "Hawk") and his Chief of Staff Branko Borković had only about 2,500 lightly armed fighters on hand to defend the city against JNA forces numbering in the tens of thousands, supported by armor, heavy artillery, and tactical aviation. They used their resources efficiently to construct an integrated defense system, including the mining of approach corridors, extensive use of roving anti-tank squads, well positioned sniper fire, heavily fortified defensive strong points in critical sectors, and systematic counterattacks.[82] The JNA's original attempts to push into this densely defended urban knot with armored spearheads were an abject failure. Under the new command of General Života Panić from late September onward, tactics were adjusted to favor infantry led assaults supported by armor and artillery and mortar fire, and advances were coordinated on multiple lines of assault. These procedures finally allowed the Serbs to fight their way into the ruined city center by mid-November, where ill-disciplined units once again did their best to discredit their cause by perpetrating massacres against cowed residents as they emerged from hiding. Serb forces had taken Vukovar, but the protracted campaign had completely disrupted the JNA's time table for winning the war, shattered whatever morale remained after the frustration in Slovenia, and allowed Zagreb to economize forces for deployment in other sectors. Upon the fall of the city Tudjman had Dedaković and Borković arrested, after they had complained publicly about being left in the lurch by the national command authority.[83] Their exploits in Vukovar were nonetheless absolutely critical to Croatia's ability to survive the JNA's onslaught in the first months of all out war.

Even with its many operational deficiencies and increasingly sharp manpower shortages, after the fall of Vukovar the JNA was in a position to attempt a two-pronged advance on the Croatian capital, launched from Vukovar through Osijek along the lines of the Drava and Sava Rivers.[84] Revealingly, no such attempt was made — Milošević's goal was not to reunite Yugoslavia by force, but to secure control of areas with significant Serb populations and bind them together within defensible confines. By linking up with the Serb rebellion inside Croatia federal forces had come to the rescue of the Republic of Serb Krajina, established geographical continuity between the Serb controlled areas inside Croatia and Serbia proper, and opened corridors of access to the Adriatic and the Danube. Not least, they had positioned themselves for the next major confrontation to spin off from the collapse of Yugoslavia — a battle for control of the Serb-dominated areas of Bosnia-Herzegovina. From November onward, the first priority was to reinforce these gains.

During the autumn of 1991, media accounts of the war began to be accompanied by maps of Croatia indicating the large Serb occupied regions that would eventually include over one-third of the national territory. Depicted graphically, the advances of the Serb party appeared decisive, but they were nothing of the sort. Vukovar may not have earned the reputation of the "Croatian Stalingrad," but its poorly armed defenders had stopped what had once been Europe's fourth largest army in its tracks for more than a month. By the time that the city had been reduced on November 17, Zagreb was probably beyond reach even had the Serbs aspired to take it — the JNA offensive that defined the war's first months culminated in Slavonia. Efforts by the JNA's 5th (Banja Luka) Corps to move north from the Sava toward Virovitica on the Hungarian border in order to secure control of both western and eastern Slavonia was checked by Croatian resistance at the town of Pakrac. The Krajina Serbs had secured control of significant territories, and expelled a large part of the indigenous Croat population, but their positions were not invulnerable. The JNA's 9th (Knin) Corps, with Ratko Mladić as Chief of Staff, was more successful in maneuvering against Zadar and Šibenik on the Adriatic coast and severing north-south communication by destroying the Maslenica bridge and piercing coastal highways. By way of contrast, the JNA's offensive against Dubrovnik, launched from neighboring Montenegro in early October, became a public relations fiasco, as ill-disciplined Montenegrin reservists and militia units wrecked havoc in the Konavle region and Croatia propagandized the brutality of artillery strikes against the splendid renaissance city for all it was worth. In the end Serb forces chose not to press home an attack, and quietly marched off toward the Bosnian front after an agreement to demilitarize the Prevlaka peninsula with UN monitoring was concluded in October 1992, with nothing to show for their adventures but loss of face. The destruction of Vukovar was a much more terrible event, but the impact of the indecisive siege of Dubrovnik was in some ways of greater significance. With its desultory shelling of the new port area from the hills above the "Pearl of the Adriatic" Serbia had lost the battle for world opinion in the unfolding Yugoslav drama, and lost it irrevocably.[85]

By the end of November a front of sorts had stabilized running along the boundaries of Serb-controlled areas in Slavonia, through the Kordun and Banija regions south of Zagreb, and into the Serb-populated Adriatic hinterland in Lika. Croatia had defended its independence, but at a high price. Vital territories stood outside of Zagreb's control, approximately half of the country's industrial infrastructure had been incapacitated or destroyed, and interdiction of the Zagreb-Split rail line running through Knin, and of transport along the Adriatic littoral, cut the country in two. The interdiction of the Zagreb-Belgrade highway, which Serb forces pierced at Okučani in late August, blocked movement along a vital European transport corridor. Croatian casualties, later estimated by President Tudjman as over 10,000 killed and nearly 40,000 wounded, were high, and one may presume, lacking reliable data, that Serb casualties were comparable.[86] Federal forces had accomplished their minimal operational objectives, but to no good purpose. No government in Zagreb would ever accept the loss of such vital national territories.[87] By December weakened and demoralized federal forces were in no condition to win the war decisively, as Kadijević had originally hoped would be the case, by developing their offensive toward Zagreb. Croatian defense forces could likewise not hope to reverse losses by advancing into areas controlled by Serb militias backed up by the firepower of the JNA. A military stalemate had been reached, which finally provided a foundation for a lasting ceasefire.

The Hour of Europe.

The fighting in Croatia unfolded parallel to an ambitious, EC-sponsored conflict management initiative. The failure of that initiative cast discredit upon European aspirations to create a common foreign and security policy, but it should be noted that the issues at stake were not all that easy to sort out. Slovenia and Croatia justified their separation from Yugoslavia on the basis of the principle of self-determination. Viewed from a less sympathetic perspective, their actions amounted to little more than unilateral armed secession. Belgrade's desire to be acknowledged as the successor of the former Yugoslav federation was not respected by the international community, but the rise of Serbian nationalism behind Milošević had critically weakened if not altogether discredited the Yugoslav idea, and Belgrade had repeatedly refused proposals for restructuring the federation on a more decentralized model. Predominantly Serb regions of Croatia (and later Bosnia-Herzegovina) insisted upon a right of self-determination, while the Serbia to which they desired to adhere refused any hint of self-determination to its Albanian minority in Kosovo. In initiating its mediation effort, the EC had no ground rules for working through these issues. It strode forward to shoulder the burden of conflict management nonetheless. In the wake of the Gulf War where Europe's role as crisis manager had been embarrassingly modest, and with the Soviet Union in a process of dissolution, the United States calling for Europe to take the lead in addressing what was perceived as essentially a European problem, and the EC's Maastricht summit on the calendar for December, the Yugoslav crisis was widely represented as "a challenge wherein the new political ambitions of the [European] Community would be submitted to a real-life test."[88] In the oft-quoted, and no doubt oft-regretted words of Luxembourg Foreign Minister and EC official Jacques Poos, the "hour of Europe" had struck.[89]

During July and August, EC mediators, represented by a new troika of foreign ministers from Luxembourg, the Netherlands, and Portugal, sought to pursue negotiations through the intermediary of the rump Yugoslav Federal Presidency.[90] On August 27, the EC ministers announced the convening of an international peace conference on Yugoslavia, conducted at The Hague from September 7 through December 12 under the direction of Lord Peter Carrington. Carrington's goal was to restructure Yugoslavia as a loose confederation of sovereign states, and his practical proposals resembled the models for confederation put forward by Slovenia, Croatia, Bosnia-Herzegovina, and Macedonia during the agony of the federation in 1990, with the addition of special guarantees for minority communities in regions where they constituted a majority of the local population (such as the Serb regions inside Croatia). Detailed arrangements would be worked out by three working groups convened at The Hague to discuss future constitutional arrangements, minority rights, and economic relations within the Yugoslav space, assisted by an arbitration committee directed by the respected French jurist Robert Badinter.[91] This proposal, the most reasonable of all the peace projects to emerge in the decade-long course of the Yugoslav conflict, was a nonstarter for all belligerents, who maintained a commitment to maximal goals and had in effect only begun to fight. Failure to achieve a negotiated arrangement along the lines suggested by the Carrington Plan before the conflict escalated beyond all control was, in the words of Florence Hartman, a "fatal error."[92] Military advantage made Belgrade especially reticent to offer concessions. In August, the Serb side opposed the extension to Croatia of the European observer mission already present in Slovenia. In early September it relented, but for unarmed civilian observers only. In mid-September Milošević rejected a proposal from Dutch Foreign Minister van der Brock calling for the interpositioning of peacekeeping forces between the warring factions. And on October 18 Serbia rejected an EC package balancing a commitment to the integrity of internal borders with respect for a right of self-determination including the creation of autonomous regions for minorities, on the specious grounds that it implied the end of the Yugoslav federation.[93]

Between July and December the EC brokered no less than fourteen ceasefire agreements, all of which were violated virtually before the ink was dry. As the level of violence intensified during September and October, frustration over Europe's inability to reverse the momentum of war grew greater. *Le Monde* described Europe's powerlessness as "pathetic," and the *Frankfurter Allgemeine Zeitung* concluded that Europe's "dress rehearsal for a common foreign policy" had become "a debacle."[94] Such conclusions were probably unfair. The lack of will to peace among the parties to conflict virtually ensured that any mediation effort, at this stage, would be an exercise in futility. But it remained the case that Europe was badly divided. Among the major powers, Germany, supported by Belgium, Denmark, and Austria, took a strong anti-Serb line and insisted on the need to offer full diplomatic recognition to Slovenia and Croatia in order to establish *faits accomplis* that Belgrade could not hope to reverse. The Holy See also lent moral support to the cause of independence for predominantly Catholic Slovenia and Croatia.[95] Great Britain, France, and Spain, fearful of the possible impact of *carte blanche* support for a policy of secession upon their own national minorities, and perhaps of expanding German influence in central Europe as well, demurred. Something like the division between Triple Entente and Triple Alliance seemed to have been reborn, with Italy straddling the fence, anxious to contain the effects of a crisis in a neighboring region but also to remain aligned with its European partners.[96] As the Maastricht summit approached, the desire to placate Bonn on the Yugoslav question in order to ensure its compliance with the project for European monetary union grew stronger, however, and Serb successes (and excesses) on the battlefields encouraged sympathy for the embattled Croats. From the beginning of December the EC was applying economic sanctions uniquely against Serbia and Montenegro, and after the conclusion of the Maastricht summit on December 10, the issue of diplomatic recognition for the secessionist republics was pushed onto the agenda.

On August 27 the EC's Badinter Arbitration Commission took on the task of developing ground rules for the deconstruction of the Yugoslav federation. The Badinter Commission issued its findings on November 29, clearing the way for secessions by describing Yugoslavia as being "in the process of dissolution," using the legal premise, derived from the experience of de-colonization, of *uti possedetis juris* to establish the legitimacy of internal, republican boundaries as emerging inter-state borders, and calling upon the federal units to submit requests for recognition in line with EC guidelines.[97] On January 11, 1992, the Commission announced its decisions. Of the four applicants, only Slovenia and Macedonia were determined to have fulfilled all criteria for recognition, while Croatia was "provisionally" certified as meeting minimum standards. Bosnia-Herzegovina was urged to conduct a referendum on independence as a condition for eligibility.[98] The rulings were legally disputable, but at this point political motives had become decisive. Bonn wanted recognition to be accorded to Slovenia and Croatia, and so it would be. Macedonia, in deference to Greek protests (including threats from Athens to veto EC initiatives should its will be defied) was left in limbo. On December 16, 1991, the EC twelve bowed to German pressure and agreed to recognize the secessionist republics on January 15, 1992. Only 8 days later, on Christmas Eve, Bonn embarrassed its allies by moving to recognize Slovenia and Croatia unilaterally.[99] The other EC members lamely followed suit on January 15. The Maastricht summit had been brought to a successful conclusion, but the pressures exerted by the Yugoslav war were having a serious impact upon European cohesion.[100]

Germany's decision to press for selective recognitions,

aggressively pursued without regard for the larger consequences, was out of character for a country that had prided itself on a commitment to multilateralism and a diplomacy of moderation and consensus.[101] Since at least 1987, however, elite opinion in Germanic Europe had been shaped by a virtual campaign of slander directed against Serbs and Serbia, the historic enemy deemed responsible for the debacle of German Balkan policy during both twentieth century world wars. In the words of the influential Balkan correspondent of the *Frankfurter Allgemeine Zeitung* Johann Reissmüller, the imperative of separation in former Yugoslavia was created by "the Serbian leadership with its oriental understanding of justice and governance," and the existence of an unbridgeable gap between "two entirely foreign cultures and civilizations, two clashing conceptions of justice and property, of governance and freedom."[102] Foreign Minister Hans-Dietrich Genscher, with family origins in the Halle region of formerly communist East Germany, was committed to the premise of self-determination that lay at the foundation of German unification, but his calculation that recognition would serve as an admonition to Belgrade and encourage an end to the fighting was misplaced.[103] Lord Carrington recognized immediately that recognition without regulation of underlying issues would destroy his fragile peace initiative, and protested loudly but in vain.[104] The inability of a single European power to muster opposition to Bonn's initiative, which was to prove disastrous in the short term, did not speak highly of the EC's readiness to assume a more significant international role.[105] Supporters of recognition continue to argue that it was a necessary response to Serb aggression, an appropriate application of the principle of self-determination, and a useful means to mobilize the international community by internationalizing the conflict. But a principle of self-determination was not consistently applied, Germany's *Alleingang* only served further to divide international opinion, and Serbia was not coerced.

Attempts to explain Bonn's haste rest upon a number of contradictory hypotheses: aspirations to win advantage in an emerging central European economic zone, to assert a more dynamic foreign policy in the wake of unification, to make up for diplomatic passivity during the Gulf War and assume a stronger leadership role in Europe, to pursue a policy of revenge against an historic enemy, to respond to domestic pressures emerging from Catholic, Bavarian, and Croatian interest groups, or to stand up to destabilizing violence on Germany's post-cold war eastern marches.[106] Some combination of these factors will have to serve — what matters are the consequences of Bonn's, and the EC's, miscalculations. Slovenia and Croatia were recognized as sovereign states, and the dissolution of Yugoslavia sanctioned, without any provision being made to address the status of Croatia's Serb minority, the prospects of the other constituent peoples of the Yugoslav federation, the legitimacy of federal instances, or the consequences for the Balkan region of Yugoslavia's precipitous fragmentation. The decade of war that followed was at least in part a consequence of these miscalculations.

Lack of results contributed to the gradual effacement of the EC's mediation role in favor of the United Nations. On September 25, 1991, in response to a request presented by Belgium, France, and Great Britain, the UN declared an arms embargo against all parties to the conflict. On October 8, Secretary General Javier Pérez de Cuéllar designated former U.S. Secretary of State Cyrus Vance as his personal representative to the region, significant in retrospect as a first step toward a more vigorous U.S. involvement in the international conflict management effort. Led by Vance the UN's role expanding rapidly, and it was under UN auspices that a fifteenth, and finally successful, ceasefire agreement was accepted by the contending factions, signed by Croatian Defense Minister Šušak and the JNA 5th Military District Commander General Andrija Rašeta on January 2, 1992, and placed into effect on the following day. The key to success, as already noted, was the emerging military stalemate. The agreement imposed a ceasefire in place, and included provisions for the monitoring of compliance by UN peacekeeping troops. In February 1992 UN Resolution 743 sanctioned the deployment of what would eventually become a 14,000 strong UN Protection Force (UNPROFOR) involving more than thirty nations, the second largest UN peacekeeping contingent ever assembled, in four noncontiguous UN Protected Areas (UNPAs) inside Croatia (eastern and western Slavonia and northern and southern Krajina — known as sectors East, West, North, and South). The original UNPROFOR headquarters, incongruously, was established in Sarajevo, soon to become a theater of war in its own right. As originally conceived, the ceasefire arrangement was supposed to serve as a prelude to a comprehensive settlement to be worked out at the Hague conference. In December, however, the Hague project collapsed, and with the eruption of war in Bosnia-Herzegovina in

1992 the UNPA arrangement and its peculiar "ink spot" distribution of protected areas was frozen in place.

The UN mandate in Croatia was defined as a classic peacekeeping mission assuming an in place ceasefire, consent of the warring parties, neutrality between former belligerents, and limiting rules of engagement confined to cases of self-defense.[107] Essential tasks included demilitarization, guarantees for the continued functioning of local authorities (to include protection of exposed communities and individuals,) monitoring the withdrawal of federal army and irregular forces from Croatia, and facilitation of refugee return. In line with these goals, JNA forces were withdrawn across the border into neighboring Bosnia-Herzegovina, and a partial attempt was made to disarm local Serb forces. Heavy weapons were placed into UN supervised weapons storage sites, from where they would, in many cases, be retrieved following the limited Croatian offensives against the Krajina during 1993. Croatia consistently opposed various aspects of the UN mission, refusing to conclude a proper Status of Forces Agreement for 3 full years and harshly criticizing UNPROFOR's performance, but the arrangement worked to its long-term advantage. As had been the case in Slovenia under somewhat different circumstances, with the withdrawal of the Federal Army, the only organized force capable of resisting an eventual Croatian reassertion of sovereignty had been removed from the game. Zagreb was now in a position to shift the balance of power to its advantage behind a UN shield, while leaving the ultimate status of the disputed territories undetermined. The president of the newly constituted Republic of Serb Krajina (created on December 19, 1991, as the result of a merger between the Serb Autonomous Regions of Baranja, Western Srem, Western Slavonia, and Krajina), Milan Babić recognized the threat that the arrangement posed to his fragile and exposed community immediately, but his opposition to the plan was overridden by Milošević, upon whom all Serb communities outside of Serbia proper remained ultimately dependent. During February 1992 Babić was unceremoniously cashiered on behalf of Milošević loyalist Martić.[108]

Babić was foresightful. The UN-brokered ceasefire was fragile from the start. Fronts remained intact, and sporadic shelling continued through 1992 and 1993. In September 1993 Croat forces launched an offensive with 6,000 troops against the so-called Medak Pocket north of Zadar, aimed at retaking the Maslenica bridge,

Zadar airport, and the Peruca hydroelectric power plant facility. The offensive was successful in the short-term, allowing a brief reopening of north-south traffic along the Adriatic littoral.[109] A ceasefire was renegotiated on March 29, 1994, but at this point the balance of forces in the theater was turning against the Serbs. When Croatia finally moved to reconquer the Krajina militarily in 1995, with vastly improved means, it was able to push UN forces aside and crush outgunned and demoralized Serb resistors, left in the lurch by Belgrade, in a matter of days.[110] Once again, intervention by the international community aimed at conflict resolution would become an objective foundation for the eventual victory of one of the contending parties.

The Destruction of Yugoslavia: A Balance Sheet.

Yugoslavia's disintegration was prepared by protracted economic decline that left citizens with little confidence in the capacity of the federation to address their basic needs. It was occasioned by the decision of republican elites to use ethnic mobilization to reinforce their hold on power. The ethnocrats prospered because of the willingness of a critical mass (though rarely an absolute majority) of citizens, politically disoriented and caught up in an atmosphere of fear, to follow them blindly.[111] In the most fundamental sense, Yugoslavs had no one to blame for the disasters of the 1990s but themselves.

The international community nonetheless was significantly involved in the events that culminated in war, and it has been forced to accept responsibility for managing the consequences. In retrospect, it is clear that leading international actors were caught by surprise by the Yugoslav conflict, and ill-prepared to deal with it. An effective effort to hold the Yugoslav federation together needed to begin well before the crisis of 1989-91. The Western powers did not make such an effort, both because they did not consider the likelihood of a breakdown of the federation to be particularly high, and because they did not view Yugoslavia as sufficiently important to merit it. Once fighting was underway, conflict management efforts were plagued by misperceptions about the nature of the problem, a lack of accord between would be mediators, scarcely disguised support for Slovenian and Croatian independence on the part of important European actors, a refusal to address the status of Serb minorities outside Serbia proper, and serious errors of judgment. The West, and the international community as represented by the UN, did not cause the demise of Yugoslavia, but their policies only succeeded in making a bad situation worse.

Misled by the discourse of Balkan marginality and caught up in the euphoria of the "end of history" supposedly ushered in by the collapse of communism, all of the great powers underestimated the potential consequences of Yugoslavia's collapse.[112] "That Yugoslav domestic chaos could give rise to one of the largest diplomatic crises since 1945," writes Marie-Janine Calic, "was an idea that virtually no one took seriously in 1991."[113] More lucid evaluations of the situation were available — the conclusions of a report by the U.S. Central Intelligence Agency leaked to the press on November 27, 1990, which predicted the collapse of Yugoslavia within 18 months followed by a bloody civil war, posed the nature of the problem with startling accuracy — but it was ignored by political leaders for whom Balkan affairs were simply not a high priority.[114] Up to the spring of 1991, by which time any attempt at preventive diplomacy was condemned to be too little and too late, distracted by the drama of the Gulf War and convinced that despite violent rhetoric the unruly Yugoslavs would eventually come around to accept some form of pragmatic cooperation, the leading world powers gave the crisis only cursory attention.[115]

Once the magnitude of events began to sink in, mediation efforts were plagued by a lack of accord over ends, ways, and means. Despite the pledges made at Maastricht, Europe's capacity to function as an international actor was revealed as inadequate. "The main lesson of the Yugoslav conflict," concluded Jonathan Eyal, "is that no coordinated European security policy exists, and that there are no effective instruments for its future coordination."[116] The degree to which the Cold War had served to impose priorities upon the European great powers was unappreciated, and the reappearance of sharply contrasting national goals seems to have come as a shock. Managing the Balkan conflict on the basis of what one analyst calls "European Political Cooperation Plus" (*ad hoc* consultations, diplomatic protests, economic sanctions, peace monitoring, and traditional mediation) would have been difficult under the best of circumstances.[117] Without agreement between the most important interested parties, it was bound to be an exercise in futility. This was revealed in the debate over recognition, where some powers strove to preserve the unity of the federation while others worked to sabotage it.

The unwillingness of the United States to take the lead in crafting consensus was another factor working against the conflict management effort. Washington's engagement was vital to effective Western policy, but U.S. foreign policy elites were uncertain about where national priorities should lie in a post-cold war environment that was still poorly understood.[118] There were strong currents of opinion that no vital U.S. interests were at stake in the region, that the Europeans would never shoulder responsibility for managing their own affairs unless forced to do so, and that "letting them fight" until clear winners and losers emerged might be a better way to recast regional equilibriums than a costly intervention.[119] The United States declined to provide strong direction for a coordinated Western policy during the first phase of the crisis and, in fact, used its influence to prevent decisive external engagement.

During the armed conflicts in Slovenia and Croatia the Soviet Union was preoccupied by domestic affairs. Soviet President Mikhail Gorbachev, caught up in a desperate effort to rescue the failing Soviet ship of state, repeatedly asserted the need to maintain the integrity of the Yugoslav federation, but his ability to influence events was declining.[120] The attempted coup of August 1991 was informed by sympathy toward Serbia as Russia's historic ally in the Balkans, but it ended as a fiasco.[121] The government of the independent Russian Federation after January 1, 1992, under President Boris Yeltsin and Foreign Minister Andrei Kozyrev, sought to align Russian Balkan policy with that of the Western democracies. In May 1992 Kozyrev visited all of the former Yugoslav republics, and signed accords establishing full diplomatic relations with Slovenia and Croatia. He also publicly asserted that responsibility for the conflict fell upon the "national-communist" leadership in Belgrade.[122] The Russian Federation voted in favor of economic sanctions against Belgrade on May 30, 1992, on July 10 it approved Yugoslavia's exclusion from the CSCE, and on September 22 supported UN Resolution No. 777 denying Belgrade the status of legal successor of Tito's federation. As relations between Yeltsin and his parliament began to disintegrate from the summer of 1992 onward, however, the government's approach to the Yugoslav crisis became a source of discord. In a series of contentious debates, the parliamentary opposition loudly affirmed Russia's traditional friendship with Serbia. "In Serbia and Montenegro," ran one typically emotional intervention, "from generation to generation the people have absorbed love and devotion for Russia with their mother's milk."[123] On June 26, 1992, the Russian Parliament passed a resolution criticizing the government for approving sanctions against Serbia, and called for their abrogation, revealing basic divisions over Balkan policy.[124] As a result of these divisions, Russia was never securely part of the Western conflict management effort in Yugoslavia. Indeed, the Russian opposition gave valuable aid and encouragement to Serb nationalism.

The lack of institutions capable of responding to the demands of the post-cold war security environment also helps to explain the ineffectiveness of Western policy. The CSCE's Paris Charter of November 1990 provided an ambitious set of premises for a new approach to the challenges of European security.[125] But, required to act by consensus and without an autonomous military arm, the CSCE was not in a position to implement policy. After the fall of the Berlin Wall, the organization swelled to include more than 50 members. It had become a "small European UN" weighed down by a burden "that it will not be able to master soon."[126] A Vienna-based CSCE Conflict Management Center created on the very eve of the crisis was quickly overwhelmed by events. The Western European Union (WEU) had only been revived as a security forum in 1984. It lacked an integrated command structure, was inadequately equipped with military assets, and possessed little political clout. Even Europe's premier security organization, and the only one with the means to act effectively in a military capacity, was at a loss when confronted with the Yugoslav imbroglio. At the outset of the crisis NATO was taking the first tentative steps toward a post-cold war identity. The Alliance was still fixed upon the traditional Article Five mission of territorial defense and was reluctant to consider out of area missions--a new NATO was on the drawing board, but it was not yet in place. Primary responsibility for managing the Yugoslav conflict therefore devolved, almost by default, upon the United Nations. But UN peacekeeping capacity was already over-extended, and the organization was not prepared to sponsor peace enforcement missions. Unfortunately, once fighting had commenced, and in the absence of a will to settlement among the belligerents, peace enforcement was the only option that promised results.

A major barrier to effective action was the near total absence of a principled foundation for peacemaking. The original justification for recognizing Slovenia and Croatia was the right of self-determination, but it was a dubious premise about which no one seemed to agree.[127] The concept was coined by Woodrow Wilson as a means for coordinating the selective dismantling of the defeated European empires of World War I, but it has never been incorporated into the code of international law. There is no consensus in place over what the conditions that qualify any one of the more than 3,000 national communities that can be identified worldwide for such a privilege might be, or whether the principle of self-determination necessarily implies a right to independence and national sovereignty. In the case of Yugoslavia, the right of self-determination was often invoked but never consistently applied. The denial of an option for self-determination to the Serbs of Croatia and Bosnia, the Croats of Herzegovina, the Kosovar Albanians, and the Albanian population of Macedonia lay at the root of much of the violence that accompanied the country's break-up. The sovereignty of the individual republics, and of inherited republican borders, was often cited as a limitation upon self-determination, but the most outspoken proponents of such perspectives were usually those with the most to gain. Particularly in Croatia, with a third of the national territory under occupation, there was a strong tendency to assert that republican boundaries were historically sanctioned, legal lines of division between sovereign entities.[128] In fact, however, administrative expediency accounted for much of the logic of the Yugoslav republican boundaries drawn up after the Second World War, which were never intended to serve as state frontiers. There was some incongruity in an international legal regime that sanctioned the dismemberment of Yugoslavia itself, while simultaneously holding up its internal boundaries as inviolable. "The country's external borders were made of cotton, its internal and regional frontiers of cement," as one disillusioned critic put it.[129]

The imperative of humanitarian intervention to defend helpless victims and enforce standards of civilized conduct has also been advanced as a justification for international engagement, but during the early phases of the conflict when the most massive abuses occurred the international community stood aside. The International War Crimes Tribunal for the Former Yugoslavia (ICTY) did not receive its statute under Chapter 7 of the UN Charter until May 1993. At least a part of the motivation for its belated convocation was to deflect criticism of Western passivity in the face of massive violence.

Moreover, it quickly became clear that all parties to the conflict were in the business of using atrocity rumors instrumentally in order to win the sympathy of a wider audience. Sorting out fact from fiction in the volatile circumstances of armed conflict is never easy. In the Yugoslav case, where efforts to demonize the enemy became a strategy of war pursued by professional public relations firms such as Ruder Finn Global Public Affairs, the challenge was particularly severe.[130]

The entire peacemaking effort was plagued by ambivalence over the role of force. A decisive intervention in the first stage of the conflict, with the goal of blocking Serbian encroachment into neighboring republics, perhaps could have nipped the crisis in the bud. But the outcome of such a response was not preordained. If conducted with inadequate forces and insufficient will, it could also have led to a military stalemate and confronted Western decisionmakers with an uncomfortable choice between escalation and withdrawal. In any case, the leading Western powers made clear from the outset that no such intervention would be forthcoming.[131] Yugoslavia's contending factions were well aware of Western reluctance, and they shaped their war plans accordingly. The major nations contributing to the peacekeeping effort were reluctant to allow their forces to be used decisively by commanders in the field. Such reluctance undermined efforts to deter warring factions contemplating escalation.

The most serious flaw in the Western conflict management effort was the absence of any kind of consistent vision for the region's future. Yugoslavia, at the heart of the southeastern European subregion, had addressed the dilemma of cultural diversity by sustaining a viable multinational federation. With the Yugoslav idea discredited, what alternatives could be brought forward as a basis for regional order? For both objective and subjective reasons, the European ideal of the nation state was unequal to the task. In the Balkans, intermingled national communities could not be pressed into ethnically homogenous national units at acceptable cost, and the legacy of enmity between peoples did not bode well for exposed minorities inside newly minted bastions of national chauvinism. Even if it could be accomplished consensually, political fragmentation along national lines would work at counterpurposes to economic development. The goal of "joining" the West, and therefore diluting national peculiarities within a larger European or Euro-Atlantic complex, was not a short-term solution. NATO and the EC were in no rush to bring the new democracies of southeastern Europe in from the cold. A united and stable Yugoslavia might have been well placed to move toward accession with Western institutions in tandem with the more advanced Central European states, but its ravaged successor states have been forced to surrender such aspirations for the foreseeable future. Even Slovenia, the most developed and stable of all the post-communist states, has been held back by chaos in the region as a whole. In its first tentative approaches to conflict management in former Yugoslavia, the Western powers set a precedent that would haunt their efforts for years to come-- reactive diplomacy focused on containment rather than cures, lack of equitable standards, inadequate commitment in view of the extent of the problem, and the absence of any kind of coherent end state as a goal of policy.

Conclusion: The Beginning of a War without End.

Slovenia succeeded in fighting its way out of Yugoslavia at relatively low cost because it enjoyed a high degree of domestic consensus about the desirability of independence, did not have to confront the dilemma of a secessionist movement on its national territory, and did not threaten the agenda of Serbian national consolidation that had become the core motivation of the Milošević regime. The lack of a tradition of animosity between Slovenes and Serbs made such an outcome easier to achieve--there were no historical grievances to be resolved, and any residual Slovenian allegiance to an experience of shared statehood was directed toward a Yugoslav ideal that was no longer politically relevant. Though Kučan and Milošević may not have plotted to "stage" a conflict in order to make separation inevitable, neither envisioned their political future within the framework of the federation. A clean break served their purposes well.

None of these conditions applied to the relationship between Croatia and Serbia. The consolidation of nationalist leaderships in Zagreb and Belgrade had been accomplished with the help of intensive media campaigns that sought to reinforce national affiliation by propagating hatred and fear. "Ancient hatreds" were not really at issue. The core themes of hate propaganda were derived from living memory — the experience of civil war between 1941-45, the real and pretended impositions of communist rule from 1945-

91, and the contemporary discourse of "Europe" which presumed to place some peoples above others in a culturally determined hierarchy of civility.[132] The national agenda with which Milošević had affiliated made a right to leave the Yugoslav federation contingent upon a willingness to surrender control over minority regions that wished to remain attached to Serbia. The mirror image of the agenda inspiring the HDZ leadership in Zagreb insisted that historic Croatian state rights could only be achieved by absorbing Serb minority regions into a unified national state ruled from Zagreb. The Serb population of Slavonia and Krajina rejected such subordination. Their will to resist was bolstered by the insensitivity of Tudjman himself, whose aggressive rhetoric, revival of symbols associated with Pavelić's Independent State of Croatia, and purge of Serbs within the state administration seemed designed to encourage the community's worst fears. These fears were promoted by Serbian nationalist propaganda emanating from Belgrade, which revived memories of Ustaša terror and held out the promise of association with a new Yugoslavia where "all Serbs could live in one state," that would of course be a Serbian state. Armed resistance was made possible by the Serb-dominated federal government, which offered encouragement to the Krajina Serbs, provided arms and munitions, and brought the JNA to bear to help defend their conquests on the ground. The result, once the Republic of Serb Krajina had established control over significant portions of Croatian territory, was a classic zero-sum conflict, with a strong emotional and mythic content that made compromise nearly impossible.

Croatia's turf war was not brought to an end by the ceasefire arrangement of January 1992. The Belgrade news weekly *Nin* described it as a "war without victors," but in fact the basic issues that had sparked conflict remained unresolved, and hostility unabated.[133] What is more, the approach to the conflict that the international community had fallen into almost by default — that of selective recognition for breakaway republics on the basis of politically designed criteria without a principled foundation and without effective guarantees — was a recipe for new disasters. Secession in Slovenia and Croatia meant the end of Tito's federation, and forced the remaining republics that wished to separate from the Serbia-Montenegro axis that had come to dominate rump Yugoslavia to choose between unpalatable alternatives. With all communities determined to avoid the worst case of subordination to a despised other, and willing to defend their cause in arms, the Pandora's Box of anarchic disassociation had been opened wide.

ENDNOTES - CHAPTER 3

1. The term "ethnocrat" is coined in Ivan Ivekovic, *Ethnic and Regional Conflicts in Yugoslavia and Transcaucasia: A Political Economy of Contemporary Ethnonational Mobilization*, Ravenna: Longo Editore, 2000.

2. Borislav designated Montenegrin as his official Yugoslav nationality, while Slobodan opted for Serbian — a measure of the relative subjectivity of these categories in Titoist Yugoslavia.

3. Vidosav Stevanovic, *Milosevic, une épitaphe*, Paris: Fayard, 2000, pp. 26-27.

4. Milošević is the subject of a number of critical biographies. Slavoljub Djukić, *Izmedju slave i anateme: Politička biografija Slobodana Miloševića*, Belgrade: Filip Višnjik, 1994, is particularly good on his early years and rise to power. See also Dusko Doder and Louise Branson, *Milosevic: Portrait of a Tyrant*, New York: Free Press, 1999; and Lenard J. Cohen, *Serpent in the Bosom: The Rise and Fall of Slobodan Milošević*, Boulder: Westview Press, 2001. Florence Hartman, *Milosevic: La diagonale du fou*, Paris: Édition Denoël, 1999, uses Milosevic as a foil for what is really a political history of the Yugoslav conflict.

5. Susan L. Woodward, *Balkan Tragedy: Chaos and Disintegration after the Cold War*, Washington, DC: Brookings Institution Press, 1995, p. 73.

6. Mark Thompson, *A Paper House: The Ending of Yugoslavia*, London: Hutchinson Radius, 1992, p. 286.

7. Tudjman's movement is reported to have received over 8 million dollars from the Croatian Diaspora during its rise to power. *Ibid.*, p. 269.

8. Marcus Tanner, *Croatia: A Nation Forged in War*, New Haven: Yale University Press, 1997, pp. 203-240, tracks Tudjman's political career.

9. Jean-Arnault Dérens and Catherine Samary, *Les conflits Yougoslaves de A à Z*, Paris: Les Éditions de l'Atelier, 2000, pp. 71-73. On June 15, 1992, Ćosić was elected by parliament as president of the new Federal Republic of Yugoslavia. As an advocate of negotiated solutions in Croatia and Bosnia-Herzegovina, and an independent personality with considerable moral stature, he quickly found himself at odds with the Milošević group, and on May 31, 1993, he was voted out of office. Dobritsa Tchossitch, *La Yougoslavie et la Question Serbe*, Lausanne: L'Age d'Homme, 1992, offers a good summary of his political views.

10. For the full text, see *Nacrt memoranduma Srpske Akademije Nauke u Beogradu*, Toronto: Srpske Narodne Odbrane, 1987.

11. Cited in Tim Judah, *The Serbs: History, Myth and the Destruction of Yugoslavia*, New Haven: Yale University Press, 1997, p. 160. See also Slavoljub Djukić, *Kako se dogodilo vodja*, Belgrade: Filip Višnjić, 1992, p. 47.

12. Cited in Hartman, *Milosevic*, p. 44.

13. Philip E. Auerswald and David P. Auerswald, eds., *The Kosovo Conflict: A Diplomatic History through Documents*, Cambridge: Kluwer Law International, 2000, pp. 10-16; and Djukić, *Izmedju slave i anateme*, p. 49.

14. Hartman, *Milosevic*, pp. 26-27.

15. Laura Silber and Allan Little, *Yugoslavia: Death of a Nation*, New York: TV Books, 1996, pp. 31-47. Stambolić remained an insightful critic of Milošević after his withdrawal from political life. His memoir, Ivan Stambolić, *Put u bespuće*, Belgrade: Radio 92, 1995, is an interesting commentary on the metamorphosis of his protégé in power. On August 25, 2000, one month prior to Milošević's overthrow, he disappeared from his residence in Belgrade. On March 28, 2003, Stambolić's remains were found in a pit in Serbia's Fruška Gora region, and on April 8, 2003, he was buried with full state and military honors in Belgrade. Investigations conducted in conjunction with the assassination of Prime Minister Zoran Djindjić have indicated that Stambolić was kidnapped and executed by five members of the Serbian Special Operations Unit, a secret police organ now disbanded.

16. The event was dubbed the "Yogurt Revolution" after the demonstrators pelted local officials with yogurt containers. The radical Serb nationalist leader Vojislav Šešelj would later claim that the entire episode was organized by the Serbian secret police. See his comments in *Velika Srbija*, No. 2, January 1995.

17. Auerswald and Auerswald, *The Kosovo Conflict*, p. 18.

18. Cited in Silber and Little, *Yugoslavia*, p. 72. The full text of the speech was published in *Politika*, June 29, 1989, pp. 3-4. See also Auerswald and Auerswald, *The Kosovo Conflict*, pp. 30-34.

19. Stevanovic, *Milosevic, une épitaphe*, p. 71. The anti-communist and Serb nationalist Jovan Rašković, leader of the Serb community in Krajina up to 1990, characterized Milošević as "a big Bolshevik, a communist, and a tyrant to the tips of his toes." Jovan Rašković, *Luda zemlja*, Belgrade: Akvarijus, 1990, p. 328.

20. On Serb nationalist ideology under Milošević, see Nebojša Popov, "Srpski populizam: Od marginalne do dominantne pojave," *Vreme*, May 24, 1993.

21. On the Marković Plan, see Mladan Dinkić, *Ekonomija destrukcije: Velika*

pljačka naroda, Belgrade: VIN, 1995.

22. Milica Uvalić, "How Different is Yugoslavia?" *European Economy*, No. 2, 1991, pp. 202-209.

23. See Woodward, *Balkan Tragedy*, pp. 47-81.

24 Hannes Hofbauer, *Balkan Krieg: Zehn Jahre Zerstörung Jugoslawiens*, Vienna: ProMedia, 2001, p. 20.

25. Cited in Ejub Štitkovac, "Croatia: The First War," in Jasminka Udovička and James Ridgeway, eds., *Burn This House: The Making and Unmaking of Yugoslavia*, Durham, NC: Duke University Press, 1997, p. 155.

26. "Tudjmanove izjave uznemirile Jevreye," *Politika*, May 5, 1990, p. 1.

27. See Gordana Suša, "Nemam domovinu, tražim neka drugu," *Borba*, February 17, 1991, p. 8. The use of the *šahovnica* as a state symbol was particularly resented. Croatian officials demonstrated sensitivity, of a particularly ineffective sort, to minority opinion by reversing the shield's red-white checkerboard alignment in order to differentiate it from the emblem used by the Pavelić regime.

28. Paul Shoup, The Future of Croatia's Border Regions," *Report on Eastern Europe*, Vol. 2, No. 48, 1991, pp. 26-33.

29. Vladimir Goati, "Politički život Bosne i Hercegovine," in Dušan Janjić and Paul Shoup, eds., *Bosna i Hercegovina izmedju rata i mira*, Belgrade: Dom Omladine, 1992, p. 55.

30. Woodward, *Balkan Tragedy*, p. 122. On the elections, whose outcome went some distance toward determining the republic's future, see Steven L. Burg and Paul S. Shoup, *The War in Bosnia-Herzegovina: Ethnic Conflict and International Intervention*, Armonk, NY: M. E. Sharpe, 1999, pp. 46-56; and Saud Arnautović, *Izbori u Bosni i Hercegovini '90*, Sarajevo: Promocult, 1996.

31. Alija Izetbegović, *The Islamic Declaration: A Programme for Islamization of Muslims and Muslim Peoples*, Sarajevo: n.p., 1990. The text describes Islam as a "normative system" and "integral way of life." Izetbegović published a more developed statement of his political and ethical views (originally composed during the 1980s) after the eruption of the Yugoslav conflict. 'Alija 'Ali Izetbegovic, *Islam Between East and West*, Ankara: International Bosnia-Herzegovina Conference, 1994. The only Yugoslav republican leader during the wars of the 1990s without a communist background, Izetbegović was briefly imprisoned in 1946 for his opposition to Titoist policies toward Bosnia's Muslim community. Upon his release he became a respected lawyer and leader of the political opposition. In 1983

he was tried, together with twelve associates, for a purported attempt to transform Bosnia-Herzegovina into an Islamic Republic, and sentenced to a 14-year term, only 2 years of which were served. The events surrounding his incarceration are described in Zachary T. Lewin, "The Islamic Revival and the Muslims of Bosnia Hercegovina," *East European Quarterly*, Vol. 17, No. 4, January 1984, pp. 437-458. For a brief biography, see Dérens and Samary, *Les conflits Yougoslaves de A à Z*, pp. 156-158.

32. Xavier Bogarel, *Bosnie: Anatomie d'un conflit*, Paris: La Découverte, 1996, pp. 45-46, and Jasminka Udovička and Ejub Štitkovac, "Bosnia and Hercegovina: The Second War," in Udovička and Ridgeway, eds., *Burn This House*, pp. 174-175.

33. Burg and Shoup, *The War in Bosnia-Herzegovina*, p. 47.

34. The republic elections are summarized in Lenard J. Cohen, *Broken Bonds: Yugoslavia's Disintegration and Balkan Politics in Transition*, 2nd ed., Boulder: Westview Press, 1995, pp. 88-162.

35. Mesić had indeed boasted of his efforts to undo the Yugoslav union, and would subsequently recount them proudly in a memoir. Stipe Mesić, *Kako smo srušili Jugoslaviju*, Zagreb: Globus, 1992.

36. "Model konfederacije," *Vjesnik*, October 6, 1990, p. 1.

37. Janez Janša, *The Making of the Slovenian State 1988-1992*, Ljubljana: Mladinska Knijga, 1994, pp. 63-68.

38. Chuck Sudetic, "Yugoslavs Push Compromise Plan," *The New York Times*, June 7, 1991, p. A5.

39. Burg and Shoup, *The War in Bosnia-Herzegovina*, p. 71.

40. Cited in Djukić, *Kako se dogodilo vodja*, p. 187, and Marco Ventura, "Jugoslavia, un omicidio perfetto," in Alessandro Marzo Magno, ed., *La Guerra dei dieci anni--Jugoslavia 1991-2001: I fatti, i personaggi, le ragioni dei conflitti*, Milan: Il Saggiatore, 2001, pp. 93-94.

41. Izetbegović was consistent in arguing, though perhaps poorly advised in concluding, that without Croatia as a balance to Serbia, Bosnia-Herzegovina would have no choice but to leave the Yugoslav federation. Arnautović, *Izbori u Bosne i Hercegovini '90*, p. 44.

42. Janez Drnovšek, *Moja resnica*, Ljubljana: Mladinska knjiga, 1996, p. 209.

43. Silber and Little, *Yugoslavia*, p. 122.

44. There is no public record of this important meeting. The results are recounted in Robert Thomas, *The Politics of Serbia in the 1990s*, New York: Columbia University Press, 1999, p. 86. On August 11, 1997, the President of the Croatian Helsinki Committee for Human Rights, Ivan Zvonimir Cicak, granted an interview to the Split-based satirical weekly *Feral Tribune* where he discussed the meeting at length. As a consequence, Cicak was placed on trial by the Croatian authorities for "disseminating false information." See "Criminal Investigation Against Ivan Zvonimir Cicak," *Advocacy Alert — Croatia*, August 1997. Tudjman and Milošević met again privately in March 1991 during a summit on the future of Yugoslavia in Tikveš, and outlined a common strategy based upon the partition of Bosnia-Herzegovina, with a small Muslim state to be left as residue. Hrvoje Šarinić, *Svi moji tajni pregovori sa Slobodanom Miloševićem 1993-1995*, Zagreb: Globus, 1999, p. 42. Obsessed with his role in history, Tudjman kept a nearly complete file of recordings of confidential conversations with colleagues conducted in the presidential office. The portions of these tapes that have been made public reveal that the Croatian President repeatedly made reference to schemes for partitioning Bosnia-Herzegovina, notably in conversation with Mate Boban and Gojko Šušak on November 28, 1993, where he speaks of trading occupied areas along the Sava for territory in western Bosnia, and as late as April 1999, when Tudjman suggested exchanging the Prevlaka Peninsula and a point of access to the Adriatic to the Serbs in exchange for Banja Luka and the Bosanska Krajina. "Croatia's Watergate Tape," *Radio Free Europe/Radio Liberty Balkan Report*, Vol. 4, No. 32, May 2, 2000. The existence of the Tudjman tapes was revealed following the HDZ's electoral defeat in 1999, but only small excerpts have been published. The Tudjman family unsuccessfully sued to have the tapes returned, but in the summer of 2002, under pressure to surrender the tapes to the International Criminal Tribunal for Former Yugoslavia in The Hague, the Croatian government made the decision to restrict all access to the documents for a period of 30 years.

45. Avramov Smilja, *Postherojski rat Zapada protiv Jugoslavije*, Veternik: Idi, 1997, p. 140.

46. *U.S. Department of State Dispatch 2*, No. 22, June 3, 1991, pp. 395-396.

47. Woodward, *Balkan Tragedy*, p. 161.

48. Thomas Manne, *Leviathan*, Vol. I, Chicago: Gateway Edition, 1956, p. 118.

49. Silber and Little, *Death of a Nation*, pp. 140-141.

50. "Acts of the Republics of Slovenia and Croatia on Sovereignty and Independence," *Yugoslav Survey*, Vol. 32, No. 3, 1991, pp. 47-56. Slovenia's parliament approved the declaration of disassociation on July 25, 24 hours earlier than originally announced, in order to allow defense forces to preempt federal reactions.

51. Janša, *The Making of the Slovene State*, p. 134.

52. Janša remains somewhat unfathomable. As a critical journalist associated with the anti-communist Slovene youth movement during the 1980s he became the *bête noire* of the Yugoslav defense ministry. In 1988 he was sentenced to a prison term for revealing state secrets in an intensely publicized political process that brought great discredit upon the Yugoslav authorities. Appointed Defense Minister at age 33 by Prime Minister Lojze Peterle after the 1990 elections, the former student "pacifist" became the architect of armed secession in 1991. Seemingly destined for a leadership role in independent Slovenia, he soon became embroiled in personal scandal, and was constrained to withdraw from political life. On his efforts to build up an autonomous Slovene armed force, see Central Intelligence Agency, Office of Russian and European Analysis, *Balkan Battlegrounds: A Military History of the Yugoslav Conflict, 1990-1995*, 2 vols., Washington, DC: Central Intelligence Agency, May 2002, Vol. 1, pp. 51-54.

53. The strategy is described by its architect in Janša, *The Making of the Slovene State*, pp. 101-113. See also the memoirs of Foreign Minister Dimitrij Rupel, *Skrivnost Država: Spomini na Domače in Zunanje Zadeve, 1989-1992*, Ljubljana: Delo-Novice, 1992, pp. 120-122.

54. James Gow and Cathie Carmichael, *Slovenia and the Slovenes: A Small State and the New Europe*, Bloomington: Indiana University Press, 2000, p. 180. Gow and Carmichael, pp. 174-184, provide a useful account of the war from the Slovene perspective.

55. Aleksander Pavković, *The Fragmentation of Yugoslavia: Nationalism and War in the Balkans*, 2nd ed., London: Macmillan, 2000, pp. 135-138. See also Woodward, *Balkan Tragedy*, pp. 166-167. Woodward posits that Yugoslav and Slovenian authorities agreed to "feign" a war in order to create a pretext for separation. Pavković, *The Fragmentation of Yugoslavia*, p. 140, describes the conflict as "a feigned war in which both sides went through a series of belligerent gestures, each with a different audience in mind."

56. On the balance of forces, see "Istina o oružanom sukoba u Slovenjii," *Narodna Armija*, Special Edition, January 26, 1991. Janša, *The Making of the Slovenian State*, pp. 239-240, remarks candidly that in the case of a full-fledged war, "the superiority of armoured units would have been paramount, and we did not have enough supplies for an anti-armour battle over greater distances." The CIA's military history of the contest speculates that in the long term the JNA effort to conquer Slovenia was a lost cause, but describes the military balance in June and July 1991 as "completely unequal." *Balkan Battlegrounds*, Vol. 1, p. 65.

57. According to the memoir of Borisav Jović, *Poslednji dani SFRJ: Izvodi iz dnevnika*, 2nd ed., Belgrade: Narodna Biblioteka Srbije, 1996, pp. 343-344, on June 30, 1991, the JNA presented an operational plan for using armed force to crush

Slovene secession. Belgrade turned down the plan, with the recommendation that force only be used as punishment and as a prelude to Slovenia's expulsion from the federation.

58. Jović, *Poslednji dani SFRJ*, p. 343.

59. *Balkan Battlegrounds*, Vol. 1, p. 68, and *Slovenija: Geografska, Zgodovinska, Pravna Politična, Ekonomska i Kulturna Podoba Slovenije*, Ljubljana: Mladinska Knjiga, 1998, p. 134.

60. "Italia e Austria attivano la diplomazia della Csce," *Corriere della Sera*, June 28, 1991, p. 6. In fact, very little grew out of this initiative. The CSCE's new, Vienna-based Center for Conflict Prevention, unprepared for a conflict on this scale, was quickly marginalized. This was an early example of the inadequacy of European institutions faced with post-cold war conflict.

61. For the text, see Snežana Trifunovska, ed., *Yugoslavia Through Documents*, Dordrecht: Martians Nijhoff, 1994, pp. 311-315.

62. He would embellish his brief tenure in office with the statement: "I have fulfilled my duty — Yugoslavia no longer exists." Cited in Cohen, *Broken Bonds*, p. 228.

63. "Bloccata la spirale dello scontro," *Corriere della Sera*, July 2, 1991, p. 3.

64. See Jill Benderly and Evan Kraft, eds., *Independent Slovenia: Origins, Movements, Prospects*, New York: St. Martin's Press, 1994.

65. Cited in Ventura, "Jugoslavia, un omicidio perfetto," pp. 93-94.

66. Mark Thompson, *Forging War: The Media in Serbia, Croatia and Bosnia-Hercegovina*, Avon: The Bath Press, 1994; and Verica Spasovska, "Der Jugoslawienkonflikt als Medienereignis: Der Einfluss der Medien auf öffentliche Meinung und Aussenpolitik," *Südosteuropa Mitteilungen*, Vol. 35, No. 1, 1995, pp. 8-17. A Serbian acquaintance of the author, the widow of a former Yugoslav diplomat from Croatia and owner of a home in Split and flat in Belgrade, reported viewing a news broadcast in Belgrade during the autumn of 1991 including graphic images of mutilated cadavers, described as the Serb victims of Ustaša terror. Upon returning to Split, she viewed the identical images on Croatian television, with the cadavers described as the Croat victims of Chetnik terror. Such abusive use of the pornography of death for political purposes, without regard to circumstance or fact, was widespread.

67. *Balkan Battlegrounds*, Vol. 1, p. 95.

68. James Gow, *Legitimacy and the Military: The Yugoslav Crisis*, New York:

St. Martin's Press, 1992, emphasizes that at this stage in the conflict the Federal Army was the initiator of all major military encounters, and that it functioned objectively as the strong arm of Milošević's political project. He interprets the high command's core motive as the desire to preserve the privileged status that derived from its role as the guarantor of the Yugoslav order. Hartman, *Milosevic*, pp. 165-170, poses a comparable argument.

69. According to one insider account, Serb paramilitaries "were all organized with the consent of Milošević's secret police and armed, commanded and controlled by its officers." Miloš Vasić, "The Yugoslav Army and the Post-Yugoslav Armies," in David A. Dyker and Ivan Vejvoda, eds., *Yugoslavia and After: A Study in Fragmentation, Despair and Rebirth*, London: Longman, 1996, p. 134. Roksanda Ninčić, *et al.*, "Drina bez Čuprije," *Vreme*, October 21, 1991, p. 20, documents the allegation. Paramilitary forces were active on all sides in the Yugoslav conflict, including Dobroslav Paraga's 15,000 strong and openly fascist Croat Defense Forces (*Hrvatske Odbrambene Snage* — HOS), and the Bosnian Muslim Green Berets, commanded by Jusuf (Juka) Prazina, like Arkan a politically connected criminal prior to the war.

70. It is sometimes asserted that these intentions were revealed by a JNA military contingency plan designated with the acronym RAM. The existence of the contingency plan was revealed well prior to the outbreak of the conflict. See "Zbrisaće nas za kugle zemaljske," *Vreme*, September 23, 1991, pp. 5-12. RAM does not conclusively demonstrate Serbian responsibility — military planning options are not necessarily indications of political intent.

71. Article 240 of the Yugoslav Constitution reads that "the armed forces of the Socialist Federative Republic of Yugoslavia defend the independence, sovereignty, territorial unity, and constitutionally determined social order." Cited from Hofbauer, *Balkan Krieg*, p. 33.

72. Velijko Kadijević, *Moje vidjenje raspada: Vojska bez države*, Belgrade: Politika, 1993, p. 88.

73. Stipe Sikavica, "The Army's Collapse," in Udovička and Ridegway, eds., *Burn This House*, p. 138.

74. James Gow, *Triumph of the Lack of Will: International Diplomacy and the Yugoslav War*, New York: Columbia University Press, 1997, pp. 19-20.

75. Borisav Jović, *Poslednji dani SFRJ*, pp. 248-253.

76. *Ibid.*, pp. 328-336.

77. In a memoir, the former president of the Yugoslav Federation Raif Dizdarević singles out Velijko Kadijević, "exceptionally ambitious and narcistic

person that he was," for "betraying" the Yugoslav idea by turning the armed forces toward Milošević and his greater Serbia ideology, "hoping to obtain a more important role, perhaps even a dominant position, in a rump Yugoslavia." Raif Dizdarević, *Od smrti Tita do smrti Jugoslavije: Svjedočenja*, Sarajevo: OKO, 1999, p. 419.

78. John Zametica, *The Yugoslav Conflict*, Adelphi Paper No. 270, London: Brassey's, 1992, is essentially correct in describing the Yugoslav People's Army as a primary victim of the conflict rather than a perpetrator. For Miloš Vasić, "The Yugoslav People's Army perished together with the Yugoslav political idea." Vasić, "The Yugoslav Army," p. 137.

79. Kadijević, *Moje vidjenje raspada*, pp. 134-136.

80. *Ibid.*, 131.

81. *Balkan Battlegrounds*, Vol. 1, p. 96.

82. *Ibid.*, p. 100.

83. Dedaković was tried before a military court for allegedly embezzling over 300,000 Deutsche Marks intended for Vukovar's defenders, but acquitted. He went on to serve as the head of the HOS military wing.

84. The Serb commander Života Panić later claimed to have urged the option upon Jović and Branko Kostić (the Montenegrin representative on the Yugoslav Presidium), but in vain. See his remarks in Ventura, "Jugoslavia, un omicidio perfetto," p. 123; and Kadijević, *Moje vidjenje raspada*, p. 137.

85. Widely publicized images of Dubrovnik under assault (to some extent engineered by Croatian defenders who used the city's medieval towers as gun placements and allegedly burnt piles of tires to create photogenic smoke effects for the international media) were used to good effect to convey the impression of a barbaric Serb invader. The bombing of the Croat presidential palace in the heart of Zagreb's old city on October 7, an action devoid of any apparent strategic logic, likewise cast discredit upon government forces. The destruction in Vukovar was much more representative, but the quiet Slavonian city lacked the media appeal of an international tourist resort or the national capital. See Misha Glenny, *The Fall of Yugoslavia: The Third Balkan War*, Harmondsworth: Penguin, 1992, p. 136.

86. On casualties in the Serb-Croat conflict, see Norman Cigar, "The Serbo-Croatian War, 1991: Political and Military Dimensions," *The Journal of Strategic Studies*, Vol. 16, No. 3, 1993, pp. 297-338.

87. Bože Čović, "Hrvatska izmedju rata i samostalnosti," *Hrvatska revija*, nos. 3-4, 1992, pp. 271-285.

88. Mihailo Crnobrnja, *Le drame Yougoslave*, Rennes: Apogée, 1992, p. 140.

89. Cited from Viktor Maier, *Wie Jugoslawien verspielt wurde*, 3rd ed., Munich: Verlag C.H. Beck, 1999, p. 395. Poos was joined in his optimism by Italian Foreign Minister Gianni De Michaelis, who suggested that the European reaction demonstrated that "when a situation becomes delicate, the Community is capable of responding as a political unit. In our view this is a good sign for the future of political union." *Ibid.*

90. On October 3, 1991, the Serb bloc moved to eliminate four vacated seats on the Titoist federal presidency. Two weeks later, on October 16, the rump presidency voted to remove the red star from Yugoslav national emblems. The federal presidency disappeared with the creation of the new Federal Republic of Yugoslavia in April 1992.

91. Henry Wynaendts, *L'Engrenage, Chroniques yougoslaves — juillet 1991-août 1992*, Paris: Éditions Denoël, 1993, pp. 123-124.

92. Hartman, *Milosevic*, p. 184.

93. Burg and Shoup, *The War in Bosnia-Herzegovina*, pp. 89-91, posit that despite his tough public façade, after the engagement of the UN in the conflict management effort beginning at the end of September, and in view of the poor performance of Serbian military units fighting outside of Serbia proper, Milošević moved away from the goal of annexing Serb-controlled regions inside Croatia toward the concept of special status for such regions under UN protection — the kind of resolution that would eventually be brokered under EC and UN auspices.

94. "L'Europe impuissante," *Le Monde*, October 9, 1991, p. 1, and Günther Nonnenmacher, "Lauter Übergänge in Europa," *Frankfurter Allgemeine Zeitung*, October 8, 1991, p. 1.

95. Christine de Montelos, *Le Vatican et l'éclatement de la Yougoslavie*, Paris: Presses Universitaires de France, 1999.

96. R. Craig Nation, "Italy and the Ethnic Strife in Central and Southeastern Europe," in Vojtech Mastny, ed., *Italy and East Central Europe: Dimensions of the Regional Relationship*, Boulder: Westview Press, 1995, pp. 55-81.

97. Relevant text in Trifunovska, ed., *Yugoslavia Through Documents*, pp. 415-417.

98. Peter Radan, "The Badinter Arbitration Commission and the Partition of Yugoslavia," *The Nationalities Papers*, Vol. 25, No. 3, 1997, pp. 537-559.

99. German recognition had been preempted by Ukraine on December 12, but Kyiv's gesture was of no importance politically. It was followed on January 13, 1992, by recognition from the Holy See in Rome.

100. The result, concluded *Le Monde*, was "not a glorious one for Europe." "Un résultat peu glorieux," *Le Monde*, January 16, 1992, p. 1. For Daniel Vernet, German pressing within the EC "allows one to conclude that Germany will no longer accept European integration conceived as a guarantee against its own potential power." Daniel Vernet, "Le retour de la 'question allemande'," *Le Monde*, December 22-23, 1991, p. 4.

101. Hanns W. Maull, "Germany in the Yugoslav Crisis," *Survival*, Vol. 37, No. 4, Winter 1995-96, pp. 99-130.

102. Johann Georg Reissmüller, *Der Krieg vor unserer Haustür: Hintergründe der kroatischen Tragödie*, Stuttgart: Deutsche Verlags-Anstalt, 1992, pp. 10, 81.

103. In a memoir of a more than 1,000 pages, Genscher only devotes several sentences to these events, among the most significant of his tenure as foreign minister. Hans-Dietrich Genscher, *Erinnerungen*, Berlin: Siedler, 1995.

104. Silber and Little, *Yugoslavia: Death of a Nation*, pp. 199-200.

105. Concern for the consequences of selective recognition was clearly articulated at the time. U.N. Secretary General Javier Pérez de Cuéllar explicitly warned that recognitions "could incite a much wider explosion," an opinion that was widely echoed in editorial opinion. See "Germany Should Hold Off," *The International Herald Tribune*, December 16, 1991, p. 8.

106. Beverly Crawford, "Explaining Defection from International Cooperation: Germany's Unilateral Recognition of Croatia," *World Politics*, Vol. 48, No. 4, July 1996, pp. 482-521. Martin H. A. van Heuven, "Testing the New Germany: The Case of Yugoslavia," *German Politics and Society*, Vol. 29, Summer 1993, pp. 52-63, offers a positive interpretation of German motivation. For a more cynical appraisal, emphasizing collusion between Zagreb and Bonn, see Nenad Ivanković, *Bonn: Druga Hrvatska Fronta*, Zagreb: Mladost, 1993.

107. Paul F. Diehl, *International Peacekeeping*, Baltimore: The Johns Hopkins University Press, 1994.

108. Srdjan Radulović, *Sudbina Krajina*, Belgrade: Politika, 1995, pp. 41-51.

109. Duška Anastasijević and Denisa Kustović, "Zločni rezultat strategije," *Vreme*, July 11, 1994, p. 23.

110. Damir Grubisa, "The 'Peace Agenda' in Croatia: The UN Peacekeeping Operation Between Failure and Success," in R. Craig Nation and Stefano Bianchini, eds., *The Yugoslav Conflict and its Implications for International Relations*, Ravenna: Longo Editore, 1998, pp. 83-108, provides an overall evaluation.

111. Paolo Rumiz, *Maschere per un massacro: Quello che non abbiamo voluto sapare della Guerra in Jugoslavia*, Rome: Editori Riuniti, 1996, pp. 39-49.

112. Francis Fukuyama, *The End of History and the Last Man*, New York: Free Press, 1992.

113. Marie-Janine Calic, *Krieg und Frieden in Bosnien-Hercegovina*, Frankfurt am Main: Suhrkamp Verlag, 1996, p. 219.

114. See Zametica, *The Yugoslav Conflict*, p. 58.

115. The author participated in a policy roundtable during March 1991 with high level U.S. and European official perspectives broadly represented, where with the exception of a few Casandras from the academic community all present accepted the comfortable conclusion that "in the end they'll work it out." The conclusion was conditioned by culturally biased assumptions — the problem was viewed as a product of typical Yugoslav disorder (*nered*), and the "Balkan mentality."

116. Jonathan Eyal, *Europe and Yugoslavia: Lessons from a Failure*, London: Whitehall Paper 19, 1993, p. 80.

117. C. J. Smith, "Conflict in the Balkans and the Possibility of a European Common Foreign and Security Policy," *International Relations*, Vol. 13, No. 2, 1996, p. 2. A systematic analysis of the European effort to develop a Common Foreign and Security Policy is provided by Jan Zielonka, *Explaining Euro-Paralysis: Why Europe is Unable to Act in International Politics*, London: Macmillan, 1998.

118. Klaus-Dieter Frankenberger, "Ohne Kompass: Der Balkankonflikt und die amerikanische Führungsrolle," *Frankfurter Allgemeine Zeitung*, May 29, 1993, p. 10.

119. James A. Baker III, *The Politics of Diplomacy*, New York: G. P. Putnam's Sons, 1995, pp. 636-637, 649-650.

120. In remarks at a dinner in honor of Spain's Felipe Gonzales on July 8, 1991, Gorbachev spoke of "destructive, backward looking nationalism and separatism" as a barrier to the ideal of a Common European Home. The remarks addressed Spanish concerns with Basque separatism, but they also reflected the parallel that the Soviet leader perceived between the Soviet Union's national dilemma and that of Yugoslavia. Cited in E. Iu. Gus'kov, ed., *Iugoslavskii krizis i Rossiia: Dokumenty,*

fakty, kommentarii (1990-1993), Moscow: Slavianskaia letopis', 1993, p. 59.

121. The Milošević regime in Belgrade embraced the August coup attempt with premature enthusiasm. See Mihailo Saranović, "Glavobolja na kvadrat," *Nin*, November 1, 1991; and Sergej Romanenko, "Raspred Jugoslavije i političke elita Rusije," in Jelica Kurljak, ed., *Ruska politika na Balkanu: Zbornik radova*, Belgrade: Institute for International Politics and Economy, 1999, pp. 105-155.

122. Risto Bajalski, "Na cijoj je strain Rusija," *Nin*, June 12, 1992; and A. V. Kozyrev, "Preobrazhenie ili Kafkianskaia metamorfoza," *Nezavisimaia gazeta*, August 20, 1992, p. 4. Defending his position before the Russian parliament on June 26, 1992, Kozyrev argued that Belgrade bore "the lion's share of guilt" for the fighting in former Yugoslavia. "Stenogramma zasedaniia verkhovnogo soveta RF po iugoslavskomu voprosu (26 iunia 1992 g.), in Gus'kov, ed., *Iugoslavskii krizis i Rossiia*, p. 89.

123. Cited by E. Iu. Gus'kov, "Krizis na Balkanakh i pozitsiia Rossii," in Gus'kov, ed., *Iugoslavskii krizisi i Rossiia*, p 40.

124. "Postanovlenie Verkhovnogo Soveta Rossiiskoi Federatsii (26 iuniia 1992 g.)." in Gus'kov, ed., *Iugoslavskii krizis i Rossiia*, pp. 111-112.

125. The Charter of Paris for a New Europe, Paris, November 21, 1990, in *The SIPRI Yearbook*, Copenhagen: SIPRI, 1991, pp. 603-613.

126. Franz Mendel, "Wo sind die Grenzens Europas?" *Europäische Sicherheit*, Vol. 3, 1992, p. 129.

127. See the insightful discussion in Woodward, *Balkan Tragedy*, pp. 199-222.

128. Ljubo Boban, *Hrvatske granice: Od 1918 do 1991 godina*, Zagreb: Školska knjiga, 1992.

129. Slobodan Despot in the postface to Vjekoslav Radovic, *Spectres de la guerre: Chose vue par un Yougoslave privé de son pays*, Lausanne: L'Age d'Homme, 1992, p. 216.

130. On the engagement of public relations firms, see Jacques Merlino, *Les vérités Yougoslave ne sont pas toutes bonnes à dire*, Paris: Albin Michel, 1993.

131. A number of options for more or less robust WEU intervention were prepared during the war in Croatia, but they were rejected by key national affiliates, led by the UK. See Trevor C. Salmon, "Testing Times for European Cooperation: The Gulf and Yugoslavia," *International Affairs*, Vol. 68, No. 2, 1992, pp. 250-251. In the U.S. the Bush administration, urged on by Chairman of the Joint Chiefs of Staff Colin Powell, ruled out military engagement from the start.

See David Halberstam, *War in a Time of Peace: Bush, Clinton, and the Generals*, New York: Scribners, 2001, pp. 34-35.

132. Alain Finkielkraut, *Comment peut-on être Croate?*, Paris: Gallimard,1992, with its evocation of an unbridgeable "cultural difference between Western and Eastern Europe" (p. 32) drawn at the line between Croatia and Serbia, and demand for European solidarity in the face of Serb barbarity, is a good example of this kind of argumentation.

133. Velizar Zečević, "Rezultati rata: Ima samo poraženih," *Nin*, January 24, 1992, pp. 10-12.

CHAPTER 4

THE LAND OF HATE:
BOSNIA-HERZEGOVINA, 1992-95

War Comes to Bosnia.

Few of the premises that informed conflict management efforts in Slovenia and Croatia applied to Bosnia-Herzegovina. Sarajevo governed a relatively underdeveloped region without the degree of self-sufficiency enjoyed by the western republics. The Bosnian "Yugoslavia in miniature" lacked even an approximate ethnic homogeneity to serve as a foundation for national identity, and, rightly or wrongly, the Islamic factor was a source of potential discord. Bosnia also confronted external threats. The departure of Macedonia and Bosnia-Herzegovina brought an end to any kind of representative Yugoslav federation. Rump Yugoslavia was for all intents and purposes a Serbian national state, planning to carve a "greater Serbia" from the flesh of its neighbors.[1] Independent Croatia formally supported Bosnian national integrity, but behind the scenes Zagreb sponsored a separatist movement among the Croat population of Herzegovina. With developed and relatively balanced economies, both Slovenia and Croatia could look forward to the prospect of independence with confidence. Lacking significant Serb or Croat minorities, Macedonia was able to declare independence and negotiate a peaceful withdrawal of the JNA from its territory during the first months of 1992. These advantages were not accorded to Bosnia-Herzegovina. Sarajevo confronted bleak economic prospects, intense intercommunal rivalry, and an imminent threat of external aggression without significant international sponsorship or real friends.

According to the census of 1991, Bosnia-Herzegovina's population consisted of 44 percent Muslims, 31 percent Serbs, 17 percent Croats, and 5 percent "other" (generally citizens who had chosen the designation Yugoslav in lieu of affiliation with a particular ethnic community). The birthrate of the Muslim community was considerably higher than that of the Croats and Serbs, and demographic trends pointed toward the emergence of a Muslim majority within one or two generations.[2] Although there were compact areas of Croat and Serb settlement, much of the population lived intermingled. This was particularly true of the Muslims, traditionally concentrated in cities and medium-sized towns.[3]

Although rates of intermarriage were high (particularly between Serbs and Croats, less so in the case of Muslims), communities maintained a strong sense of identity. Bosnia-Herzegovina had a tradition of tolerance based upon the ideal of *komšiluk* (good neighborliness), but it was a tradition that reinforced rather than diluted communal affiliation.[4] The history of Bosnia was filled with ethnic friction — the great Bosnian writer Ivo Andrić once referred to his country as "the land of hate." Mistrust between communities was exploited during the civil war of 1941-45, and many of the worst atrocities of the period were perpetrated on Bosnian soil. Despite decades of peaceful cohabitation under Tito, the poisoned legacy of the war years remained alive. Ethnic mobilizations during 1990-91 reopened fault lines and heightened fear. The radical nationalist wing of the Bosnian Croat faction made no secret of its desire to affiliate with an independent Croatia. The Bosnian Serb leadership refused to accept association with what they perceived to be an aspiring Islamic state.[5] Izetbegović and his entourage were not willing to approve a partition of Bosnia-Herzegovina that would leave them with a small, land-locked territory that did not reflect their real weight within the population. They aimed to preserve a unitary state that the Muslim community, with its growing demographic weight, could eventually come to dominate. All sides were uncompromising and prepared to fight to achieve their goals.

The threat of violence was particularly acute due to Bosnia-Herzegovina's special place in Yugoslav military policy. Titoist strategic culture was rooted in the legacy of World War II partisan resistance, adapted after 1948 to the threat of invasion from the Soviet bloc. Mountainous and centrally located, Bosnia-Herzegovina was structured from 1968 onward as a sanctuary for guerrilla-style resistance to a would-be invader. Approximately 50 percent of Tito's JNA was permanently stationed in Bosnia-Herzegovina, and the republic was the site of over 55 percent of Yugoslavia's military industries and munitions depots. Like other Yugoslav republics, Bosnia-Herzegovina maintained a Territorial Defense organization, which upon the eruption of hostilities split along communitarian lines, providing each of Bosnia's three constituent nations with the kernel of an autonomous armed force. Bosnians were disproportionately represented within the JNA officer corps, at the end of 1991 an estimated 200,000 citizens were believed to have had access to arms, and spontaneously organized Defense Leagues were proliferating.[6] When the war began in the spring of 1992, 45 separate paramilitary formations representing all three major ethnic communities were able to take the field.[7] It should have been obvious that it would be impossible for Bosnia to sever its ties with Yugoslavia without courting violence. In a diary entry for March 26, 1990, Milošević confidant Borisav Jović had already concluded that in the event of a breakup "Bosnia-Herzegovina cannot survive as a sovereign state, nor can a struggle for control of its territory unfold without loss of blood."[8]

As had been the case with the Serb minority in Croatia, though with less justification (Bosnia initiated no discriminatory measures against its Serb population), the Serb community inside Bosnia-Herzegovina was an outspoken opponent of any project for separation that would leave it a minority within an independent state. On October 15, 1991, when the representatives of the SDA and HDZ within the Bosnian parliament pushed through a "declaration of sovereignty" including a right of secession, Bosnian Serb leader Radovan Karadžić challenged the deputies with the extraordinary statement that the declaration represented the "road to Hell" where "the Muslim nation may disappear altogether."[9] Karadžić was born in 1945 in Montenegro, and arrived in Sarajevo at age 15, where he went on to build a successful career as a sports psychologist, including a stint as advisor for the Sarajevo professional soccer squad. During the political ferment of 1990 Karadžić briefly supported the creation of a Bosnian Green Party, before shifting to a nationalist position and aligning with the newly created Serbian Democratic Party (SDS). The violent rhetoric that laced his October speech was only too typical. Visibly enthused by his role in the political limelight, Karadžić would become a driving force for war in 1992, and uncompromising proponent of Serb nationalist demands thereafter.[10]

In September, Karadžić's SDS sponsored the creation of four Serb Autonomous Regions (*Srpske Autonomne Oblasti* or SAOs) within Bosnia on the model of the Serb Krajina, and on October 26 unveiled a Parliament of the Serb Nation in Bosnia chaired by Momčilo Krajišnik.[11] A plebiscite on November 10 resulted in an overwhelming refusal of separation from Yugoslavia, and on December 21 a

Serb Republic of Bosnia-Herzegovina (*Republika Srpska u Bosni i Hercegovini*) was declared into being with the announced intention of maintaining association with Belgrade. The Croat community followed the same road. The HDZ originally announced its support for a sovereign Bosnia-Herzegovina, but in November it mimicked the Serbs by creating two Croat Autonomous Regions, dubbed the Croatian Community of Herceg-Bosna (*Hrvatska Zajednica Herceg-Bosna*) and Bosanska Posavina. Izetbegović claimed to represent the ideal of a multicultural Bosnia, but he worked to insure Muslim domination of Bosnian institutions, and supported the secessionist aspirations of the Sanjak branch of his movement inside Serbia, the Muslim National Council of Sanjak (*Muslimansko Nacionalno Vjeće Sandžaka*), which organized a referendum on self-determination on October 25, 1992.

Both the Serb and Croat initiatives were declarations of war against the ideal of a unitary state. On May 6, 1992, Karadžić met with Mate Boban, a former clothing store manager who had displaced the more moderate Stjepan Kljujić at the head of the HDZ on February 1, 1992, in Graz, Austria to discuss a partition of Bosnia-Herzegovina to their mutual advantage.[12] Collusion between Serbs and Croats at the expense of the Muslim community would go a long way toward explaining the logic of the war that would follow. Karadžić described Bosnia-Herzegovina coldly as "an artificial state created by the communists."[13] Later in 1992 Boban argued for the abolition of the Bosnian presidency on the grounds that "today Bosnia-Herzegovina has practically ceased to exist as a state, and when there is no state, there is no need for a president."[14]

In the last week of February 1992 the United States abandoned its reticence about the dissolution of Yugoslavia, and opted to support Bosnian independence. Following the fighting in Croatia, Washington confronted strong domestic pressure to oppose Serb aggression, and key leaders were increasingly influenced by explanations of the sources of the conflict that highlighted Belgrade's responsibility. In his memoir, U.S. Ambassador Warren Zimmermann speaks of the need to resist the "Serbian game plan" to create an enlarged "Serboslavia."[15] Support for a breakup of the federation along republican boundaries brought Washington into alignment with its European allies, and seemed to provide a convenient premise for managing the Yugoslav problem as a whole. Urged on by an international community now led by the United

States, Sarajevo conducted its referendum on independence on February 29-March 1, 1992.[16] The results were ominous. The Muslim and Croat communities voted overwhelmingly for independence--of the 63 percent of the electorate that participated, 99.4 percent voted in support of the proposition — but the Bosnian Serb boycott was also nearly unanimous. As was the case during the republic-level election of 1990, final tallies corresponded almost exactly to the proportional weight of Bosnia's major ethnic communities. On the basis of this outcome and in an atmosphere of tension marked by incidents of violence and provocative rhetoric, the Bosnian government and its collective presidency, led by Muslim faction leader Izetbegović, declared independence on March 27. Within little more than a week the gesture was rewarded by formal recognition on the part of the EC and the United States. On April 30, Bosnia-Herzegovina became the 52nd member of the CSCE, and on May 22 it was admitted to the United Nations.

Acknowledgement of Bosnian independence was offered without guarantees for the new state's security or gestures to assuage the concerns of its Serb and Croat communities. Such guarantees and gestures were urgently needed. SDS activists determined to resist separation from Yugoslavia began to erect barriers in Sarajevo in the first days of March, following a shooting incident at a Serb wedding celebration.[17] Fighting between Croat and Serb militias and regular forces in the Bosanksa Krajina, Posavina, and eastern Bosnia erupted shortly thereafter, and immediately after the declaration of independence skirmishes between Serb militias and local police forces reinforced by Muslim militias and criminal gangs broke out in the outskirts of Sarajevo.[18] On April 4 Izetbegović threw down the gauntlet by ordering the mobilization of all reservists and police forces in Sarajevo, prompting a call from the SDS for Serbs to evacuate the city. Two days later the shelling of Sarajevo from Serb artillery emplacements on the surrounding heights was initiated. In these first, confused weeks of war the government's ability to maintain public order collapsed as Serb, Croat, and to a lesser extent Muslim nationalist factions waged local encounters to secure positions of advantage and appointed crisis committees to supplant instances of vested authority. On April 7 the Assembly of Serbian People in Bosnia-Herzegovina, meeting in Banja Luka, declared the independence of the Serb Republic of Bosnia-Herzegovina — renamed the Serb Republic (*Republika Srpska*) on August 13, 1992

— and the Serb representatives Biljana Plavšić and Nikola Koljević resigned from the Bosnian collective presidency. The stage was set for a struggle pitting the Bosnian government and presidency under the control of the SDA against the Bosnian Serbs, aided and abetted from Belgrade. The HDZ publicly supported the government in Sarajevo, and on April 7 Zagreb accorded Bosnia-Herzegovina diplomatic recognition, but simultaneously sought to reinforce the autonomy of Herceg-Bosna with the intent of promoting its eventual attachment to the Croat *domovina*.[19] That goal was partially realized on July 3, 1992, when Herceg-Bosna declared itself to be an independent state with its own flag (identical to the Croatian national banner) and armed forces.

Bosnia-Herzegovina's secession meant war. It was a war that, in its initial stages, the government in Sarajevo was not prepared to fight, and that the international community that had encouraged separation lacked the will to contain. At the critical juncture before a retreat from the precipice became impossible, the only party to raise a voice in protest were the citizens of Bosnia themselves. On April 5-6, after a week of country-wide demonstrations, tens of thousands of protestors assembled before the Bosnian Parliament in Sarajevo to demand new elections and a policy of reconciliation. The crowd was dispersed on the evening of April 6 by sniper fire, probably leveled by both SDS and SDA gunmen, with eight killed and over fifty wounded.[20] The young student Suada Dilberović, shot down by a sniper while attempting to flee from the parliament area across the Vrbanja Bridge (now renamed in her honor) is conventionally cited as the first victim of the war. Demonstrators briefly broke in to the first floor of the parliament building and created a Committee of National Security pledged to oppose ethnic mobilization, but lacking official backing they were left to twist in the wind. Isolated and without resources, the committee was forced to disband on April 9.[21] Thus was dispersed, without a gesture of solidarity or word of regret from the international community that would wax so eloquent in the years to come over Bosnia's Calvary, a last effort to revive the tradition of a civic and multicultural Bosnia-Herzegovina.

Marching on the Drina.

Several generations of Yugoslavs grew up with the mythology of armed resistance to occupation during World War II, reflected in a

154

steady diet of partisan films and public ceremonies. These evocations of heroic struggle were often clumsy, but not insubstantial. Despite instrumentalization for political purposes, the partisan tradition was imposing and in some ways ennobling. It was a significant source of cohesion within Tito's multinational federation.[22]

The fighting that swept across Bosnia-Herzegovina between 1992 and 1995 became a travesty of that tradition, with entire communities mobilized behind their most extreme and uncompromising elements in a disorganized struggle for demeaning ends. Armed with international recognition, and in view of Serb and Croat assaults, the Sarajevo government, and the Muslim community for which it was the most significant institutional representative, could at least claim a right of self-defense. But Izetbegović also pursued a more contested agenda — to preserve Bosnia-Herzegovina as a unitary state in defiance of the will of its Serb and Croat minorities. Driven forward by corrupt warlords, imposed upon civilian communities who would bear the lion's share of costs without being granted any real responsibility for shaping the course of events, and passively observed as a kind of perverse entertainment by the more fortunate citizens of the developed world, the Bosnian conflict has been described by numerous commentators as a "post-modern" war. If the post-modern condition is equated with the absence of meaning and cynical manipulation, where "war is won by being spun," the description is apt.[23]

All of Bosnia's national communities began to prepare for war well prior to the outbreak of hostilities, and with fighting underway their armed contingents quickly grew into full-fledged armies.

In the spring of 1991 the Izetbegović leadership created a Patriotic League (*Patriotska Liga*) as an organ for self-defense, formally representing Bosnia-Herzegovina as a whole but in fact dominated by the Muslim faction. During the summer the League was subordinated to a Council for the National Defense of the Muslim Nation based in Sarajevo.[24] At the outset, the Patriotic League had approximately 35,000 personnel at its disposal, coordinated by a rudimentary organizational structure.[25] The Patriotic League, territorial defense forces loyal to Sarajevo, and armed police units combined on July 5, 1992, to form the Army of Bosnia-Herzegovina (*Armija Bosne i Hercegovine* — ABH) under the command of the Muslim (with origins in the Sanjak) General Šefer Halilović. Originally, the ABH high command had a distinct multi-national character with the Bosnian Croat Stjepan Šiber as Chief of Staff and the Bosnian Serb Jovan Divjak as his deputy. Over time, as the Bosnian Muslim community came under greater pressure and the prospects of building a viable multinational state came to seem more remote, the ABH's Islamic character became more pronounced. Its units were often raised locally, and deployed to defend their areas of origin. According to Divjak, in May 1992 the ABH commanded over 75,000 soldiers, and by 1994 had grown to nearly 250,000.[26] From the outset, however, and consistently throughout the years of conflict, the ABH was poorly armed. Bosnia-Herzegovina was the only Yugoslav republic where territorial defense forces were effectively disarmed in the course of 1990. A stock of small arms was extracted from captured JNA barracks in Travnik, Visoko, Zenica, Tuzla, and Bihać during the first weeks of war, but the ABH lacked access to armor, heavy artillery, aircraft, and communications assets. The shortfall of heavy weapons prevented the ABH from evolving into a real combined arms force and left it at a considerable disadvantage confronting better prepared adversaries.

Bosnian Croat military units were formed to help resist Serb encroachments inside Croatia during 1991. In the first months of 1992 they were attached to a Croat Defense Council (*Hrvatsko Vjeće Odbrane* − HVO) with its headquarters in Kiseljak, subordinated to the leadership of the HDZ and under the command of General Milivoj Petković. On July 21, 1992, the HVO was made part of the combined defense forces of Bosnia-Herzegovina, but collaboration with the ABH was minimal. From the outset the HVO was directly controlled by the emerging Croatian Army chain of command, under the former partisan fighter General Janko Bobetko.[27] At the war's outbreak the HVO controlled about 20,000 combatants, organized by municipality, and supported by about 5,000 militiamen attached to Paraga's HOS commanded by Blaž Kraljević.[28] Friction between the HVO and the HOS was evident from the start, and eventually Zagreb would take steps to reassert control over its unruly militia forces, including the arrest of Paraga, the assassination of military coordinator Ante Paradžik, and the murder of Kraljević (together with eight members of his staff) on August 9, 1992. From 1993 onward, the HOS ceased to be a significant military factor.

At the onset of fighting in April 1992, the Serb faction in Bosnia-Herzegovina was represented by the JNA, a variety of volunteer militias, Bosnian Serb territorial defense forces, and Interior Ministry elements. On May 19, after being denounced by Sarajevo as an army of occupation, the 5th Corps of the JNA was ordered to withdraw into rump Yugoslavia, but in a transparent ploy, officers and soldiers of Bosnian origin, amounting to 80 percent of the total contingent after a series of planned personnel transfers, were left behind and integrated in the newly minted Army of the Serb Republic (*Vojska Republike Srpske* — VRS).[29] Serb forces in Bosnia numbered over 100,000, equipped with approximately 500 tanks, 400 heavy artillery pieces (over 100 mm.), 48 multiple rocket launchers, 350 120 mm. mortars, 250 armored personnel carriers and infantry fighting vehicles, 120 fighter-bombers, and 80 light attack and observation helicopters.[30] The VRS possessed an effective General Staff (*Glavni Štab*) under Chief of Staff General Manojlo Milovanović, which would provide a critical advantage in the fighting to come. The SDS also created an armed militia on the basis of existing territorial defense assets and volunteer units, armed and organized by the JNA, numbering about 60,000 by early April 1992, supplemented by 15,000 armed police and supported by paramilitary units penetrating Bosnia from Serbia proper. These varied units, coordinated by the JNA command structure and supported by JNA firepower, would be militarily dominant in the first phase of the war.

On 8 May, simultaneously with a major purge of the JNA high command, the former JNA officer Ratko Mladić, of Bosnian origin and distinguished by his service in Dalmatia during 1991, replaced the moderate Milutin Kukanjac as VRS commander in chief. Mladić was a relatively little-known figure at the time of his appointment, but he was popular with his soldiers and regarded as a tough operational commander with a front line style and swagger. The depredations of his troops in the Bosnian conflict, and particularly the interview that he accorded to the BBC on 2 July 1993, during which the Bosnian general, relaxed and effusive, opined in a racially offensive manner about an emerging Muslim threat, came closer to revealing the real man.[31] There was never any doubt that the VRS was Mladić's army, and his relations with Karadžić were never particularly good — Mladić's real loyalty lay with Milošević in Belgrade.[32] The VRS did not receive the kind of overt military support that the HV provided to the HVO, however. Though it did offer certain kinds of assistance, the VJ never deployed large combat formations into Bosnia.

Though standards of professionalism improved as the conflict dragged on, all of the Bosnian formations were make shift armies, with major shortcomings that often prevented the accomplishment of militarily essential tasks. The Muslims' lack of heavy weaponry forced them onto the defensive, seeking to maintain the integrity of some kind of national sanctuary while rallying international support. The Serbs seized control of large swaths of territory in the war's first months, but once the defenses of their opponents had been bolstered they found themselves overextended, with over 1,000 kilometers of frontline and without sufficient reserves to break through contested areas by storm. As the smallest of the forces in the field, the HVO remained dependent upon the support of HV units. Despite the Serbs' initial advantages, the military inadequacies of all forces placed strategies of annihilation beyond reach, and almost guaranteed that some kind of stalemate would ensue.

Although the underlying issue that motivated the fighting was the character, or very survival, of the Bosnian state, the campaigns were waged within local theaters for control of terrain. This meant securing contested areas for one's own ethnic faction — hence the phenomenon of ethnic cleansing whereby military control became synonymous with terrorist assaults upon local populations intended to provoke mass flight.[33] By the summer of 1993, former Yugoslavia counted over 4 million refugees and displaced persons.[34] Poland's Tadeusz Mazowiecki, appointed on October 6, 1992, to head the UN Expert Commission on Human Rights Violations in Bosnia-Herzegovina, was correct in remarking that "ethnic cleansing is not a consequence of this war, but rather its goal."[35]

None of the parties to the conflict possessed sufficient forces to maintain extended fixed fronts or execute large-scale operational maneuver. Fighting therefore developed around individual battle zones, often focused on urban complexes encircled by hostile forces and subjected to artillery fire and harassment by snipers but rarely taken by assault. After the first chaotic months, when the Bosnian Serbs enjoyed a short-lived strategic advantage (due to careful preparation, material superiority, and the fact that the VRS inherited control over 50 percent of Bosnian territory), all belligerents were forced to fragment their forces and make do with modest tactical advances.[36] The role played by paramilitary forces was striking, though all militia formations were integrated into larger operational plans coordinated by the respective "national" commands. The Bosnian conflict was a civil war waged by three contending factions whose mutual relations shifted back and forth from hostility to cooperation depending upon the configuration of forces within individual battle areas. It was a primitive war, characterized by sieges, limited offensives, and purposeful atrocities. The contest for territory took on a cultural dimension, marked by the intentional destruction of historical monuments and cultural artifacts — it has been estimated that by the end of 1992 up to 70 percent of the architectural inheritance of Bosnia-Herzegovina had been damaged or destroyed, including over 300 mosques, 150 Orthodox churches, and 50 Catholic churches.[37] Destruction of the Ivo Andrić monument in Višegrad by the Bosnian Muslims, the dynamiting of the 16th century Ferhadija and Arnaudije mosques in Banja Luka by the Bosnian Serbs on the night of May 5-6, 1992, the Serb shelling of the Bosnian National Library, the *Većnica*, in Sarajevo and destruction of thousands of irreplaceable historical manuscripts on the night of August 25-26, 1992, immediately preceding the opening of the London Conference on Former Yugoslavia, the targeting of the 16th century stone bridge (*Stari most*) in Mostar by Croat artillery in November 1993 — these are only particularly egregious examples of the widespread cultural vandalism.[38] Many of these atrocities had an explicitly anti-Muslim character, and were justified as acts of historical revenge directed against the Ottoman legacy, "the continuation in an extreme form of a process of de-Islamization that had begun decades earlier."[39]

Despite the confused nature of the fighting, the strategic goals of the warring factions were clear. The Serb and the Croat factions aimed at securing compact territories that could be controlled militarily and eventually accorded autonomy and attached to their respective homelands. That meant a de facto partition of Bosnia-Herzegovina between Serbia and Croatia, the agenda vetted by Tudjman and Milošević, and Boban and Karadžić, in their respective meetings of March 25 and May 6.[40] The absence of honor among thieves ensured that the project could not unfold to the satisfaction of the would-be partitioners. But the plan suffered from a more crucial flaw. Given the traditional distribution of peoples, any attempt at partition would either condemn a significant part of the Muslim population to discrimination inside hostile ethnic states, or confine it within a small, land-locked, and economically nonviable mini-state. The Muslim party sought to ward off such outcomes at all costs, by maintaining control of the capital, insisting upon the integrity of Bosnia-Herzegovina, banking on international recognition as a guarantor of survival, and resisting Serb and Croat territorial encroachments wherever possible.[41] At the outset of hostilities, Sarajevo controlled only about 15 percent of Bosnian territory and was clearly outgunned. Its status as the legitimate government of a sovereign Bosnia-Herzegovina was nonetheless a significant asset, and one that would become more meaningful as time went on.

The Bosnian Serbs' goal was to establish control over a belt of contiguous territory in the Bosanska Krajina region of western Bosnia, and in eastern Bosnia, securing linkage with Serbia and opening an area of access from the confluence of the Drina and the Sava eastward through Banja Luka toward Knin. Thus constituted, the "Serb Republic" would be attached to Serbia proper along the Drina, and divided from Croat and Muslim regions by the Una, Sava, and Neretva rivers. It would be a single, integrated territory, possibly with part of a divided Sarajevo as its capital, which could eventually be joined to what remained of the Yugoslav Federation in an approximation of a greater Serbia.[42]

In order to achieve this goal, the Serb faction needed to accomplish several tasks. The first was to secure control of the frontier with Serbia along the valley of the Drina, an area of mixed population with numerous towns with a Muslim majority. In the first weeks of April Serb paramilitary formations, aided by regular units of the JNA, pushed into municipalities such as Zvornik, Višegrad, Bratunac, Srebrenica, and Foča, beating down inadequate defenses and interning, murdering, terrorizing, and expelling the Muslim populations. Other towns in the Drina valley, including Goražde, and Žepa, were placed under siege. The fall of Bijeljina, a small town in northeastern Bosnia 15 kilometers from the Serbian border with a population of about 40,000, opened the season of massacres. Moving into an ethnically mixed community about a third of whose residents were Muslim, Arkan's Tigers presided over the slaughter of hundreds of local residents and the expulsion of survivors before surrendering the region to JNA contingents complicit with the greater Serbia agenda.[43] The results of the campaign in the Drina valley were significant, but not decisive. In some cases (Zvornik, Višegrad) resistance was swept aside in a matter of days. In others (Foča), where local defenders were more effectively armed and organized, weeks were required before control could be secured. The Serbs succeeded in opening a corridor from Zvornik to Serb-controlled areas surrounding Sarajevo, but in May and June overextended

VRS forces were pushed out of Srebrenica and besieged in Doboj. A counteroffensive during the summer rolled back some of these losses, but in the Srebrenica-Žepa and Višegrad-Goražde-Foča areas the ABH was able to hold on to local enclaves. Despite their successes, Serb forces already seemed to lack both the manpower and the will to force well-defended urban concentrations.

Simultaneous with the assault in eastern Bosnia, and utilizing similar methods, control was established over much of the Bosanska Krajina, an area populated primarily by Serbs but with important Muslim and Croat minorities, contiguous with the Serb-controlled areas of Croatia in the Kninska Krajina and Slavonia.[44] On April 3 the regional center Banja Luka was occupied by the JNA, purged of Muslim and Croat residents, and transformed into the political center of a Serb-dominated western Bosnia. Between May-July 1992 in the Prijedor-Sanski Most-Ključ area of western Bosnia the 1st Krajina Corps of the VRS committed some of the worst atrocities of the war, systematically "cleansing" the area of Croat and Muslim minorities.[45] Muslim and Croat forces held on to a salient south of Banja Luka keyed on the town of Jajce, but in the autumn a three-pronged VRS offensive, aided by disaccord between Croat and Muslim defenders, pushed into the city center. After 4 days of heavy fighting, Jajce fell on October 29.

In May and June Serb forces also attempted to move into the Bihać region in the extreme northwest corner of Bosnia (sometimes referred to as the Bihać pocket or Cazinska Krajina), predominantly Muslim and bounded by the Una River and the Croat-Bosnian border. Serb forces took Bosanska Krupa and Bosanski Novi on the Una and entered the Grabez plateau east of Bihać city before bogging down in the face of coordinated resistance. By December, the Bihać pocket had been reduced to a small triangular area completely surrounded by Serb forces, but effectively defended by perhaps 10,000 combatants in six Muslim brigades organized as the ABH's 5th Corps, together with a battalion-sized Bosnian Croat unit controlled from nearby Zagreb.

Eastern Bosnia and the Bosanska Krajina were linked by the Posavina region, south of the Sava along the border between Bosnia and Slavonia. Clashes in Posavina between Serb and Croat forces erupted on the right bank of the Sava in Bosanski Brod during March. Control of what would become known as the Posavina or Northern Corridor, which established geographical contiguity between the emerging Serb entities of Croatia and Bosnia-Herzegovina and northern Serbia, was a strategic imperative. Here too the Serbs used militia units to seize control of areas surrounding the corridor and expel non-Serb inhabitants, hoping to consolidate their gains by pushing forward the heavy forces of the JNA. They were, however, required to ward off offensives south of the Sava launched by the HV, which in April and May moved through Bosanski Brod into Derventa and Modriča, temporarily cutting off passage along the corridor and dividing Serb-controlled areas in Bosnia into two parts. Subsequent fighting saw some of the largest pitched battles of the entire war. In October the VRS finally forced HV and HVO forces out of Bosanski Brod (some argue that the Croat withdrawal was the result of a collusive bargain according to which Serb forces agreed simultaneously to withdraw from the Prevlaka peninsula adjacent to the Gulf of Kotor in southern Croatia), and by December a tenuous hold on the corridor had been reestablished. The Serbs would henceforward be required to defend these gains by committing a significant portion of their reserves.

The Serbs' ability to open the corridor was a major success, achieved in the face of numerically superior Croat and Muslim forces due to greater military professionalism, more effective organization, and superior firepower. The position remained highly vulnerable nonetheless, and throughout the war it would be a contested area whose exposure ensured that Serb war aims remained unsecured. The Serb failure to take the towns of Gradačac and Orašje, to the south and north of the corridor west of Brčko town, denied their position strategic depth.[46] The brutal campaign of ethnic cleansing that preceded military occupation made any claim to control the area fundamentally illegitimate. Moreover, from a Muslim perspective Posavina was viewed as a vital link between central Bosnia and the Danube basin and central Europe — a position critical to the long-term viability of the Bosnian state that could not be allowed to remain in the hands of the enemy.

Another important prize remained elusive. On May 2 the Serbs failed in an attempt to fight their way into the Muslim strongholds of central Sarajevo, and were forced to fall back and consolidate positions in the northern and eastern approaches. This left the Bosnian capital encircled but intact in the hands of the Izetbegović government. The subsequent contrast between the Bosnian Serbs' isolation in their village capital of Pale (a resort community with only 6,000 residents overlooking the capital from the hills on its eastern outskirts to which Karadžić withdrew his headquarters in the spring of 1992) and their rivals' situation in the historic capital would serve to undermine the Serb faction's credibility.

Also on May 2-3, in a bizarre incident all too typical of the confusion surrounding the onset of war, upon his return to Sarajevo Airport from the EC Conference on Bosnia-Herzegovina in Lisbon, Izetbegović was seized and detained as a hostage by the JNA. After complex negotiations, he was eventually bartered in exchange for a pledge by the Bosnian government to lift the blockade on the Lukavica Barracks headquarters of the 2nd Army District in downtown Sarajevo. Izetbegović was released, but during the withdrawal of Serb forces from Lukavica Muslim territorial defense units opened fire, killing a number of officers and soldiers as well as civilian bystanders.[47] In a memoir, ABH commander Halilović interprets the circumstances as part of a failed coup intended to replace Izetbegović with a leader (probably Fikret Abdić, who was present in the city as the events unfolded) willing to ally with the Serb party as a means to avoid war — an assertion that cannot be demonstrated conclusively, but that corresponds to what had long been a current of opinion supportive of cooperation with Bosnian Serbs within the Muslim leadership.[48] The objective consequence of the incident was quite different. The Serbs' disregard for standards of diplomacy, and the Muslims' violation of the ceasefire accord at Lukavica, resulted in a significant escalation of hostilities. The outcome reconfirmed Izetbegović as uncontested leader of the Muslim faction, reinforced his determination to resist Serb pressure, and sowed even more seeds of mistrust among Bosnia's warring factions.

Despite its failure to partition Sarajevo, and to unseat the Izetbegović government, the VRS maintained control of artillery emplacements on Sarajevo's surrounding heights, from whence it was able to prosecute the daily bombardments and partial siege of the city that would become one of the most visible features of the Bosnian conflict. The strategic logic of the Serb attacks, which after May 1992 were never coordinated with any kind of systematic effort to seize control of the city, remains difficult to fathom.[49] Sarajevo was not vital to the Bosnian Serbs' military goals, and maintaining the siege consumed a good deal of manpower that could perhaps have been employed more usefully on other fronts. Divjak estimates that the Serbs assigned 29,000 effectives to the siege of Sarajevo to cover 64 kilometers of front — too small a force to seize and hold an area where an advantage in armored forces would be neutralized by the difficulty of maneuver, but a drain on their ability to function in other theaters.[50] Sarajevo was not the only Bosnian city subjected to besiegement, but it quickly became a focal point of international attention, and the site for numerous visits by international dignitaries and celebrities determined to exhibit their humanitarian credentials — beginning with the highly publicized visit of French President François Mitterrand on June 28-29. The Serb decision to surrender control over Sarajevo Airport to the United Nations in the wake of Mitterrand's visit on June 29 enabled greater media access to the city and enhanced its stature as an international *cause célèbre*. The siege of Sarajevo served to demonstrate the precariousness of Bosnia's legally constituted government, but, like the siege of Dubrovnik during the previous year, it had a devastating impact upon the credibility of the Serb cause.

While the Muslim party struggled to hang on in central Bosnia and Sarajevo, the HVO maintained its positions in the north and pressed Serb forces out of western Herzegovina. A military cooperation agreement between Izetbegović and Tudjman concluded in May, and the rapid consolidation of the ABH from May onward, enabled Croat and Muslim forces to reinforce their positions in central Bosnia. On June 15, Croat forces entered Mostar, destroying the city's main Orthodox cathedral and 17 mosques while Serb units withdrew toward Trebinje in eastern Herzegovina. On June 15 the HVO negotiated a statement of cooperation with the local Muslim leadership, aptly described by Edgar O'Ballance as "an example of classic Machiavellian perfidy."[51] Within a week Boban had declared the Croatian Community of Herceg-Bosna autonomous, and on October 25 Mostar was named its capital. The tide of the war had not turned, however, as the Serb summer counteroffensive made clear. Along the Croatian border to the north, only the Bihać pocket remained outside of Serb control.

By the end of 1992 a first phase in the history of the Bosnian conflict had culminated with the Serb faction dominating nearly 70 percent of the national territory. The HVO, precariously aligned with Muslim forces, controlled the predominantly Croat areas of western Herzegovina, while Izetbegović found his authority reduced to a small area in central Bosnia stretching from Tuzla

164

to Kiseljak, Sarajevo, and the handful of exposed eastern Bosnian enclaves. The territorial gains of the Serb party created the illusion of success, but in fact each of the belligerents had for the time being achieved minimal goals. The Serbs had carved out a Bosnian Serb Republic and established a link between Serb controlled regions from Belgrade to Knin, but they had not eliminated resistance and ended the war. The Croats had established a redoubt in Herzegovina, but their military position was weak and the alliance that they had established with the Muslim party on the verge of collapse. Despite a sequence of defeats, the Muslims maintained control of the national capital, and were building a more capable army that, with the benefit of interior lines of communication, had demonstrated its capacity to defend core areas in central Bosnia, and even (in Gradačac, Bihać, and the Brčko suburbs) to score small tactical successes. The rough territorial division that this situation defined would remain basically unaltered until the strategic balance was transformed by international intervention in 1995.

In January 1993 fighting inside Croatia briefly flared as units of the HV moved to seize Zadar's Zemunik airport and the Maslenica gorge in spite of the integrity of the UN Protected Area and in defiance of UN protests. The intention was to reconstruct the Maslenica Bridge, destroyed by the Serbs in November 1991, and to open traffic along the Adriatic *magistrala* linking Zagreb to Split. By the summer of 1993 the Croatians had put a 300-meter pontoon bridge in place, but in August it was rendered unusable by Serb shelling. The Maslenica offensive was nonetheless a harbinger of things to come. It demonstrated Zagreb's dissatisfaction with the UN-supervised status quo, and determination to impose change.

In Bosnia, the Serb faction focused its operations during the 1993 campaigning season on efforts to broaden the Posavina Corridor and consolidate areas of control in the Drina valley. In both cases, limited successes were achieved. By August, Croat and Muslim defenders had been pressed southwest of Brčko, and the Serbs' area of access widened by some five kilometers. Fighting in the Drina valley was initiated by the Muslim faction, when on January 7, 1993, the local commander Naser Orić, only 25 years old but distinguished by his service as former bodyguard to none other than Slobodan Milošević, launched a series of raids from within the Srebrenica enclave, burning villages, massacring civilians, and setting the stage for what would become a tragic vendetta. The Serbs responded by closing on

165

Srebrenica and threatening to seize it, advancing by April 15 to within several kilometers of the city center. In response to international pressure the assault was called off, and the status quo preserved, but the exposure of the eastern Bosnian enclaves had been clearly demonstrated.[52] In May the VRS pushed toward the Žepa enclave, and in July severed supply lines leading into Goražde. Operations were subsequently developed toward Mounts Igman and Bjelašnica on the outskirts of Sarajevo, with the latter falling to a combined arms offensive including helicopter assault on August 1, threatening Muslim supply routes into the beleaguered capital, which ran across the exposed Mount Igman road and through a newly constructed tunnel passing under the airport. Within days, under international pressure, the VRS agreed to vacate their threatening positions to UNPROFOR forces. Much sound and fury accompanied these operations, but in the larger picture they had very little impact on the strategic balance. The cumulative burden of protracted military operations was nonetheless taking its toll on overextended Bosnian Serb forces, and on September 10, 1993, several Serb units mutinied in Banja Luka, demanding better treatment and a more efficient military effort.[53]

The most significant strategic development of the 1993 campaigning season was the breakdown of the Croat-Muslim alliance and the emergence of a series of new battle areas in central Bosnia. Friction between Croat and Muslim forces had been endemic since the beginning of the conflict. Already in the autumn of 1992, Croats and Muslims were at odds over the distribution of weapons from captured JNA casernes, and in October local fighting erupted in Novi Travnik, Prozor, and Vitež. Central Bosnia as a whole was an ethnically mixed area where a single ethnic group could rarely claim a decisive numerical advantage, and Croat and Muslim forces were often collocated in disputed urban areas, tenuously allied but subordinate to competing chains of command. The radical wing of the Croat national movement made no secret of its desire to bring as much as possible of Bosnia-Herzegovina into association with Croatia proper — in late January 1993 a Croat member of the Bosnian presidium, Mile Akmadžić, declared Bosnia-Herzegovina to be "clinically dead."[54] Earlier in the month, provoked by the desire to expand control of terrain as a prelude to UN and EU sponsored peace negotiations, Croat-Muslim fighting erupted in Gornji Vakuf, a majority Muslim town in the midst of an area designated by international negotiators in Geneva to become a Croat controlled canton. In April the Croat-Muslim contest became a war within the war, when, sparked by a shooting incident in Zenica, the HVO abandoned restraint and launched an offensive designed to terrorize local Muslim populations and seize control of key territory and transport corridors in central Bosnia.

On April 16, HVO forces perpetrated a deliberate massacre of the inhabitants of the predominantly Muslim village of Ahmići in western Bosnia's Lašva valley, surrounding the area to prevent flight, moving through the town and systematically killing residents with small arms fire, burning the village to the ground, and dynamiting the minaret of the central mosque.[55] The atrocity, described in one study as "the Guernica of the Bosnian conflict," inaugurated a campaign of ethnic cleansing.[56] By summer the HVO, aided and abetted by HV formations, was engaged in a struggle for control of the Lašva valley corridor, with fighting in and around Fojnica, Kiseljak, Vitez, and Zenica. Government forces, still lacking heavy weaponry but with a local manpower advantage, stood up to the pressure well, and in June a Muslim counteroffensive regained Travnik and moved on to Kakanj, Bugojno and Prozor. Desperate Croat resistance now led to blind reprisals, culminating in yet another incident of massacre, in the Muslim village of Stupni Do during October 1993.

Between May 1993 and January 1994 the HVO also prosecuted a siege of Muslim-controlled east Mostar (the city's old Ottoman Quarter), in tandem with the Serb siege of Sarajevo, albeit without attracting the same kind of international notoriety (though in February the UN threatened the Croats with sanctions).[57] East Mostar held out, and, like the VRS around Sarajevo, the HVO never dared to venture an all out assault. During this phase of the war, Serb and Croats forces sometimes entered into tacit alliances of convenience in local theaters of operation, but also continued to confront one another on other fronts.[58]

Over time, the course of the Croat-Muslim war in central Bosnia became increasingly favorable for the Muslim faction. From June 1993 onward new ABH commander Rašim Delić injected a note of self-confidence into Muslim strategic planning, creating the 7th Muslimski and 17th Krajina Brigades by enlisting highly motivated refugees from other parts of Bosnia and using them repeatedly to spearhead assaults. By September the momentum of the Croat offensive had been reversed, with the ABH once again in control of significant parts of central Bosnia and the HVO in disarray, its ability to survive increasingly dependent upon the direct intervention of the HV. Strategic decision had not been achieved, however. In November Croat counterattacks recouped some lost ground, and at the moment of the February 1994 truce that brought an end to the fighting, both sides were locked into something like a standoff. In a larger sense, the contest had only worked to the advantage of the Bosnian Serb party, which was able to use the strife between its adversaries to consolidate gains elsewhere — but not, it is worth noting, to strike decisively at Muslim strongholds and win the war.

The Muslim faction lost ground when disagreement with Izetbegović over acceptable terms for a negotiated peace settlement led local strongman Fikret (Babo) Abdić, speaking from Velika Kladuša inside the Bihać pocket, to declare an Autonomous Province of Western Bosnia on September 27, 1993. Abdić, the central figure in the Agrokomerc banking scandal that traumatized Yugoslavia in 1987, had outpolled Izetbegović in the Bosnian presidential elections of 1990, but surrendered the position due to political disagreements with the SDA. He was above all a businessman who feared the effect of war without end upon the commercial interests of his western Bosnian fiefdom. Immensely popular locally and with ties to both Zagreb and Belgrade, Abdić called upon government troops stationed in the enclave to join his cause, and was successful in prompting the defection of two full ABH brigades, both raised from the area of Velika Kladuša. He negotiated ceasefires with Tudjman and Milošević, and, with a small private army of about 5,000, combatants organized in six brigades managed to fight off several ABH offensives. In the spring of 1994, however, the Muslim 5th Corps under General Atif Dudaković succeeded in regaining control of most of the pocket, forcing Abdić back into his stronghold of Velika Kladuša.[59] During the first months of 1994, no less than five independently commanded military formations were active in the small territory of the Cazinska Krajina — Abdić's breakaway Muslim forces, Dudaković's 5th Corps of the ABH, the HV, the VRS, and the Serb Army of the Krajina (supported by Belgrade and operating from base areas across the border in close cooperation with the VRS).[60] The outbreak of fighting within the Muslim camp, and the sequence of shifting associations between Croat, Serb, and Muslim forces, revealed the degeneration of the Bosnian conflict into a series of confused struggles for local control, with alliances of convenience blurring any sense of larger purpose, and with no end in sight.

Hope Is Not a Peace Plan.

On January 6, 1992, Lord Carrington proposed that separate talks on Bosnia-Herzegovina be opened in the framework of the EC mediation effort in Croatia, scheduled to shift its venue from The Hague to Brussels. Two rounds of exploratory discussions were conducted in Lisbon, Portugal (Portugal having assumed the EC's rotating presidency at the turn of the year) under the auspices of the diplomat José Cutilheiro on February 21-22 and March 7-8. With the impending Bosnian referendum serving as a spur to action, the overriding concern of mediators was to block a spiral of conflict. To that end, a blueprint was proposed that sought to come toward the minimum goals of all contending parties. Bosnia-Herzegovina was defined as a unitary state, but with three constituent units, defined by ethnicity and with territorial integrity — one Bosnia with three parts (*Bosna cela iz tri dela*) as some cynics chose to put it. Three-and-a-half years later, after war had reduced the republic to ruins, the international community would impose a framework for peace with the same foundation, but in the spring of 1992 the idea of cantonization, in effect a kind of soft partition arrangement, was premature. While accepting the need to negotiate, Izetbegović was opposed to any concession to the premise of communal division or federalization. Stjepan Kljujić, who represented the HDZ in the first Lisbon sessions, was also a champion of Bosnian unity, but upon departing the discussions he was replaced by the Croat nationalist Boban. The SDS had supported a partition arrangement in Bosnia-Herzegovina throughout 1991, but with the exigency, unacceptable to its negotiating partners, that the Serb community receive control over up to 70 percent of the national territory.[61] In Sarajevo on March 18-19, with war clouds looming, Cutilheiro managed to cajole all faction leaders into signing a Statement of Principles for New Constitutional Arrangements for Bosnia and Herzegovina that embodied the premise of ethnic compartmentalization, but no effort was made to define the contours of the subunits in question.[62] The fatal issue of control over terrain was simply not addressed in a diplomatic expedient which Burg and Shoup describe as characterized by "almost total confusion."[63] In a matter of days the communal leaders had withdrawn their support, and the Cutilheiro plan languished.[64]

The intensity of violence in Bosnia-Herzegovina from the spring of 1992 onward took observers by surprise, and provoked hasty efforts to bring the fighting under control. These efforts were weakened from the start by constraining assumptions about the nature of the conflict. The most basic was the assignment of nearly all responsibility to the Serb faction and to its presumed sponsor in Belgrade, accused of forwarding a "Serbian project systematically to create, through violence that included ethnic cleansing, the borders of a new, ethnically homogenous set of contiguous territories" that could eventually be incorporated into a greater Serbia.[65] The premise of Serb guilt was articulated in a long list of official pronouncements. On May 11 the EC's Council of Ministers assigned responsibility for the violence in Bosnia-Herzegovina to the JNA and "the authorities in Belgrade." One day later the CSCE issued a Declaration on Bosnia-Herzegovina that condemned Belgrade and the JNA for "clear, gross, and persistent violations" of CSCE principles and commitments. On May 15 UN Security Council Resolution No. 752 decried external interference in Bosnian affairs and requested an immediate ceasefire, and on May 20 the U.S. State Department urged sanctions as a response to "protracted Serbian aggression."[66] The interpretation was not incorrect in and of itself — the Serb faction bore heavy responsibility for the course of events. But the perception of *exclusive* Serb responsibility quickly came to dominate interpretations of the entire Yugoslav problem, with unfortunate side effects. The complexity of underlying issues was obscured by one-dimensional explanations focused on Serb imperialism, the obstructionism practiced by competing factions was downplayed or ignored, and the need to come toward Serb concerns as a part of an enduring settlement was made more difficult.

The case against the Serb faction was strengthened by the shelling of a bread line in downtown Sarajevo on May 27, 1992, killing 16 and leaving 140 wounded, and by revelations in July and August concerning Serb inspired ethnic cleansing and the mistreatment of prisoners in detention camps.[67] These exposés created an ethical climate that was unpropitious to pragmatic diplomatic bargaining. On August 13 the UN Security Council unanimously adopted Resolution No. 771 condemning violations of international humanitarian law in Bosnia-Herzegovina, and requested that information concerning such violations be submitted to UN authorities. But growing outrage over Serb conduct did not affect the international consensus opposing military intervention. NATO estimates, perhaps designed to dampen enthusiasm, indicated that a force of at least 460,000, including 200,000 Americans, would be required to reverse the Serb offensive, and neither the U.S. administration of President George Bush nor its European allies judged that the interests at stake were sufficient to justify such a commitment.[68] Warren Zimmermann, who served as the last U.S. ambassador in Yugoslavia, suggests that "the use of force was simply too big a step to consider."[69] As late as December 1992, NATO reiterated its opposition to troop deployments in Bosnia-Herzegovina.[70] On May 13 UN Secretary General Boutros Boutros-Ghali submitted a Report on Bosnia-Herzegovina based upon the findings of Undersecretary Marack Goulding that urged humanitarian assistance but characterized the situation as "tragic, dangerous, full of violence, and confusing," and therefore inappropriate for UN sponsored peace operations.[71] Bosnian Foreign Minister Haris Silajdžić spoke to an emergency session of the Islamic Conference Organization on June 17 to request intervention in the name of Muslim solidarity, but responses were noncommittal.

The refusal to consider military means meant that the international community was not prepared to administer the only remedy that corresponded to its preferred diagnosis of the Yugoslav pathology. What it supplied instead was a long series of feeble gestures — UN resolutions (no less than 54 UN resolutions on the Yugoslav conflict were issued by December 1993), sanctions, embargos, peacekeepers where there was no peace to keep, celebrity visits to embattled Sarajevo, empty threats, and endless mediation — that produced considerable sound and fury but did little to deter the dynamic of conflict on the ground.

Even if a large-scale military intervention could have been mounted, it is not clear that it would have sufficed to bring the conflict to an end. Belgrade's aspiration to create a greater Serbia was a part of the problem, but not the whole. Milošević had taken to the hustings on behalf of Serb nationalism as a means to consolidate power, but he had no sincere commitment to the Serbian national cause. His influence over the Serb entities in Croatia and Bosnia-Herzegovina, though considerable, was not absolute. Zagreb's role in the Bosnian conflict, complicated by the priority accorded to recouping control over the UNPAs inside Croatia, was nearly identical to that of Belgrade. James Gow has argued that a lack of will was the fatal weakness of international mediation in Bosnia, and he is correct to the extent that a will to act was woefully lacking.[72] But it is also necessary to consider what courses of action would have contributed to achieving a lasting peace. A settlement imposed at the Serbs' expense at the outset might have prevented an escalation of the conflict, and saved lives, but lacking a larger concept for reestablishing regional order it would not have resolved the manifold dilemmas created by Yugoslavia's disintegration.

In lieu of a decisive intervention, the international community sought to contain the conflict by isolating the Federal Republic of Yugoslavia and reducing its ability to aid and abet a war effort, while simultaneously supporting a humanitarian relief effort to address the human dimensions of the tragedy — a policy of "containment with charity" in the bitter phrase of Susan Woodward.[73] The arms embargo imposed during the war in Croatia in September 1991 was maintained despite concern that it disadvantaged the Muslim faction. Economic sanctions against the Federal Republic of Yugoslavia imposed by the EC in November 1991 were reinforced on May 30, 1992, by UN Security Council Resolution No. 757, blocking commercial transactions, freezing credit, and closing down international air travel. Another UN resolution of April 17, 1993, deepened the sanctions and tightened controls.

In the early summer of 1992 the UNPROFOR mandate was extended to Bosnia-Herzegovina. The original purpose of the deployments was to support the delivery of humanitarian assistance, but the mission was steadily expanded to include the protection of Sarajevo Airport, mounting guard for convoys, oversight of ceasefires, monitoring of military exclusion zones, and deterrence of local aggression. In July 1992, at UN request, the Western European Union and NATO agreed to enforce the economic embargo by monitoring shipping on the Danube and along the Adriatic coast (*Operation Otranto*), and in November the mandate was extended to include "Stop and Search" missions. On October 9, 1992, the United States gained approval for UN Security Council Resolution No. 781, imposing a No Fly Zone over Bosnia-Herzegovina that NATO would eventually agree to enforce. UN Security Council Resolution No. 816 of March 31, 1993, granted NATO aircraft permission to shoot down planes violating no-fly restrictions. In December 1992 the UN approved the creation of a third UNPROFOR command in

Macedonia, to be based along the border between Macedonia and Serbia and intended as a preventive deployment to deter aggression. Three hundred fifteen U.S. soldiers joined the contingent in the summer of 1993 as Operation ABLE SENTRY, the first time ever that U.S. soldiers were committed to an operation under UN command.

These initiatives deepened the international community's engagement, but did not provide effective tools for shaping the conflict environment. Instead, lack of consensus concerning priorities, limited mandates, and aversion to risk encouraged mission creep. When UNPROFOR commander Phillippe Morillon of France was temporarily detained by outraged citizens demanding protection during a visit to the Muslim enclave of Srebrenica on March 11, 1993, he took the personal initiative of declaring the city a UN "Safe Area." In June, with UN approval, the designation was extended to Sarajevo, Goražde, Srebrenica, Tuzla, Žepa, and Bihać. Unfortunately, the term safe area was a euphemism, used to describe what were in fact encircled and indefensible enclaves, teeming with displaced persons and with a combined population of over 1.2 million. In direct contravention of the safe area concept, several of the enclaves were used by Muslim forces as sanctuaries for launching raids against Serb-held territories. By assuming responsibility for their protection, UNPROFOR had "saddled itself with a responsibility it was not prepared to honor" and extended its mandate to the breaking point.[74]

Cumulatively, these measures did little to slow down the war. Arms, petroleum, and lubricants found their way into the hands of combatants despite the international embargo. The warring factions bartered among themselves for needed supplies, especially in the area of the enclaves. UNPROFOR was frustrated by divisions at the command level, a lack of intelligence and communications assets in theater, and restrictive rules of engagement inappropriate for the kind of peace support functions that it was asked to carry out. Between April 1992 and May 1994, no less than 77 ceasefires were negotiating between warring parties, all of which were broken in short order. Sanctions did serious damage to the Serbian economy, but also had the effect of strengthening popular affiliation with Milošević by allowing him to blame Yugoslavia's misfortunes upon foreign enemies. Preventive deployment in Macedonia provided reassurance to Skopje, but given the multiple pressures to which Belgrade was being subjected there was no real threat to deter. The concept of the safe area was a gesture of solidarity with the Muslim population under assault, but UNPROFOR, and the governments of the contributing powers that stood behind it, was not prepared to make good on its promises — only 7,000 of the 34,000 peacekeepers pledged to defend the safe areas ever arrived in theater.

The diplomatic track originally developed by Lord Carrington was broadened in August 1992 with the creation of a new mediation forum under joint EC and UN auspices. A London-based International Conference on Former Yugoslavia (ICFY) sponsored by the EC, UN, CSCE, and Islamic Conference Organization, and including over 30 national delegations, launched the initiative on August 26-27. The conference drew up a list of 12 principles to guide the peacemaking effort, and created a Permanent Committee co-chaired by Lord David Owen for the EC and Cyrus Vance for the UN, six working groups to address specific aspects of the crisis, and a secretariat with seats in Geneva, Switzerland. In a meeting in Geneva on September 3, the Permanent Committee incorporated three representatives each from the EC and CSCE, representatives of the five permanent members of the UN Security Council, one representative of the Islamic Conference Organization, two representatives of countries bordering the war zone, and Lord Carrington. So constituted, the ICFY represented a considerable (and cumbersome) bureaucratic apparatus, established as a permanent forum devoted entirely to the challenge of peacemaking.

The first major initiative of the ICFY was the so-called Vance-Owen Peace Plan, unveiled at a meeting in Geneva on January 3, 1993 where Karadžić, Boban, and Izetbegović represented the Bosnian factions, and presidents Dobrica Ćosić and Tudjman the Federal Republic of Yugoslavia and Croatia. In retrospect, Vance-Owen appears as a desperate effort to rescue the idea of a unitary state by making limited concessions to the premise of ethnic partition. According to the plan, Bosnia-Herzegovina would be divided into ten provinces — three Serb, three Muslim, two Croat, and one Croat-Muslim, plus the "mixed" city of Sarajevo. Each province would have a governor representing the dominant community plus two vice governors representing the minority communities. Considerable local autonomy was accorded to the provinces, and the central government was intentionally kept weak. The ethnic factions were asked to surrender weapons within their own "home" provinces as a step toward demilitarization, and an international police force was to be organized to ensure order. The plan had notable attractions. It addressed Serb aggression by reducing the extent of the three Serb cantons to 43 percent of the national territory and keeping them physically divided, thus preventing the emergence of a consolidated Bosnian Serb area with the potential to affiliate with neighboring Yugoslavia. Bosnia-Herzegovina was sustained as a unitary state, and a context for reversing at least some of the consequences of ethnic cleansing was put in place. Both Tudjman and Milošević bought into the plan — the territorial provisions were generous to the Croat community, and the Serbian leader (who had probably made the calculation that the plan could never be enforced) was willing to sacrifice Pale's maximal demands in exchange for a lifting of international sanctions against the Federal Republic of Yugoslavia.

Despite its promise, the Vance-Owen Peace Plan was not acceptable to all local actors, and did not generate consensus within the international community. The Bosnian Serbs rejected the arrangements out of hand. Izetbegović, with characteristic indecisiveness, begrudgingly expressed a willingness to consider the terms, but left no doubt as to his dissatisfaction.[75] Most significantly, the United States refused to support the project on the grounds that it awarded Serb aggression. The alternative offered by the Clinton administration, still in the process of defining its approach to the Bosnian problem and torn by conflicting motives, became known as "Lift and Strike" — lifting the arms embargo against the Muslim party in order to allow it to organize a more effective defense (a policy that demanded collaboration with Croatia to ensure access for arms transfers) and selective air strikes under NATO auspices to punish Serb violations.[76] In his memoir, David Owen lambastes what he calls a U.S. policy of "lift and pray" as "outrageous" and a "nightmare" intended to sabotage the mediation effort in order to cater to domestic interest groups.[77] According to some accounts, a reading of Stephen Kaplan's *Balkan Ghosts* had convinced the U.S. president that engagement of U.S. ground forces in the Bosnian quagmire was to be avoided at all costs.[78] Whether or not Kaplan's book was responsible, the judgment was seconded by key figures in the U.S. security establishment.[79] Whatever the motivation, the U.S. call for a selective end to the arms embargo, coupled with a refusal to commit troops to the peacekeeping mission where its European allies were already significantly engaged, created trans-Atlantic friction.

The Vance-Owen Peace Plan's complexity was unavoidable in view of the tangled issues on the table, but complexity may have worked against acceptance by making implementation seem so distant a possibility as not to merit concessions. The refusal of the international community to pledge significant resources to enforce the plan in the event of implementation was also a serious draw back. Most decisive, however, was the continued lack of commitment to a negotiated outcome on the part of the warring factions themselves. Only the Croats offered unambiguous support for a plan that satisfied nearly all of their territorial ambitions. The Muslim faction remained noncommittal and unenthusiastic, even after the plan was adjusted to come toward its territorial demands, and the Serbs were consistently rejectionist. In retrospect it is not clear that, even with a green light from Pale, the plan could have been enforced on the ground.

No such green light was forthcoming. Under pressure from his patron Milošević and Greek president Konstantin Mitsotakis, at the conclusion of a two day session conducted on May 1-2, 1993, in Athens, Karadžić agreed to accept the arrangement, pending approval by the Bosnian Serb parliament in Pale.[80] The condition proved to be decisive — on May 5-6, after a burly debate described by Laura Silber and Allan Little as a "dark farce," with opposition led by Biljana Plavšić and Ratko Mladić, the Bosnian Serb deputies voted 51-2 (with 12 abstentions) to reject the plan.[81] A public referendum subsequently affirmed the result. During the Pale debates, Milošević cut the sorry figure of a sorcerer's apprentice unable to control the forces of aggrieved nationalism that he had helped to conjure up. His unprincipled diplomacy was now beginning to run against the tides of the anarchic fragmentation that the willful destruction of Yugoslavia had provoked.

The Bosnian Serb rejection of the Vance-Owen Peace Plan corresponded with Vance's resignation as UN envoy and replacement by the Norwegian Thorvald Stoltenberg. In August 1993 the ICFY presented a new Owen-Stoltenberg Peace Plan that took a step away from the ideal of a unitary Bosnia-Herzegovina by recommending the creation of a three-part confederation, 51 percent of which would be controlled by the Bosnian Serbs, 30 percent by the Muslims, and 16 percent by the Bosnian Croats, with the remaining 3 percent representing the municipalities of Mostar and Sarajevo, to be placed under international (EC and UN respectively) control. The plan had its origins in a June proposal originating in Zagreb and Belgrade, calling for the transformation of Bosnia-Herzegovina into a "union of three republics," that was approved by Tudjman and Milošević, albeit with the proviso that the individual units be granted a "right to self-determination."[82] The project was originally refused by the Muslim side, but revised to incorporate some of Izetbegović's key demands, including an outlet to the Adriatic accorded by the Croat side, and a corridor of access to the Goražde enclave promised by the Serbs. On September 20, 1993, on board the HMS *Invincible* in the Adriatic, the Serbian and Croatian leaders and Momir Bulatović of Montenegro, together with Izetbegović, Karadžic, and Boban representing the Bosnian factions, accepted the Owen-Stoltenberg proposals in principle, with the condition that plebiscites on self-determination could be conducted after a 2-year waiting period. Back on shore, Izetbegović reconsidered his position, and ultimately opted to reject the plan after the Bosnian parliament had undermined its logic by affixing additional conditions as prerequisites for support. In November 1993, pressured by concern for the humanitarian consequences of a third winter of war, a French-German initiative, eventually dubbed the European Union "Action Plan," (on November 1, 1993, the European Community was officially renamed the European Union--EU) sought to revive the Owen-Stoltenberg approach by increasing pressure on the Muslim faction to accept an agreement that satisfied most of its territorial demands, and offering to suspend sanctions against Yugoslavia in exchange for greater flexibility on territorial issues. In the background of these talks, secret exchanges under European sponsorship concerning the Serb-occupied parts of Croatia were underway in Norway — an exchange that came to an abrupt halt when Tudjman publicly announced that concessions to Croatia's Serb minority would be limited to "local cultural autonomy."[83] These various efforts were nonstarters, and by December it was clear that an EU initiative had once again led to "abject failure."[84]

The travail of international mediation in the Bosnian conflict during 1992-1993 can be attributed to several factors. First and most fundamental, a will to peace was still absent among the contending Bosnian factions. The Croat faction was willing to sign on to agreements that satisfied its territorial demands, but not to make sacrifices in order to win the acquiescence of its rivals. Commitment to prosecute the war in central Bosnia left the HDZ without positive diplomatic options. The Serb faction defied external pressure and clung desperately to the territorial gains that it had achieved in the first months of combat. With its essential goals accomplished and a strong military position that only an unlikely external intervention seemed capable of reversing, and in the absence of any coherent concept for ending the war diplomatically, Pale saw little use for compromise. In the summer of 1993, with Mostar under siege and the Muslims' strategic position temporarily declining, Izetbegović began to entertain concessions, but only reluctantly. As the Muslims' military fortunes improved, willingness to compromise melted away. All parties to the conflict continued to perceive the war instrumentally, as a means toward the achievement of political goals. The "hurting stalemate" of conflict management theory, where the costs of continued engagement are perceived to outweigh achievable strategic gains, had not yet been reached.[85]

The initiatives of the international community were also inconsistent. The Yugoslavia idea had been sacrificed on the alter of a putative right of national self-determination, but self-determination was rejected as a mechanism for conflict resolution in the case of Bosnia. The varied ICFY peace proposals, based upon the premise that aggression should not be rewarded by sanctioning the consolidation of ethnically pure enclaves, recommended reconfiguring Bosnia-Herzegovina as a kind of Yugoslavia in miniature, a federative association of cantons or provinces with a weak central government and civil service defined by ethnic quotas. Such a solution did not satisfy the core demands of any of the parties to the conflict. The Serb and Croat factions wanted self-determination and the right to attach to their national homelands. The Muslims wanted a unitary state with a strong central government. All parties were willing to fight for their agendas, and the international community was not prepared to take decisive steps to impose peace. Though UNPROFOR deployments grew from 1500 troops in August 1992 to over 23,000 by 1995, they were never sufficient to the task at hand. The international embargo intended to prevent arms transfers into the conflict zone was ineffective. A variety of routes continued to bring arms and munitions to the contending armies, which managed to increase the size and sophistication of their arsenals as the conflict progressed.[86] Sanctions against Serbia and Montenegro damaged the fabric of the national economy and pressed large numbers of citizens into poverty, but did not affect the well-being of ruling elites.[87] They had some impact upon Milošević's decision to support a negotiated solution, but his own strategic calculation that the war had served its purpose of helping consolidate power, and now placed its exercise at risk, would no doubt have been made with or without the added impetus that sanctions provided. The creation of the International Tribunal for the Former Yugoslavia (ICTY), finally charted in May 1993, was in principle a groundbreaking gesture toward a more exigent international war convention, but the ICTY was insufficiently funded, understaffed, and pursued its dossiers too slowly to make a real difference. Humanitarian relief efforts helped to address the suffering created by years of war, but a significant portion of official aid was siphoned off by criminal elements associated with the warring factions and never reached its intended goal. The most efficient aid programs were conducted by non-governmental organizations (NGOs) and volunteer associations that avoided official channels and sought to work directly with individuals in need.

Another reason for lack of progress, as in the Croatian conflict during 1991-92, was disaccord among the powers. Only the United States and NATO were in a position to provide decisive leadership. But the Bush administration was not convinced of U.S. stakes in the conflict, and, during its first year in office, the Clinton administration was indecisive, anxious to align with the Muslim cause on moral grounds, but deterred by the potential costs of unilateral engagement.[88] By opposing the Vance-Owen peace initiative, the United States ensured its failure, but it was not able to produce a credible alternative. The Lift and Strike option was contested from the start, and after an unsuccessful tour of European capitals by Secretary of State Warren Christopher during May, during which the U.S. initiative met with near unanimous rejection, it had no substance as policy at all. Almost by default, the least common denominator of containment with charity continued to prevail.

An Endgame Strategy.

On February 5, 1994, a mortar shell landed in the Markale market in Sarajevo, killing 65 and wounding over 200. Ghastly images of the carnage were broadcast worldwide. Serb sources were quick to suggest that the Muslims had staged the atrocity to win sympathy, and circumstances made it difficult to assign responsibility definitively. General Michael Rose, commander of the UNPROFOR for Bosnia-Herzegovina, stated that an analysis of the crater did not allow conclusions concerning the trajectory of the shell, and Yasushi Akashi, special envoy of the UN Secretary General, expressed "certain doubts" about the round's origin.[89] But the act was consistent with a long-established pattern of Bosnian Serb shelling, and Pale was immediately condemned in the court of world opinion.[90] In retrospect, by galvanizing the international community and reviving U.S. determination to lead, the incident seems to have functioned as a cathartic event, shattering the acquiescence that had hindered international conflict management efforts in the past.

A first consequence was to energize NATO as a strategic actor. On February 7, the Atlantic Alliance set a 10-day ultimatum for the withdrawal of Serb heavy weapons and mortars from a twenty kilometer "total exclusion zone" around Sarajevo. As an alternative, the Serbs were instructed to establish nine weapons storage sites outside the zone, to be controlled by UNPROFOR but accessible in case of a Bosnian Muslim attack. After complicated negotiations, the Bosnians Serbs finally agreed to comply with these conditions, but only begrudgingly and with the support provided by some 400 Russian soldiers moved into Sarajevo from the Russian UNPROFOR contingent in Croatia's UNPA-East.[91] NATO's intervention had forced the Russians hand — Moscow had no desire to cede ground in Bosnia to an organization that it still regarded as an international competitor. In principle Russian engagement helped to establish the peacemaking effort on a broader international foundation, but it also posed complications by making it necessary to coordinate policy with Moscow's agenda.

The Sarajevo crisis arrived at a delicate moment for the Russian Federation. As Yeltsin's relations with his parliament disintegrated during 1992, policy toward the Yugoslav crisis became a more important source of discord.[92] With the conflict in Bosnia heating up, small numbers of Russian mercenaries, inspired by the 19th century Pan-Slav tradition and sponsored by ephemeral national-patriotic organizations with political connections, made their way to Yugoslavia to fight for the Serb cause.[93] During the latter months of 1992 and 1993, the debate over relations with Serbia became more strident. On September 23, 1992, the chair of the parliament's Constitutional Commission, Oleg Rumianstev, described policy toward Serbia as "a betrayal of Russian interests."[94] Foreign Minister Kozyrev's bizarre speech before the CSCE foreign ministers conference at Stockholm on December 14, 1992, in which he pretended to support extreme nationalist positions in order to dramatize "the danger that threatens our course in post-communist Europe," added fuel to the fire.[95] One of the main shocks offered in the speech was a condemnation of sanctions against Yugoslavia and the assertion that Russia would consider "unilateral measures" if they were not lifted. "In its struggle," the Russian foreign minister intoned, "the present government of Serbia can count on the support of great Russia."[96] This phrase was singled out for special condemnation by the chair of the parliament's Committee on International Relations and Foreign Economic Affairs, Evgenii Ambartsumov, for whom Kozyrev's exercise in diplomatic irony sounded suspiciously "like an ultimatum delivered to the Serbian leadership."[97] For the most outspoken parliamentary critics, the government's policy was "tragic" and a "criminal" mistake that sullied "our traditional ties with Serbia, Slavic ties and Orthodox ties."[98] Under domestic pressure, in 1993 Russian diplomacy in former Yugoslavia became more active. Special envoy Vitalii Churkin, who had made only two visits to former Yugoslavia in all of 1992, was constantly underway between the former Yugoslav republics from the first months of 1993 onward. In May 1993, Kozyrev visited Belgrade for the first time in nearly a year.[99]

In October 1993 the conflict between president and parliament was resolved after a fashion when Yeltsin resorted to a cannonade to disperse his recalcitrant deputies after they had occupied the "White House" serving as the seat of government in Moscow. Two months later, in hastily scheduled national elections, the ultra-nationalist, and rhetorically pro-Serb Liberal Democratic Party led by Vladimir Zhirinovskii received the highest percentage of votes in balloting by party list.[100] During a visit to Serbia and Montenegro during the first week of February 1994, Zhirinovskii drenched his audiences in bombast, adopting the rhetoric of Serb nationalism by intoning that "Russia and Serbia have only two enemies, Catholicism from the West and Islam from the East," and evoking, during public remarks at Brčko, a Russian "secret weapon" capable of terrorizing the West.[101] Yeltsin's decision to abandon the pro-Western orientation that had inspired Balkan policy in the past, and to come toward the Bosnian Serb position at least symbolically, was an attempt to co-opt the popular sentiments that Zhirinoskii's posing encouraged. Under the gun of the NATO ultimatum, Yeltsin put his prestige on the line by directly contacting Milošević and Karadžić and offering Russian support to encourage compliance. The result seemed to be a triumph for Russian diplomacy. Russian units were greeted in Bosnia by cheering crowds, and the pullback of Serb weapons proceeded smoothly.[102] The moral, from a Russian perspective, was clear: "The Serbs had not yielded to the ultimatum, to the U.S.A., or to the West as a whole, but they were willing to listen to the opinion of their traditional Russian partner."[103] Serb nationalist opinion rejoiced that after 3 years of "disorientation, despair, pain, and dissatisfaction," Moscow had realized that "historically tested and friendly relations" with the Serbs corresponded to "the vital requirements and long-term national and state interests of Russia."[104] There was a good deal of wishful thinking built into these assessments, but for the time being Russia's diplomatic ploy seemed to increase the diplomatic stakes in the Bosnian crisis considerably.

Partisans of a stronger U.S. role viewed Russia's initiative as obstructive, and regretted that, by defusing the Sarajevo crisis prematurely, it had preempted a more decisive confrontation with Serb forces. Behind the scenes a major reformulation of U.S-Bosnian policy was nonetheless underway.[105] By the beginning of 1994 the conflict had begun to impact more viscerally upon substantial U.S. interests — stability in Europe, the viability of the Atlantic Alliance, relations with Russia, reputation in the Muslim world, and America's stature as global leader. Moreover, the Clinton administration was looking forward to mid-term elections and had begun to be concerned about the potential for the Bosnian imbroglio to damage its standing with the electorate. This combination of interests was too potent to ignore, and it provoked a concerted effort to devise an effective strategy for bringing the conflict under control. According to the emerging U.S. policy framework put together after the Sarajevo ultimatum, NATO would become the focus of a strategy of coercive diplomacy aimed specifically at the Serb faction and its territorial dominance inside Bosnia-Herzegovina, judged to be the single biggest obstacle to a negotiated peace.

In February-March 1994, building on the momentum of the Serb withdrawal from the outskirts of Sarajevo, Western pressure achieved the reopening of Tuzla Airport, with Russian observers brought in to monitor compliance. Though justified as a means to facilitate the delivery of humanitarian aid, the gesture also had strategic significance — Tuzla was a bastion of support for a unified, multinational Bosnia-Herzegovina, and it would eventually become the focus of the U.S. military presence in the region. On February 27, in line with the strategic reappraisal underway, two NATO aircraft shot down four Yugoslav *Jastreb* jet fighters that had trespassed the no-fly zone near Banja Luka. This was the first combat action undertaken by the Alliance since its establishment in 1949, and a harbinger of things to come. On April 10-12, NATO launched a set of three symbolic air strikes against Serb positions during fighting in the Goražde enclave, and on April 22, with Goražde still under siege, committed to ensure the defense of the Žepa, Tuzla, Bihać, and Srebrenica safe areas.[106] A Serb attack against a French armored vehicle during fighting around Sarajevo provoked a NATO a response against a derelict Serb tank destroyer inside the exclusion zone on September 22. The vehicle was selected from a target list by Yasushi Akashi and the attack was never considered to be more than a symbolic gesture. Though militarily ineffective (some did not hesitate to call it pathetic), the action could nonetheless be interpreted as a signal of resolve. On November 21 NATO aircraft attacked the Udbina airbase in the Kninska Krajina, from which Serb air strikes had been launched against Bihać, and did more substantial damage, even if strikes were limited to the airfields only, and targeted areas were quickly repaired. These raids were followed on November 23 by strikes against the radar facilities (but not launchers) at three Serb SAM sites in the Bihać area.

The West's more assertive military posture was matched by a new diplomatic approach. In January 1994 representatives of the Muslim and Bosnian Croat factions came together under U.S. auspices in the Petersberg conference center near Bonn. Three months later, on March 18, 1994, a Washington Agreement announced the creation of a Bosnian Croat-Muslim Federation. This agreement, concluded between the Croat HDZ and Muslim SDA factions, was the result of patient prodding from Washington.[107] It brought an end to the year-long war between Croat and Muslim forces in central Bosnia and Herzegovina, where Muslim forces had scored significant advances since the preceding summer, and allowed the two factions to make common cause against the Bosnian Serbs. Neither the HDZ nor the SDA had changed its nationalist stripes, or abandoned long-term goals. The Croat faction was won over with promises of economic confederation with Croatia, and by the opportunity to escape from a military stalemate in which it could not hope to prevail.[108] The SDA was attracted by the military advantages of a ceasefire. In order to insure cooperation, on February 8, 1994, the Tudjman regime engineered the ouster of hard liner Boban as HDZ faction chief on behalf of the more accommodating Krešimir Zubak.[109] The Washington Agreement was an arrangement of convenience that allowed the HDZ and SDA to concentrate upon a common adversary.[110] Despite pledges of good intentions, including an agreement to combine their respective armed forces in a new "Federation Army," the federation did not give rise to common institutions or a meaningful commitment to cohabitation. It did, with the assistance of UNPROFOR monitors, allow contending Muslim and Croat forces in central Bosnia to disengage, and permit the siege of Mostar to be lifted. Military pressure against Serb positions was correspondingly increased. Strategically, the accord created an objective foundation for the U.S. determination to direct cumulative pressure against the Bosnian Serbs, and ultimately, by allowing a territorial division within the province that did not work egregiously to the Muslims' disadvantage, made the option of a soft partition easier to contemplate. Ivo Daalder describes it as "the [U.S.] administration's first successful Bosnian initiative."[111]

In April 1994 a new international negotiating forum known as the Contact Group was formed to concentrate attention on Bosnian peace initiatives and create a context for collaboration among the great powers. The original members were the United States, the United Kingdom, France, Germany, and the Russian Federation.[112] The perceived need for the Contact Group was a reflection of the frustration that combined UN-EU efforts under the ICFY had engendered over the past year.[113] Though the group's first sessions gave rise to familiar wrangling over ends and means, in late May its members met with the Bosnian factions in Talloires, France, and began to work out the outline of a peace arrangement. Almost overnight the Contact Group, which provided a mechanism for engaging Russia more directly in the mediation effort, seemed to have supplanted the ICFY as a consultative forum and facilitator for conflict management.

By July the Contact Group had produced a new framework for peace negotiations, based upon a proposed 51/49 percent territorial split between the Muslim-Croat Federation and the Bosnian Serbs.

The plan was another attempt to square the circle by maintaining a unitary Bosnia-Herzegovina while granting territorial status and political identity to its constituent ethnic nations. It was originally presented on July 6 as a take it or leave it ultimatum, with a 2-week period for consideration and a promise of punitive action against recalcitrant parties. The Bosnian Muslim and Croat factions, now increasingly amenable to Washington's lead, and calculating that the Bosnian Serbs would reject the scheme in any case, bought in to the plan without conditions. The Milošević government, whose ability to pressure the Bosnian Serbs was considered to be critically important, supported the concept.[114] But the Bosnian Serbs, who were asked to make territorial concessions but also rewarded with international recognition and the capacity to retain independent armed forces, remained recalcitrant. The July 20 deadline was repeatedly extended as the Serb faction raised new conditions. Finally, after another overwhelmingly negative popular referendum conducted at the beginning of August, Pale refused to accept the terms. Blinded by its territorial conquests and apparently incapable of thinking strategically, the Bosnian Serb leadership had become an immovable object blocking any and all negotiated options. The central strategic challenge for international mediators, in line with what had become the preferred U.S. approach, now became how to coerce the Bosnian Serbs to trade land for peace.

Fighting continued as these diplomatic initiatives unfolded. In March and April, triggered by Muslim raiding into Serb-controlled territory, a Bosnian Serb offensive pressed toward Goražde, the largest and best defended of the eastern Bosnian safe areas. Swollen to a population of over 70,000 including refugees, hosting the important *Podjeba* munitions factory complex, and the closest Muslim-held territory to Serbia proper, the enclave was considered to be of great strategic importance. By mid-April Goražde was in the range of Serb artillery fire and appeared to be on the verge of falling. On April 23 UN special envoy Yasushi Akashi, perhaps concerned for the fate of UNPROFOR soldiers inside the enclave, refused a request from NATO Secretary General Manfred Wörner to use NATO airpower to force the Serbs back.[115] By April 26 Bosnian Serb forces began to withdraw on their own initiative — General Mladić was once again hindered by the lack of sufficient infantry to overrun fixed defenses — and fighting within the enclave came to a halt.[116] The precarious situation of the enclaves had been demonstrated yet

185

again, however, and mistrust between the UNPROFOR and NATO command structures was aggravated. In the U.S. perspective, the perception that only credible counter force would serve to reduce Serb pretensions was greatly strengthened.

During the summer, violations of the Sarajevo exclusion zone by both sides multiplied, and in August and September fighting swirled around the beleaguered city. Bosnian Serb actions, which included repeated efforts to close Sarajevo airport and the single road leading out of the city to the UN logistics base in Kiseljak, could be interpreted as a direct challenge to the UN mandate for Bosnia-Herzegovina, originally intended to support the delivery of humanitarian assistance. On several occasions UNPROFOR commander Rose threatened air strikes against both belligerents to punish violations of the exclusion zone. Simultaneously, a coordinated Muslim-Croat offensive retook Kupreš in central Bosnia, and fighting erupted around Donji Vakuf, Glamoč, and Bosansko Grahovo. In July, the ABH's 5th Corps under General Atif Dudaković achieved a major victory by beating down resistance in the Bihać pocket and forcing Abdić to withdraw to the Serb-controlled Krajina. Inspired by success, on October 26 Dudaković launched a drive to break out from the pocket into central Bosnia, but ran headlong into a Bosnian Serb counter-offensive that by late November threatened to overrun Bihać itself. Once again an acrimonious debate erupted among the Western allies over the feasibility of a NATO air response in defense of a safe area under siege, with General Rose ultimately refusing the air strike option as incompatible with his peacekeeping mandate. The crisis was defused, but not resolved, at the 11th hour by another voluntary Serb withdrawal. Patience with UNPROFOR's self-imposed caution was growing thin, however, and Washington's determination to use NATO as a means for forcing Serb compliance had now fully matured.

Despite a more assertive U.S. posture, as 1995 dawned the Bosnian conflict remained a troublesome issue in U.S. domestic policy, and a divisive dilemma for trans-Atlantic relations. With presidential elections now on the horizon, the Republican-controlled Congress defied administration policy by voting to lift the arms embargo against the government of Bosnia-Herzegovina unilaterally. Key European allies were simultaneously signaling their unwillingness to maintain commitments to UNPROFOR in the event that the Americans, without ground forces in the theater that would be subject to reprisals, should break ranks and supply arms to one of the belligerents. The U.S. was committed to support an UNPROFOR pullout with its own forces — a potentially costly undertaking with all the trappings of an election year nightmare.[117] Under the circumstances, the option for decisive engagement that had ripened over the past year appeared less risky than futile attempts to maintain the status quo, or abject withdrawal. Meanwhile, the arrogance of the Serb conquerors seemed to know no bounds. On February 19, 1995, against a background of pervasive popular suffering, the gangster Arkan, architect of Serb ethnic cleansing, married the popular singer Ceca in an ostentatious public ceremony in Belgrade's Intercontinental Hotel.[118] As the organized criminal element within the Milošević regime became ever more blatant, the case for increased international engagement became more compelling.

The central strategic problem remained how to force Serb withdrawal from contested territories in order to create a more equitable balance on the ground. NATO air power could not win and hold terrain without the support of ground maneuver forces, the Western allies were not about to undertake a large-scale theater campaign, and the HVO and ABH were only capable of sustaining local offensives. But there was a force in the theater ready to take the field against the Serbs. This was the HV, increasingly competent operationally, motivated to liberate Croatian territory under Serb control, and ready to carry the battle into Bosnia if asked. In an interview of November 18, 1994, Tudjman had signaled his interest in an internationally supervised division of spoils in Bosnia, speaking of the need for a "new Congress of Berlin" that would allow the Serbs to surrender western Bosnia up to the Vrbas River in exchange for control of the eastern Bosnian enclaves (Žepa, Srebrenica, and Goražde) and a right to attach the Republika Srpska to Serbia proper.[119] This agenda could easily be combined with the concept of a military offensive intended to right the strategic balance and create a foundation for negotiated solutions. In the spring of 1995 the moderate wing of Tudjman's HDZ, led by Josip Manolić and Stipe Mesić, broke away in protest against the regime's growing authoritarianism and corruption. Eventually the split would lead to the HDZ's political effacement, but in the short-term it had the effect of removing temperate voices opposed to military solutions. With his communist background, authoritarianism, and crude nationalism

Tudjman was in most ways a mirror image of Milošević. But transit rights in Croatia, with its long Adriatic coastline and access to the Bosnian interior, was vital to the Western conflict management effort, and the Croatian leadership was anxious to further cooperation with the West. Over the past year, with U.S. assistance offered both through official channels and the Virginia based private contractor Military Professional Resources, Inc. (staffed by an impressive list of former U.S. military commanders), the HV had been transformed into a competent armed force.[120] It would now be tasked with the work of what the U.S. diplomat Robert Frasure called the "junk yard dog" in applying land power as a coercive tool against the Serb redoubts in Slavonia, Krajina, and Bosnia-Herzegovina.[121]

In the first days of May 1995 Croatian forces attacked Sector West of the Republic of Serb Krajina (western Slavonia) in a coordinated offensive designated Operation FLASH *(Bljesak)*. On May 1 Croatian forces launched assaults along the Zagreb-Belgrade highway between Novo Gradiška and Okunčani, and by May 3 Jasenovac, Pakrac, and Okunčani had fallen, while tens of thousands of Serb refugees poured across the border into Serbia proper. Resistance by Serb defenders, betrayed by their political leaders, abandoned by their military commanders, and left without a hint of support from Belgrade, was quickly overcome. On May 3, at the noon hour, 11 *Orkan* missiles were fired from the territory of the Kninska Krajina against Zagreb, killing one and wounding 40. The military relevance of the rocket strikes was minor, but once again an egregious act of violence insured that the Serbs would lose the battle of public opinion. During Operation Flash the HV demonstrated its ability to achieve decisive operational success. Perhaps more importantly, the much-ballyhooed Serb autonomous region was exposed as a house of cards, corroded from within by corruption and incapable of defending itself.[122] Croatia's precipitous action was criticized internationally, but it was a first step toward coercing a Serb drawback as a prerequisite for a negotiated settlement.

In late May NATO aircraft launched several attacks against Bosnian Serb targets to enforce a ceasefire in the Sarajevo exclusion zone. In retaliation, Pale seized approximately 400 UN peacekeepers as hostages. Some of these hostages were chained to potential targets in the guise of human shields, albeit only for the time required to take photographs that would subsequently make the tour of the world. The images served to make the point that should air strikes continue, UN personnel were vulnerable. They were an effective instrument of intimidation and propaganda. The action was a profound humiliation, the nadir of frustration for the entire UN peacekeeping effort, but it also became a catalyst for more decisive intervention. On June 3 the defense ministers of fourteen member-states of the EU and NATO agreed to create a Rapid Reaction Force to protect UNPROFOR contingents from further harassment, and at the end of July the British-French led force was redeployed from bases in central Bosnia to Mount Igman, at a critical juncture of the Sarajevo front.

On July 11 and 25, the Bosnian Serbs upped the ante by seizing the UN safe areas of Srebrenica and Žepa, in the former case pushing aside a small force of 429 Dutch Blue Helmets and massacring over 8,000 prisoners in the worst single atrocity of the entire Bosnian conflict (and in all of Europe since the Second World War).[123] The Serb attack on Srebrenica was not unprovoked — the enclave had not been demilitarized and was used as a base for staging raids against Serb villages during which atrocities were committed. The bloodbath of July 1995 was the culmination of a long-running vendetta, but it was not just another in a long line of atrocities. The premeditated nature of the massacre, the extent of the killing, and the arrogant demeanor of the conquerors combined to make it a unique, and uniquely horrible, event, and an appropriate symbol for the degenerate nature of the Serb national agenda as it was pursued during the Bosnian war.

Once again, Serb aggression was abetted by operational confusion on the part of UNPROFOR. The UNPROFOR command was not willing to approve timely NATO air attacks on the Srebrenica front, and the limited strikes launched on July 11 were too little and too late.[124] The small Dutch UNPROFOR contingent, after verifying the Serb attack, came under fire from Muslim positions while attempting to report to its headquarters. Incapable of resisting a major combined arms offensive, confused about responsibility, and unaware of the intent of Serb commanders, the Dutch opted not to conduct a suicidal resistance, and withdrew from the city to their operational base at Potočari, some six kilometers to the north, followed by a desperate throng of refugees. In view of the aftermath, the lack of meaningful resistance might appear craven, but there was little that the handful of peacekeepers on hand, or pinprick air strikes, could have done to prevent the Srebrenica massacre.[125] The international community, which had originally pledged 7,000 peacekeepers to Srebrenica, had never taken measures to ensure that its safe areas were safe in fact as well as in name. Following Srebrenica, the Žepa enclave, defended by a grand total of 68 Ukrainian Blue Helmets, fell in a matter of days.

The larger enclave of Goražde appeared to be next in line, but the limits of Western acquiescence had now been reached. The seizure of the enclaves was in line with the U.S. effort to rationalize areas of control as a foundation for peace negotiations, but totally unacceptable in view of the consequences. At a session of July 26 in Brussels, the North Atlantic Council pledged "prompt and efficient" action in the event that Goražde was attacked. Already overstretched following their offensives against Srebrenica and Žepa, the Bosnian Serb forces held back. The West's response would not be launched from within the indefensible enclaves of eastern Bosnia, but rather in a theater were Pale was much more exposed.

In July and August a large-scale HV offensive, codenamed Operation STORM (Oluja), overran the entire Republic of Serb Krajina, seizing the capital Knin and driving the remnants of its armed forces across the border in disarray.[126] On July 30 HVO and HV units moved against the villages of Grahovo and Glamoč, placing themselves within artillery range of Knin and cutting the road attaching the city to the Serb controlled hinterland. A frantic diplomatic effort aimed at forestalling a test of arms followed, but to no avail. The United States had laid the groundwork for the operation, and, though it remained publicly noncommittal, it did nothing to constrain Zagreb. Milošević, who had urged Babić and Martić to come to terms with Zagreb for more than a year, privately assured Tudjman that Serbia would not respond.[127] The Bosnian Serbs, under severe military pressure, were in no position to react, and UNPROFOR forces in place did not even think about the option of resistance. With overwhelming force on hand and in the absence of effective diplomatic or military constraint, Tudjman used hastily assembled, UN sponsored negotiations in Geneva as a forum for articulating unilateral demands.[128] On August 4, 25 HV brigades rolled into the Krajina and broke what resistance could be mustered in a matter of hours. The consequences of the military operations were not excessive given the scope of the undertaking — Croatian sources cite 174 killed and 1,430 wounded on the part of the HV, against perhaps several thousand Serbs killed. But the worst was yet to come. From August 3 onward, a line of refugees over 40 kilometers long formed at the frontier crossing leading into Bosnia-Herzegovina, and eventually upwards of 180,000 Serbs would flee the province under duress, the worst single incident of ethnic cleansing in the entire sequence of Yugoslav wars. Among the 9,000 or so Serbs that remained, hundreds, mostly defenseless senior citizens, were murdered by Croat Special Forces in the weeks to come. Thousands of homes, some of them, ironically, belonging to Croat refugees who had fled the province in 1991 (if not marked by the initials HK, signifying *Hrvatska Kuča* — Croatian Home), were burned.[129] On August 27 Tudjman celebrated his victory with a shameful speech at the Knin castle, mocking the Krajina Serbs as "those ones that disappeared in 3 or 4 days, without taking time to gather their underwear," and cursing the pathetic refugees as "a malignant tumor in the heart of Croatia, destroying the Croat national essence."[130]

The Croatian junkyard dog was a compromising ally, but the successes achieved by Operation Storm opened up prospects for a decisive turnaround in former Yugoslavia. Coordinated offensives by Croatian and Muslim forces into the Bosanska Krajina followed the fall of Knin, and in a matter of weeks the territorial stalemate that had prevailed since the summer of 1992 was broken. On August 28 another gratuitous shelling incident in Sarajevo provided the Western Alliance with its own *casus belli*, and on August 30 NATO initiated a bombing campaign, designated Operation DELIBERATE FORCE, focused on disrupting Bosnian Serb communication assets and breaking the siege of Sarajevo. The raids were substantial — in 2 weeks of concentrated attacks, NATO aircraft flew 3,315 sorties and 750 attack missions directed against 56 target complexes.[131] Assisted by the strikes, Muslim and Croat ground forces were able to accelerate their advance. As a result, the 51/49 percent territorial division that was at the foundation of the Contact Group's peace plan came to be mirrored by realities on the ground. Decisive intervention inspired by the United States and spearheaded by NATO air power had restored a regional balance of power, and in so doing created an objective foundation for a negotiated peace.[132]

Military action was paralleled by a U.S. led diplomatic initiative.[133] An outline of the U.S. "Endgame Strategy" was presented to key European allies and the Russian Federation by a high-level delegation led by National Security Advisor Anthony Lake during a whirlwind

191

tour through London, Paris, Bonn, Rome, Sochi (a Russian Black Sea resort), Madrid, and Ankara in the second week of August. The plan proposed a comprehensive settlement for the Bosnian crisis that included maintaining a unitary Bosnia-Herzegovina with a capital at Sarajevo, that would be internally divided between "entities" representing the Croat-Muslim federation and the *Republika Srpska* defined territorially according to the Contact Group plan. The project was made in the United States but welcomed by the allies, no doubt overjoyed to ride behind forceful American leadership. Moscow's public reactions were harshly critical — a parliamentary resolution condemned the "genocide" being perpetrated against the Serbs, and Yeltsin remarked that NATO actions in the Balkans could "ignite the flames of war in Europe."[134] But Russia had failed in the effort to impose constraint, and its protests had no visible effect. Yeltsin sought to restore his damaged credibility by offering to sponsor a summit conference bringing Yugoslav leaders together in Moscow, but the session was not looked upon favorably in Washington and was never convened.[135] In the original itinerary for Lake's tour of Europe, Russia was not even placed on the agenda.[136]

The next step was to sell the project to Balkan regional leaders, a task assigned to the forceful Richard Holbrooke, uninvolved in the genesis of the project but respected for his toughness. Between August and November, Holbrooke led a team of U.S. diplomats on a diplomatic shuttle between Balkan capitals that was successful in clarifying details of the project to the interested parties, and eventually, with the help of a good deal of head banging, bringing them on board.[137]

On 5 October Clinton was able to announce a 60-day ceasefire, to be accompanied by the creation of a NATO-led Peace Implementation Force (IFOR). The stage was now set for the proximity talks conducted under strict U.S. supervision at Dayton, Ohio from November 1-21. No leniency was granted to the warring factions. Though present during the deliberations, the Bosnian Croat and Serb delegates were not permitted to function as direct parties in the talks — their interests were represented by Zagreb and Belgrade. Remarkably, at the 11th hour Milošević intervened personally to break a logjam by agreeing to assign all of Sarajevo and a portion of the outlying hills, including districts that the Serb faction had controlled from the outset of fighting, to the Muslims.[138] The critical issue of control over the Brčko choke point, which could not be resolved by consensus, was placed into the hands of international arbitrators. When all else failed, strong-arm tactics were an option — Izetbegović had to be physically coaxed by U.S. negotiators to sign the document acknowledging the existence of the Republika Srpska.[139] Such methods were crude but effective. The Dayton Peace Accord was initialed at the conclusion of the conference, and formally signed in Paris on December 14. During the Paris sessions a leftover issue from the Serbian-Croatian conflict was resolved by the accord concluded on November 12 in the Slavonian town of Erdut, establishing mechanisms for the peaceful transfer of eastern Slavonia, Baranja, and western Srijem back to Croatian sovereignty, a process that was completed without incident in the course of 1996

Dayton was the result of a purposeful U.S. strategy of coercive diplomacy put into place from early 1994 onward. The elements of the strategy, which included interlinked economic, military, and diplomatic tracks, included the maintenance of sanctions against Belgrade as a means for turning Milošević away from the project for a greater Serbia that had inspired the war's first phase, covert arming of the ABH, support for a build up of the HV, the Washington Agreement brokering a limited but strategically significant Croat-Muslim accord, the threat of air strikes as a means of channeling Serb behavior, limited air strikes as a form of punishment, and eventually a decisive application of air power to trip the military balance in tandem with the ground offensives launched by Croat and Muslim forces. Economic means were used to soften Belgrade's resolve and deter any temptation to intervene. Military means were used to break the Serb party's territorial dominance inside Bosnia and create a balance on the ground propitious to a negotiated outcome (Washington also exerted pressure on its Muslim and Croat protégés to limit offensive operations outside of Banja Luka once a viable strategic balance had been achieved). The combination of U.S. air power and the ground offensive undertaken by a regional ally achieved a decisive strategic result without engaging U.S. forces in ground combat, and would eventually be touted as a model for intervention in other regional contingencies. The key to the U.S. diplomatic strategy, ironically after years of berating the Bosnian Serb leadership and insisting that ethnic cleansing would not be rewarded, consisted of series of concessions to the Serb party — courting Milošević with a pledge to lift sanctions in exchange for bringing around intransigents in Pale, and a new willingness to entertain Bosnian Serb strategic goals, including control over a geographically contiguous territory constituting nearly half of the country (considerably more than the Serb faction would have been accorded under the terms of the Vance-Owen plan, for example) and recognition of the Republika Srpska as a legitimate international entity. Finally, the United States agreed to underwrite a negotiated peace with its own armed forces. The United States had brokered peace by redrawing the strategic balance inside Bosnia, committing itself to overseeing the peace process, and accepting a soft-partition arrangement that addressed the minimal conditions of all parties. These concessions were critical to the ability of the international community to sell Dayton to the contending factions. They would come to haunt the project as the task of peacemaking gave way to peace building. Imposing peace was well within the capacity of a unified and purposeful West inspired by American leadership. Sustaining a process of reconciliation between embittered and resentful rivals would prove to be an entirely different kind of challenge.

The Dayton Peace Process.

The Dayton Accord offered an agenda for peace, not a finished architecture. It is therefore most useful to speak of a Dayton approach to peace-building, multilateral but subject to strong U.S. influence and with complementary civilian and military components. The most striking aspect of the accord was the sharp division of labor between its military and civilian sectors, the former led by NATO and the latter by the UN-sponsored High Representative charged with overseeing civilian implementation. At Dayton, the United States was insistent about avoiding the kind of paralyzing reliance upon UN direction that had discredited UNPROFOR, and the Dayton Accord explicitly denied any responsibility in the military sector to the Office of the High Representative, stating that the High Representative "shall have no authority over the IFOR and shall not in any way interfere in the conduct of military operations."[140] In order to make the accord more palatable in the United States, IFOR's original mandate was limited to 1 year, a polite fiction that the architects of the project could hardly have taken seriously.

Politically, the Dayton Accord formalized the same tradeoff between state sovereignty and the federative principle that had characterized Western peace plans since 1992. In principle, the new Bosnia-Herzegovina was a unitary state. In fact, it was subject to a soft partition, divided between the Bosnian Federation (Croat and Muslim) covering 51 percent of the territory and the Republika Srpska covering 49 percent. The central government, with its seat at Sarajevo, consisted of a rotating presidency, a bicameral parliament, and a constitutional court. Its effective authority was limited to the conduct of foreign affairs, international commerce, and fiscal policy. By way of contrast, the Bosnian Federation and the Republika Srpska (referred to in the Dayton context as the entities) were accorded considerable prerogatives — to grant citizenship, maintain armed forces, and pursue "special parallel relationships" with third parties (i.e., Croatia and Yugoslavia) so long as these relationships did not jeopardize the sovereignty and territorial integrity of Bosnia-Herzegovina. Indicted war criminals were barred from holding any military or elective office (a clause inserted with the specific intention of blocking access to leadership positions for the Bosnian Serbs Karadžić and Mladić). The people of Bosnia-Herzegovina were in principle accorded the right to move freely throughout the entire national territory, and the goal of resettling refugees in their places of origin was cited.

The success story of the Dayton process came in the military sector. Operation JOINT ENDEAVOR, conducted from the autumn of 1995 under the command of NATO's Supreme Allied Commander Europe (SACEUR) with a 57,000 strong Implementation Force including nearly 20,000 Americans, was effective in enforcing a cession of hostilities and providing a safe and secure environment for the peace process to unfold. The IFOR was specifically tasked to separate hostile forces; mark and monitor a four-kilometer wide Zone of Separation (ZOS) between the two Bosnian entities; affect territorial adjustments by specifying inter-ethnic boundaries and overseeing the turnover of transferred territories; patrol the ZOS and supervise the withdrawal of forces and heavy weapons into garrisons and cantonment areas; ensure the withdrawal from the theater of foreign forces (in particular international Islamic units supporting the Muslim faction); and enforce compliance with other aspects of the treaty. The IFOR's mandate was limited, and the limits were rigorously respected — a consequence of U.S. concern with mission creep that contributed to the peacekeeping effort's credibility, but also reduced its effectiveness.

IFOR got off to a slow start with deployment delays (and corresponding cost overruns) occasioned by severe weather conditions (slowing the construction of a crucial bridge over the Sava), conflicting priorities (European rail refused to prioritize rail traffic bound for Bosnia during the holiday season and a French rail strike blocked the transfer of heavy freight cars bound for Bosnia), and the planning constraints imposed by the Dayton time lines (which necessitated heavier than intended reliance upon airlift in place of ground transport). Despite these problems, by February 1996 IFOR was deployed in four countries (Bosnia-Herzegovina, Croatia, Hungary, and Italy), and its mission was well underway.

IFOR's first commander, U.S. Admiral Leighton Smith, characterized the purpose of the mission as to ensure "an absence of war and an environment in which peace has a chance."[141] In these admittedly narrow terms, IFOR's performance can be described as an outstanding success. The ZOS and inter-entity boundaries were established without major incident, and the zone effectively patrolled by ground, air, and static post observation. POW exchanges were completed on schedule despite considerable acrimony on all sides. The cantonment of heavy weapons and repositioning of forces within entity boundaries was concluded within the Dayton time line, the positioning of weapons in unauthorized locations and establishment of illegal check points was banned, and foreign forces were withdrawn from the theater. IFOR also made contributions in repairing bridges, roads, and airports, and numerous other civic projects (surveys, repair of power generation and distribution systems, medical care, etc.). It encompassed a significant civil affairs mission including the publication (inside the U.S. sector) of a trilingual newspaper entitled *Herald of Peace*, and numerous other activities designed to further reconciliation. On IFOR's watch the possibility for armed confrontation between opposing factions was reduced to practically zero. Bosnia's cemeteries ceased to fill up with victims, and the prerequisites for a lasting peace were established. These were impressive achievements by any standard.

Some military tasks remained elusive or subjects of controversy. An arms control regime was negotiated on the Dayton time table in June 1996 using the Conventional Forces in Europe (CFE) agreement as a model. According to the agreement, each of the armed factions agreed to accept fixed limits on five categories of weaponry — tanks, armored personnel carriers, attack helicopters, heavy artillery (over

75 mm.), and combat aircraft—according to an agreed ratio of apportionment. The goal of the agreement was to maintain a stable strategic balance, but implementation proved to be difficult, and all sides continued to engage, with varied degrees of success, in a competition to maintain their military capacity behind the scenes.[142] The U.S. approach to the problem included a Train and Equip Mission on behalf of the Croats and Muslims, intended to provide the armed forces of the federation with the wherewithal to stand up to the forces of the Serb Republic and "to prevent war by creating a military balance in Bosnia" according to James Pardew, the State Department official originally assigned to head the program.[143] Simultaneous with the arms control process designed to reduce overall levels of armaments, the United States committed to providing federation forces with consignments of rifles, machine guns, radios, and heavy weapons including 45 M60 A3 tanks, 80 M113 Armored Personnel Carriers, 15 UH-1H helicopters, and 840 AT-4s. Turkey agreed to provide on the ground training, and some Arab states promised financial support. But the program was plagued by problems from the start. The federation proceeded slowly toward the creation of a functioning Muslim-Croat ministry of defense (a joint ministry was established in June 1996 but remained little more than a façade), and Islamic influence upon the Izetbegović clan remained a source of concern. The United States withheld a consignment of arms on shipboard off the Croatian coast for nearly a month in October-November 1996 until its demands for the dismissal of Bosnian Deputy Minister of Defense Hasan Čengić, accused of maintaining ties to Iran, were acted upon.[144] Key U.S. allies expressed unanimous opposition to the program. "These arms are a recipe for war," argued an anonymous Western European ambassador. "Maybe not this year or the next, but one day American-made tanks will be rolling across Bosnia's plain, and what will Washington do then?"[145]

For the time being such Cassandra-like prophesies remained barren, and the frictions and frustrations associated with IFOR's peacekeeping mission were far outweighed by positive contributions. NATO's IFOR mission was extended for an additional 18 months in December 1996 under a reduced but still potent Stabilization Force (SFOR), and in 1998 SFOR's mandate was extended indefinitely. Cumulatively, international engagement in Bosnia-Herzegovina since 1995 has represented a groundbreaking exercise in multilateral peacekeeping that deserves careful assessment.

To begin, it should be noted that the original designation of an *implementation* force has some significance. The oft-reiterated purpose of the mission was to implement an already existing political settlement and defend a ceasefire in place. It would be incorrect, however, to perceive Operation JOINT ENDEAVOR as an exercise in classic peacekeeping. NATO forces insisted upon full prerogative to use decisive force whenever it was deemed necessary by the command authority, without the need to turn to the UN hierarchy for approval. The heart and soul of the original deployments was the U.S. First Armored Division, a unit clearly superior to any other force in the theater and determined to override local obstruction. The real operational concept of Joint Endeavor was to enter with intimidating power and force consent, a concept more in line with peace enforcement via intimidation and compulsion than peacekeeping. The concept was effective. Neither IFOR nor SFOR has been challenged militarily, and they have suffered remarkably few casualties.[146]

Though approved by the UN Security Council, the operation was completely subordinated to NATO under the overall command of the Supreme Allied Commander Europe (SACEUR — during the IFOR mandate U.S. Army General George Joulwan). As such it provided a model for the use of a regional security organization as the leading force in a peace operation conducted under UN auspices.[147] It also provided a trial by fire for something resembling NATO's Combined Joint Task Force (CJTF) concept. In July 1993 U.S. Senator Richard Lugar famously remarked that in the post-cold war period NATO needed to go "out of area or out of business."[148] The CJTF concept was developed as a means for making out of area non-Article Five missions feasible, as well as strengthening the Alliance's European pillar by widening the area of responsibility for the European allies.[149] As combinations of forces drawn from NATO and non-NATO member states, subordinated to a NATO headquarters in a limited duration peacekeeping mission, IFOR and SFOR demonstrated the potential for this kind of operation. In Bosnia, NATO began the process of "redesigning itself for selective intervention missions," a significant recasting of the purpose of the Alliance.[150]

Joint Endeavor imposed special responsibilities upon Britain and France, which together with the United States were assigned control of territorial sectors inside Bosnia: a northern sector covered by two brigades of the U.S. First Armored Division with its headquarters near Tuzla and including the Posavina corridor; a southwestern sector covered by the UK including Bihać and Banja Luka; and a southeastern sector covered by France including Sarajevo and Goražde. IFOR placed French forces under direct NATO command for the first time since 1966 and at the outset their participation seemed to indicate an evolution of French defense policy toward acceptance of the NATO framework as the core of European security planning.[151]

IFOR and SFOR have also presided over large multilateral coalitions with more than forty participating states, many of them also associated with NATO's Partnership for Peace program. A significant part of the mission was staged out of southern Hungary, not long before an integral part of the Warsaw Pact. Overall, the implications of international participation in the NATO-led peacekeeping effort were considerable. "The wide participation in the implementation force," suggested U.S. Secretary of Defense William Perry, "is a symbol of the new Europe. The effort will define how security in Europe is going to be handled for decades to come. In effect, we will be defining what post-cold war Europe is all about and how its security will be assured."[152]

IFOR and SFOR likewise provided a working model for security cooperation between Russia and the West that was all the more positive in light of the sparring over Balkan policy that preceded it. The Western intervention that set the stage for Dayton was presented as a *fait accompli* that a weakened Russian Federation, lacking strong leadership and preoccupied with its own military engagement in Chechnya, was powerless to resist. Moscow was left with no choice but to involve itself in the Dayton process in order to retain at least a symbolic presence in a region where it has important interests at stake. It did so by negotiating a special agreement allowing a Russian brigade to attach to IFOR in the U.S. sector subordinated directly to the U.S. (rather than NATO) chain of command.[153] The pro-government *Izvestiia* mocked Russia's willingness to enforce an accord that it had originally criticized as "Operation Fig Leaf," and Russia's independent press interpreted the outcome as a humiliating defeat.[154] But Moscow had at least limited losses by finding a way to engage in the peacekeeping process on its own terms. On the ground, Russian-American military collaboration in Bosnia proved encouraging. To pose Russian military engagement in the Balkans as a model for future cooperation may be overly optimistic given the special circumstances that pertain, but it may at least be described as a good example.[155]

How the example evolves will in some measure be determined by the long-term success or failure of Western engagement. By 1997 the specifically military tasks assigned to NATO peacekeepers had been accomplished. Simultaneously, the process of political reconciliation and nation-building for which a ceasefire was intended to be a prerequisite was visibly in disarray. IFOR and SFOR had succeeded in imposing a truce and blocking a renewal of hostilities, but the Dayton process as a whole had failed to create the prerequisites for a self-sustaining peace — a failure that was reflected by the indefinite extension of the SFOR mandate. As a framework for peace building, the Dayton Accord was seriously flawed.

The nature of the flaws was no mystery. Acceptance of a quasi-partition arrangement to smooth the way toward a ceasefire had the perverse effect of reinforcing nationalist extremism. The Croat, Muslim, and Serb communities retained independently controlled armed forces, and remained under the direction of the same uncompromising leaders that had waged the war. Elections conducted under the supervision of the High Representative and the OSCE in 1996 reinforced the nationalist element in all three camps, giving new legitimacy to tribunes of exclusion such as the Serb Momčilo Krajišnik and the Croat Dario Kordić.[156] The same process was at work within Izetbegović's SDA, whose Islamic character became more pronounced once the constraints of military campaigning were lifted. The purge of the moderate Haris Silajdžić and his followers from party offices was one of many indications of this evolution. The Serb exodus from the Sarajevo suburbs, which saw the overnight departure of over 90 percent of the community once Serb forces were withdrawn (of approximately 6,000 Serbs once resident in the Vogošca district only some 600 are estimated to have remained, and of over 17,000 in Ilidža fewer than 100), was in some ways imposed by the Serb side as a matter of policy (IFOR allowed the exodus to be conducted with the aide of Serb army trucks), but it was also encouraged by Islamic extremists and included several stoning incidents. Political consolidation in post-Dayton Bosnia was allowed to go forward within the divided ethnic communities. Institutions of central governance were hemmed in by ethnic counter-mobilizations, constrained by intrusive international oversight, and effectively marginalized.

The same kind of ambiguities applied to the Bosnian Federation, which was revealed to be a forced marriage of convenience to which neither party maintained any real allegiance.[157] The divided city of Mostar was the living symbol of the federation's infirmity. The city was subjected to EU administration beginning in July 1994, and mandated to unite its Croat and Muslim sectors into a multiethnic administration. EU direction brought improvements in infrastructure and living conditions, but the city was not united. The Rome Accord of February 1996, generated under U.S. pressure, imposed a weak truce upon the feuding Croat and Muslim authorities, who repeatedly provoked incidents along the city's de facto ethnic dividing line, but only at the cost of shrinking the already small common area in the city center and after a humiliating confrontation with rioters in which EU administrator Hans Koschnik (who would subsequently resign his post in frustration) was briefly held hostage.[158] With its Old Bridge still broken in mid-span, post-Dayton Mostar offered an ironically appropriate postcard image for what had become an incorrigibly divided society.[159]

Other unresolved issues also blocked progress. The Dayton process called for the status of the Posavina Corridor and the disputed town of Brčko to be fixed by an arbitration committee, but both sides regarded the issue as a vital interest and a final decision was repeatedly postponed.[160] Transparent inter-entity boundaries and refugee return were key goals, but the creation of "ethnically pure" enclaves had been a major war aim of all belligerents, and progress toward reversing the consequences of years of ethnic cleansing was negligible. Police and mob violence were used by all sides to force out the unwanted, and special efforts were made to frustrate internationally sponsored pilot projects for refugee return in places such as Travnik, Jajce, and Stolac. The mayor of Jajce, to cite one example, was driven from office by Croat extremists after agreeing to the return of 200 Muslim refugees. In Bosnian villages of Gajevi and Jusići (located adjacent to the Posavina Corridor and therefore of strategic significance) in November 1996, hundreds of Muslims attempting an organized return to their former homes were blocked and fired upon by Serb police. IFOR troops intervened and halted the ingress until applications for return were verified, but when the process resumed in February and March 1997, it was frustrated by further episodes of mob violence.[161] The refugee problem was further exacerbated by the war-ravaged physical environment. Many of the homes to which refugees aspired to return were little more than burned out shells, without access to water, electricity, or public services. There was also the spiritual burden of the war, which virtually forced returning refugees to assume the role of colons and adapt an exclusionary ethnic affiliation that many preferred to reject, and often made resettlement an impossible choice even if physical circumstances permitted. UN High Commissioner Carlos Westendorp would later describe the reluctance of the international community to push harder for refugee return as its single largest failure in post-Dayton Bosnia-Herzegovina.[162] Several million land mines were scattered over Bosnia-Herzegovina at the conclusion of hostilities, and though mine marking and removal was initiated under Dayton and major transportation arteries were cleared, the size of the task was daunting. De-mining was technically not designated as an IFOR tasking--a National Mine Agency was created to address the problem under international sponsorship — but progress continued to depend upon the stability underwritten by an international military presence.

The Dayton process depended upon economic reconstruction and development to reinforce popular support for the peace process, but efforts to generate growth in the wake of the conflict were broadly unsuccessful.[163] Several years into the process *per capita* income was estimated to be at 25 percent of pre-war levels. Nearly half of the pre-war population of 4.6 million counted as refugees or internally displaced persons. Bosnia's total population was estimated at 3.5 million, a 23 percent reduction from the prewar level, with unemployment of over 60 percent. The legacy of physical destruction left behind by the war was immense: industrial production was reduced by 90 percent, with 80 percent of power generators destroyed or out of operation, 40 percent of bridges destroyed, and 60 percent of housing, 50 percent of schools, and 30 percent of health care facilities damaged. Donor conferences hosted by the EU and World Bank managed to meet targets for development assistance, but the sums in question were only a drop in the bucket. Weak governance and the disruption of normal economic activity were exploited by the organized criminal elements that had mushroomed in the course of the war, and the criminalization of basic economic activity (as was the case throughout former Yugoslavia and indeed much of the post-communist Balkans) soon became another barrier to recovery.[164]

The ICTY was not formally associated with the Dayton process, but the Dayton Accord mandated signatories to "cooperate" with its work, which was generally viewed as an integral part of the peace building effort. The assumption was that without some kind of retribution for those responsible for the worst atrocities of the war, Bosnia would never be able to clear the slate and engage in a process of reconciliation.[165] The premise can be challenged. Revenge is a powerful motive, but it may contribute to polarization was well as renewed empathy, particularly when the results are not judged to be equitable by all concerned. To achieve maximum effect, the judgments of the tribunal needed to be swift, credible, and fair. But the tribunal itself was granted no authority to arrest, the responsibility for which devolved upon the international military contingents active in Bosnia and the entities themselves. As a result, only a small minority of more than eighty indicted suspects were apprehended and brought to The Hague under the IFOR and first SFOR mandates. Critics immediately labeled the tribunal an exercise in hypocrisy, created in order to deflect public criticism at a moment when the Western conflict management effort was going badly, maintained as a means for placing pressure upon the factions, and ultimately transformed into a self-perpetuating institution with a momentum and vested interests of its own.[166]

An Ambiguous Peace.

Between 1992-95 the war in Bosnia-Herzegovina claimed hundreds of thousands of casualties. Millions were driven from their homes and consigned to the status of displaced persons and refugees.[167] Unrelenting hate propaganda, systematic ethnic cleansing, recurrent massacre, and widespread cultural vandalism make the Bosnian tragedy a narrative of rare inhumanity. Fought out in the heart of Europe, under the scrutiny of an intensely curious (though often curiously insensate) international media, the conflict and its aftermath dominated the international security agenda for years. At Dayton the United States and its allies succeeded in imposing a fragile truce upon the warring factions, but failed to construct a viable framework for peace building. Eight years after the end of hostilities Bosnia-Herzegovina remains occupied by a NATO-led peacekeeping force, with the goal of a self-sustaining peace still apparently out of reach.

The task of facilitating a resolution of the Bosnian conflict was always tremendously difficult. The complex and emotional nature of the issues at stake, the important role played by poorly disciplined irregular forces, the ill-will with which local actors entered into negotiations, and the pervasiveness of war propaganda and disinformation combined to make the conflict particularly opaque and intractable. Despite these challenges, international mediation during the conflict must be characterized as a failure. The international community did not foresee the consequences of disassembling Yugoslavia in the absence of arrangements for resolving the many issues of citizenship and identity that the elimination of federal institutions was bound to create. Recognition of a sovereign Bosnia-Herzegovina without guarantees for its security was a recipe for disaster. Subsequent efforts to end the fighting were hampered by the inadequacy of international institutions, lack of accord among the major powers, and reluctance to contemplate decisive military measures when peace enforcement had become the only viable mechanism for conflict resolution. Much of the mediation effort was reactive and crisis-driven, lacking the inspiration of a larger strategic concept and insensitive to the ways in which the war fit into emerging regional and global security frameworks. U.S. diplomacy was to some extent paralyzed by disagreements about the nature of post-cold war world order and the way in which regional conflicts such as that in the Balkans should affect strategic priorities absent any kind of clear and present danger to hard U.S. interests — a dispute which in some ways has yet to be resolved. The Dayton Accord that eventually brought the conflict to a close was a triumph of U.S. statecraft, but it was obtained at the cost of a series of compromises and concessions (a willingness to cut deals with autocrats such as Tudjman and Milošević, recognition of the Republika Srpska despite its abysmal war record, soft partition as a foundation for domestic order in post-Dayton Bosnia) that risked to make effective post-conflict peace building more difficult.

The first and most obvious victim was Bosnia-Herzegovina itself, and the ideal of multiculturalism that many presumed it to embody.[168] Dayton may have been envisioned, as Rahda Kumar suggests, as "an interim solution offering a breathing space for rationality to return as fear ebbed," but it was in essence a soft partition arrangement, and historical precedent indicates that "the process of partition has inexorably drawn communities further apart."[169] The primary purpose of the accord was to impose peace, and the result "resembled an armistice between warring states more than a social compact for the rebuilding of Bosnia."[170] Though the Dayton institutions may yet permit Bosnia-Herzegovina to reclaim some of its traditional stature as an arena for cultural interaction and ethnic cohabitation, experience to date has been mixed.

The Balkan region as a whole also suffered from the inadequacies of the Dayton process. The fighting in Bosnia-Herzegovina was successfully contained within the boundaries of the republic, but the impact of the war upon the region was profound. A major failure of the Dayton Accord was the degree to which it focused almost exclusively upon solutions for Bosnia and ignored the waves of instability that the conflict had stirred up in surrounding areas. The economic consequences of the war undermined prospects for post-communist transition in much of Southeastern Europe. Dayton had the objective effect of reinforcing Milošević, whose irresponsible policies remained a threat to regional order. It did little to address the extreme fragility of the various statelets and regions aspiring to statehood — Macedonia, Montenegro, Kosovo, and the Bosnian entities themselves — that had emerged in the southern Balkans as a result of Yugoslavia's dissolution. Revealingly, an effort to place the Kosovo problem on the Dayton agenda was rejected as an unnecessary source of complications.

Dayton also failed to resolve Washington's Balkan dilemmas. The United States was drawn into the Bosnian conflict against its best judgment. In the end it played a decisive role in shaping the outcome, but its commitment to security management and peacekeeping responsibilities did not rest upon a solid foundation. Domestic critics castigated the administration for committing the United States to a "geopolitical backwater" where vital national interests were not at stake, and pushed for hard partition as a prelude to disengagement.[171] Washington was vital to the viability of the Dayton project but not unconditionally committed to its success. As a result, soon after the conclusion of the accord familiar frictions over burden sharing and political direction between the United States and its European allies reappeared.[172]

The Dayton Accord brought an end to the fighting in Bosnia-Herzegovina, and this was no small accomplishment. It did not succeed in providing a viable concept for rebuilding the state, recasting regional order, or blocking the spiral of conflict to which the disintegration of multinational Yugoslavia continued to give rise. The consequences of these failings would soon make themselves felt.

ENDNOTES - CHAPTER 4

1. In conversation with Borisav Jović on June 28, 1990, Milošević evoked the possibility of creating a new, Serb dominated Yugoslavia without Slovenia and Croatia, "which would have nearly 17 million inhabitants, sufficient for European circumstances." Borislav Jović, *Poslednji dani SFRJ: Izvodi iz dnevnika*, 2nd ed., Belgrade: Narodna Biblioteka Srbije, 1995, pp. 161.

2. In the 1961 census, Muslims made up 26 percent of the population; Serbs, 43 percent; and Croats, 22 percent. Srdjan Bogosavljević, "Bosna i Herzegovina u ogledalu statistike," in Dušan Janjić and Paul Shoup, eds., *Bosna i Herzegovina izmedju rata i mira*, Belgrade: Dom Omladine, 1992, pp. 31-47.

3. Adolph Karger, "Das Leopardenfell: Zur regionalen Verteilung der Ethnien in Bosnien-Herzegowinien," *Osteuropa*, Vol. 42, No. 12, 1992, pp. 1102-1111.

4. See Xavier Bougarel, *Bosnie: Anatomie d'un conflit*, Paris: La Découverte, 1996, pp. 81-86, and Rusmir Mahmutćehajić, *Dobra Bosna*, Zagreb: Edition Durieux, 1997. Mahmutćehajić argues for a sovereign, unitary Bosnia-Herzegovina based upon an overarching national identity transcending ethnic and confessional division.

5. See the interview with Momčilo Krajišnik, "Jugoslavija ili rat," in *Danas*, August 6, 1991, pp. 29-31.

6. Marie-Janine Calic, *Krieg und Frieden in Bosnien-Herzegovina*, Frankfurt am Main: Edition Suhrkamp, 1996, p. 89.

7. Most of these formations were closely linked to the emerging Bosnian Serb, Croat, and Muslim chains of command. For a description of the process in the Serb case see "Kako su formirane dobrovoljačke jedinice u Srbiji," *Borba*, November 20-21, 1993, pp. 111-112. By 1994, according to UN sources, the number of paramilitary formations active in Bosnia-Herzegovina had increased to 83 (53 Serb, 13 Croat, and 14 Muslim). UN Commission of Experts, Annex III.A, p. 267, n. 259. From Tim Judah, *The Serbs: History, Myth and the Destruction of Yugoslavia*, New Haven: Yale University Press, 1997, p. 185.

8. Jović, *Poslednji dani SFRJ*, p. 72.

9. The text appeared in the Sarajevo based *Oslobodjenje*, 15 October 1991, p. 1. See also Laura Silber and Allan Little, *Yugoslavia: Death of a Nation*, London: TV

Books, 1996, p. 215.

10. Jean-Arnault Dérens and Catherine Samary, *Les conflits Yougoslaves de A à Z*, Paris: Les Editions de l'Atelier, 2000, pp. 163-164.

11. Kasim I. Begić, *Bosna i Hercegovina od Vanceove misije do Daytonskog sporazuma (1991-1996)*, Sarajevo: Bosanska Knjiga, 1997), pp. 56-60.

12. Zdravko Tomac, *Tkoje ubio Bosnu? Iza zatvornih vrata*, Zagreb: Birotisak, 1994, p. 37.

13. "Jeder hasst hier jeden: Bosniens Serben-Führer Radovan Karadžić über Vergewaltigungen, Vertreibung und den Genfer Friedensplan," *Der Spiegel*, January 25, 1993, pp. 122-123.

14. Mate Boban, "Samostalna i konfederativna BiH," *Večernji list*, October 22, 1992, p. 9.

15. Warren Zimmermann, *Origins of a Catastrophe: Yugoslavia and its Destroyers--America's Last Ambassador Tells What Happened and Why*, New York: Random House, 1996, pp. 191-192.

16. The dominant political forces inside Bosnia's Muslim community had consistently reiterated their unwillingness to remain within a truncated, Serbian-dominated Yugoslavia. See Fahrudin Djapo, "Miloševića 'Grose' Srbija," *Bosanski pogledi*, 15 August 1991, p. 3. German pressure to resolve the crisis in Croatia through "preventive recognition" thus had the effect of radically foreclosing Bosnia's options. "[Bosnian President Alija] Izetbegović was thus forced by German-led EC policy into the same mistake that Tudjman had made voluntarily — he embarked upon secession from Yugoslavia without securing prior agreement from the Serbs." Misha Glenny, *The Fall of Yugoslavia: The Third Balkan War*, London: Penguin, 1992, p. 151.

17. Xavier Bougarel, "Bosnia and Hercegovina — State and Communitarianism," in David A. Dyker and Ivan Vejvoda, eds., *Yugoslavia and After: A Study in Fragmentation, Despair and Rebirth*, London: Longman, 1996, p. 101. In the wedding incident, a Serb bridegroom was shot and killed, and an Orthodox priest wounded, by a Muslim convinced that the celebration in the city's old Muslim quarter, the Baščaršija, which included a display of Yugoslav flags, was a provocation. Pouring oil on the flames, Momčilo Krajišnik described the shots as "a great injustice aimed at the Serb people." Cited in Silber and Little, *Yugoslavia: Death of a Nation*, p. 205.

18. Organized criminal gangs or "neighborhood bands" (*mahalske bande*) led by flamboyant "Godfathers" such as Jusuf "Juka" Prazina, Musan "Caco" Topalović, and Ramiz "Ćelo" Delalić, were vital to the city's defense, but prone to

exploit their influence to extort profit. In October 1993 ABH Commander Rašim Delić expelled Prazina and closed down Topalović's and Delalić's "9th and 10th Mountain Brigades." Topalović was killed under suspicious circumstances, and Delalić arrested and sentenced to a prison term. Prazina went on to fight on the Mostar front, but was eventually forced into exile and assassinated by his own bodyguard in Belgium during January 1994. Delalić has since emerged from incarceration and taken up employment as a restauranteur.

19. Zlatko Dizdarević, "Bosnia Erzegovina 1992-1993," in Alessandro Marzo Magno, ed., *La Guerra dei dieci anni. Jugoslavia 1991-2001: I fatti, i personaggi, le ragioni dei conflitti*, Milan: Il Saggiatore, 2001, p. 162, calls it Tudjman's "double game."

20. Bougarel, *Bosnie*, pp. 57-58, and Mira Beham, *Kriegstrommeln*, Munich: Medien, Krieg und Politik, 1996.

21. Željko Vuković, *Ubijanje Sarajeva*, Belgrade: Kron, 1993, and Silber and Little, *Death of Yugoslavia*, pp. 226-229.

22. Milovan Djilas, *Wartime: With Tito and the Partisans*, London: 1977, presents a fair-minded portrait of the partisan tradition that to some extent debunks official mythology. The abusive use of the partisan tradition for purposes of political mobilization is mocked in Emir Kusturica's great film, *Underground.*

23. Michael Ignatieff, *Virtual War: Kosovo and Beyond*, New York: Metropolitan Books, 2000, p. 196.

24. Central Intelligence Agency, Office of Russian and European Analysis, *Balkan Battlegrounds: A Military History of the Yugoslav Conflict, 1900-1995*, 2 vols., Washington, DC: Central Intelligence Agency, May 2002, Vol. 1, p. 130.

25. Alija Izetbegović later claimed that at its origin the Patriotic League commanded between 30,000 and 40,000 combatants. Izetbegović Speech to the Second Congress of the Party of Democratic Action, in *Dnevni Avaz* (Sarajevo), September 9, 1993.

26. Divjak is cited in Dizdarević, "Bosnia Erzegovina 1992-1993," p. 172.

27. Janko Bobetko, *Sve Moje Bitke*, Zagreb: Vlastita Naklada, 1996, pp. 212-230. In September 2002 the 83-year-old Bobetko became the oldest and most senior level Croatian official indicted by the International Criminal Tribunal for Former Yugoslavia, charged with responsibility for atrocities against civilians committed by troops under his command during HV operations in the Medak pocket southwest of Zagreb in September 1993. Ian Traynor, "Croatia Refuses to Hand Over General Accused of War Crimes," *The Guardian*, September 25, 2002.

28. Belgrade's estimates at the time were considerably higher, citing a force of about 50,000-60,000 combatants. *Balkan Battlegrounds*, Vol. 1, p. 132.

29. Jović, *Poslednji dani SFRJ*, pp. 420-421.

30. *Balkan Battlegrounds*, Vol. 1, pp. 129-130.

31. Extracts from this interview appear in the BBC documentary *The Death of Yugoslavia*. U.S. General Wesley Clark describes Mladić as "coarse and brutal." Wesley K. Clark, *Waging Modern War: Bosnia, Kosovo, and the Future of Combat*, New York: Public Affairs, 2001, p. 40. For a brief biography, see Dérens and Samary, *Les conflits Yougoslaves*, pp. 217-218.

32. *Balkan Battlegrounds*, Vol. 1, pp. 141-142.

33. For a portrait of Serb ethnic cleansing in the first months of the war in the Zvornik area (a particularly egregious case) see Hans Trotter, *et al.*, 'Ethnische Sauberungen' in der nordostbosnischen Stadt Zvornik von April bis Juni 1992, Vienna: Ludwig Baltzman Institute for Human Rights, 1994. A Muslim perspective on ethnic cleansing in eastern Bosnia is provided by Nijaz Mašić, *Istina o Bratuncu: Agresija, genocid, i oslobodilačka borba 1992-1995*, Tuzla: Opština Bratunac sa Privreminim Sjedištem u Tuzli, 1996.

34. UN statistics recorded 4.25 million refugees and displaced persons, dispersed throughout former Yugoslavia and Europe: 2.33 million in Bosnia-Herzegovina, 613,000 in Croatia, 520,000 in Serbia, 32,000 in Macedonia, 33,000 in Slovenia, and 750,000 in Europe (324,000 of whom were located in Germany). Calic, *Krieg und Frieden*, pp. 121-122.

35. Interview mit dem UNO-Beauftragten Tadeusz Mazowiecki, "Nicht die gesamte serbische Nation beschuldigen," *Süddeutsche Zeitung*, December 19, 1992, p. 12. For the Mazowiecki commission report see Tadeusz Mazowiecki, "Massive Human Rights Violations in Former Yugoslavia," in *U.S. Policy Information and Texts*, No. 133, October 30, 1992, *Final Report of the Commission of Experts Established pursuant to Security Council Resolution 780* (1992). The report assigns the Serbs preponderant, but not unique responsibility for ethnic cleansing and associated crimes against humanity. Norman Cigar, *Genocide in Bosnia: The Politics of "Ethnic Cleansing,"* College Station, TX: Texas A&M University Press, 1995, locates the root of the phenomenon in what is described as Belgrade's purposefully genocidal campaign to create a greater Serbia.

36. See Christopher Collinson, "Bosnian Army Tactics," *Jane's Intelligence Review*, Vol. 6, No. 1, January 1994, pp. 11-13.

37. "Više od lomače," *Vreme*, November 23, 1992, pp. 50-51.

38. The fate of Mostar's Old Bridge has become an appropriate symbol for this aspect of the conflict. See Mišo Marić, "Pogubljeni most," *Vreme*, January 3, 1994, pp. 28-29.

39. Mark Mazower, *The Balkans: A Short History*, New York: The Modern Library, 2000, p. xxxviii.

40. Miloš Minić, *Dogovori u Karadjordjevu o podeli Bosne i Herzegovine*, Sarajevo: Rabić, 1998. Tudjman and Milošević met privately at Karadjordjevo and left no public record of their discussion. The dialogue would continue — according to Tudjman's *chef de cabinet* the two leaders met on 18 separate occasions during the course of the war up to 1995. Vidosav Stevanovic, *Milosevic: Une épitaphe*, Paris: Fayard, 2000, p. 217. According to Boris Raseta, the arrangement would also have regulated the situation inside Croatia via partition, with Zagreb granted control of western Slavonia and Krajina, and Belgrade control over Posavina and eastern Slavonia. Boris Raseta, "The Questions Over Slavonija, "*Balkan War Report*, No. 33, May 1995, pp. 3-8. Tudjman and Milošević were also in periodic telephone contact during the war in Bosnia-Herzegovina. Private communication to the author from a Yugoslav official.

41. The partition arrangement for Bosnia-Herzegovina worked out by Tudjman and Milošević was vetoed without appeal by Izetbegović. See Milan Milošević, "Bespuća Raspleta," *Vreme*, July 18, 1994, pp. 14-18.

42. Karadžić specified Serb war aims in a speech and interview delivered in 1995, commenting upon the outcome of the war in terms of original goals. Banja Luka Srpska Televizija, September 12, 1995.

43. These actions were consciously intended to intimidate. Arriving in Zvornik several days later, Arkan called upon its defenders to surrender or "experience the fate of Bijeljina." Cited in *Balkan Battlegrounds*, Vol. 1, p. 137.

44. According to the Yugoslav census of 1981, the population of the Bosanska Krajina was 63 percent Serb, 15 percent Muslim, and 9.5 percent Croat.

45. Preparations are meticulously documented in Smail Čekić, *The Aggression in Bosnia and Genocide Against Bosnians, 1991-1993*, Sarajevo: Ljiljan, 1994.

46. It has been suggested that the absence of more effective Croat pressure against these exposed positions provides further evidence of Serb-Croat collusion. Steven L. Burg and Paul S. Shoup, *The War in Bosnia-Herzegovina: Ethnic Conflict and International Intervention*, Armonk, NY: M. E. Sharpe, 1999, p. 198.

47. Silber and Little, *Yugoslavia: Death of a Nation*, pp. 231-243.

48. Šefer Halilović, *Lukava strategija*, Sarajevo: Maršal, 1997, pp. 62-63.

49. Susan L. Woodward, *Balkan Tragedy: Chaos and Dissolution after the Cold War*, Washington, DC: The Brookings Institution Press, 1995, p. 235, suggests that the Serb faction sought to efface multicultural Sarajevo because it "stood as a mockery to national exclusiveness." Bosnian Serb leader Momčilo Krajišnik seemed to confirm this judgment in a 1994 interview, asserting that; "The significance of Sarajevo for our struggle is immense. Here it is being demonstrated that there is no future for any kind of unitary state. Here we are concerned with two cities, two states." "Ljudi i vreme: Momčilo Krajišnik," *Vreme*, November 28, 1994, p. 55.

50. Cited in Dizdarević, "Bosnia Erzegovina 1992-1993," pp. 173-174.

51. Edgar O'Ballance, *Civil War in Bosnia 1992-94*, New York: St. Martin's Press, 1995, p. 65.

52. See the account in Burg and Shoup, *The War in Bosnia-Herzegovina*, pp. 140-142.

53. Bougarel, *Bosnie*, p. 130. The revolt was immediately contained and did not spread. For the agenda of the mutineers see *Vreme*, September 20, 1993. Pacifist demonstrations were also reported in September 1993 in the Bosnian Muslim communities of Tuzla and Zenica. "Opstanak, daleko od Sarajeva," *Borba*, November 1, 1993.

54. Mile Akmadžić, "Država BiH u kliničkoj smrti," *Borba*, January 26, 1993, p. 9.

55. Robert Stewart, *Broken Lives: A Personal View of the Bosnian Conflict*, London: HarperCollins, 1994, pp. 278-299. The local Croat commander, General Tihomir Blaskić, would subsequently be sentenced to a 45-year prison term by the ICTY, the most severe punishment meted out by the Tribunal to date. Published portions of the Tudjman Tapes seem to indicate that a substantial knowledge of the events existed at the highest level, and that systematic efforts were made to falsify and cover them up. Yomiuri Shimbun, "Tudjman's Dark Secrets Surfacing," cited from *www.balkanpeace.org/cib/cro/cro10.shtml*.

56. *Balkan Battlegrounds*, Vol. 1, p. 192.

57. Vanesa Vasić-Janeković, "Život u Stupici," *Vreme*, October 18, 1993, pp. 32-33.

58. Begić, *Bosna i Hercegovina*, pp. 140-142, suggests that under Croat pressure during the summer of 1993, the Muslims seriously considered pursuing a strategic alliance with the Bosnian Serb faction, or if that were not possible, requesting the declaration of a UN protectorate over Bosnia-Herzegovina.

59. Abdić was eventually arrested in Croatia in June 2001 and accused of operating detention camps and perpetrating torture against his Muslim opponents during the war. In July 2002 he was convicted by a Croatian court in Karlovac of war crimes and sentenced to a maximum of twenty years in prison. "Bosnian Warlord Guilty," *The Guardian*, August 1, 2002.

60. Burg and Shoup, *The War in Bosnia-Herzegovina*, pp. 155-156.

61. The SDS published a map depicting a partition arrangement in December 1991, with 70 percent of the territory assigned to the Serb faction. See Robert M. Hayden, "The Partition of Bosnia and Herzegovina," *Radio Free Europe/Radio Liberty Research Reports*, Vol. 2, No. 22, May 28, 1993, pp. 4-6.

62. "Izjava o principima za novo ustavno uredjenje BiH," *Oslobodjenje*, March 19, 1992, p. 1.

63. Burg and Shoup, *The War in Bosnia-Herzegovina*, p. 111.

64. U.S. Ambassador Zimmermann would later claim that he conveyed to Izetbegović his government's formal support for the European initiative, but also offered the personal query: "If you don't like the agreement, why are you willing to sign it"? Ljiljana Smaijlović, "Intervju: Voren Zimerman — Moja Uloga u Bosni," *Vreme*, No. 192, June 27, 1994, pp. 16-18. Zimmerman's coyness is sometimes cited as an example of emerging U.S. sympathy for Muslim grievances.

65. Gow, *Triumph of the Lack of Will*, pp. 42-43.

66. Citations from Brana Markovic, *Yugoslav Crisis and the World: Chronology of Events January 1990-October 1995*, Belgrade: Institute of International Politics and Economics, 1996, pp. 39-41.

67. Roy Guttman, *A Witness to Genocide*, New York: Macmillan, 1993. Guttman was Newsday's foreign correspondent in Bosnia in the summer of 1992, and received a Pulitzer Prize for his revelations of abuses in Serb detention camps.

68. These attitudes would carry through the campaigns of 1992 and 1993. For a sampling of U.S. opinion see Henry Kissinger, "Yugoslavia: Before Sending Troops, Marshal the Arguments," *International Herald Tribune*, September 21, 1992, p. 5, and Mark Helprin, "Stay Out of Bosnia," *The Wall Street Journal*, September 21, 1993, p. 12. Opinion within the Bush administration was also affected by concern for the impact of a major international involvement on the eve of a reelection campaign.

69. Zimmermann, *Origins of a Catastrophe*, p. 158.

70. See *The Washington Post*, December 11, 1992, p. A52.

71. Markovic, *Yugoslav Crisis*, p. 41.

72. Gow, *Triumph of the Lack of Will*.

73. Woodward, *Balkan Tragedy*, p. 325 .

74. Silber and Little, *Yugoslavia: Death of a Nation*, p. 275.

75. "Osam Izetbegovićevih uvjeta za potpisivanje Vance-Owenovog plana," *Vjesnik*, March 27, 1993. p. 31.

76. Secretary of State Warren Christopher provided an outline of the policy of the new administration toward Bosnia-Herzegovina during February 1993 that avoided radical new directions — despite the rhetoric of the electoral campaign, where Clinton had criticized the policies of his predecessor. U.S. Department of State, Office of the Assistant Secretary, *Statement by U.S. Secretary of State Warren Christopher*, February 10, 1993, pp. 2-4. Lift and Strike would not be formalized as a policy until May 1993, following the collapse of hopes to implement the Vance-Owen Plan. Burg and Shoup, *The War in Bosnia-Herzegovina*, pp. 250-251.

77. David Owen, *Balkan Odyssey*, New York: Harcourt, Brace & Co., 1995, pp. 112 and 161-163.

78. Elisabeth Drew, *On the Edge: The Clinton Presidency*, New York: Simon & Schuster, 1994, pp. 157-158. The perception was reinforced after the firefight in Mogadiscio on October 3, 1993 that resulted in the deaths of 18 U.S. Army Rangers.

79. See in particular Colin Powell's op-ed commentary in *The New York Times*, September 28, 1992, p. A1.

80. Silber and Little, *Yugoslavia: Death of a Nation*, pp. 276-290.

81. *Ibid.*, p. 285.

82. Burg and Shoup, *The War in Bosnia-Herzegovina*, pp. 265-266.

83. Srdjan Radulović, *Sudbina Krajina*, Belgrade: Dan Graf, 1996, p. 70.

84. Burg and Shoup, *The War in Bosnia-Herzegovina*, p. 283.

85. I. William Zartman, "The Unfinished Agenda: Negotiating Internal Conflicts," in Roy Licklider, ed., *Stopping the Killing: How Civil Wars End*, New York: New York University Press, 1993, p. 24.

86. Iran and Saudi Arabia were important sources of arms and support for the Muslim faction. Shipments moved across Turkey and were often airlifted into Croatia and trucked into Bosnia, with Croat forces taking a standard 30 percent cut as a reward for their cooperation. The Clinton administration turned a blind eye to these transfers, and to the presence of Iranian Mujahideen in the ranks of Bosnian forces, from 1992 onward. Douglas Jehl, "U.S. Looks Away as Iran Arms Bosnia," *The New York Times*, April 15, 1995, p. A3; and John Pomfret and David B. Ottaway, "U.S. Allies Fed Covert Arms to Balkans," *The Manchester Guardian Weekly*, May 19, 1996, p. 20. Bosnian Vice President Ejup Ganić would later assert that the Russian Federation was the largest single arms supplier for the Bosnian government during the war, and that Iranian transfers, though important, were not "decisive." Ben Barber and James Morrison, "Bosnian: Russians Top Arms Suppliers," *The Washington Times*, February 2, 1997, p. 1.

87. Miroslav Prokopijević and Jovan Teokarić, *Ekonomske sankcije UN: Uporedna analiza i slučaj Jugoslavije*, Belgrade: Institut za Evropske Studije, 1998.

88. National Security Advisor Anthony Lake, for example, argued that support for the Bosnian Muslims would serve to strengthen the U.S. position in the Muslim world as a whole. Drew, *On the Edge*, p. 144. After the terror attacks against New York and Washington, DC, of September 11, 2001, and the initiation of a global War Against Terrorism, the administration of George W. Bush was quick to point to support for the Muslim cause in Bosnia as evidence that the United States did not conduct an "anti-Muslim" foreign policy.

89. The charge that on occasion the Muslim faction deliberately attacked its own people in order to affect international opinion and encourage intervention, obviously highly sensitive and difficult to adjudicate, has been leveled repeatedly. See the account by former U.S. commander Charles G. Boyd, "Making Peace with the Guilty: The Truth About Bosnia," *Foreign Affairs*, Vol. 74, No. 5, September-October 1995, pp. 22-38; and Burg and Shoup, *The War in Bosnia-Herzegovina*, pp. 164-169.

90. Miloš Vasić, "Masakr na Markalama," *Vreme*, February 14, 1994, pp. 10-14.

91. Marković, *Yugoslav Crisis and the World*, pp. 116-118.

92. Opposition to Yeltsin's pro-Western orientation was carefully and hopefully noted in Belgrade. See Djuro Bilbija, "Rusija 'protiv' Rusije," *Borba*, October 7, 1992, p. 4. Skeptics commented caustically upon Milošević's "myopic" reliance upon the eventual emergence of a "Slavic, Orthodox, and pro-Serbian Russia" capable of functioning as a real strategic ally. Ranko Petković, "Bratstvo ili interes?" *Nin*, October 8, 1993.

93. See the accounts by Aleksei Chelnokov, "Ispoved' russkogo naemika,"

Izvestiia, March 10, 1994, p. 5; and Il'ja Levin, "Neopanslavism: Mutuality in the Russian-Serbian Relationship," in Paul Shoup and Stefano Bianchini, eds., *The Yugoslav War, Europe and the Balkans: How to Achieve Security?*, Ravenna: Longo Editore, 1995, pp. 73-82.

94. Cited in E. Iu. Gus'kov, "Krizis na Balkanakh i pozitsiia Rossii," in E. Iu. Gus'kov, ed., *Iugoslavskii krizis i Rossiia: Dokumenty, fakhty, kommentarii (1900-1993)*, Moscow: Slavianskaia letopis', 1993, p. 47.

95. The text of the speech, and Kozyrev's subsequent explanation of his motives, are in "Vystuplenie A. V. Kozyreva na vstreche Ministrov inostrannykh del SBSE (Stokgol'm, 14 dekabria 1992 g.)," in Gus'kov, ed., *Iugoslavskii krizis i Rossiia*, pp. 128-129.

96. *Ibid.*

97. *Ibid.*, p. 131. During 1992 and 1993 Ambartsumov and his committee sought in vain to develop a compromise position between the pro-Western line of the government and the parliamentary opposition.

98. *Ibid.*, pp. 195, 212.

99. Borko Gvozdenović, "Nova misija Rosije," *Politika*, May 18, 1993, p. 4.

100. Upon assuming his seat in the new Russian parliament, Zhirinovskii made his position crystal clear: "I am for Serbia, my party is for Serbia, and our parliamentary groups are likewise for Serbia." Cited in Borko Gvozdenović, "Ruska Duma zatražila ukidanje sankcija protiv Jugoslavije" *Politika*, January 22, 1994, p. 4.

101. Cited in D. Vuković, "Tajno oružje za neprijatelje Srba," *Borba*, February 2, 1994, p. 1.

102. Veselin Simonović, "Srbi i Rusi," *Vreme*, February 28, 1994, pp. 33-38.

103. Dmitrii Gornostaev, "Khotia i khrupkii, no mir," *Nezavisimaia gazeta*, February 22, 1994, p. 1.

104. Savva Zhivanov, "Rossiia i iugoslavskii krizis: Vzgliad iz Belgrada," *Nezavisimaia gazeta*, July 19, 1994, p. 5. See also N. Smirnova, "Balkany i politika Rossii: Istoriia i sovremennost'," *Mirovaia ekonomika i mezhdunarodnye otnosheniia*, No. 5, 1994, pp. 110-116.

105. Anthony Lewis, "This Ultimatum is Modest, More Needs to be Done," *International Herald Tribune*, February 12, 1994, p. 6. On the reformulation of U.S. policy see Ivo. H. Daalder, *Getting to Dayton: The Making of America's Bosnia Policy*,

Washington, DC: Brookings Institution Press, 2000, pp. 23-26.

106. The limits of collaboration between Russia and the West were already revealed during these events. Moscow protested strongly against lack of consultation, and what it interpreted as unilateral punishment being meted out to the Serb faction. Mikhail Karpov, "Moskva po-prezhnemu zhdet ot OON pol'noi informatsii," *Nezavisimaia gazeta*, April 15, 1994, p. 1.

107. George Rudman, "Backtracking to Reformulate: Establishing the Bosnian Federation," *International Negotiation*, Vol. 1, No. 3, 1996, pp. 525-545. For symbolic purposes, the Bosnian Serbs were also invited to join the federation. Their parliament in Pale, to no one's surprised, refused the invitation in a formal vote on April 23, 1994.

108. Croatia also received a $125 million World Bank loan in reward for its cooperation. *Balkan Battlegrounds*, Vol. 1, p. 227.

109. Boban's death from a heart attack was announced during 1997. It was widely speculated at the time that he had not in fact died, but merely adopted a new identity in order to avoid extradition to The Hague. "Mate Boban," *Bošnjački vremeplov*, in *www.bosona.com/mate.htlm*.

110. Burg and Shoup, *The War in Bosnia-Herzegovina*, pp. 292-298; Silber and Little, *Yugoslavia: Death of a Nation*, pp. 319-323; and Owen, *Balkan Odyssey*, pp. 255-292.

111. Daalder, *Getting to Dayton*, p. 27.

112. Italy was denied a place in the Contact Group at the request of the other European associates. In 1996, after a considerable amount of complaining from Rome (which carried a special responsibility in conflict management efforts due to geographical proximity), Italy joined the group as a sixth member.

113. David Owen suggests that the Contact Group concept was inspired by the successful experience of international mediation in Namibia during 1977. Owen, *Balkan Odyssey*, p. 277.

114. An editorial in the regime-friendly *Politika* on July 31 urged Pale to accept the plan. On August 4 Belgrade announced that its border with the Republika Srpska would be closed in retaliation for the Bosnian refusal, and threatened economic sanctions.

115. Burg and Shoup, *The War in Bosnia-Herzegovina*, p. 150.

116. Mladić may also have been handicapped by illness during the fighting in Goražde, or preoccupied by the recent suicide of his 23-year-old daughter Ana in

Belgrade. "Politika Samoubistva," *Vreme*, April 11, 1994, pp. 9-10. On April 24 the ICTY indicted both Mladić and Karadžić for war crimes and genocide.

117. As recounted in Richard Holbrooke, *To End a War*, New York: Random House, 1998, pp. 4-21. Holbrooke suggests that the decisive push toward U.S. engagement was provided by the realization that even without such an engagement U.S. forces would be required to go into harms way to assist an UNPROFOR withdrawal. The possibility of U.S. forces being subjected to casualties while presiding over defeat during an election year was more than sufficient to energize the Clinton administration into more decisive action. Burg and Shoup, *The War in Bosnia-Herzegovina*, p. 160, assert unambiguously that: "It was the growing threat of this withdrawal that provided the catalyst in 1995 for the American effort to end the fighting."

118. On January 15, 2000, in this same hotel, Arkan would be assassinated with his wife at his side.

119. Hrvoje Šarinić, *Svi moji tajni razgovori sa Slobodom Milošević*, Zagreb: Globus International, 1999, p. 178. According to the author, U.S. negotiators subsequently urged Zagreb to press their would-be Muslim allies to consider surrender of the eastern Bosnian enclaves in the context of an overall settlement. *Ibid.*, p. 184. See also *Balkan Battlegrounds*, Vol.1, pp. 265-279.

120. Spokespersons for Military Professional Resources Inc. emphasize that no members of the organization ever engaged in combat operations on behalf of Croatia, though one independent commentator notes that their council and technical support was "more important than a trainload of artillery." Alessandro Marzo Magno, "La reconquista della Krajina," in Magno, ed., *La Guerra dei dieci anni*, p. 259. See also Chris Black, "U.S. Veterans' Aid to Croatia Elicits Queries," *The Boston Globe*, August 13, 1995, p. 12; Charlotte Eager, "Invisible United States Army Defeats Serbs," *The Observer*, November 5, 1995, p. 25; and Yves Goulet, "MPRI: Washington's Freelance Advisors," *Janes Intelligence Review*, July 1, 1998, p. 38.

121. Frasure's remark is rendered in Holbrooke, *To End a War*, p. 73.

122. "Pad Zapadne Slavonije," *Vreme*, May 8, 1995, pp. 8-17; and Magno, "La Reconquista della Krajina," pp. 253-265.

123. Jan Honig and Norbert Both, *Srebrenica: Record of a War Crime*, New York: Penguin Books, 1997; and David Rohde, *Endgame: The Betrayal and Fall of Srebrenica, Europe's Worst Massacre Since World War II*, New York: Farrar, Straus and Giroux, 1997.

124. The Russian parliament nonetheless passed a near unanimous resolution condemning the air strikes as "open support for one side to the conflict" and calling

for unilateral Russian withdrawal from economic sanctions against Yugoslavia. *Gosudarstvennaia Duma: Stennogramma Zasedanii*, No. 117, July 12, 1995, pp. 51-52.

125. Norbert Both, *From Indifference to Entrapment: The Netherlands and the Yugoslav Crisis, 1990-1995*, Amsterdam: Amsterdam University Press, 2000, pp. 181-242. A carefully documented study of the role of the Dutch Battalion at Srebrenica undertaken by the Netherlands Institute for War Documentation, critical of the unit's comportment but also sensitive to the degree to which it had been left on its own to manage an impossible situation, was published in April 2002. The appearance of the study provoked the resignation of the Dutch government. *Srebrenica, A 'Safe' Area: Reconstruction, Background, Consequences and Analyses of the Fall of a Safe Area*, Amsterdam: Netherlands Institute for War Documentation, April 2002.

126. A critical evaluation of the campaign is offered by Giacomo Scotti, *Croazia, Operazione Tempesta: La "liberaziione" della Krajina ed il genocidio del popolo serbo*, Rome: Gamberetti Editrice, 1996.

127. Šarinić, *Svi moji tajni razgovori*, pp. 199-203. These assurances provide yet another illustration of the collusive strategies pursued by the two former communist leaders throughout the conflict.

128. *Ibid.*, p. 266.

129. Raymond Bonner, "War Crimes Panel Finds Croat Troops 'Cleansed' the Serbs," *The New York Times*, March 21, 1999, p. A1.

130. Cited in Magno, "La riconquista della Krajina," p. 281.

131. Colonel Robert C. Owen, ed., *Deliberate Force: A Case Study in Effective Air Campaigning*, Maxwell Air Base, Alabama: Air University Press, January 2000. Of the sorties, 2,285, or 65 percent, were flown by U.S. aircraft. Strike aircraft were required to fly "above the range of low-level air defenses, and none were lost." Bruce R. Nardulli, Walter L. Perry, Bruce Pirnie, John Gordon IV, and John G. McGinn, *Disjointed War: Military Operations in Kosovo, 1999*, Santa Monica, CA: RAND, 2002, p. 12.

132. Attila Hoare, "A Rope Supports a Man Who is Hanged: NATO Air Strikes and the End of Bosnian Resistance?" *East European Politics and Society*, Vol. 12, No. 2, Spring 1998, pp. 203-221.

133. The genesis of the "Endgame Strategy" inside the U.S. interagency process is described by Daalder, *Getting to Dayton*, pp. 81-112.

134. "Boris Eltsine evoque une aide de la Russie aux Serbes bosniaques et durcit le ton sur l'élargissement de l'OTAN," *Le Monde*, September 9, 1995, p. 4.

135. "Boris El'tsin popravil svoiu Balkanskuiu initsiativu," *Izvestiia*, August 11, 1995, p. 1. Tudjman expressed interest in the project, but immediately withdrew under Western pressure. A subsequent effort to organize a summit under Russian auspices in October 1995 had to be cancelled after Yeltsin was incapacitated by a heart attack.

136. Scott Parish, "Twisting in the Wind: Russia and the Yugoslav Conflict," *Transition*, No. 14, November 3, 1995, p. 26.

137. Holbrooke's account in *To End a War* may be considered the definitive narrative of these negotiations.

138. The sacrifice of Sarajevo did not conflict with the logic of partition that Belgrade seems to have pursued from the outset of the fighting. Already in January 1995, in conversation with a Croat confidant, Milošević is reported to have remarked that "Sarajevo cannot become a Serb city." Šarinić, *Svi moji tajni razgovori*, p. 201.

139. Interview by the author with U.S. negotiators, Brussels, Belgium, June 2000.

140. *The Dayton Peace Agreement*, Annex 10, Article II.8.

141. Admiral Leighton Smith JNR USN, "IFOR: Half-Way Through the Mandate," *RUSI Journal*, August, 1996, p. 13.

142. Jeffrey D. McCausland, "Arms Control and the Dayton Accords," *European Security*, Vol. 6, No. 2, Summer 1997, pp. 18-27.

143. Cited in John Pomfret, "U.S. Starts Delivery of Heavy Weapons to Bosnia's Muslim-Croat Forces," *The Washington Post*, November 22, 1996, p. 44. U.S. negotiators originally opposed the Train and Equip option, but Sarajevo made it a nonnegotiable condition of support for the Dayton Accord.

144. John Pomfret, "Disputed Bosnian Officials Removed," *The Washington Post*, November 20, 1996, p. 28.

145. Cited in Pomfret, "U.S. Starts Delivery of Heavy Weapons."

146. *Military Security in Bosnia-Herzegovina: Present and Future*, Washington, DC, The Atlantic Council of the United States, Vol. VII, No. 11, December 18, 1996.

147. Dick A. Leurdijk, "Before and After Dayton: The UN and NATO in the Former Yugoslavia," *Third World Quarterly*, Vol. 18, No. 3, 1997, pp. 457-470.

148. Cited from Stephen R. Rosenfeld, "NATO's Last Chance," *The Washington Post*, July 2, 1993, p. A19.

149. Charles Berry, "NATO's Combined Joint Task Forces in Theory and Practice," *Survival*, Vol. 38, No. 1, 1996, pp. 81-97. Berry defines the CJTF as "a multilateral, multiservice, task-tailored force consisting of NATO and possibly non-NATO forces capable of rapid deployment to conduct limited duration peace operations beyond Alliance borders, under the command of either NATO's integrated military structure or the Western European Union." (p. 86). Though the deployments in Bosnia-Herzegovina were not designated as a CJTF, they closely corresponded to this definition.

150. Robert J. Art, "Why Western Europe Needs the United States and NATO," *Political Science Quarterly*, Vol. 111, No. 1, 1996, p. 32. See also G. L. Schulte, "Former Yugoslavia and the New NATO," *Survival*, Vol. 39, No. 1, 1997, pp. 19-42.

151. Robert P. Grant, "France's New Relationship with NATO," *Survival*, Vol. 38, No. 1, 1996, pp. 58-80. Paul Cornish could conclude, prematurely as it transpired, on the basis of French participation that "France has declared that the best hope for a well-organized, meaningful, and above all cost-effective European security structure lies, first and foremost, in NATO rather than in some exclusively European politico-military institution or formation." Paul Cornish, "European Security: The End of Architecture and the New NATO," *International Affairs*, Vol. 72, No. 4, 1996, p. 757.

152. William J. Perry, "The Iron Logic of Our Bosnian Involvement," *Defense '96*, Issue 1, 1996, p. 13.

153. Moscow refused to subordinate its soldiers to the NATO command structure as a point of pride. For details of the arrangement see *Krasnaia zvezda*, November 11, 1995, pp. 1-2.

154. *Izvestiia*, November 11, 1995, p. 1; Semen Vasilievskii, "Bol'shie poteri i malenkie dostizheniia," *Nezavisimaia gazeta*, December 8, 1995, pp. 4-5; and Yuri Borko, "The Old World: Consolidation with a Back-Glance at Russia," *New Times*, January 1996, pp. 18-20.

155. Sergei A. Baburkin, "The Bosnian Crisis and the Problem of U.S.-Russian Military Cooperation," *Mediterranean Quarterly*, Fall 1996, pp. 97-112; and Sharyl Cross, "Russia and NATO Toward the Twenty-First Century: Conflicts and Peacekeeping in Bosnia-Herzegovina and Kosovo," *The Journal of Slavic Military Studies*, Vol. 15, No. 2, June 2002, pp. 1-58.

156. Henry Kissinger, "America in the Eye of a Hurricane," *The Washington Post*, September 8, 1996, p. 26, described the impeding elections as a "travesty" and

recommended some variant of partition as an alternative to imposed cohabitation. The Office of the High Representative in Bosnia responded by labeling his critique "an almost certain recipe for a new war." "Response to Dr. Henry Kissinger's Article in the Washington Post of September 8," Office of the High Representative, Sarajevo, September 14, 1996, cited from *www.ohr.int/articles/a960914a.htm*.

157. Brendan O'Shea, "Bosnia's Muslim/Croat Federation: A Step in the Right Direction or Another Recipe for Disaster?" *Studies in Conflict and Terrorism*, Vol. 19, No. 4, 1996, pp. 403-412; and J. Stephen Morrison, "Bosnia's Muslim-Croat Federation: Unsteady Bridge Into the Future," *Mediterranean Quarterly*, Vol. 7, No. 1, 1996, pp. 132-150. An alternative perspective is provided by Daniel Serwer, "Bosnia: Peace by Piece," *Strategic Forum*, No. 81, 1996, pp. 1-4.

158. See Office of the High Representative, *Agreement on Mostar*, February 18, 1996, cited from *www.ohr.int/docu/d960218d.htm*.

159. "Mostar — daleko od zelja," *Republika*, No. 272, November 1-15, 2001, pp. 1-3.

160. Ranko Petrović, "Arbitration for the Brčko Area," *Review of International Affairs*, Vol. 47, No. 47, July 15-August 15, 1996, pp. 12-13. After postponements in April 1997 and February 1998, the arbitration committee finally made its decision on March 4, 1999. Following a plan developed by the independent International Crisis Group, Brčko was declared a "neutral" city and placed under the jurisdiction of the central state institutions of Bosnia-Herzegovina. It was thus removed from the jurisdiction of the Republika Srpska, but not granted to the Federation. An international administration was to be kept in place in the city "indefinitely," the entire district was to be demilitarized, and freedom of movement guaranteed (a point that was now a vital interest of the Bosnian Serbs) by SFOR. Inhabitants of the city (mostly Serb) and the environs (mostly Muslim) were free to choose their entity affiliation. Thomas Hofnung, *Désespoirs de paix: L'ex-Yougoslavie de Dayton à la chute de Milosevic*, Anglet: Atlantica, 2001, pp. 115-124.

161. The incidents were controlled by joint U.S.-Russian military action. See Mike O'Conner, "2nd Day of Bosnia Fighting is Worst Since '95 Pact," *The New York Times*, November 13, 1996, p. 1; Bill Sammon, "Bombs May Delay Muslims' Move Back Home," *European Stars and* Stripes, January 23, 1997, p. 1; Cindy Elmore, "Serbian Mob Levels Muslim Settlement," *European Stars and Stripes*, March 4, 1997, p. 1; and J. P. Barham, "Last Muslim Structure in Gajevi Burned Down," *European Stars and Stripes*, March 13, 1997, p. 1.

162. Carlos Westendorp, "Kosovo: las lecciones de Bosnia," *Politica Exterior*, Vol. 13, No. 70, July-August 1999, pp. 45-49.

163. Christine Wallich, "Policy Forum: Bosnia--After the Troops Leave," *The Washington Quarterly*, Vol. 19, No. 3, 1996, pp. 81-86.

164. John R. Lampe, Susan L. Woodward, and Mark S. Ellis, *Project on Bosnian Security and U.S. Policy in the Next Phase: Bosnian Economic Security After 1996*, Washington, DC:, East European Studies, The Woodrow Wilson International Center for Scholars, and The Atlantic Council of the United States, 1997.

165. Theodor Meron, "The Case for War Crimes Trials in Yugoslavia," *Foreign Affairs*, Vol. 72, No. 3, 1993, pp. 122-135.

166. Vojin Dimitrijevic, "The War Crimes Tribunal in the Yugoslav Context," *East European Constitutional Review*, Vol. 5, No. 4, Fall 1996, pp. 85-92. The courts was also accused of a "selective and historically unjust" anti-Serb bias--over half of the original indictees were Serbs. See Peter Brock, "The Hague Experiment in Orwellian Justice," *The Mediterranean Quarterly*, Vol. 7, No. 4, Fall, 1996, p. 62.

167. See the discussion of various casualty estimates in Burg and Shoup, *The War in Bosnia-Herzegovina*, pp. 169-170.

168. The tragedy of Bosnian multiculturalism is evoked in a considerable literature produced during the war. See Noel Malcolm, *Bosnia: A Short History*, New York: New York University Press, 1994; Robert J. Donia and John V. A. Fine, Jr., *Bosnia and Hercegovina: A Tradition Betrayed*, New York: Columbia University Press, 1994; and Ivan Lovrenović, *Unutarna zemlja: Kratki pregled kulturne povijesti Bosne i Hercegovine*, Zagreb: Durieux, 1998. Bougarel, *Bosnie*, pp. 25-52, portrays the conflict as a fatal consequence of Bosnia's communitarian tradition against the background of the collapse of central authority.

169. Radha Kumar, *Divide and Fall? Bosnia in the Annals of Partition*, London, Verso, 1997, p. 34. Kumar's study provides a useful comparative analysis of partition arrangements in the Indian sub-continent, Palestine, Ireland, Cyprus, and Bosnia-Herzegovina.

170. Burg and Shoup, *The War in Bosnia-Herzegovina*, p. 415.

171. Ted Galen Carpenter and Amos Perlmutter, "Strategy Creep in the Balkans: Up to Our Knees and Advancing," *The National Interest*, Vol. 44, Summer, 1996, p. 59; and Michael O'Hanlon, "Bosnia: Better Left Partitioned," *The Washington Post*, April 10, 1997, p. 25.

172. Susan L. Woodward, "The United States Leads, Europe Pays," *Transition*, Vol. 2, No. 14, July 12, 1996, pp. 12-16.

CHAPTER 5

WAR AND REVENGE IN KOSOVO, 1998-99

Kosova-Republic.

The inability of the Dayton negotiators to place the peace process in Bosnia within a strategic framework for the region as a whole proved to be a major failing. Yugoslavia's fragmentation had not yet run its course, and in the absence of a comprehensive settlement new challenges to the territorial status quo were certain to arise. One of these challenges, launched following the Dayton Accord in the Serbian province of Kosovo, would culminate, after several years of escalating tension, in a fourth Balkan war.

Few crises have been more consistently predicted than the one that erupted in Kosovo during the winter of 1997-98. Milošević had set off the process leading to the disintegration of the Yugoslav federation by abolishing Kosovo's autonomy in 1989 and subjecting the Kosovar Albanian majority to a demeaning occupation. The situation was untenable, and the observation that in Yugoslavia "everything started with Kosovo and everything will finish with Kosovo" quickly became a commonplace.[1] After Dayton, when United Nations' sanctions against Serbia and Montenegro were lifted without any reference to the situation in the province, support for radical alternatives grew. Given a tradition of Kosovar Albanian uprisings stretching back over several centuries, a turn to armed resistance was inevitable.

Kosovo's symbolic significance in Serbian national mythology, heavily Albanian demographic balance, and abject poverty made it a trouble spot from the moment of incorporation into the Serbian dynastic state in 1913. Albanians fought against Serbs during both 20th century world wars, and the province was only reintegrated into Titoist Yugoslavia at the end of the Second World War after the suppression of local resistance.[2] For two decades after the war Kosovo was subject to intrusive police controls under the authority of the Serb communist Aleksandar Ranković. The ouster of Ranković in 1966, after revelations of abuse of office, cleared the way for more open expressions of dissent that were not long in arriving. Tito reacted to protest demonstrations in 1968 with a policy of liberalization, permitting the display of the Albanian national flag as a Kosovar emblem, restructuring the University of Priština as a predominantly Albanian institution, channeling investment into the area in a vain attempt to close the development gap, and in the 1974 constitution granting Kosovo virtually full self-administration. These were hopeful initiatives, but expanded autonomy, paralleled by the elevation of a new, ethnically Albanian provincial leadership, created opportunities for provocations against the Serb minority.[3] Discrimination against Kosovar Serbs was never remotely as severe as what would eventually be depicted in the Serbian media, and presumed by the public, but it was deeply resented.[4]

In 1981, demonstrations by Kosovar Albanian students at the University of Priština spilled over into a general uprising.[5] The underlying cause of unrest was the failure of Yugoslav social policy to address the dilemmas of underdevelopment and discrimination.[6] Politically, the Kosovar Albanian response took the form of a classic ethnic mobilization. The leading slogan of the 1981 demonstrations became "Kosova-Republic," expressing the demand that Kosovo be elevated to the status of a seventh Yugoslav republic — an administrative transformation that would have granted Yugoslav Albanians the status of a constituent nation, including a notional right of secession.[7] The Albanian rising was the first major challenge to Yugoslav institutions of the post-Tito era, and it was put down harshly, with mass arrests and administrative reprisals against real and suspected sympathizers.[8]

The repression of 1981 created a generation of Kosovar Albanian resistors for whom Yugoslavia itself had become the enemy. In the mid-1980s a so-called Enverist faction (named for Albanian dictator Enver Hoxha) coalesced around a Marxist-Leninist position favoring armed struggle and a war of national liberation. In retrospect it appears that the movement's Marxist orientation was opportunistic. Beneath the radical veneer a group of militant nationalists, committed to a tactic of political violence in pursuit of the goal of a greater Albania, and with financial support from the Kosovar Albanian diaspora in Western Europe, was in the process of forming. Friction between Serbs and Kosovar Albanians provided a constant backdrop to the long agony of Yugoslav federalism during the 1980s, and under Serb occupation from 1989 onward Kosovo became a cauldron of injustice and anger, a vivid example of the dilemma of frustrated nationalism in a context of intercultural diversity that lies at the basis of the entire Balkan regional dilemma.[9]

The Kosovo Liberation Army.

From 1989 resistance to Serb domination was led by the Paris-educated university professor Ibrahim Rugova and his Democratic League of Kosovo (LDK). Rugova and a handful of associates, including the intellectuals Rexhep Qosja, Fehmi Agani, and Bujar Bukoshi, created the LDK in the wake of Milošević's abrogation of Kosovo autonomy with the explicit goal of forwarding national independence. On July 2, 1990, the Kosovo Assembly formally declared the province to be "an independent and equal entity within the framework of the Yugoslav federation," and was immediately dissolved and condemned as illegal by the Federal Presidency.[10] Several days later, on July 5, the group reconvened underground as the "Assembly of Kosova." Eventually, on September 21, 1991, it would declare the "Republic of Kosova" to be "a sovereign and independent state." This action was confirmed by a referendum conducted in defiance of Serbian authority from September 26-30 in which 87 percent of eligible voters were claimed to have participated, with 99.87 percent voting in support.[11] As the dominant force within the shadow government, the LDK promoted a strategy of nonviolent resistance that acknowledged Kosovo's weakness and exposure by refusing direct confrontations with the authorities, but simultaneously strove to signal the Kosovar Albanians' refusal to bend to the hegemony of Belgrade, denying the legitimacy of federal institutions, refusing participation in Yugoslav elections, and seeking to build up alternative national institutions run by the Kosovar Albanian majority. In elections of March 1992, once again conducted underground in defiance of a Serbian ban, Rugova was chosen president and his LDK, with 74.4 percent of the vote, won a clear majority in a self-proclaimed national parliament. Working within Kosovo's traditional clan structure, Rugova was successful in deflecting calls for more active resistance, and in March 1998 he was re-elected as shadow president. His party's emphasis upon the moral force of the Kosovar Albanian national cause was perhaps too successful — relative calm may have encouraged the illusion that the status quo in Kosovo was in some way sustainable, and made preventive action to head off a crisis seem less urgent. Rugova was however entirely unsuccessful in obtaining meaningful concessions from Milošević, who for his part was subjected to little pressure from the West to be more accommodating. Late in 1992, against the background of war in Croatia, President George Bush addressed a one sentence "Christmas Warning" cable to Milošević and his top military commanders, asserting that "in the event of conflict in Kosovo caused by Serbian actions, the United States will be prepared to employ military force against Serbians in Kosovo and in Serbia proper."[12] In view of Washington's reluctance to intervene in the conflict underway in Croatia, the statement, issued by a lame duck administration without reference to specific circumstances, may well have been taken with a grain of salt. Throughout the 1990s international pressure did not significantly affect Belgrade's determination to repress Kosovar Albanian national aspirations.

The suppression of Kosovo autonomy, the imposition of Rugova's nonviolent approach, and the preoccupation of the international community with the conflicts in Croatia and Bosnia-Herzegovina created a political vacuum that militants were quick to fill. In 1993 a so-called Kosovo Liberation Army (KLA) emerged from the radical wing of the Kosovo national movement as a focus for active resistance. The KLA combined Enverist radicals with their roots in the political contestation of the 1980s and Kosovar Albanians who had fought together with Croat and Muslim formations in Croatia and Bosnia or had been alienated by Milošević's strong-arm tactics, with Kosovo's native *kaçak* tradition of local resistance to central authority.[13] The rise of the KLA was a product of cumulating frustration with the inability of Rugova's strategy to achieve results, underlined by the failure of the Dayton peace conference to address the Kosovo dilemma in any meaningful way.[14] Its lowest common denominator was armed struggle, and in February 1996, with a core of about 150 militants, the organization launched a campaign of violence with a series of shootings and bomb attacks, in Priština, Vučitrn, Kosovska Mitrovica, Peć, Suva Reka, Podujevo, and elsewhere, against Serbian police stations, military casernes, post offices, and Kosovar Albanians suspected of collaboration with the oppressor. On January 16, 1997, in a symbolically significant incident, an auto bomb attack seriously wounded the new rector of what was now the Serb-administered University of Priština, Radivoje Papović. By October 1997 more than 30 Serbs and Kosovar Albanians had fallen victim to assaults, the central regions of Donji Prekaz and Drenica had become KLA controlled sanctuaries, and *The New York Times* was speaking of an organization "ready to wage a secessionist war that could plunge this country [the Federal Republic of Yugoslavia] into a crisis rivaling the conflict in Bosnia."[15] On November 28, 1997, the shadowy organization revealed itself publicly when three masked and uniformed fighters appeared in Lhausa and spoke briefly, before the cameras of Tirana television, at the funeral of KLA activist Halit Gecaj, a victim of the Serbian police.

The KLA's strength at the beginning of 1998 was estimated at around 500 active members, organized in small, mobile cells and often acting in groups of three to five rebels. The occasional violence perpetrated by the organization would probably not have become a major threat, had it not been for two precipitating events. The first was the collapse of the Albanian government in the spring of 1997 following the implosion of a state sponsored pyramid investment scheme. In the ensuing riots military casernes were looted and perhaps as many as a million light arms distributed to the population at large.[16] The tradition of bearing arms has deep roots among the Gheg clans of northern Albania and Kosovo, and many of the weapons found their way into the hands of KLA fighters, smuggled across the difficult terrain dividing Albania from Kosovo, or via western Macedonia. The second precipitating event was the decision by Yugoslav authorities to launch a campaign to suppress armed resistance. A police action on January 22, 1998, failed in the attempt to arrest Adem Jashari, the head of a powerful clan in the Drenica region whose defiance of authority was as much a part of the kaçak tradition as it was of KLA grand strategy, but who had become a symbol of local independence. An armed assault against the Jashari clan's redoubt in Donji Prekaz followed on March 5, leaving 58 dead in its wake including 18 women and 10 children under the age of 17.[17] The bloodbath had the predictable effect of galvanizing resentment, and in its wake the KLA mushroomed, according to some, possibly exaggerated estimates coming over the next several months to control as many as 20,000 armed fighters, and over 40 percent of the province's territory. In the narrow confines of Kosovo, however, its lightly armed militants were no match for the disciplined military forces of a modern state. Belgrade seems to have allowed the KLA to over extend and expose itself. In June 1998, the Yugoslav Army launched a counter offensive, massing over 40,000 troops operating with tanks, helicopters, heavy artillery, and mortar fire, that gathered momentum as it progressed and by late summer seemed to be on the verge of breaking organized resistance once and for all.[18]

Despite every possible warning, the major Western powers were unprepared for the flare up when it actually occurred. Throughout the 1990s Kosovo had been what Tim Judah calls "the place that the diplomats knew they should do something about, but were not sure what and anyway had more important things to do."[19] Numerous plans for compromise, including a partition arrangement that would have assigned a northeastern corridor to Serbia and allowed the remainder of the province to opt for either independence or attachment to Albanian, were developed during the 1990s, but none were consistently pursued.[20] Opportunities for preventive diplomacy were allowed to slip away, and international conflict management efforts were belated and reactive. The one serious attempt to address the situation in Kosovo preemptively was undertaken by the Rome-based Catholic religious order Sant'Egidio, which made some progress in developing an agenda for educational reform, useful in its own terms but insufficient to reverse a dynamic of confrontation.[21]

During 1997, as the KLA began to surface, the primary concern of U.S. policymakers was the need to cultivate Milošević's support for the ouster of the hardline leadership of the Republika Srpska, perceived to be blocking implementation of the Dayton Accord. Milošević was rewarded for cooperation by diplomatic concessions including approval for direct charter flights to the United States by the Yugoslav national airline, the reopening of a Yugoslav consulate in the United States, and an increase in the number of Yugoslavs allowed to participate in UN activities in New York. When U.S. special representative Robert Gelbard came to Belgrade on February 23, 1998, to announce these blessings, he added the observation that the KLA was "without any questions a terrorist group." In his public remarks, the U.S. emissary went out of his way to reiterate the point, stating that "having worked for years on counterterrorist activity, I know very well that to look at a terrorist group, to define it, you rip away the rhetoric and just look at actions. And the actions of this group speak for themselves."[22] Terrorist organizations had a specific status as pariahs in U.S. law, and declaratory policy was unequivocal — no tolerance, no compromise, no mercy. Although in private Gelbard conveyed to Milošević U.S. displeasure with Serbian heavy handedness and urged restraint, Washington seemed to be implying that the Kosovo problem would be left to the discretion of Belgrade, albeit within the bounds of prudence.

The Serbian blitz against the KLA was launched within a week of Gelbard's remarks, and the escalation of violence from February 1998 onward presented Western policymakers with a different kind of dilemma. The severity of Serbian reactions, which included the destruction of villages, execution of prisoners, and terrorization of the local population, was judged to be disproportionate.[23] In the immediate aftermath of the Serbian offensive influential voices in the U.S. media were raised calling for "a decisive international response," and, as the extent of violations became clear, sympathy for the Kosovar Albanian position became stronger.[24] Washington shifted direction to take account of these reactions. On March 4, Gelbard ascribed "overwhelming responsibility" to the government of Yugoslavia and described Serbian aggression as something "that will not be tolerated by the United States."[25] During a visit to London on March 7, Secretary of State Madeleine Albright urged "immediate action against the regime in Belgrade to ensure that it pays a price for the damage it has already done," and on March 13 National Security Advisor Sandy Berger specified that Milošević would be receiving the "escalating message . . . that the international community will not tolerate violent suppression of the Kosovans."[26]

Unfortunately, the KLA was a problem in its own right. The KLA was not a unitary movement with clear lines of internal authority. It was directed by a faceless leadership whose international allegiances were suspect and long-term aspirations unclear. As the political expression of a chronically divided society, the KLA was split along clan lines, between regional sub-groupings, and between émigré and internal lines of responsibility. The conflict in Kosovo also had significant implications for the Albanian Question as a whole. By 1998 former Albanian Prime Minister Sali Berisha, once the darling of the West for his outspoken anti-communism and publicly supportive of Rugova's LDK while in power, but *persona non grata* since the collapse of his corrupt personalist regime in the spring of 1997, had become one of the KLA's most visible supporters.[27] Berisha's political base lay in the Gheg regions of northern Albania, and the primarily Gheg Kosovar Albanian national movement was a logical ally in his continuing struggle against the predominantly Tosk leadership of new Albanian Prime Minister Fatos Nano. On the regional level, the KLA's political agenda could hardly have been more provocative: independence for Kosovo grown from the barrel of a gun as the first step toward the creation of a greater Albania including all or part of Albania proper, Serbia (Preševo, Bujanovac, Medvedja), Montenegro (Dukagjin, Plav, Rozaj), the Republic of Macedonia (Tetovo, Gostivar), and Greece (Chamuria). For Washington, whose regional policy had been constructed around the rubric to "restore stability," this was the agenda from hell. The KLA was launching an assault on the fragile equilibrium of the post-Dayton order in the entire southern Balkans that threatened to make Kosovo "the tinderbox of a general Balkan war."[28]

There was, of course, an Albanian Question to be considered, and the goal of a greater Albanian was not necessarily unacceptable in its own terms.[29] What was unpalatable were the means to which the KLA had resorted. To embrace the cause of the KLA in the midst of an ongoing armed struggle would set an unfortunate precedent for other frustrated separatist or irredentist movements tempted by a resort to arms. The logic of ethnic division that the KLA program espoused contrasted with the goal of reintegration inspiring the Dayton process in Bosnia-Herzegovina. Any progress toward independence threatened to subvert the neighboring Republic of Macedonia, with an Albanian minority constituting up to 30 percent of the population, concentrated in western Macedonia in districts physically contiguous with Kosovo, and with close links to the Kosovar Albanians reaching back to the days of shared citizenship inside federal Yugoslavia. Not least, support for the insurrection risked to set the stage for what might become an armed confrontation with Milošević's Serbia. Despite these risks, the Clinton administration stepped forward to revive the rhetoric of the 1992 Christmas Warning and present Belgrade with a stark choice between backing down or confrontation with the United States and its allies.

In the wake of the terrorist attacks against the United States launched on September 11, 2001, the challenge of terrorism has taken on a new weight in U.S. national security policy, and sympathy for organizations such as the KLA, which use irregular forces and violence against civilians to promote strategies of armed resistance in complex regional contingencies, has been reduced to practically nil. In his defense before the International Criminal Tribunal for Former Yugoslavia (ICTY) in The Hague, Milošević has emphasized the terrorist character of the KLA, including references to the organization's contacts with Osama bin Laden's al-Qaeda terror network and the engagement in Kosovo of al-Qaeda militants

trained in Afghanistan.[30] Reading history backward in this manner —
has its risks — U.S. policy during the Kosovo crisis was focused
upon the implications of the conflict itself, not necessarily its larger
ramifications or the weight of what may have been perceived as a
marginal engagement by what were at that point omnipresent al-
Qaeda operatives. The extremist character of the KLA, and its ties
to international terror networks with a powerful anti-American
commitment, nonetheless call attention to the contradictions of
Western policy during the genesis of an intervention that would
eventually be portrayed as a moral crusade, but that in fact was
driven by an ambiguous choice between unpalatable options.

Five Minutes to Midnight.

The Western powers were not anxious to engage in Kosovo,
but as Yugoslav reprisals continued, a hands-off attitude was
judged to be unsustainable. The severity of Serbian repression was
destabilizing. By the autumn, military operations had produced
over 200,000 internally displaced persons, and threatened to
provoke a humanitarian disaster should fighting be prolonged
through the winter months.[31] The West had justified its intervention
in Bosnia-Herzegovina on the premise that forceful ethnic cleansing
was unacceptable in modern Europe. Inaction in the face of the
events in Kosovo seemed to risk invalidating the *raison d'être* of
its considerable Balkan engagement. In addition, the KLA was a
reality that could not be ignored. Under siege, large segments of
the Kosovar Albanian population flocked to its banner, calling into
question Rugova's ability to represent his nation, and raising the
specter (perhaps encouraged by faulty intelligence estimates) of a
national insurrection sweeping out of control.

During the first weeks of the Serbian crackdown the premises of
Washington's approach to the problem were recast. Castigation of
the KLA as terrorist was quietly set aside, though the organization's
maximal agenda was not endorsed. Simultaneously, the anti-
Serbian edge of Western policy was reasserted. Serbian repression
was criticized and already on occasion interpreted not merely as an
exaggerated reaction to a domestic insurgency, but as a campaign
with genocidal intent directed against the Kosovar Albanian
population as a whole. Nonetheless, efforts were made to maintain
some kind of balance between the parties to conflict. During the

early stages of the fighting Washington sought to distance itself from both belligerents, to encourage dialogue between the Yugoslav government and Rugova's LDK, and to contain the fighting within the territory of the Federal Republic of Yugoslavia — moderate goals that could eventually be combined in the framework of a coherent policy response.

U.S. policy in the first phase of the crisis was built upon the assumptions that the KLA agenda for national independence was unacceptable, and Serbian repression disproportionate. The presumption that only domestic issues were at stake was rejected in light of massive human rights abuses and their implications for stability in the region, and the pursuit of a military solution on the part of both belligerents was condemned as a recipe for frustration. The preferred alternative was a diplomatic solution, including legal adjudication of human rights abuses mediated through the good offices of the West.[32] Rugova's LDK was considered the most legitimate representative of the Kosovar Albanians, and Washington placed considerable pressure on the organization (with only limited success), to build a more broadly based advisory board and distance itself from KLA extremism.[33]

On the Serbian side, there was no one to turn to other than the familiar devil Milošević, who once again assumed center stage as his country's primary interlocutor with the West. Though the terms of a solution were in principle to be left to the interested parties to determine, Washington made no secret of its preference for what Gelbard described on March 26, 1998, as "some form of enhanced status for Kosovo, within the borders of the Federal Republic of Yugoslavia."[34] Belgrade was characteristically defiant, and on April 23, 1998, the Milošević regime conducted a popular referendum in which 94.7 percent of the electorate rejected international mediation. Despite Serbian intransigence, however, the approach to the conflict articulated by Washington during the fighting of spring 1998 would be maintained with a great deal of consistency through the twists and turns that followed.

Concern for the spillover effects of the Kosovo conflict was greatest in neighboring Albania and Macedonia, and it was here that Western containment efforts were concentrated. Since 1992, the United Nations Preventive Deployment Force in Macedonia (UNPREDEP), made up primarily of U.S. and Scandinavian units deployed along the Macedonian-Serbian border, had been kept in place with the intent of monitoring any attempted Serbian move southward. When the normal extension of the UNPREDEP mandate was discussed in the UN Security Council in November 1997, however, the United States bowed to pressure from the Russian Federation and agreed to terminate the deployments after a final extension of nine months. Moscow's opposition was based upon the argument that progress toward stabilization in Bosnia-Herzegovina had made preventive deployments less necessary, but it also rested upon a calculated concern over the implications of a long term U.S. military presence in the area, and for the generally anti-Serb tenor of Western policy.

Faced with the need to find alternatives, Washington introduced a post-UNPREDEP package that included efforts to improve the combat readiness of Macedonian forces through expanded security assistance (the United States unilaterally increased its own security assistance allotment for Macedonia from $2 million to $8 million annually), and an expanded Partnership for Peace (PfP) individual partnership program, including an intensified agenda of joint exercises, strengthened military to military contacts, and the possibility of expanding Macedonia's Krivolak firing range into a permanent PfP center for peacekeeping training. This program was being discussed at the moment when large-scale violence erupted in Kosovo in February 1998, making the continued relevance of preventive deployments obvious to all. At the end of August 1998 the UNPREDEP mandate was renewed by consensus. The feuding over renewal had nonetheless revealed contrasting priorities within the international community, and did not bode well for the prospects of cooperation in the event of a crisis. Moreover, the issue of containing the Kosovo conflict at the Macedonian frontier, a task for which UNPREDEP was not equipped, was left unresolved.

In May 1998, with the situation becoming more explosive by the day, a NATO survey team undertook a preliminary study to estimate the feasibility of a preventive deployment in Albania. In April 1998, Belgrade and Tirana began to exchange accusations over the Kosovo problem, with Albanian Prime Minister Fatos Nano speaking of Serb responsibility for "pathological and traditional violence," and Yugoslav UN ambassador Vladislav Jovanović accusing Tirana of giving support to the KLA.[35] Blocking weapons trafficking and preventing the KLA from using Albania as a sanctuary seemed to be goals worth pursuing, but the NATO study concluded that upwards of 20,000 soldiers, combined with a major effort to build transportation corridors and ensure supply lines in an isolated and underdeveloped area, would be required to control the border. On the basis of these estimates NATO ruled out the option.[36] In a short time it would be required to make a much greater contribution of soldiers and material, and to fight a major war, in an effort to resolve the problems that preventive measures were intended to head off.

The Western effort to contain the Kosovo conflict in its early phases was spelled out by the May 28, 1998, Declaration on Kosovo issued at the NATO ministerial in Luxembourg.[37] The measures recommended included: (1) expanded PfP assistance to help the national armed forces of both Macedonia and Albania secure their frontiers; (2) a NATO-PfP joint exercise to be conducted in Macedonia during September 1998; (3) the establishment of a PfP partnership cell in Tirana and the conduct of a small PfP-led exercise during August; (4) the opening, beginning in July, of a permanent NATO naval facility at the Albanian port of Durrës; and (5) a commitment to expand UN and OSCE surveillance in the region. These measures were sufficient to prevent a short-term expansion of the conflict beyond the borders of Kosovo, but not to dampen the brush fire that was now blazing within the troubled province itself.[38]

Diplomatic alternatives were pursued through both bilateral and multilateral channels. At the first signs of trouble, the six-member International Contact Group was brought back to center stage as a vehicle for coordinating Balkan policy. In a statement of March 9, 1998, the Contact Group condemned "the use of excessive force by Serbian police against civilians" as well as "terrorist actions by the Kosovo Liberation Army" and outlined a series of measures intended to encourage dialogue.[39] Similar language appeared in UN Security Council Resolution 1160, promulgated on March 31, which condemned excessive use of force against civilians, imposed an arms embargo against the Federal Republic of Yugoslavia, and concluded with the vague threat of "additional measures" in the absence of progress toward a settlement.[40] The North Atlantic Council (NAC) issued its first statement on the problem on March 5, 1998, expressing "profound concern" and pledging engagement to prevent escalation and "promote security and stability."[41] At the end of May, the NATO ministerial in Luxembourg defined the situation in Kosovo as "unacceptable," and in June the EU foreign ministers agreed, together with the United States, to impose a ban on investments and to freeze Serbian foreign assets.[42] The ICTY was accorded the authority to investigate and prosecute violations in Kosovo, and during July its head prosecutor, Louise Arbour, announced that the situation in the province met the standards of an "armed conflict" where the laws of war would apply.

The United States weighed in diplomatically through its ambassador to Macedonia Christopher Hill, who took the lead in coordinating diplomatic communication inside Kosovo with representatives of the KLA and LDK. Special envoy Holbrooke was also brought back into the limelight as a channel to the leadership in Belgrade. At a May 15 meeting between Milošević and Rugova organized under Holbrooke's auspices, Belgrade formally committed itself to discussions with representatives of the Kosovar Albanian community.[43] Urged on by Washington, on June 12 the International Contact Group, joined by the foreign ministers of Canada and Japan, drew up a ten-point program, including calls for: (1) an immediate cease-fire; (2) international monitoring; (3) access for the UN High Commissioner for Refugees and international NGOs; and (4) dialogue between Belgrade and the Kosovar Albanians under the auspices of international mediators.[44] The negotiations led nowhere, however, and the momentum of the Serbian offensive unfolding on the ground was not discernibly slowed.

The missing ingredient appeared to be coercion. In its efforts to build a united front of opposition to the Serbian crackdown, Washington was successful in creating a façade of unity among key Western allies around the lowest common denominator of respect for international humanitarian law. Soon, however, military action as a means to compel Serbian compliance was being evoked. On June 15-16, 1 day prior to a scheduled visit by Milošević to Moscow, NATO conducted an exercise in the skies over Macedonia and Albania entitled Operation DETERMINED FALCON, demonstrating its capacity to react with air power to provocations on the ground. NATO foreign ministers also announced the scheduling of PfP exercises in Albania for August and September. During a summer visit to Moscow German Foreign Minister Klaus Kinkel upped the ante by remarking that in the event that the situation in Kosovo did not improve military intervention might be necessary, noting that it was already "five minutes to midnight."[45] On June 16, following talks with Russian President Boris Yeltsin, and on the basis of a commitment "on the necessity of preservation of the territorial integrity and respect of sovereignty of the Federal Republic of Yugoslavia," Milošević agreed to grant access to the province to 150 international observers organized under OSCE auspices as the Kosovo Diplomatic Observer Mission (KDOM).[46] At this point a combination of diplomatic pressure and threats of force seemed to be bearing fruit.

Appearances were deceiving, and it quickly became apparent that in the case of Kosovo a military option would be highly disputatious. Whatever the violations for which it was responsible, Yugoslavia was a sovereign state engaged in putting down an armed insurrection on what was acknowledged as its own territory. External intervention on behalf of an armed secessionist movement would create a disturbing precedent. Any kind of military strikes against Serbia would inevitably contribute to the campaign of the KLA, an effect that Washington and its allies were anxious to avoid. And there were significant sources of dissension. Russia, clinging to its historical role as protector of the Serbs in an effort to salvage some leverage in the region, rejected the military option point blank, refused to sanction air strikes against Yugoslavia in UN or OSCE forums, and warned of "serious international consequences" should NATO act without a formal international mandate.[47] NATO asserted a right to intervene regardless, on the basis of existing UN resolutions and in a case of urgent humanitarian necessity, but it was not internally united. Behind the scenes numerous allies, including Denmark, France, Germany, Greece, Italy, and Spain, expressed reluctance to engage the Alliance without approval from a mandating authority.[48]

The orchestrated campaign of coercive diplomacy reached its culmination in the autumn. On September 23 the UN Security Council (with China abstaining) passed Resolution 1199 describing the situation in the province as a "threat to peace and security in the region" that demanded "immediate action" on behalf of peace, and calling for a ceasefire, withdrawal of Yugoslav forces from Kosovo, free access for the international community, and the return of refugees and internally displaced persons.[49] On the following day, NATO defense ministers meeting in Villamoura, Portugal, issued Activation Warnings for two different kinds of military responses, described as *Limited Air Response* (short term, punishing retaliation aimed at fixed targets such as headquarters, communication relays, and ammunition drops) and *Phased Air Campaign* (a five-phase air operation moving from the suppression of Yugoslav air defenses through attacks against major force components). These options rested upon an extensive NATO planning effort that had been underway since June 1998, and that had produced a palette of no less than 40 air campaign variants.[50] Western policy had now shifted toward compellence, with NATO in the role of enforcer.

On October 1 the NAC issued an Activation Request for both limited and phased air options, and at U.S. urging, NATO began the process of decision on the issuance of Activation Orders (ACTORDs). Several days later a long-awaited report from UN Secretary General Kofi Annan was sharply critical of the "wanton killing and destruction" in Kosovo, and in its wake Holbrooke presented Milošević with an ultimatum demanding an immediate pullback.[51] In an address to the Cleveland Council on World Affairs on October 9, Deputy Secretary of State Strobe Talbott provided a rationale for the use of force by defining the situation in Kosovo as "a clear and present danger to our vital national interests."[52] On October 13, confronting what appeared to be an imminent threat of attack, Serbian President Milan Milutinović announced acceptance in principle of a compromise, including a pullback of heavy weapons and major force contingents, return to normal peacetime police monitoring, and a pledge of proportionate response to provocation.[53] The NAC, pushed forward by Secretary General Solana, nonetheless went ahead with its ACTORD decision, accompanied by a 96-hour "pause" to allow Belgrade to demonstrate good intentions. An agreement signed by Yugoslav Foreign Minister Vladislav Jovanović and OSCE representative Bronislav Geremek on October 16 permitted the creation of a 2000-member OSCE Kosovo Verification Mission (KVM), which was endorsed by the UN Security Council 1 week later, and the launching of a NATO air surveillance mission to monitor compliance.[54] Belgrade dragged its feet on disengagement, but under pressure eventually accepted NATO's conditions intact.[55] On October 27 the NAC finally suspended its programmed air strikes. The relevant ACTORDs were not cancelled, however, with NATO reserving the right to execute them at a later date if necessary. Several weeks later a Kosovo Verification Coordination Center was established in order to reinforce "liaison, planning, coordination and information exchange" with NATO.[56] Coercive diplomacy, ratcheted up to the point of an imminent threat of air attack, seemed to have pushed Milošević to his breaking point.

The exercise in coercion placed considerable strain on the Western Alliance. The kind of friction inherent in the use of NATO in an intrusive peace enforcement capacity was made clear in the days immediately following Belgrade's concessions by the revelation of what was presented as a serious breach of security. NATO staff officer and French Major Pierre-Henri Bunel was accused of passing targeting data for eventual air strikes on to Belgrade, an action interpreted by some as the product of "a dominant climate within French military circles of sympathy for the Serbian cause" born of empathy for a traditional ally.[57] The speaker of the Russian parliament Gennadi Seleznev stated bluntly that in the event of military action against Belgrade he would initiate legislation to withdraw from the Permanent Joint Council defining a special relationship between Russia and NATO. The issue of NATO intervention was the first significant foreign policy decision for the new German governing coalition of Chancellor Gerhard Schröder and Foreign Minister Joschka Fischer, both, in their youth, self-proclaimed pacifists and opponents of NATO. While committing to respect alliance commitments, Berlin asserted the right to repose the issue in the future, and was particularly insistent about the need to keep diplomatic options open.[58] Perhaps most significant in the long-term, a joint Anglo-French declaration on European defense signed in Saint Malo, France, on December 4, 1998, reflected disgruntlement with Washington's forcing inside the Alliance by urging the EU to create "the capacity for autonomous action backed up by credible military forces, the means to use them and readiness to do so in order to respond to international crises."[59] This was a first step in the direction of an autonomous European Security and Defense Policy separate and distinct from that defined by the Atlantic Alliance.

In retrospect it is clear that the Western conflict management effort in Kosovo was belated and ineffective. It was also seriously confused about ends and means. During most of the 1990s, Rugova's adherence to a policy of nonviolence gave the Kosovar Albanian faction considerable moral authority and provided space for proactive policies designed to soften Serbian repression in the context of an overall regional settlement. By the time that the issue was pushed onto the international agenda during 1998 hopes for a negotiated outcome had all but evaporated, and between Kosovar Albanian extremism and Serbian brutality, there was very little to choose. A decade of conflict and broadening Western engagement had made the Balkans too seminal a region to allow for a do-nothing option. The Serbian side was uniformly perceived as being primarily responsible, Western patience with Milošević and his cynical maneuvering had long since grown thin, and further toleration for Serbian defiance was not judged to be desirable. But the precedent of terrorist violence and armed secession being established by the KLA was disturbing. Lodged between a rock and a hard place, during the first phase of the Kosovo crisis U.S. diplomacy sought to impose a weak compromise through the threat of coercion. In very short order, the limitations of the approach would become painfully clear.

War and Revenge.

The Holbrooke-Milošević accord was concluded a full 8 months after the Serbian campaign of repression had been launched. By the time that crisis diplomacy was cranked up to confront the problem, large swaths of Kosovo had already been devastated by war, some 750 Kosovar Albanians killed, and over 200,000 internally displaced persons set on the road to nowhere. Under the circumstances, and given the effort that had been expended to assemble an apparatus of coercion, the accord itself was remarkably tepid. Yugoslav authorities agreed to pull their special military units out of the province, but the withdrawal came after the KLA infrastructure had been reduced to tatters and at the onset of the winter season where serious campaigning would be much more difficult. The Serbs were permitted to maintain police and military levels equivalent to those in place under what had been a virtual martial law regime prior to February 1998. Compliance was to be monitored by the 2,000 unarmed members of the KVM, assisted by an air verification mission coordinated by NATO and designated as Operation EAGLE EYE.[60] The modest contingent of observers threatened no one, and had itself to be protected by a 1,500 member extraction force, dubbed Operation DETERMINED GUARANTOR, led by the French and based in Macedonia.[61] The accord included pledges by the Serbs to engage in good faith negotiations with Kosovar Albanian representatives aimed at reestablishing local self-government with a 3-year time frame for the restoration of Kosovo's autonomy, a general amnesty for resistance fighters, cooperation with the work of the UN war crimes tribunal to identify responsibility for violations of the laws of war, the convening of elections for the autumn of 1999, and a program to facilitate the return of refugees and internally displaced persons. These guidelines were by no means punitive — Belgrade could have lived with them without any fear of loss of control within the province.

There were at least two wild cards standing in the way of a peaceful settlement. The first was the KLA itself, in no way a party to the October accord, and committed to continue its campaign of armed resistance despite setbacks. The second was the determination of the authorities in Belgrade to press their advantage and put paid to Kosovar Albanian resistance when the opportunity presented itself. The KLA had accumulated a good deal of international sympathy in its unequal struggle with the Yugoslav authorities and was anxious to make use of it. Milošević had watched closely as NATO struggled with the "appalling and unenviable choice" to intervene, and was aware that alliance cohesion was weak.[62] The October accord did not effectively constrain either party to the conflict, and the small KVM contingent that moved slowly into place lacked the means to demand respect. By January 1999 only 800 of the 2,000 observers originally pledged had arrived, and when the mission was withdrawn in March, it had not grown beyond 1,400.[63] As in Bosnia-Herzegovina, the international community had moved to address symptoms rather than underlying problems. A different approach might have provided for a more robust presence of alliance ground forces adjacent to Kosovo as a mechanism for intimidation, or even worked to secure Belgrade's approval for a full-fledged international protectorate inside the province that would have assured its continued attachment to Yugoslavia. Such solutions were rejected by the Clinton administration, which sought to minimalize U.S. exposure and placed its bets on bluff. Without mechanisms to enforce respect for the accord, whether to prevent the Kosovar Albanians from exploiting partial Serbian compliance to their own advantage, or to block Serbian reprisals in the face of new provocations, the October bargain was condemned to failure.

Predictably, as Serbian forces pulled back as agreed, KLA fighters moved forward to occupy the vacated terrain. Soon sporadic fighting had resumed. In December, Serbian "training exercises" near Podujevo, undertaken without prior notification to the OSCE, developed into larger scale offensive operations against KLA units in clear violation of the October understanding. The seminal event in the new escalation occurred on January 15, 1999, in the village of Račak in the rebellious Drenica region, where a Serbian punitive action left 45 civilians dead, including two women and a 12-year-old boy.

The question of what exactly happened in Račak has been hotly contested. The version of events announced to the world in the immediate aftermath of the killing suggested that Serbian units in pursuit of a small KLA contingent occupied the village and massacred its inhabitants as an admonition to those tempted to offer sanctuary to the guerrillas.[64] One of the first international observers to arrive on the scene was the former U.S. ambassador William Walker, now serving as head of the OSCE KVM force. Upon viewing the corpses of the victims, Walker flew into a rage, accusing the Serbian side of conducting a willful massacre, and announcing his convictions via telephone to U.S. leaders.[65] There was some impropriety in Walker's communication with American decisionmakers in view of his primary responsibility to the OSCE, but it is the substance of his report, and the political uses to which it was put, that is, most vividly disputed. Broadcast around the world, Walker's judgment went far to condition public sentiment for an eventual military campaign against Serbia. Within days, the U.S. Department of State would condemn the event as a "massacre of civilians by Serb security forces," while NATO Secretary General Solana spoke of "a flagrant violation of international humanitarian law."[66] Subsequent international investigations of the incident have however failed to produce forensic evidence that would indicate that a massacre occurred, and suggest that it remains possible (as Serb observers had argued at the time) that the cadavers displayed at Račak were those of fallen resistance fighters and innocent bystanders killed in the fighting, gathered together from over a wider area by villagers under KLA direction, and presented as victims of a purposeful massacre with the express purpose of swaying international sentiment against the Serbs.[67]

Whether or not the events at Račak were intentionally manipulated or misrepresented to strengthen the case for Western intervention, they cast discredit on Serbian forces and increased pressure for an international response. On January 15, with the fighting at Račak underway, the U.S. National Security Council defined its goals in the crisis as to "promote regional stability and protect our investment in Bosnia; prevent the resumption of hostilities in Kosovo and renewed humanitarian crisis; [and] preserve U.S. and NATO credibility."[68]

General Wesley Clark echoed this conclusion in his evaluation of the impact of Račak by suggesting that in the wake of the killing "NATO's credibility was on the line."[69] All of the U.S. goals were placed at risk by the disintegration in course, and least of all could the Alliance allow the perception that it had once again, as in Bosnia, become complacent in view of a policy of massacre. Meeting in London on January 29, ministers representing the International Contact Group cut to the chase by demanding that representatives of Yugoslavia and the Kosovar Albanians come together under international auspices for proximity talks at the French château of Rambouillet, located in the environs of Paris.[70] On January 30 the NAC issued a statement lending its support to the Contact Group initiative and threatening a forceful response in the event of non-compliance. It also granted NATO Secretary General Solana full authority to approve air strikes against targets within the Federal Republic of Yugoslavia if events so merited — an important derogation of responsibility that in effect negated the possibility for a single-member veto to block action.[71] The stage was once again set for an exercise in coercive diplomacy that was intended to conclude with a Western-imposed peace plan.

The plan itself, drawn up by the Contact Group and closely modeled on the Dayton Accord, consisted of a framework agreement establishing guidelines for a peace process, accompanied by a number of annexes treating specific aspects of implementation.[72] The key security and civilian implementation annexes were the source of considerable behind the scenes squabbling among the Western allies, with differences emerging over the familiar issue of a UN mandate, the role of NATO (whose representatives were banned from the Rambouillet sessions by the French hosts), distribution of responsibility between the security component of an implementation mission and its civilian component, and the extent of U.S. participation in a proposed Kosovo occupation force. The Rambouillet sessions were underway for a full week before final texts had been agreed upon. This was not necessarily a critical lapse in view of the fact that the program was not intended as a working text open to discussion — it was presented as an ultimatum to take or leave under threat of reprisals. But the differences between the allies over the substance of the agreement did not bode well.[73]

In its final form the Rambouillet accord called for an immediate cession of hostilities; the partial withdrawal and demilitarization of all armed forces inside Kosovo; guarantees of civil rights; and a peace settlement that would grant Kosovo expanded autonomy within Yugoslavia in the short term, and allow a binding referendum on the province's final status after 5 years. The security annex provided for the occupation of the province by a NATO-led international force, based upon a status of forces contract that would also provide for a right of access to the entire territory of the Federal Republic of Yugoslavia. To the surprise and chagrin of the mediators present, these terms were not accepted by either of the parties to the negotiations. The Serbian delegation, without high level representatives and totally dependent upon approval from Belgrade, accepted the plan in outline but raised numerous objections to various aspects of implementation. Milošević was clearly anxious to avoid any agreement that would allow for the deployment of NATO forces on Yugoslav territory.[74] The Kosovar Albanian delegation, uncomfortably combining representatives of the KLA and LDK, and headed by KLA hard liner Hashim Thači, objected to any arrangement that would leave Kosovo a part of Yugoslavia, even for an interim period.[75] The intransigence of the parties was a diplomatic embarrassment that seemed to indicate the limits of Western leverage.

Faced with a potential failure that would compromise the entire mediation effort, the original 23 February deadline for an accord was extended and a new round of talks scheduled for March 15 in the Kleber Center in Paris. During the intervening weeks, Western efforts were directed almost entirely toward bringing Thači and the Albanian delegation around. The winning argument appears to have been that without the Kosovar Albanians on board, punitive military strikes against Serbia would have to be suspended. Holbrooke visited Belgrade on March 10 and conveyed the message that without Serbian compliance, military action was inevitable. At the second round of talks at the Kleber Center from March 15-19, the Kosovar Albanian delegation delivered its promised signature, while the Serbs demurred and called for continued dialogue.[76] The United States offered 28,000 NATO peacekeepers, including 4,000 U.S. soldiers, to supervise a negotiated settlement, but the real focus of the American effort was to win over the KLA as a means to sanction punitive strikes against Serbia.[77] Upon departure from Paris after the conclusion of the sessions on March 19, the Serbian delegation denounced the terms of the accord as a Western ultimatum in violation of international law.[78] Simultaneously, Serbian forces began to mass in and around Kosovo in what appeared to be preparations for a confrontation.[79]

The Rambouillet proximity talks had failed to produce a negotiated accord, but they were successful in creating a pretext for military action. Immediately upon the departure of the Yugoslav delegation, the machine of war was set into motion. On March 19 the KVM was withdrawn from Kosovo, and on March 21 Holbrooke arrived in Belgrade to deliver a final admonition to Milošević, who dutifully refused to receive him. On March 23 Solana directed the SACEUR, U.S. General Wesley Clark, to begin air operations against Yugoslavia. One day later, in the mist and rain of an early Balkan spring, Operation ALLIED FORCE was launched.

The decision to resort to force in Kosovo remains controversial, in part because Serbian motives during the events leading up to hostilities can only be inferred. Western goals were clearly stated and unquestionably defensible, but the means chosen to pursue them were debatable. NATO had launched an attack against a sovereign state engaged in suppressing a domestic insurgency without a convincing international mandate. During the year preceding the attack, approximately 2,000 people had died as a result of violence associated with the uprising in the province — tragic, but far from the "genocidal" violence that some denounced. The UN High Commissioner for Refugees established that some 250,000 Kosovar Albanians had chosen to leave their homes under duress — likewise tragic, but hardly a humanitarian disaster of unprecedented dimensions.[80] The legitimacy of NATO's appeal to urgent humanitarian necessity as a justification for action was therefore open to question.[81] The Rambouillet plan contained conditions (freedom of operation for NATO forces throughout the entire territory of Yugoslavia and the designation of a binding referendum on Kosovo's final status that would almost certainly result in a choice for independence) that would have been difficult for any government in Belgrade to accept.[82] It was moreover presented as an ultimatum under threat of force, in contravention of international legal precepts, which do not recognize agreements concluded as a result of coercion. By intervening against one party to a civil dispute, NATO adopted an objectively partisan stance that belied its own rhetoric of neutrality. The most detailed Western account of U.S. decisionmaking during the crisis argues baldly that the purpose of Rambouillet was not to promote a diplomatic accord, but rather "to create a consensus in Washington and among the NATO allies that force would have to be used."[83] For its many critiques, by precluding diplomatic options and precipitating events before the threat of force could be made credible, Rambouillet became "a text book example of how not to conduct diplomacy."[84]

It remains the case that Serbia's aggressive approach to the Kosovo problem was clearly a problem. Fighting over the past year had already created a wave of refugees that threatened to throw neighboring states into chaos, and the situation only promised to grow worse. NATO's initiative could therefore reasonably be portrayed as a legitimate reaction to a "pending humanitarian catastrophe" created by the willful policies of a defiant Belgrade.[85] Though the air war option may not have been an optimal response in purely military terms, it was the only response that was politically feasible, and some kind of riposte was absolutely necessary. Even at lower levels of violence, Belgrade's provocations were a challenge to NATO, the anchor for U.S. forward presence in Europe and the keystone of the continent's security architecture. In October 1998 coercive diplomacy had been tried and failed. Now it was the turn of coercion pure and simple.

Operation ALLIED FORCE.

The military confrontation between NATO and Yugoslavia opened with significant strategic miscalculations on both sides.

Allied terms for conflict termination were defined at the outset of the contest and adhered to with great consistency thereafter: an end to violence and military operations in Kosovo, withdrawal of Serbian military and police forces, acceptance of a NATO-led international monitoring force, return of refugees and internally displaced persons, and commitment to a political framework on the basis of the Rambouillet accord, including expanded autonomy for a democratic Kosovo inside the Yugoslav federation. This was a "Serbs out, NATO in, refugees back" scenario that the Alliance would stick with to the bitter end. Political goals were linked to a military strategy that focused upon the use of air power to suppress defenses and allow unhindered NATO operations in Yugoslav air space, isolate the Yugoslav Third Army inside Kosovo and degrade its combat capacity, and coerce acceptance of NATO peace terms. In the words of U.S. President Clinton, in his address to the nation announcing the commencement of air operations, NATO forces were tasked to "demonstrate the seriousness of NATO's opposition to aggression," deter Milošević from "escalating his attacks on helpless civilians," and "damage Serbia's capacity to wage war against Kosovo by seriously diminishing its military capabilities."[86]

In the wake of the Kosovo conflict, U.S. Air Force Lieutenant General Michael Short, Commander of Allied Air Forces Southern Europe and the U.S. 16th Air Force headquartered in Aviano, Italy, during the campaign, criticized his political masters for failing to develop "clear political objectives" to guide military commanders.[87] Short's assertion is in some ways unfair — in Kosovo, the political end state that military force was intended to facilitate was articulated about as clearly as circumstances permitted. What was less than clear were the appropriate means for achieving stated objectives. Key NATO allies were uncomfortable from the start with the resort to air attacks to coerce a fellow European state. The Clinton administration was convinced that limited bombing strikes would suffice to force Serbian compliance, but loath to follow the logic of coercion to the end of unconstrained warfare, possibly including conventional ground combat operations.[88] As a result, NATO made a conscious decision to go to war with one hand tied behind its back. U.S. decisionmakers were particularly concerned with the fragility of public support for a protracted war in the Balkans, and for the impact of a costly and indecisive contest upon alliance cohesion. In the summer of 1998 alliance planners developed a full range of military options for contingencies in Kosovo, but U.S. political leaders publicly ruled out any commitment of ground forces in a "nonpermissive" environment.[89] According to a study prepared by the RAND Corporation on behalf of the U.S. Army, ground options were never seriously considered during the planning process. The report states unequivocally that: "from mid-1998 onward, not only was this option [ground operations] shelved, no serious contingency planning for air-land operations was undertaken. The exclusive planning focus was on air and missile strikes."[90] In his March 24 address Clinton announced peremptorily that "I do not intend to put our troops in Kosovo to fight a war."[91] On that foundation, limited air strikes were initiated on the basis of what would soon prove to be the unfounded assumption that several days of bombing would suffice to convince Milošević that capitulation was his best option. On the evening of March 24, speaking to a national television

246

audience, Secretary of State Madeleine Albright was forthright in declaring to the U.S. public, but also to its adversaries in a theater of war, that "I don't see this as a long-term operation."[92] The United States aspired to stage a punitive action, not to wage war in the classic sense. The "whole purpose of the NATO effort," in the words of General Clark, "was to empower diplomacy."[93] As a consequence, its military operations unfolded under rules of engagement that have been described as "uncompromisingly restrictive."[94]

During the air war in Kosovo, allied combat commanders were instructed to avoid casualties at all costs.[95] NATO air attacks were never entirely successful in suppressing layered and redundant Serb air defense systems, including the threat of radar-guided surface to air missiles, and to reduce risk, during most of the campaign air strikes were launched from above a medium altitude ceiling of 5,000 meters. These precautions made it possible to limit losses, and during the campaign only two NATO aircraft were downed by hostile fire, but the price was decreased operational efficiency, and at least one well-publicized incident where the difficulties of visual discrimination from high altitude led to a tragic targeting error. Misgivings on the part of some alliance members and the lack of a valid mandate made NATO particularly sensitive to the issue of collateral damage, imposing restrictions on the kinds of targets that commanders were allowed to attack, and creating opportunities for sanctuary that Serbian forces were able to exploit. Procedures for target approval involving all of the NATO allies, thrown together hastily after the initiation of hostilities, proved to be especially cumbersome and led to what the chair of the NATO Military Committee, German General Klaus Naumann, would later call "a lowest-common-denominator approach" to target selection.[96] The assumption that punitive strikes would do the job, difficulties in suppressing air defenses, politically imposed conditions dictating minimal losses, restrictive rules of engagement, and the inevitable constraints associated with coalition warfare, excluded reliance upon preferred U.S. Air Force doctrine, recommending the application of overwhelming force against a full spectrum of targets from the outset of a campaign.[97]

Working within these constraints, the SACEUR developed plans for a three-phase air campaign. In Phase I, antiaircraft defenses and command posts would be targeted. Phase II was to extend attacks to strategic infrastructure beyond the 44th parallel. In Phase III Belgrade itself would come under attack. The plan actually implemented on March 24 envisioned strikes against a modest total of 50 pre-approved targets, and presumed that 2 to 4 days of bombing would suffice to provide Milošević with a face-saving pretext to pull out after having offered token resistance. Unfortunately, it quickly became apparent that the Serbian leader had no such intention, and that the intensity of the campaign as it had been planned would not be sufficient to achieve U.S. goals.

What followed in the first weeks of the campaign, in the words of one critic, was a "chaotic, unscripted, and confused" effort to adapt to the unforeseen.[98] General Clark spelled out the alternative to a strategy of intimidation in a briefing on March 25, arguing for the need "to systematically and progressively attack, disrupt, degrade, devastate . . . and destroy" Serbia's ability to wage war.[99] This represented a significant escalation of military goals that many allied political leaders were not prepared for. It was not until the NATO summit in Washington on April 23 that the Alliance formally approved an intensification of the air operation by expanding the target set to military-industrial infrastructure and other strategic targets, and committing to the deployment of additional aircraft. By this point, hopes for a short war had long since been discarded.

Yugoslav miscalculations were even more severe. Milošević may well have been surprised when NATO mustered the will to launch its original attack. Upon the initiation of hostilities his strategy became to hunker down and limit damage, seek to disrupt the allied war effort asymmetrically, and hope for friction within the Alliance to create pressure for a compromise peace. The Serbian population predictably rallied behind its leadership with the nation under attack. Large demonstrations expressing scorn for NATO's air war were organized in Belgrade and other urban centers, the wrecked fuselage of a downed F-117 "Stealth" fighter was prominently displayed as a trophy, and citizens paraded in the streets with small targets pinned to their lapels to symbolize defiance. Anti-war sentiment was also manifested in Western Europe — using NATO as an instrument for waging war against a neutral European state was an inherently risky undertaking, and one that was bound to stir up resentment. In 4 days of bombing raids against Iraq in December 1998 (Operation DESERT FOX) conducted mainly by the United States and the United Kingdom, punitive air attacks were used to demonstrate political will but without seeking any kind of decisive strategic result. Milošević may have convinced himself that a similar demonstration was what the West had in mind in the case of Yugoslavia, and that by weathering the initial storm, while banking on declining allied cohesion as the war effort became more demanding, his position in a negotiated settlement would be strengthened.[100]

Most dramatically, the campaign of ethnic cleansing within Kosovo was radically expanded. Within days of the first air strikes, tens of thousands of Kosovar Albanians fled from their homes in a ghastly exodus that would quickly reach near biblical proportions. By the end of the war, according to the UN High Commissioner for Refugees, 848,100 refugees had left the province — approximately 40 percent of the total population. The majority of these hapless victims were pushed across the border into Montenegro, Macedonia, or Albania, where makeshift camps were hastily set up to care for them. Though it would later be claimed that the problem had been foreseen, the internationally community was clearly unprepared for a wave of refugees of this dimension.[101]

Western sources, citing classified intelligence reports, have argued that the massive ethnic cleansing was carefully planned and had already been set in motion, under the designation Operation HORSESHOE, in the days prior to March 24.[102] This explanation was made public by the office of German Defense Minister Rudolf Scharping in the first days of the conflict, and it has served ever since to deflect criticism that the Alliance's military action had provoked the very humanitarian disaster its was intended to head off. In light of the Bosnian precedent, it was hard not to believe the worst of the Serbian leadership. "In Kosovo," wrote J. Bryan Hehir in the midst of the conflict, "prefigured by the ethnic cleansing of Bosnia, the world . . . knows exactly what is happening, and we know who is responsible."[103] Milošević had an obvious motive. The flood of refugees disrupted alliance planning, and forced a significant commitment of resources to emergency relief. Had he been able to break Alliance will and negotiate a ceasefire with the refugees still dispersed outside the borders of Kosovo, Milošević would have affected a decisive shift in the demographic balance within the disputed province to Serbia's advantage. But the Western powers also had a strong vested interest in justifying their decision to intervene on the basis of preplanned and egregious Serbian transgressions that they were not in a position to control. Indeed, some commentators have questioned whether an operational plan dubbed "Horseshoe" ever existed except as a product of Western disinformation.[104] During his trial in The Hague, Milošević has challenged the existence of the plan by noting that the Western sources describing it rendered the term "Horseshoe" with the Croatian *potkovica* rather than the more common Serb variant *potkova*.[105] This was a linguistically dubious assertion, that was perhaps intended to impress the judges more than fellow Serbs, but the ICTY proceeded on its own behalf to exclude documents outlining plans for Operation HORSESHOE as potential forgeries.

Without access to Serbian archival sources that could presumably shed a more definitive light on the issue, the assumption of premeditation and careful planning does not correspond to what we know about how the expulsions actually occurred. Rather than unfolding in a coordinated and systematic manner, there were widespread regional variations. Some communities were expelled en masse while others were barely affected. Local reprisals and the undisciplined comportment of soldiers seeking to wreck revenge upon communities judged responsible for the NATO attacks played an important role in individual cases. As in Bosnia, ill-disciplined paramilitary forces were responsible for some of the worst abuses. Though it is impossible to relieve Milošević of ultimate responsibility, many of the refugees fled out of simple fear of being caught up in a war zone. Tim Judah comes closest to our actual knowledge of events when he suggests that "haphazard expulsion plans . . . coupled with . . . the 'we'll f . . . them' attitude, plus fighting, terror, and lack of food and all the other circumstances of the war led to the exodus."[106]

What is beyond dispute is that by provoking the exodus, whether purposively or haphazardly, Milošević had cast down a gauntlet that the Western Alliance could not fail to pick up, solidifying public opinion in support of the war effort and virtually ensuring his own eventual defeat. Televised images of the teaming refugee encampments became an enduring symbol of the war, and galvanized international sentiment in much the same way that the shelling of Sarajevo had done several years earlier. The impact of these events was magnified in the short term by undocumented but widely dispersed reports of massacres. Subsequent investigations failed to substantiate the rumors, but their effect was considerable, and the spectacle of mass flight was undeniable and damning. Yugoslavia had purchased a short-term disruption of the allied campaign by casting itself as a pariah. In consequence support for the allied war effort was strengthened, Serbian hopes to achieve substantial support from the Russian Federation were shattered, and alliance cohesion was reinforced.

During Operation ALLIED FORCE combined air operations were carried out by 14 allied states, in what was, by far, the largest and most sustained combat operation in NATO history. At the outset, 214 U.S. aircraft and 130 allied aircraft were readied at European bases, augmented by B-2s operating from the continental United States. By June the total number of U.S. aircraft operating in the theater had grown to 731, while the allied contribution had more than doubled to over 300. The Combined Air Operations Center controlled operations from its base with the 5th Tactical Air Force in Vicenza, Italy.

Between March 24 and June 10, in 78 days of around-the-clock operations, NATO pilots flew nearly 38,000 sorties, including over 14,000 strike missions. U.S. aircraft flew about two-thirds of the sorties, and dominated key functions such as reconnaissance, suppression of air defenses, and strikes with precision guided munitions. Strike operations were mainly carried out by land-based aircraft, but Navy carrier-based aviation, Marine shore-based and sea-based aircraft, and cruise missile ships and submarines also played a role. The high proportion of support to strike sorties was a product of the special circumstances of a limited air campaign in a difficult theater — protective air patrols in multiple locations were organized as a matter of course, distances between targets and air bases required numerous tanker support sorties, and intensive use was made of reconnaissance and early warning and control aircraft. Remarkably, only two aircraft failed to return to base, and there were no allied combat fatalities.[107] Approximately 500 noncombatants died as a result of errant attacks, a regrettable outcome, but in view of the intensity and duration of the campaign also a tribute to the care taken to limit collateral damage to the extent possible.[108] The intensive use of precision strike systems, which accounted for over half of munitions expended, was critical in this regard. Nonetheless, a number of highly publicized incidents of accidental strikes against civilians (including a refugee truck convoy), the deliberate targeting of civilian infrastructure, the decision to allow strikes to be launched only from above 5,000 meters, decreasing accuracy but reducing pilot risk, and the environmental damage caused in Yugoslavia and neighboring countries by oil and chemical spills generated considerable controversy.[109]

Despite the escalating intensity of attacks, NATO's goals of suppressing air defenses, reducing Serb combat capacity, and compelling acceptance of peace terms remained elusive. The Yugoslav command and control network was well protected and redundant.[110] Poor weather, typical for the region in the spring season, and difficult terrain, made the acquisition and identification of targets a challenge. Considerable energy was drawn into humanitarian assistance operations in the face of the refugee crisis (Operation ALLIED HARBOR), a commitment that would last for the duration of the conflict and beyond.[111] Units of the Serbian Third Army deployed inside Kosovo, including some 40,000 soldiers and 300 tanks, dispersed into smaller units, hid during the day, maneuvered at night, and successfully limited vulnerability.[112] By April the neat strategy of compellence on the basis of which operations had commenced had given way to a war of attrition, with the allied coalition seeking desperately for politically acceptable and operationally feasible means to up the ante. As the war became more protracted, political pressure inevitably grew.

Frustration over the lack of initial success gave rise to a clash of perspectives between SACEUR Clark and Air Force General Short. Short expressed disgruntlement with the incremental character of the air campaign, and urged attacks against the "head of the snake" including governmental offices in Belgrade and strategic infrastructure. Clark did not oppose this line of thought, but he was concerned about the impact on alliance cohesion. The SACEUR believed that efforts to break Milošević's will through strategic bombing needed to be complemented by efforts to deny him the means to act by attacking Serbian ground forces, the "top priority of the campaign" because it struck at the enemy's real center of gravity.[113] His conviction was if anything reinforced by pressure from the North Atlantic Council to focus strikes against the Yugoslav Third Army inside Kosovo as a means to provoke military withdrawal. This meant a serious commitment to degrade Serbian forces deployed inside Kosovo — a waste of air assets in "tank plinking" in Short's dismissive jargon.[114] In retrospect, Clark's hope that air power could be used significantly to degrade Serbian forces inside Kosovo may have been overly optimistic. Estimates published during the campaign claimed that up to a third of Serbian heavy armaments positioned in Kosovo were destroyed by allied bombing, but subsequent evaluations make it clear that the real extent of attrition was considerably less.[115]

In the end, the approaches favored by Clark and Short would be tried simultaneously. On April 3, NATO missiles destroyed the Yugoslav and Serbian Interior Ministries in downtown Belgrade. Thereafter, the Serbian capital would remain under intermittent attack. Attacks on bridges, refineries, industrial complexes, and the national energy grid followed. On April 23, NATO attacked the Serbian state television building in Belgrade, killing 11 civilian employees. The attack was justified on the grounds that the facility was used to disseminate war propaganda, but it was an unusual step that has become the most criticized of all NATO initiatives during the war.[116] The decision to attack national infrastructure, in a campaign where the greatest military alliance in the history of the world found itself at war with a small and isolated Balkan state with 11 million residents and a level of military spending at about one-twentieth that of its adversary, was without question an unusual one. Its impact upon the Serbian people, who had never been consulted about the decisions that led to war, and upon the long-term economic well-being of Serbia and the entire Balkan subregion, was profoundly negative. Given the decision to rule out ground operations, however, this was arguably the only military option available to achieve the Alliance's stated goals.

Targeting the capital was not without risks. On May 7 NATO strike aircraft, misled by a breakdown in the process of identifying and validating targets, attacked the embassy of the People's Republic of China in downtown Belgrade, killing three and wounding twenty. The Alliance immediately apologized for what it called a "terrible mistake," and on May 9 President Clinton wrote to Chinese President Jiang Zemin to offer regrets.[117] Protestations of good intent were to no avail. In the days following the bombing, the Chinese denounced the action as "a gross violation of China's sovereignty," while mobs in Beijing and other Chinese cities raided and ransacked U.S. government offices with the implicit support of their government.[118] Beijing has consistently rejected official explanations of the incident and clung to the assertion that the embassy was targeted purposively in order to "send a message." Though Sino-American relations have weathered the storm, the impact of the incident was profound, a form of collateral damage for which the allied coalition was in no way prepared.

Despite alliance friction, systematic attacks against infrastructure and the promise of national ruin should the campaign be allowed to drag on indefinitely placed significant, cumulating pressure on decisionmakers in Belgrade. Efforts to degrade Serb forces inside Kosovo made considerably less progress. In response, and at the SACEUR's urging, discussion of a ground war option continued to surface despite consistent declaimers by spokespersons for the Clinton administration.

On March 26 General Clark requested the deployment of U.S. Army Apache helicopters to basing areas in Macedonia as a means for launching deep strikes against Serbian ground forces deployed in Kosovo.[119] The request was controversial, and in fact the Army, Air Force, and Marine Corps all expressed nonconcurrence with the deployment of Apaches without an accompanying ground maneuver force, a requirement according to Army doctrine but contrary to the U.S. desire to avoid ground operations in the Kosovo case. The National Security Council overrode such opposition, and President Clinton approved the request on April 3. Already on March 29, however, overwhelmed by refugees and concerned with the implications of serving as a staging post for combat operations, Skopje refused to grant consent to basing rights. As a result the Army's *Task Force Hawk* was reassigned to Tirana's Rinas airport, which was already hosting humanitarian aid operations (NATO's Operation ALLIED HARBOR and the U.S. Operation SHINING HOPE) and lacked the infrastructure required to host it effectively. After an intensive material buildup that absorbed over 25 percent of the airlift devoted to the campaign as a whole, including the deployment of 6,200 troops and 26,000 tons of equipment as force protection assets and for infrastructure support, more than three times initial estimates, 22 Apaches were finally deployed as an Army Aviation Brigade Combat Team by April 24. From the start, resistance to their use in a nonconventional combat environment was intense. The "no casualties" constraint was not consistent with the nature of the mission to which the Apaches were to be assigned, potential collateral damage from Apache strikes risked alienating allied and public opinion, the cost-benefit ratio for tank hunting under difficult operational circumstances was viewed by some as unpromising, the lack of an accompanying ground maneuver element was unconventional, and qualms about the potential for the use of the Apaches to become a step toward a larger ground campaign were strong.[120] The crash of an Apache during a mission rehearsal on April 26, and a subsequent training accident on May 5 during which two Apache crew members died, threatened to turn a deployment that was initiated to considerable fanfare into a public relations nightmare. In the end the Apaches were withdrawn without ever going into action.[121]

Efforts to plan for the eventuality of more extensive ground operations ran head long into both political and logistical constraints. U.S. and NATO planners were not authorized to conduct traditional campaign planning for ground operations, and no land component commander was ever designated during the campaign. Once it became clear that air operations were not having the desired effect, ground options were considered, but only in a series of "assessments" that lacked the rigor of the formal planning process.[122] Moreover, approaching the theater posed critical logistical challenges. The most logical line of operations ran from the Greek port of Thessalonica up the valley of the Vardar (Axios), to Skopje. Use of the corridor, however, was problematic. Polls indicated that well over 90 percent of Greek citizens opposed the war, and the government of Constantine Simitis in Athens, though willing, was hard pressed to maintain solidarity with the Alliance. Macedonia was not comfortable supporting a campaign waged on the side of the KLA in view its own restive Albanian minority. As a result, both Greece and Macedonia resisted allowing their national territories to be used as staging areas for combat operations. Belgrade was exposed to an attack from the north staged out of Hungary, but such a venture would have represented a considerable escalation that NATO was not prepared to accept.[123] It was also unpopular in Hungary, which sought to fulfill its commitments as a new member of the Alliance (formal accession had occurred only 1 week prior to the initiation of hostilities), but feared for the well-being of the sizable Magyar minority in Yugoslavia's Vojvodina region. The only other option was to move across Albania, through relentless terrain nearly devoid of infrastructure, along a single lane highway traversing dozens of inadequate bridges and other obstacles. This was an option that U.S. planners were willing to contemplate, but it demanded a time-consuming commitment to prepare the ground. By the time discussion of a ground option began in earnest, the window of opportunity for initiating operations prior to the onset of winter weather conditions had practically closed.[124] Political constraints were also a factor. The Clinton administration feared the consequences of a land war, and, among the NATO allies, only the United Kingdom spoke out publicly in favor of a ground campaign in the event that other options fell short.[125]

In the final weeks of Operation ALLIED FORCE a local offensive staged by KLA units under loose allied supervision along the Albanian-Kosovo border in the Mount Pastrik area, designated as Operation ARROW and intended to open a route of access toward Priština and enable the KLA to link up with sympathizers in the interior, had the effect of drawing Serbian heavy forces into the open and exposing them to air attack, including B-52 strikes. Some observers have interpreted these actions as a significant contribution to the cumulating pressure that would eventually cause Milošević to bow to the will of his opponents, but they were of limited scope and culminated with the repulse of KLA forces to near their starting positions.[126] Subsequent searches found no trace of destroyed VJ equipment.[127] The KLA lacked the weight to become a decisive force in the campaign and was not in a position to sustain operations against the better equipped Yugoslav Army.

Concern for the increased exposure of ground assets may nonetheless have been one factor among many that eventually motivated Belgrade to opt for a negotiated solution. The presence of the Apache force as the potential spearhead of a ground invasion, planning efforts aimed at preparing a ground offensive, and highly visible attempts to prepare Western publics for such an option, could not but have had some impact upon Milošević and his advisors. The threat of ground operations, though unrealized, helped set the stage for conflict termination.

Military efforts were paralleled from the start by intense diplomatic activity. In public pronouncements, NATO remained unyielding concerning its conditions for a cessation of combat operations. Privately, concern for the possibility that operations might have to be prolonged through the winter gave impetus to the diplomatic track. Milošević had demonstrated his capacity to take punishment and maintain the cohesion of his armed forces. The deadline for a commitment to ground operations before the onset of winter was fast approaching. Without a quick end to hostilities, the physical survival of the hundreds of thousands of Kosovar Albanian refugees clinging to existence in makeshift camps was at risk. And with a critical mass of Kosovar Albanians eliminated or scattered to the winds, the goal of the Serbianization of Kosovo would be close to realization. Under these conditions, Serbian acceptance of allied conditions would look more like victory than defeat.

The effort that would eventually open the door to a negotiated settlement was spearheaded, surprisingly but not incongruously, by the Russian Federation. From the onset of the Kosovo crisis, Moscow had used its limited leverage in an attempt to keep Western responses within a diplomatic framework. On March 31, 1998, it approved UN Security Council Resolution No. 1160, but conditioned support by insisting upon the elimination of any reference to a "threat to international peace and stability" that could justify international military action under Chapter VII of the UN Charter. In June, after considerable debate, Moscow agreed to the ten-point program drawn up by the Contact Group calling for a ceasefire, international monitoring, and a negotiated settlement, as a means to encourage moderation. At a June 16 summit in Moscow, Yeltsin told Milošević "unequivocally" that Yugoslavia could not rely on Russian support if it did not heed Russian council, and pressure from Moscow was useful in convincing Serbia to grant access to the Kosovo Diplomatic Observer Mission.[128] But any talk of military pressure as a means to coerce compliance remained anathema. Russia's approval for UN Security Council Resolution No. 1199 on September 23, 1998, was conditioned by the assertion that the resolution did not condone a resort to force. In early October, the Kremlin warned that it would use the veto to block any resolution authorizing use of force by the United Nations in Kosovo.[129] Given this background, the launching of Operation ALLIED FORCE could be construed as a challenge to Russia's self-perception as a great power with special interests in the Balkan region.

The tone for initial Russian reactions was set by Prime Minister Evgenii Primakov, who on March 23 requested that his flight, en route to Washington for a biannual meeting with U.S. Vice President Al Gore, be turned around in mid-air when he learned that military action against Serbia was imminent. The dramatic action was popular with the Russian public, but it was a gesture of futility. Russia's ambassador to the UN Sergei Lavrov condemned NATO's "unacceptable aggression" at an emergency session of the Security Council, and on March 26 Russia cosponsored (with Belarus and India) a UN draft resolution that demanded an end to air strikes and return to diplomacy.[130] The resolution was only supported by three of the fifteen Security Council members (Russia, China, and Namibia), and NATO's determination to pursue the military effort remained unshaken.[131] At the end of March, Russia sent several intelligence gathering ships into the Mediterranean to monitor the conflict, a gesture of independence that was suspect in NATO circles but peripheral to the course of the war.[132] Primakov also paid a visit to Milošević in Belgrade, but his diplomatic initiative was rejected out of hand by the Alliance.[133] In early April Yeltsin publicly remarked that continued military operations could lead to a new world war, Moscow suspended all relations with NATO, and editorial opinion railed against the United States as a "new Goliath" for whom "force is the only criterion of truth."[134] But verbal excess was no substitute for effective policy. Russia's opposition to the NATO war effort left it isolated, and the Kremlin, consistent with its approach to the Balkan dilemma from the origins of the conflict, was not prepared to risk its relationship with the West on behalf of a putative Serbian ally.

A turning point arrived on April 14, when Yeltsin appointed former Prime Minister Viktor Chernomyrdin as special Russian peace envoy in the region, undercutting Primakov's initiatives and leading in short order to his dismissal from office and political marginalization.[135] Chernomyrdin immediately abandoned Primakov's anti-Western rhetoric, made clear to Belgrade that it could not count upon open-ended Russian support, and assiduously worked toward a compromise arrangement that would increase Russia's diplomatic leverage, offer Belgrade face-saving concessions, and if possible bring the bombing to an end.

A diplomatic bargain became increasingly attractive to the Alliance as the pursuit of a military solution became more protracted. German Foreign Minister Fischer and National Security Advisor Michael Sterner took a first step in this direction in mid-April, traveling to Moscow and returning on the same day upon which Chernomyrdin assumed the post of special envoy with a six-point program that sought to bring peace negotiations back under the aegis of the UN, and attract Belgrade by offering a 24-hour bombing pause as a prelude to a ceasefire.[136] The program was rejected by the Alliance, but it had posed the challenge of engaging Russia in international mediation efforts. On April 25, the final day of NATO's muted 50th anniversary summit in Washington, DC, Clinton responded to a phone call from Yeltsin by proposing that Chernomyrdin be brought into a joint mediation effort with U.S. counterparts. Two days later U.S. Deputy Secretary of State

Strobe Talbott was in Moscow to consult with Chernomyrdin and Russian Foreign Minister Igor Ivanov concerning the terms of a possible accord.[137] In the first week of May Chernomyrdin arrived in Washington, where, in discussions with American officials, it was determined that he join with Talbott in representing NATO and Finnish President Martti Ahtisaari on behalf of the EU as a negotiating team.[138] On May 6 the foreign ministers of the G-8 outlined a direction for these initiatives in a political declaration calling for a negotiated solution balancing "a substantial autonomy for Kosovo in respect of the Rambouillet accord and the principle of the sovereignty and territorial integrity of the Federal Republic of Yugoslavia."[139]

Between mid-May and early June, a series of meetings between Ahtisaari, Talbott, and Chernomyrdin became the forum within which a coordinated Western peace initiative was forged.[140] The third of these sessions was held in Joseph Stalin's infamous retreat in the Moscow suburb of Kuntsevo, where despite the intimidating setting it was the U.S. envoy who laid down the law that any negotiated agreement would have to fit within the outline of NATO's conditions for peace.[141] When Chernomyrdin traveled to Belgrade for talks with Milošević on May 27, he was able to insist in good faith that a modest inflection of NATO conditions as an incentive for cooperation was the best that the Serbs could hope for. In the peace proposal finally accepted by Milošević on June 3, these inflections were indeed modest, but not insignificant.[142] Yugoslavia was forced to surrender physical control of the disputed province, but Belgrade could claim to have defended Serb honor and assured that Kosovo would remain, even under NATO occupation, an integral part of the Federal Republic of Yugoslavia. With Milošević's accord, on June 9 a Military Technical Agreement defining the terms of a ceasefire was initialed, and on June 10 the agreement was incorporated into UN Security Council Resolution No. 1244, which brought a formal end to the war.[143] Simultaneously, NATO air strikes were suspended.[144] Operation ALLIED FORCE had been waged to a successful conclusion, though not in the way that those who conceived it had originally intended.

Why had Milošević caved in? The question is significant, but not easy to answer given our present level of knowledge. In a careful analysis of the problem, Stephen Hosmer places primary emphasis upon the cumulative effect of the allied bombing campaign, and particularly attacks against "dual use" targets, including electrical grids and water facilities.[145] The efficiency of the air campaign, and the spectacle of the progressive destruction of much of the country's critical infrastructure, was no doubt compelling.[146] Whether it justifies maintaining the option of including such targets in future U.S. war plans, as Hosmer urges, is perhaps an open question. Nor is it clear that the attacks against infrastructure were ultimately decisive. The possibility of a ground offensive, aimed at affecting a forced entry in order to occupy and liberate Kosovo, must also have been a factor in the Serbian strongman's calculations. Fear of isolation, once the Russians had made clear that there were limits to their patience, may also have been a relevant concern. Without Russia in its corner, Belgrade had few positive alternatives. The indictment of Milošević and four other top Yugoslav officials by the ICTY at the end of May, imposed by the Tribunal in spite of concerns in Washington that by consigning the leadership to pariah status their willingness to compromise might be reduced, has also been cited as a pointed symbolic gesture that brought home the possible personal consequences of continued defiance.[147] Not least, the bitter pill of capitulation was sweetened by Western concessions. NATO's desire to bring the campaign to an end before tensions within the Alliance built up to the breaking point motivated a softening of the Rambouillet terms that may in the end have made them palatable, though just barely, to beleaguered Yugoslavia. Finally, the Serbian leadership may have concluded that once the bombing campaign was brought to a halt, and with continued Russian backing, it could deflect the peace process toward a more positive outcome. Milošević had already completed a massive expulsion of Kosovar Albanians that would have worked to his advantage should it have been allowed to stand. A Russian zone of occupation in occupied Kosovo might also have become the foundation for a partition arrangement that would at least give Belgrade something to show for its efforts, and validate the leadership's claim to have stood up for the national cause.

The Aftermath: Victory or Compromise?

NATO was quick to claim that Belgrade had capitulated, and that the peace settlement fully corresponded to its own conditions for a ceasefire. In his address to the nation on Kosovo delivered upon the cessation of hostilities on June 9, President Clinton asserted that "the demands of an outraged and united international community have been met" and hailed "a victory for a safer world, for our democratic values, and for a stronger America." Clinton also pledged to "finish the job" by engaging in an effort to build peace in the war torn province, an effort that the complex nature of the peace agreement itself risked to compromise.[148] For despite the allies' justified satisfaction, Milošević had not surrendered unconditionally. The Chernomyrdin-Ahtisaari agenda was significantly different from that which had inspired the original Rambouillet accord, and provided the Serbian party with some prerogative to defend its interests even in the wake of military defeat.

First, the entire process of conflict management had been brought back under the aegis of the UN. The plan eliminated Rambouillet's call for a binding referendum on independence after five years. Any determination of Kosovo's final status would now have to be approved by the UN Security Council, where Russia exercised the right of veto. Annex B of the Rambouillet accord granted NATO forces the right to operate throughout the entire territory of the Federal Republic of Yugoslavia. That right was reduced by the Chernomyrdin-Ahtisaari project to Kosovo alone. The Kosovo Peacekeeping Force (KFOR) sanctioned by the project was now to be placed under joint NATO-UN auspices, and the OSCE was granted significant authority as the civil component of the international presence in the province. Supervision of refugee return would also be conducted under the auspices of the UN, rather than NATO. In the interim, the text reiterated that Kosovo was considered to be an integral part of the Federal Republic of Yugoslavia.

By working to represent Serbian interests, Russia had secured for itself the familiar role of great power sponsor, and achieved its minimum goal of maintaining leverage over the direction of the peace process. The encroachment was noted in Western capitals with concern. In the short term, resistance to Russian intrusion was manifested in an absolute refusal to accede to the request for a separate Russian occupation zone inside Kosovo, on the grounds that Russian sympathy for the Serbian position could lead toward a de facto partition of the province. "The danger," in the words of General Clark, "was that the Russian would gain a separate sector that they would turn into a separate mission favoring the Serbs."[149] Frustrated by its inability to obtain control of an occupation zone, on June 11-12 Moscow sent an expanded airborne company (approximately 200 paratroopers) on short notice from Bijelina in Bosnia-Herzegovina across the Drina to occupy Priština's Slatina airport in advance of the arrival of the British-led KFOR contingent. The operation seems to have been inspired by Chief of the General Staff General Anatolii Kvashnin, who used direct access to Yeltsin to win approval for the operation, which was initiated without Foreign Minister Ivanov or Prime Minister Sergei Stepashin being informed. The intent was to reinforce the original deployment via air, bringing several thousand soldiers to bear at a critical point in order to make a defiant statement concerning Russia's regional role and to expand its strategic options.[150] Clark, perceiving "the future of NATO" to be at stake, argued for the need to use U.S. Apache helicopters to interdict the arriving force by blocking runways.[151] British Lieutenant General Michael Jackson, commander of the Allied Command Europe Rapid Reaction Corps, challenged these prescriptions, insisting, in a head-to-head confrontation, that "I'm not starting World War III for you."[152] Such pyrotechnics were both unfortunate and unnecessary. The Russian plan had neglected the need for over flight permission from Bulgaria, Romania, and Hungary, which was promptly refused, leaving the small contingent at Slatina isolated and at the mercy of arriving KFOR units. Having made its point in a manner of speaking, and aware of its forces' exposure, the Kremlin was more than happy to beat a diplomatic retreat.[153] The episode nonetheless made clear the fragility of Russia's engagement with the Western peacemaking effort, the dissatisfaction of influential elements within the security establishment with a subordinate role, and the determination of NATO to keep the reins firmly in its own hands.

NATO won the war in Kosovo.[154] Yugoslavia was shattered by the cumulative effect of air strikes that it was powerless to resist. Milošević's forces were compelled to withdraw from the province, which was immediately occupied by KFOR. Hundreds of thousands of Kosovar Albanian refugees were permitted to return to their homes, and the humanitarian disaster so feared at the outset was headed off with thousands, or tens of thousands, of lives spared as a consequence. The conflict itself was contained, and in the short-term its impact upon the surrounding region was not allowed to escalate out of control. NATO affirmed its capacity to stand united under adversary, and to fight and prevail. Its 50th anniversary summit, held in April 1999 at a low point in the military campaign, approved a new strategic concept that championed out of area peace support operations, and reconfirmed a commitment to build a new NATO as the centerpiece of Europe's post-cold war security architecture. In purely military terms, and despite the unresolved debates over strategic choices, its pursuit of the war effort was exemplary, as the outcome, combined with the absence of any NATO combat fatalities, dramatically attests.

In was not clear that NATO had positioned itself effectively to win the peace. Despite his miscalculations and blunders, Milošević remained in power. In the end air power proved sufficient to compel Serbian withdrawal, but it had only opened the door for an important commitment of ground forces, designated as Operation JOINT GUARDIAN, with a challenging mission before them. The allies had committed themselves to administer what had in effect become another Balkan protectorate, at great expense and for the foreseeable future. After insisting upon the rapid withdrawal of the entire Yugoslav military and police apparatus that had been responsible for maintaining public order in the past, KFOR was left alone to manage a seething cauldron of resentments. In the initial phase of the war, NATO's air war had patently failed to prevent Serbian atrocities directed against the Kosovar Albanians. One year after the initiation of the KFOR mission, only about a third of the approximately 200,000 Serbs who lived in the province prior to the bombing campaign were estimated to remain, many of them withdrawn into an enclave adjacent to the Serbian border in the north. The victory of the Kosovar Albanians had led in short order to a campaign of reverse ethnic cleansing, that also affected Kosovo's Roma, Turkish, and Goranci minorities, and made a mockery of allied intentions to recreate an authentically multicultural environment.[155] The KLA was formally disbanded in September 1999, with a small remnant of 5,000 members (3,000 active, 2,000 reserve) converted into a Kosovo Protection Corps charged with missions such as disaster relief, search and rescue, and the reconstruction of infrastructure (but not, formally at least, with policing responsibilities). The hard core of the organization remained intact nonetheless, apparently undeterred from the pursuit of its maximalist agenda for a greater Albania. NATO hoped to use Operation ALLIED FORCE to illustrate its new security concept sanctioning out of area operations to promote regional stability. But the trauma associated with the war, combined with the costs and risks associated with an open-ended deployment of ground forces, made it more likely that the operation would be regarded as an exceptional case rather than as a model. The final status toward which Kosovo was moving remained ambiguous, with prospects for either full independence or reintegration into a tolerant and multicultural Serbia increasingly distant. One distinguished American commentator, remarking on the contradictions between NATO's purported goals and the campaign's discernable outcome, described the war against Yugoslavia, as an act of policy, as "a perfect failure."[156]

The secondary effects of the conflict were also significant. The accidental bombing of the Chinese embassy in Belgrade was a military blunder and a diplomatic embarrassment of the first order that Beijing did not hesitate to exploit.[157] The stand off with the Russian company in Priština was ominous. The downing of major bridges across the Danube conjured up images of the devastation of World War II, something that all Europeans had pledged never to allow again, and by blocking commercial navigation imposed a heavy burden on the entire regional economy. The imbalance of forces in the theater, and the virtual absence of allied casualties, was noted by some ethicists as the reflection of a resort to "violence which moralizes itself as justice and which is unrestrained by consequences" that had transformed "the expectations that govern the morality of war" itself.[158] Ironically, military effectiveness may have contributed to undermining America's image as a benign arbiter whose power was set in the service of humanitarian goals. Serbia had been driven into a black hole, from which it will have to be lifted at Western expense if a healthy Balkan regional order is ever to be recreated. U.S. relations with the European allies were also strained — although NATO had prevailed in the conflict, the long term effects upon alliance cohesion were potentially quite negative. The inevitable complications of coalition warfare, and striking military capabilities gap between the United States and its European allies, led some to question whether the Alliance could ever be an effective instrument for waging war.[159] Europe read the lessons in its own way, and in the wake of the conflict the EU moved with a new sense of purpose to forward its project for an autonomous European Security and Defense Policy, a long-term commitment to strategic independence with serious implications for the transatlantic bargain that has always stood at NATO's foundation.

Even short, victorious wars can give rise to ambiguous outcomes and unintended consequences. Operation ALLIED FORCE was a success in military-operational terms, but it was fought as a limited war and concluded with a tactical compromise. It provides what may be a typical case study of what Wesley Clark describes as "modern war," waged for the ambiguous goals of "regional stability and humanitarian assistance," where "adversaries are not major and the issues at stake do not threaten the immediate national survival of the great powers."[160] Such conflicts will rarely receive full and unambiguous national commitment and support, and they have and will continue to present military planners with special challenges and responsibility. Although victory, in conventional military terms, may be nearly a foregone conclusion, strategies for winning modern wars must be coupled with equally robust strategies for winning the peace. Such strategies will need to include intrusive preventive diplomacy, effective coalition building and burden sharing, access to a wide range of military capabilities spanning the entire spectrum of conflict, and a long-term commitment to post-conflict peace building. The absence of such integrated strategies has been a chronic failing of Western diplomacy throughout the protracted Balkan crisis. The West's Kosovo engagement represented yet another opportunity to move beyond reactive, crisis driven responses toward a more complex and effective approach — an opportunity that might yet be seized.

ENDNOTES - CHAPTER 5

1. Miranda Vickers, *Between Serb and Albanian: A History of Kosovo*, New York: Columbia University Press, 1998, p. 289.

2. Spasoje Djaković, *Sukobi na Kosovu*, Belgrade: Narodna Kniga, 1984, and Paul Shoup, *Communism and the Yugoslav National Question*, New York: Columbia University Press, 1968, pp. 104-111.

3. See Roberto Morozzo della Rocca, *Kosovo: La Guerra in Europa*, Milan: Guerini, 1999, p. 53.

4. Julie A. Mertus, *Kosovo: How Myths and Truths Started a War*, Berkeley: University of California Press, 1999, pp. 100-114, illustrates the process with reference to the 1985 Martinović case, where a Serbian peasant working his field was purportedly attacked by Kosovar Albanian assailants who forced a bottle into his rectum, a gesture judged to be evocative of the symbolically-charged Ottoman practice of impalement.

5. *Ibid.*, pp. 17-55.

6. See in particular Michel Roux, *Les Albanais en Yougoslavie: Minorité nationale, territoire et developpement,* Paris: Fondation de la Maison des Sciences de l'Homme, 1992.

7. Kosova is the Albanian designation for the province. Use of the Albanian designation, for some at least, has come to imply support for Kosovar Albanian national aspirations. Serbs sometimes refer to the province as Kosovo-Metohija, or Kosmet. The Greek term *metoh* refers to church properties and evokes the significant monastic holdings of the Serbian Orthodox Church in the area. I use the term Kosovo as the most common international designation without any intent to cast judgment concerning its final status.

8. Vickers, *Between Serb and Albanian,* pp. 197-213.

9. Despite its relative backwardness and isolation, Kosovo's status as a focus for Serbian nationalism and flash point for armed conflict has generated a large literature describing the region's history. The Kosovo problem is evoked from a Serbian perspective in Dimitrije Bogdanović, *Knijga o Kosovu,* Belgrade: Serbian Academy of Arts and Sciences, 1986. Recent studies inspired by the breakup of Yugoslavia include Marco Dogo, *Il Kosovo: Albanesi e Serbi — Le radici del conflitto,* Lungra di Cosenza: Marco Editore, 1992; Noel Malcolm, *Kosovo: A Short History,* New York: New York University Press, 1998; and Vickers, *Between Serb and Albanian.*

10. Philip E. Auerswald and David P. Auerswald, eds., *The Kosovo Conflict: A Diplomatic History through Documents,* Cambridge: Kluwer Law International, 2000, pp. 43-47.

11. *Ibid.*, pp. 56-59.

12. *Ibid.*, p. 65; and David Binder, "Bush Warns Serbs not to Widen War," *The New York Times*, December 28, 1992, p. 1.

13. Tim Judah, *War and Revenge,* New Haven: Yale University Press, 2000, p. 117.

14. Rugova responded critically to the armed campaigns of the KLA, asserting that "We must chose nonviolence, not only because it is the proper choice, but because it is the necessary choice." His political opponent, Adem Demaçi, a former political prisoner in Titoist Yugoslavia linked to the KLA leadership, responded by labeling Rugova "the architect of all our political failures," and insisting "I will not condemn the tactics of the Kosovo Liberation Army because the path of nonviolence has gotten us nowhere." Cited from Chris Hedges, "Kosovo Leader

Urges Resistance, But No Violence," *The New York Times*, March 13, 1998. See also Hashim Thaqi, "Kosova," in William Joseph Buckley, ed., *Kosovo: Contending Voices on Balkan Intervention*, Grand Rapids, MI: William B. Eerdmans Publishing Company, 2000, pp. 189-191. These tensions within the Kosovar Albanian leadership would remain unresolved throughout the conflict. See also "Roots of the Kosovo Insurgency," *AUSA Background Brief*, No. 82, June 1999.

15. Chris Hedges, "Albanians Inside Serbia Set to Fight for Autonomy," *The New York Times*, October 19, 1997, p. 15.

16. Philip Smucker, "Albanian Weapons Cross to Kosovo," *The Washington Times*, April 8, 1998, p. 1; and Jens Reuter, "Die internationale Gemeinschaft und der Krieg in Kosovo," *Südost Europa*, Vol. 47, Nos. 7-8, July-August 1998, p. 289.

17. Chris Soloway, "Serbia Attacks Ethnic Albanians," *The Washington Post*, March 6, 1998, p. 1; and Tim Judah, "A History of the Kosovo Liberation Army," in Buckley, ed., *Kosovo*, p. 112.

18. Chris Hedges, "Milosevic Moves to Wipe Out Kosovo Rebels," *The New York Times*, June 2, 1998, p. 1.

19. Judah, *War and Revenge*, p. 92.

20. Michel Roux, "Spartire il Kosovo? Elementi per un dossier," *Limes*, No. 2, 1999, pp. 199-213.

21. Hans-Georg Ehrhart and Matthais Z. Karadi, "Wenn brennt der Balkan? Plädoyer für eine komplexe Präventionspolitik im Kosovo-Konflikt," *Frankfurter Rundschau*, March 25, 1998. The texts of the agreements on education negotiated under the auspices of Sant' Egidio appear in Auerswald and Auerswald, *The Kosovo Conflict*, pp. 78-79, 121-123.

22. See "Progress in Bosnia," *The Washington Post*, January 22, 1998, p. 20; and Justin Brown, "As Balkans Tense, a US Twist," *The Christian Science Monitor*, March 3, 1998; and the text of Gelbard's remarks in Special Representative Robert S. Gelbard, Press Conference, Belgrade, Serbia and Montenegro, February 23, 1998, cited from *http://www.state.gov/www/policy_remarks/1998/980223_gelbard*.

23. See the eyewitness accounts in "Kosovo: l'horreur en Europe," *Le Monde*, October 28, 1998, pp. 1-3.

24. Cited from "A Warning to Heed," *The Christian Science Monitor*, March 4, 1998.

25. Cited in R. Jeffrey Smith, "US Assails Government Crackdown in Kosovo," *The Washington Post*, March 5, 1998, p. 23.

26. Cited from Steven Erlanger, "Albright Tours Europe to Whip Up Resolve to Punish Yugoslavians," *The New York Times*, March 9, 1998; and Barbara Slavin, "Berger: US Goal is to Keep Kosovo from Spilling Over," *USA Today*, March 13, 1998, p. 8.

27. Chris Hedges, "Kosovo Rebels Find Friend in Former Albanian President," *The New York Times*, June 10, 1998, p. A8.

28. Anthony Lewis, "Remember 1991," *The New York Times*, March 16, 1998.

29. Credible cases for an independent Kosovo are offered by Nicholas X. Rizopoulos, "An Independent Kosovo: Waiting for Another Navarino?" *World Policy Journal*, Vol. XV, No. 3, Fall, 1998, pp. 13-16; and Paul Garde, "Il faut donner au Kosovo la maîtrise de son destin," *Le Monde*, October 24, 1998.

30. In cross-examination before the Hague tribunal, Milošević read an FBI document dated December 2001 to this effect. See Tommaso di Francesco, "Milosevic, scontro tra i 'giudici'," *Il Manifesto*, March 10, 2002, p. 1; and "Milosevic sieht Verbindung bin Ladins mit der UCK: Verwicklung der Kaida in Kosovo-Krieg?" *Neue Zürcher Zeitung*, March 9, 2002. See also "KLA Rebels Train in Terrorist Camps: Bin Laden Offers Financing, Too," *The Washington Times*, May 4, 1999, p. A1.

31. Mike O'Connor, "Thousands of Refugees Flee Serb Mountain Attack," *The New York Times*, August 5, 1998, p. A3.

32. See "Establishing a Durable Peace in the Balkans," U.S. Department of State, Bureau of European and Canadian Affairs Home Page, December 7, 1998, in *www.state.gov/www/regions/eur/bosnia/index.htlm*.

33. In spite of this pressure, the LDK continued to support cooperation with the KLA in building broadly representative national institutions. Its platform in the autumn of 1998 called for full national independence after a phase of transition, during which an international protectorate would be set up to guarantee the well being of Kosovo's Serb minority. See "President Rugova's Press Conference," *Kosova Daily Reports* No. 1605, November 6, 1998, pp. 1-2.

34. In a press conference with Jeremy Greenstock, Political Director, United Kingdom Foreign Commonwealth Office, Pristina, Serbia and Montenegro, March 26, 1998. Cited from: *http://www.state.gov/www/policy_remarks/1998/980326_gelbard*.

35. Philip Smucker, "Albanian Guerrillas are Ready to Do or Die," *The Washington Post*, April 27, 1998, p. 1.

36. R. Jeffrey Smith, "NATO Albania Deployment Less Likely," *The Washington*

Post, May 28, 1998, p. 30.

37. Auerswald and Auerswald, *The Kosovo Conflict*, pp. 170-172.

38. Ron Jensen, "NATO Foreign Ministers Weighing Kosovo Options During 2-Day Talks," *European Stars and Stripes*, May 28, 1998, p. 2.

39. Auerswald and Auerswald, *The Kosovo Conflict*, pp. 111-114.

40. *Ibid.*, pp. 139-142; and John M. Goshko, "Arms Embargo on Yugoslavia: U.N. Security Council Seeks to Prevent More Violence in Kosovo," *The Washington Post*, April 1, 1998, p. 24.

41. Auerswald and Auerswald, *The Kosovo Conflict*, pp. 98-99.

42 *Ibid.*, p. 171.

43. Guy Dinmore, "U.S. Envoy Arranges Kosovo Peace Talks," *The Washington Post*, May 14, 1998, p. 25.

44. Auerswald and Auerswald, *The Kosovo Conflict*, pp. 189-190; and Justin Brown, "Aiming NATO At Serb Advance," *The Christian Science Monitor*, June 11, 1998, p. 1.

45. Cited in Stefan Troebst, *Conflict in Kosovo: Failure or Prevention? An Analytical Documentation*, Flensburg: European Center in Minority Issues, 1998, pp. 784-785.

46. Auerswald and Auerswald, *The Kosovo Conflict*, pp. 196-197.

47. Celestine Bohlan, "Russia Vows to Block the U.N. from Backing Attacks on Serbs," *The New York Times*, October 7, 1998.

48. Ivo H. Daalder and Michael E. O'Hanlon, *Winning Ugly: NATO's War to Save Kosovo*, Washington, DC: Brookings Institution Press, 2000, p. 45, make a distinction between a "Catholic" faction (France and Italy) demanding a mandate, a "Lutheran" faction (the U.K. and eventually Germany) acquiescing reluctantly to an emergency response, and an "Agnostic" faction (the United States) arguing that a mandate was not absolutely necessary.

49. Auerswald and Auerswald, *The Kosovo Conflict*, pp. 250-253.

50. Benjamin S. Lambeth, *NATO's Air War for Kosovo: A Strategic and Operational Assessment*, Santa Monica: RAND, 2001, pp. 11-12.

51. Auerswald and Auerswald, *The Kosovo Conflict*, pp. 260-273. See also "Les

allies s'apprêtent a donner l' "ordre d'action" aux militaries," *Le Monde*, October 13, 1998; and Barbara Crosette, "Serbs Continue Kosovo Terror, Annan Asserts," *The New York Times*, October 6 , 1998, p. 1.

52. Deputy Secretary Strobe Talbott, Kenyon C. Bolton Memorial Lecture to the Cleveland Council on World Affairs, Cleveland, Ohio, October 9, 1998. Cited from *http://www.state.gov/www/policy_remarks/981009_talbott_forpol.htm11/6/98*.

53. Auerswald and Auerswald, *The Kosovo Conflict*, pp. 292-294.

54. *Ibid.*, pp. 299-303. The OSCE commitment included "readiness to consider in an urgent manner any further specific steps necessary to meet the requirements for efficient verification in Kosovo." See Organization for Security and Cooperation in Europe, Permanent Council, Decision No. 259, October 15, 1998, and Decision No. 263, October 25, 1998, in *www.osce.org/news/pcdec259.htm* and *www.osce.org/news/pcdec263.htm*.

55. In a meeting with Milošević in Belgrade on October 20, Wesley Clark abruptly informed the Yugoslav president that "If you don't withdraw, Washington is going to tell me to bomb you, and I'm going to bomb you good." Wesley K. Clark, *Waging Modern War: Bosnia, Kosovo, and the Future of Combat*, New York: Public Affairs, 2001, p. 148.

56. Javier Solana, "Remarks at the Inauguration of the Kosovo Verification Coordination Centre, November 26, 1998, cited from *www.nato.int/docu/speech/1998/s981126a.htm*.

57. Rémy Ourdon, "Six années de liaisons dangereuses franco-serbes," and Jacques Isnard, "Un officier français de l'OTAN est accuse d'espionnage au profit des militaries serbes," *Le Monde*, November 4, 1998, p. 4. Bunel, dismissed from the service, responded to the accusations in a bitter denunciation of NATO policy in the Balkans. Pierre-Henri Bunel, *Crimes de guerre à l'Otan*, Paris: Edition 1, 2000.

58. Sabrina P. Ramet and Phil Lyon, "Germany: The Federal Republic, Loyal to NATO," in Tony Weymouth and Stanley Henig, eds., *The Kosovo Crisis: The Last American War in Europe?* London: Reuters, 2001, pp. 83-105.

59. Maartje Rutten, ed., *From St. Malo to Nice--European Defence: Core Documents*, Paris: Western European Union Institute for Security Studies, May 2001, pp. 8-9.

60. Bruce R. Nardulli, Walter L. Perry, Bruce Pirnie, John Gordon IV, and John G. McGinn, *Disjointed War: Military Operations in Kosovo, 1999*, Santa Monica: RAND, 2002, p. 16.

61. Jacques Isnard, "750 soldats français pour protéger l'OSCE au Kosovo," *Le Monde*, November 5, 1998. Madeleine Albright defined the arrangement on

October 27 as keeping NATO "overhead and next door." Secretary of State Madeleine K. Albright, Remarks on Kosovo, October 27, 1998, Office of the Spokesman, U.S. Department of State. Cited from *http://secretary.state.gov/www/statements/1998/981027.html*.

62. Judah, *War and Revenge*, p. 178.

63. Giulio Marcon, *Dopo il Kosovo: Le guerre nei Balcani e la costruzione della pace*, Triete: Asterios Editore, 2000, p. 37.

64. Questions about the accuracy of this version of events were nonetheless raised in the immediate aftermath of the events. See Christophe Châtelot, "Questions sur le massacre de Racak," *Le Monde*, February 11, 1999.

65. Wesley Clark describes his telephone communication with Walker, beginning with the phrase "Wes, we've got trouble here," in his memoir. Clark, *Waging Modern War*, p. 158.

66. Auerswald and Auerswald, *The Kosovo Conflict*, pp. 411-412.

67. See Tiziana Boari, "Racak, bugia di Guerra," *Il Manifesto*, February 6, 2001, p. 5. U.S. CIA reports had already specified that many KLA actions were intended to provoke reprisals in order to encourage foreign intervention. See Barton Gelman, "How We Went to War," *The Washington Post*, national weekly edition, April 26, 1999, pp. 6-9.

68. Cited from Barton Gellman, "The Path to Crisis: How the United States and its Allies Went to War," *The Washington Post*, April 18, 1999, p. A31.

69. Clark, *Waging Modern War*, p. 161.

70. Auerswald and Auerswald, *The Kosovo Conflict*, pp. 471-473.

71. *Ibid.*, pp. 477-478.

72. *Ibid.*, pp. 434-461.

73. Italian Prime Minister Massimo D'Alema would later argue that a strategy which avoided ultimatums, but increased the number of OSCE observers and systematically built up an intimidating ground force in Macedonia, would have had a much greater chance of preventing the kind of massive ethnic cleansing that actually occurred and fulfilling NATO's stated humanitarian purpose. Massimo D'Alema, *Gli italiani e la guerra*, Milan: Mondadori, 1999, p. 49.

74. "M. Milosevic réitère son refus de troupes étrangères au Kosovo," *Le Monde*, February 18, 1999.

75. Christophe Châtelot, "Des représentants de l'UCK prédisent l'echec des pourparlers de Rambouillet," *Le Monde*, February 19, 1999.

76. The heavily edited Serb version of the text, and conciliatory statement of March 5, appear in Auerswald and Auerswald, *The Kosovo Conflict*, pp. 608-610.

77. For the final text, *Ibid.*, pp. 542-590.

78. *Ibid.*, pp. 665-666.

79. For an insider's account of Rambouillet, see Marc Weller, "The Rambouillet Conference on Kosovo," *International Affairs*, Vol. 75, No. 2, April 1999, pp. 225-239.

80. Cited from R. Jeffrey Smith, "Belgrade Rebuffs Final Warning," *The Washington Post*, March 23, 1999.

81. For diverse perspectives see Catherine Guichard, "International Law and the War in Kosovo," and Adam Roberts, "'Humanitarian War' Over Kosovo," *Survival*, Vol. 41, No. 2, Summer 1999, pp. 25-29, 104-107; Hilaire McCourbey, "Kosovo, NATO and International Law," *International Relations*, Vol. 14, No. 5, August 1999, pp. 29-46; Reinhard Merkel, ed., *Der Kosovo-Krieg und das Völkerrecht*, Frankfurt am Main: Suhrkamp, 1999; and Dieter S. Lutz, ed., *Der Kosovo-Krieg: Rechtliche und rechtsethische Aspekte*, Baden-Baden: Nomos Verlagsgesellschaft, 2000.

82. Western negotiators have subsequently argued that the freedom of movement clause in Annex B of the accord was part of a standard status of forces agreement, that it was always considered to be open to negotiation, and that during the talks it was never raised as an object of disagreement by the Serbian delegation. See "Rubin, Hill on Kosovo at U.S. Institute for Peace March 23," U.S. Department of State, International Information Programs, Washington File, March 24, 2000. The way in which the clause was perceived by Serbian negotiators may have been quite another matter.

83. Daalder and O'Hanlon, *Winning Ugly*, p. 85.

84. Christopher Layne, "Miscalculations and Blunders Lead to War," in Ted Galen Carpenter, ed., *NATO's Empty Victory: A Postmortem on the Balkan War*, Washington, DC: CATO Institute, 2000, p. 15.

85. General Wesley K. Clark, "When Force is Necessary: NATO's Military Response to the Kosovo Crisis," *NATO Review*, Summer 1999, p. 15.

86. Auerswald and Auerswald, *The Kosovo Conflict*, pp. 729-733; and Francis X.

Clines, "NATO Opens Broad Barrage Against Serbs as Clinton Denounces 'Brutal Repression'," *The New York Times*, March 25, 1999, p. A1.

87. Elaine M. Grossman, "Short: U.S., NATO Lacked Clear Political Objectives in Kosovo War," *Inside the Pentagon*, May 25, 2000, p. 1. During the campaign Short was subordinate to General Wesley Clark as Supreme Allied Commander Europe (SACEUR) and Commander in Chief, U.S. European Command, to Clark's air component commander General John P. Jumper as Commander U.S. Air Force Europe, and to General James O. Ellis, Commander, Allied Forces Southern Europe and Commander in Chief, U.S. Naval Forces Europe.

88. President Clinton went on public record stating that "the thing that bothers me about introducing ground troops into a hostile situation--in Kosovo and the Balkans--is the prospect of never being able to get them out." Interview with Dan Rather, March 31, 1999, cited in Nardulli, *et al.*, *Disjointed War*, p. 23.

89. U.S. Department of Defense, *Report to Congress: Kosovo/Operation Allied Force After-Action Report*, Washington, DC: U.S. Government Printing Office, January 31, 2000, pp. 15-16.

90. Nardulli, *et al.*, *Disjointed War*, p. 3. The report elaborates: "Forced-entry ground operations were effectively ruled out by both senior NATO political authorities and U.S. political and senior military leaders by the summer of 1998. With the exception of some broad estimates on what types of forced-entry land operations might be considered and what they would require, neither NATO nor the United States planned for land invasion from June 1998 until after Operation ALLIED FORCE began in March 1999." *Ibid.*, p. 14.

91. Auerswald and Auerswald, *The Kosovo Conflict*, p. 732.

92. Cited from John T. Correll, "Assumptions Fall in Kosovo," *Air Force Magazine*, June, 1999, p. 4.

93. Clark, *Waging Modern War*, p. 121.

94. Lambeth, *NATO's Air War for Kosovo*, p. 22.

95. Clark, *Waging Modern War*, p. 183, notes that the imperative not to lose air crews was described as the "first measure of merit" in the operation.

96. Cited from James Kitfield, "War-Making By Committee," *National Journal*, May 8, 1999, p. 4.

97. This was the kind of approach originally supported by General Short, who called for striking the "head of snake" in Belgrade by hitting power stations and government ministries in the first wave of stacks. See Dana Priest,

The Commanders' War: The Battle Inside Headquarters," *The Washington Post*, September 21, 1999.

98. Dana Priest, "Tensions Grow With Divide Over Strategy," *The Washington Post*, September 21, 1999, p. 1.

99. U.S. Army General Wesley Clark, SACEUR, NATO Briefing, March 25, 1999.

100. Lambeth, *NATO's Air War for Kosovo*, p. 9.

101. Catherine Simon, "Le HCR en accusation," *Le Monde*, May 18, 1999. Clark, *Waging Modern War*, pp. 176-177, corroborates the absence of allied planning for shielding civilians under the circumstances that developed after March 24.

102. William Drozdiak, "Serb Offensive was Meticulously Planned," *The Washington Post*, April 11, 1999, pp. A1, A26-27.

103. J. Bryan Hehir, "Kosovo: A War of Values and the Values of War," in Buckley, ed., *Kosovo*, p. 399.

104. See in particular Heinz Loquai, *Der Kosovo-Konflikt--Wege in einem vermeidbaren Krieg: Die Zeit von Ende November 1997 bis März 1999*, Baden-Baden: Nomos Verlagsgesellschaft, 2000.

105. Rémy Ourdan, "Milosevic se pose en victime d'un 'crime contre la vérite'," *Le Monde*, February 16, 2002.

106. Judah, *War and Revenge*, p. 250.

107. *Report to Congress: Kosovo/Operation Allied Force*, pp. 78-99.

108. William M. Arkin, "Civilian Deaths in the NATO Air Campaign," Human Rights Watch, *http://hrw.org/hrw/reports/2000/nato*. Clark, *Waging Modern War*, p. 297, plausibly describes Operation ALLIED FORCE as "the most precise and error-free campaign ever conducted."

109. See, for example, Mario Vargas Llosa, "La Guerra inútil," *El Pais*, May 17, 1999, p. 4.

110. For an assessment of efforts to suppress the Yugoslav integrated air defense system see *Report to Congress: Kosovo/Operation Allied Force*, pp. 64-71.

111. "Les moyens manquent toujours face aux 910,000 réfugiés du Kosovo," *Le Monde*, May 13, 1999.

112. *Report to Congress: Kosovo/Operation Allied Force*, pp. 60-63.

113. Clark, *Waging Modern War*, pp. 241-242.

114. John Tirpak, "Short's View of the Air Campaign," *Air Force Magazine*, September 1999.

115. "L'OTAN a détruit 31 percent des armes Lourdes au Kosovo," *Le Monde*, May 21, 1999; Richard J. Newman, "The Bombs that Failed in Kosovo," *U.S. News and World Report*, September 20, 1999; John Barry and Evan Thomas, "The Kosovo Cover-Up," *Newsweek*, 15 May 2000, pp. 23-27; and Nardulli, *et al.*, *Disjointed War*, pp. 48-49.

116. "Bombes contre images . . .," *Le Monde*, April 25-26, 1999.

117. Auerswald and Auerswald, *The Kosovo Conflict*, pp. 960-961.

118. *Ibid.*, pp. 955-956.

119. Clark, *Waging Modern War*, pp. 227-228.

120. Dana Priest, "Army's Apache Helicopter Rendered Impotent in Kosovo," *The Washington Post*, December 29, 1999, p. 1.

121. For a thorough evaluation of Task Force Hawk, see the account in Nardulli, *et al.*, *Disjointed War*, pp. 57-97.

122. *Ibid.*, pp. 38-40.

123. Clark, *Waging Modern War*, p. 307.

124. *Ibid.*, pp. 316-339, details the effort to define a ground option. The planning variant underway from the beginning of June called for massing a force of 175,000-200,000 soldiers in Albania and Macedonia, prepared to move into Kosovo on September 1. This was a very ambitious target.

125. Jacques Isnard, "La Grande-Bretagne plaide de nouveau en faveur d'une intervention terreste de l'OTAN," *Le Monde*, May 19, 1999.

126. Paul C. Forage, "The Battle for Mount Pastrik: A Preliminary Study," *The Journal of Slavic Military Studies*, Vol. 14, No. 4, December 2001, pp. 57-80; and Clark, *Waging Modern War*, pp. 327-328. Clark views the KLA offensive as an opportunity that NATO forces failed to exploit due to reluctance to engage the U.S. Apache force.

127. Nardulli, *et al.*, *Disjointed War*, p. 56.

128. Cited from Oleg Levitan, "Inside Moscow's Kosovo Muddle," *Survival*, Vol. 42, No. 1, Spring 2000, p. 132. See the joint statement issued by Yeltsin and Milošević in Auerswald and Auerswald, *The Kosovo Conflict*, pp. 196-197.

129. Celestine Bohlan, "Russia Vows to Block the U.N. from Backing Attack on Serbs," *The New York Times*, October 7, 1998, p. A8.

130. Auerswald and Auerswald, *The Kosovo Conflict*, pp. 744-745; and Barton Gellman, "U.S., Allies Launch Air Attack on Yugoslav Military Targets," *The Washington Post*, March 25, 1999, p. A1.

131. Auerswald and Auerswald, *The Kosovo Conflict*, p. 748.

132. In his memoir, Wesley Clark refers to this modest flotilla flamboyantly as a "Russian battle group." Clark, *Waging Modern War*, p. 212.

133. See his press statement of March 31 in Auerswald and Auerswald, *The Kosovo Conflict*, p. 761.

134. Judith Matloff, "Russia's Tough Talk Unsettles the West," *The Christian Science Monitor*, April 12, 1999, p. 1; and A. Matveyev, "Washington's Claim to World Leadership," *International Affairs*, Vol. 45, No. 5, 1999, p. 53.

135. Primakov was dismissed as prime minister on behalf of interim replacement Sergei Stepachin on May 12, 1999, with the Kosovo conflict still underway. See François Bonnet, "En limogeant M. Primakov, M. Eltsine ouvre une crise majeure en Russie," *Le Monde*, May 13, 1999.

136. Auerswald and Auerswald, *The Kosovo Conflict*, pp. 863-868.

137. Sharon LaFraniere, "American, Russian Seek Kosovo Solution," *The Washington Post*, April 28, 1999, p. 21.

138. According to Daalder and O'Hanlon, *Winning Ugly*, pp. 168-169, the proposal to engage Ahtisaari in the effort came from Madeleine Albright. Strobe Talbott, *The Russian Hand: A Memoir of Presidential Diplomacy*, New York: Random House, 2002, p. 314, credits himself with the choice. In Talbott's account, Sandy Berger is reported to have described the combination of Chernomyrdin and Ahtisaari as a "hammer and anvil" between which Milošević could be beaten into submission.

139. Auerswald and Auerswald, *The Kosovo Conflict*, p. 944.

140. Talbott, *The Russian Hand*, pp. 317-321.

141. Martin Walker, "Revealed: How Deal Was Done in Stalin's Hideaway," *The Guardian*, June 5, 1999.

142. Auerswald and Auerswald, *The Kosovo Conflict*, pp. 1078-1081.

143. *Ibid.*, pp. 1101-1106.

144. Reconfirmed a year later as "Military Technical Agreement between the International Security Force ("KFOR") and the Governments of the Federal Republic of Yugoslavia and the Republic of Serbia," June 9, 2000, in *www.stratfor.com/crisis/kosovo/specialreprosts/special84.htm*.

145. Stephen T. Hosmer, *The Conflict Over Kosovo: Why Milosevic Decided to Settle When He Did*, Santa Monica, CA: RAND, 2001, pp. 133-134.

146. Rebecca Grant, *The Kosovo Campaign: Aerospace Power Made it Work*, Arlington, VA: The Air Force Association, September 1999, offers an enthusiastic perspective on the role of air power in the conflict.

147. The text of the indictment appears in Auerswald and Auerswald, *The Kosovo Conflict*, pp. 1005-1027.

148. Text of Clinton's Address to the Nation on Kosovo, June 9, 1999, in *www.stratfor.com/crisis/kosovo/specialreports/special86.htm*.

149. Clark, *Waging Modern War*, p. 348.

150. Vladimir Mukhin, "Rossiiskii desant operedil natovskii kontingent," *Nezavisimoe voennoe obozrenie*, 18 June 1999.

151. Clark, *Waging Modern War*, p. 388.

152. *Ibid.*, p. 394.

153. Igor' Korotchenko and Andrei Korbut, "Kompromiss mezhdu NATO i Rossiei naiden," *Nezavisimoe voennoe obozrenie*, June 25, 1999.

154. Daalder and O'Hanlon, *Winning Ugly*, make the strongest case to this effect.

155. David Rohde, "Kosovo Seething," *Foreign Affairs*, Vol. 79, No. 3, May/June 2000, p. 70. See also Marcus Gee, "Europe's Whipping Boy: Kosovo Gypsies Live in Fear of Albanian Revenge," *The Globe and Mail*, March 23, 2000.

156. Michael Mandelbaum, "A Perfect Failure: NATO's War Against Yugoslavia," *Foreign Affairs*, Vol. 78, No. 5, September/October 1999.

157. Francis Deron, "Pékin entend obtenir des 'compensations' politiques après l'erreur de l'OTAN," *Le Monde*, May 14, 1999.

158. Michael Ignatieff, *Virtual War: Kosovo and Beyond*, New York: Metropolitan Books, 2000, pp. 161, 163.

159. The United States flew 60 percent of total sorties in Operation ALLIED FORCE, but 80 percent of strike sorties, 90 percent of advanced intelligence and reconnaissance missions, and 90 percent of electronic warfare missions. U.S. forces fired over 80 percent of the precision guided weapons used in the conflict, and 95 percent of the cruise missiles. Anthony Cordesman, *Lessons and Non-Lessons of the Air and Missile War in Kosovo*, Washington, DC: Center for Strategic and International Studies, 1999.

160. Clark, *Waging Modern War*, p. 419.

CHAPTER 6

GREECE, TURKEY, CYPRUS

Brother Enemies.

Greece and Turkey are integral parts of Southeastern Europe and both played active roles as regional powers during the turbulence of the 1990s. Following the breakup of Yugoslavia, Athens strove to maintain some degree of solidarity with the Orthodox Christian peoples of the region including Serbia, while Ankara aligned with Muslim communities under siege.[1] Both tended to view the other's search for influence as threatening — Balkan engagement was often interpreted as the manifestation of a grand strategy of encirclement.[2] The more extreme interpretations of this ilk were intended primarily for public consumption, however. Rhetoric aside, Greek and Turkish authorities took pains to keep their regional policies aligned with the Western powers, and to avoid being dragged into confrontation.

In the best of all possible worlds, Greece and Turkey would be pillars of stability amidst the turbulence of the Balkans and the eastern Mediterranean. Both states enjoy privileged access to European institutions. Levels of well-being lag behind the standards of the most advanced European states, but in the regional context Greece and Turkey are in leadership roles. Athens and Ankara have powerful state traditions with strong cultural foundations, and multiple assets that could be brought to bear to promote regional development. These assets have to some extent been squandered due to the inability of Greeks and Turks to move beyond a history of enmity. For much of the post-war period Athens and Ankara have been archrivals whose antagonism has approached the level of preoccupation. Rather than contributing to a resolution of the southeastern European security dilemma, Greece and Turkey have been among its main progenitors.

Greek-Turkish rivalry is unusual in that the protagonists are very unevenly matched. Greece is a small Balkan state with a population of 10.5 million. Turkey has a more complex Eurasian character, with a large and rapidly growing population of over 65 million. Greece is a member of both NATO and the EU, and relations with institutional Europe dominate its international agenda. Turkey is also a NATO member, and a candidate for EU membership, but it has a long

Asian frontier and a difficult geostrategic situation "at the center of a crescent-shaped wedge of territory stretching from Kazakhstan to the Gulf and Suez and finally to the North African coast, containing the most volatile collection of states in the world."[3] Greek security policy is focused on local challenges. Turkey is an aspiring mid-level power with prospects that match its ambitions. Ankara has assumed significant commitments in the Caucasus and Central Asian regions since the break up of the USSR. Relations with neighboring Iraq and Syria are troubled, and ties to the Arab world as a whole have been damaged by an emerging strategic link to Israel.[4] Greece is reasonably stable domestically, while Turkey continues to struggle with the rise of political Islam, a sharp economic downturn, and the demands of its Kurdish minority.[5]

Greece and Turkey maintain high levels of readiness and burdensome military expenditures. At the end of the 1990s Turkey devoted 3.8 percent of its Gross Domestic Product to defense spending and Greece 4.7 percent (against a NATO average of 2.2 percent), and both sides had initiated ambitious force modernization programs. There is nonetheless little doubt that Turkey has the wherewithal to prevail in a direct confrontation. Turkish GDP is approximately 1.5 times that of Greece, and militarily it enjoys something like a 4-1 ratio of superiority with 594,000 soldiers in arms (477,000 in land forces, 63,000 in the air force, and 54,000 in marine forces) compared to a Greek force of 168,700 (116,000 on land, 33,000 in the air, and 19,700 at sea). Greek policy toward Turkey, and the burden of preparedness that has been associated with it, has been dominated by the need to deter a powerful and potentially hostile neighbor.

Unresolved tensions impact negatively upon Ankara's foreign policy agenda as well. Turkey's long-standing goal of accession to the EU has repeatedly been sacrificed to the pursuit of its rivalry with Greece. In view of the challenges that it confronts on other fronts, eternal bickering with Athens might well be portrayed as a luxury, if not an extravagance. Rivalry persists all the same, irrespective of the constant ministrations of NATO, the good will of innumerable mediators and profferers of good offices, the objective needs of the conflict-torn Balkan region, and the best interests of almost all those involved.

There are at least two reasons why this is so. First, though it is sometimes concerned as much with symbol as with substance,

Greek-Turkish rivalry is deeply rooted and complex. The underlying issues that propel animosity are neither trivial nor straightforward, and they defy facile solutions. Second, the rivalry is set in a larger spatial and temporal context. Greek-Turkish relations are often discussed on the basis of "ancient hatred" assumptions that emphasize their timeless character — what Henry Kissinger has called the "atavistic bitterness" and "primeval hatred of Greeks and Turks."[6] But the relationship is also dynamic. It has been marked by periods of détente as well as fits of tension, and is at present very much conditioned by circumstances specific to the post-cold war period, including the dynamic of regional instability produced by the Balkan crisis of the 1990s.

The dawn of a new millennium has seen movement towards Greek-Turkish rapprochement that is a source of promise for the entire region. But decades of rivalry and complex unresolved issues cannot be swept off the table overnight. The Greek-Turkish relationship remains a key to peace building in southeastern Europe that must be carefully monitored and, to the extent possible, shaped to encourage compromise solutions that allow both parties to realize their potential as neighbors, partners, and forces for regional stability.

Historical and Cultural Dimensions.

Greek national identity rests upon three pillars: the legacy of Hellenism, the Byzantine and Orthodox Christian heritage, and the national revival of the modern period. The classical legacy is timeless, and in some sense universal. The Byzantine Empire was Greek in language and in spirit, and its collapse in the face of the Ottoman assault is almost universally regarded as an epic tragedy and the prelude to a dark age of cultural effacement, the *Turkokratia* or age of Turkish domination. Modern Greek nationalism is a product of the 19th century national revival, waged as a bitter struggle against Ottoman overlordship. The first Greek national state, created in 1830, only represented about one-third of the Hellenic people of the Balkans. Thereafter, modern Greece was constructed piece by piece, as the consequence of a long sequence of wars, diplomatic maneuvers, and uprisings forwarding *enosis*, or union with the Motherland, inspired by the *Megali Idea* (Great Idea) of uniting all the Hellenic peoples of the eastern Mediterranean in a single state.

This process was coterminous with the long decline of Ottoman civilization. In Turkish national memory, it is linked with a gradual loss of great power status and cultural preeminence. For the Turks, Byronic Pan-Hellenism is considered to have been little more than a convenient justification for great power meddling in the affairs of the empire, an attempt that would culminate at the end of the First World War in an effort to incorporate former Ottoman territories into the European colonial system. The modern Turkish Republic is regarded as the product of a successful effort to resist dismemberment, led by Mustafa Kemal (Atatürk) and associated with the assertion of a specifically Turkish national idea.

The tragic culmination of the *Megali Idea* coincided with that assertion. The division of the Ottoman Empire envisioned by the Versailles peacemakers included a partition of Anatolia, with the projected creation of a Kurdish national state in the east, and a 5-year mandate granted to a Greek expeditionary force in Smyrna (Izmir), center of the ancient Hellenic communities of the western coastal areas.[7] These plans were challenged by Kemal, who drew upon his military connections to build up an independent armed force and rally a Turkish national movement out of the reach of the allies in Ankara. In 1922 the Greek expeditionary force imprudently opted to advance on Kemal's headquarters, pillaging Turkish communities along its route. Decisively defeated on the Sakarya River, it was driven back into Smyrna in disarray. The occupation of the city degenerated into violence, including massacres of the Greek and Armenian populations and a conflagration that destroyed much of the old harbor area. The remnant of the Greek expeditionary force was withdrawn by sea. Without protection, Greek communities in Turkish held territory throughout Anatolia were subjected to harassment and reprisals.[8]

The Treaty of Lausanne brought an end to the conflict in 1923 by sanctioning state sponsored ethnic cleansing — over 1.5 million Greek and Turkish citizens were required to relocate across the newly drawn border as part of an organized transfer of populations. Though it is sometimes presented as a solution, the forced migrations only exacerbated relations between communities in the long run. For the Turks, the events of 1919-23 are commemorated as the War of National Independence, whose outcome ensured the consolidation of a viable Turkish national state. For the Greeks they are the "catastrophe," a cataclysmic defeat that brought a violent end to the millennial Hellenistic civilization of Asia Minor. Like other countries whose national idea rests upon a cult of martyrdom derived from a long and only partially realized struggle for independence, modern Greek national identity has been culturally constructed around a myth of resistance to a barbaric, alien, and permanently menacing other. In the case of Turkey, national identity has been defined against the foil of rivalry with an eternal Greek enemy, always ready to take advantage of Turkish weakness, and simultaneously resented and scorned.[9]

Outside the context of this mythic structure, of course, Greek-Turkish relations have been subject to greater nuance. The peace of Lausanne was followed by a phase of rapprochement under Turkish President Kemal and Greek Prime Minister Eleftherios Venizelos, architects of war in 1919 but now seeking to prioritize domestic reform. The policy survived its architects, and Greek-Turkish feuding was not a significant factor in international relations from 1930-55.[10]

It was only with the rise of anti-British national agitation on the island of Cyprus in the mid-1950s that Greek-Turkish rivalry made a comeback. In the post-World War II period, both Greece and Turkish had become modernizing societies subject to traumatic social change including rapid urbanization, progress toward universal literacy, and the rise of mass political cultures where the evocation of an invented national tradition displayed against the foil of the despised rival played well in public forums. On both sides, political elites manipulated national sentiments to further their quest for power, in the process conjuring up a strategic rivalry that would take on a life of its own.

The Wine Dark Sea.

The core of Greek-Turkish rivalry has been the struggle for control of Homer's wine dark sea, the Aegean and eastern Mediterranean. It is by any measure a vital interest for both sides. For Greece, the sea constitutes an essential part of the nation, attaching the Greek mainland to major islands and island groups. For Turkey, the Aegean covers the north-south maritime artery linking the Dardanelles to the Mediterranean coast including the port of Izmir, and the air corridors providing access for civil aviation toward the west. Today, the Aegean and eastern Mediterranean have assumed additional geostrategic significance as the western pole of an emerging commercial axis stretching east and southward toward the Caspian Sea and the Persian-Arabian Gulf. Marcia Christoff Kurop argues that "the eastern Mediterranean and the Persian Gulf form a single entity with Turkey and Egypt providing a continental and maritime bridge between Europe and the Middle East."[11] For Margarita Mathiopoulos, the Aegean is "a geopolitical region of vital interest" as "NATO's corridor of stability between Europe, the Middle East, and the former Soviet Asian territories."[12]

In the recent past stability has been in short supply. By imposing population transfers and delineating spheres of influence, the Lausanne treaty created a kind of equilibrium in the region. That equilibrium began to unravel with the emergence of the Cyprus question in the 1950s, which reposed the issue of strategic control over maritime space. By the 1970s a long list of points of discord had emerged that defy resolution to this day.

1. Sovereignty and the Militarization of Strategic Islands.

There are approximately 3,000 Greek islands in the Aegean Sea, of which only about 130 are inhabited. At Lausanne in 1923 and in the 1947 Treaty of Paris, which transferred the Dodecanese island group from Italy to Greece, Athens agreed to keep only lightly armed security forces on western Aegean islands and to refrain from the construction of fortifications. The militarization of selected islands was nonetheless begun in 1964, and by the 1970s over 25,000 Greek soldiers were stationed in the Dodecanese adjacent to Turkey's Mediterranean coast, on Lemnos, Samothrace, and smaller islands near the entrance to the Dardanelles, and on certain central Aegean islands.

Greece has argued according to the *clausala rebus sic stantibus* that the Montreux Straits Convention of 1936 lifts the demilitarized status of islands adjacent to the Dardanelles; that Turkey is not a signatory to the 1947 Treaty of Paris and that therefore the Dodecanese can be armed; and that, especially in the wake of the Cyprus occupation of 1974 and the creation of a 4th Aegean Army unattached to NATO on the eastern coast of the Turkish mainland with its headquarters in Izmir in 1975, Greece perceives a Turkish threat to which it may legitimately react in self-defense under Article 51 of the UN Charter. Turkey has responded that the demilitarization of eastern Aegean islands is a condition of Greek sovereignty; that no essential change in circumstance has occurred; that the Paris treaty also applies to nonsignatories; that the Montreux Convention does not change the status of Lemnos and adjacent islands; and that there was no prior Turkish threat motivating Greek actions--Ankara has only undertaken countermeasures in the face of severe Greek provocation. These issues remain unresolved, and the militarized islands are points of constant friction.

The problem is complemented by disputes over sovereignty. The maritime frontier between the Dodecanese group and the Turkish coast was precisely delineated in a 1932 agreement between Italy and Turkey, but since April 1996 Ankara has posed concerns about "gray zones" of undetermined sovereignty further to the north, where the terms of the 1923 Lausanne agreement are less specific, as well as in the Sea of Crete. The Turkish demand for adjudication has been portrayed as a maneuver to obtain leverage with an eye upon a future comprehensive resolution of Aegean issues, but it also has a strategic dimension.[13]

2. *Delimitation of the Continental Shelf.*

The Aegean seabed became an object of contention following the discovery of oil deposits off the island of Thasos in 1974. Bilateral negotiations began in 1981 but were broken off at Greek initiative in 1987. Turkey responded by initiating seismic activities and drilling in disputed areas, giving rise to a sharp crisis in the spring of that year. Since 1987 the issue has become less acute, due in part to the modest extent of the resources in question, but it is far from having been resolved. Athens argues that (a) the islands facing the Turkish mainland are a part of Greece, and Greek lands must be considered to be an integral whole; (b) the Geneva Convention of 1958 on the continental shelf specifies that islands possess continental shelves; and (c) the continental shelf border between Turkey and the adjacent Greek islands must be based on the equidistance principle measured from the nearest Turkish coast. If applied, these premises would give Greece effective control over nearly all the Aegean Sea, leaving only a narrow coastal strip for Turkey.

In response, Ankara has argued that (a) islands located on the natural prolongation of a continental land mass do not have continental shelves of their own; (b) the 1982 Law of the Sea Convention disallows consolidation of Aegean islands with continental Greece by forbidding an "archipelago regime" or "national integrity" principle; (c) there is no rule of law or logic that dictates an "equidistance principle" between small islands and a large adjacent land mass, and (d) the Treaty of Lausanne mandates a balance permitting each side to utilize the sea on an equitable basis. A broad range of factors specific to the character of the Aegean, including its semi-closed character, the Greek archipelago regime, the distribution of natural resources, mutual security interests, and lines of communication must be considered in delimiting a continental shelf. Turkey's ideal solution would impose a line of division allowing it to exploit a significant part of the eastern half of the seabed. Ankara has, however, consistently refused Greek requests to bring the issue before the International Court of Justice. It has preferred to seek a bilateral agreement, perhaps less due to the merits of the legal case than of fear for the potential implications of a court ruling for other unresolved disputes, notably its differences with Syria and Iraq over control of the waters of the Euphrates.[14]

3. *Territorial Waters.*

At Lausanne, territorial waters in the Aegean were extended for only three miles. In 1936, Greece unilaterally expanded its territorial waters to six miles, and following World War II Turkey reciprocated. Today, with the six-mile limit as standard, Greece possesses 48.86 percent of the Aegean and Turkey possesses 7.47 percent, leaving 48.85 percent as international waters. The 1985 Law of the Sea Treaty, which Turkey has refused to sign, allows a 12-mile extension of territorial waters, the extension that Turkey applies to its Mediterranean and Black Sea coastlines. In 1995 the Greek parliament asserted its right to enforce a 12-mile limit in the Aegean, a gesture that Ankara promptly labeled a *casus belli*. Although the Turkish response was aggressive, Greece's original claim was clearly provocatory. The imposition of a 12-mile limit would bring together Greek territorial waters between the Cyclades and Dodecanese archipelagos, giving Athens hypothetical control over a vital north-south line of communication, as well as maritime access to the Black Sea.

The issue is nonetheless more symbolic than real. The extent of effective control that a 12-mile limit would bring is not necessarily all that great. International law does not permit interdiction of peaceful commercial traffic, or even the passage of warships, except in cases of strong tension or open conflict. A 12-mile extension is moreover opposed by almost every other power with naval interests in the Aegean, and not least the major NATO powers. If the issue persists, it is in some measure because of its implications for the related problem of national airspace.

4. *Airspace Control.*

International law and the Chicago convention of 1944 require that the extent of national airspace correspond to the extent of territorial waters. Since 1931 Greece has asserted a national airspace limit of ten miles, valid for both continental Greece and the Greek archipelago, despite its formal adherence to six-mile territorial waters. From 1974 onward, Turkey has protested against this incongruity, and reinforced its position by systematically conducting over-flights in the four-mile gray zone. These interventions are regularly challenged by Greek aviation, leading to instances of mock combat and occasional clashes. Disputes over airspace have given rise to other sources of tension, including differences over air corridors in the Istanbul-Athens flight region, international flight routing, terminal areas, and military flight issues such as early-warning borders, command and control areas, and flight maneuvers. The argument directly affects flight borders for two NATO commands, the south-central NATO headquarters in Izmir (Izmir also hosts Turkey's 6th Allied Tactical Air Force) and the 7th Tactical Air Force in Larisa, Greece.

5. *Treatment of Minorities.*

Greece and Turkey have been chronically at odds over the treatment accorded to their respective minorities. Despite the population transfers carried out under the terms of the Lausanne treaty, a sizable Turkish minority remained in western Thrace (in 1923 the Muslim population of western Thrace was estimated at 130,000, out of a total regional population of 190,000) together with a Greek population of over 100,000 in Istanbul, as well as smaller minorities of 7,000 and 1,200, respectively, on the Turkish islands of Bozcaada (Tenedos) and Gokceada (Imbros). Lausanne made specific reference to these "Muslim and non-Muslim" minorities and guaranteed them the right to maintain autonomous religious, cultural, and educational institutions.

The Greek side is fond of pointing out that the Greek population of Istanbul has been reduced today to under 10,000, and that only 250 Greeks remain on Gokceada and 100 on Bozcaada, while the

Muslim population of western Thrace has remained fairly stable at around 120,000. Ankara retorts that a natural rate of increase would have more than doubled the population of western Thrace were it not for mass migration provoked by a Greek policy of denial of identity and systematic repression. The numbers are disputed, and the climate of hostility that infects Greek-Turkish relations allows little space for flexibility.[15]

Athens has reacted to international criticism of its policy in western Thrace by offering a number of concessions including educational incentives and limited self-government, but it refuses to designate the minority in question as Turkish, clinging instead to the "Muslim" designation used in the text of the Lausanne treaty. According to Greek sources, about half of the community are of Turkish descent, 35 percent are Bulgarian speaking Pomaks (Muslim Slavs), and 15 percent are Muslim Roma. The concerned peoples have a long list of grievances that includes the expropriation of land by the Greek state, denial of citizenship to individuals returning from trips abroad, educational discrimination, refusal of the right of election for local religious leaders or Muftis (in 1990 Greece suspended the election of local Muftis in favor of appointment by the state), and electoral gerrymandering aimed at denying the Turkish minority fair representation.[16] The status of the Greek minority and Orthodox Patriarchate in Istanbul remain sore points with Greek public opinion, and, as an ethnically Turkish region that is territorially contiguous with Turkey proper, western Thrace is militarily exposed and a point of potential leverage in the larger Greek-Turkish strategic competition.

The precedent most often cited to evoke a Turkish threat to western Thrace is that of Cyprus, where a Turkish expeditionary force, in defiance of international opinion, has maintained control of an ethnically Turkish enclave on an island with a majority Greek population for over a quarter century. The Cyprus problem is importantly affected by disputes over sovereignty in the Aegean, but is has a distinct character and great symbolic weight. Cyprus has become the most polarized, embittered, and intractable of all the issues that continue to set Greeks and Turks at odds.

The Green Line.

The beautiful island of Cyprus, mythical birthplace of Aphrodite, has an important location some 80 kilometers off of Turkey's southern Mediterranean coast and a complex history that reflects its strategic importance. Culturally and socially, like the larger Balkan region of which it is in fact a part, it has been subjected to waves of external influence, including periods of Byzantine, Venetian, Hellenic, Turkic, and British predominance. From 1571-1878 the island was part of the Ottoman Empire, but at the Congress of Berlin in 1878 it was leased to Britain for use as a naval basing area. Cyprus was annexed by London in 1918 and declared a crown colony in 1925.

The population of Cyprus today is around 830,000, divided between a Greek majority representing about 80 percent of the total and a Turkish minority representing 18 percent. These communities traditionally lived interspersed throughout the island, which included numerous mixed villages. The anti-colonial movement launched in the 1950s, however, was simultaneously a Greek nationalist movement that sought to link the call for independence to the goal of *enosis*, or attachment to Greece. Turkish Cypriot leaders responded with a call for *taksim*, or partition. These divergent political agendas quickly became the source of intercommunal friction.

In August 1955 the United Kingdom, which sought to resist Cypriote self-determination but whose personnel on the island were coming under attack, attempted to address the problem by convening a conference bringing together representatives of Greece and Turkey in London. At the conference, Britain offered an arrangement for partial self-government under British sovereignty that was not fully acceptable to either party. Perhaps more importantly, with deliberations in progress a bomb exploded at the Turkish consulate in Thessalonica (in the immediate vicinity of the house in which Atatürk was born). This act of terrorism was eventually discovered to have been a Turkish provocation, responsibility for which became one of the items in the bill of indictment brought against then Prime Minister Adnan Menderes that would lead to his execution by hanging in September 1961, after his government was overturned by a military putsch. The immediate consequence was a series of anti-Greek pogroms in Izmir and Istanbul, where over 2,000 Greeks were killed and many more driven from the city as refugees.[17] In a pattern that would repeat itself in former Yugoslavia decades later, these bloody proceeding polarized public opinion and contributed to a process of ethnic mobilization that would make rational resolution of disputes nearly impossible.

Between 1956-60 the tone of Cypriot politics was set by the terrorist anti-British agitation of the National Organization of Cypriot Fighters (EOKA) led by Georgios Grivas, a retired army colonel with extreme right-wing political affiliations. After a British expeditionary force of over 30,000 soldiers proved insufficient to control the violence, London moved toward an agenda for separation. A February 1959 Zurich agreement between Greece and Turkey defined a formula for independence that was formalized in a Treaty of Guarantee signed in London in 1960. The treaty identified Greece, Turkey, and the United Kingdom as guaranteeing powers with the right to intervene, severally or unilaterally, in defense of its provisions, and drew up basic articles for a constitutional order. According to the terms, the U.K. would retain two military base areas (which it still maintains), while Greece and Turkey were permitted to garrison 950 and 650 soldiers respectively on the island. The constitution specifically forbade attachment to another state (placing Cyprus alongside Austria as the only countries in the world whose sovereignty has been thus circumscribed). It also defined a power-sharing arrangement inspired by the premises of ethnic quotas and balancing, according to which a Greek Cypriot would serve as president and a Turkish Cypriot as vice president, with four Greek Cypriot and three Turkish Cypriot ministers. Thirty percent of the seats in the House of Representatives were reserved for the Turkish Cypriot minority, 40 percent of commissions in the National Guard, and 30 percent of positions in the police force and civil service. The president and vice-president were each accorded the right to veto legislation, and separate communal municipalities were established in the five largest Cypriot towns. These arrangements sought to reassure the Turkish Cypriot minority by granting it limited autonomy and disproportionate representation within key national bodies. In August 1960 the Greek Cypriot Archbishop Makarios III became the first president, and the Turkish Cypriot Fazıl Küçük the first vice-president, of an independent Republic of Cyprus.[18]

The Cypriot constitution was flawed, and it quickly proved to be nonviable in practice. Makarios launched the crisis that undermined his country's fragile equilibriums on November 30, 1963, after repeated deadlocks over matters of policy, by proposing 13 amendments designed to curtail many of the special advantages accorded to the Turkish Cypriot minority. Within a matter of weeks communal strife exploded in the capital of Nicosia, driven forward by the harassment of Turkish Cypriots at the hands of Greek extremists, including efforts to ethnically cleanse whole districts by using intimidation and coercion to force residents from their homes. In reaction the Turkish Cypriots withdrew from all governmental institutions and began to establish armed enclaves as nodal points for self-defense. These events have been interpreted by some as the product of a Greek Cypriot strategic design, known as the Akritas Plan, intended to place the Turkish Cypriot community on the defensive and provoke a collapse of the constitutional order.[19] In 1964 a UN multilateral peacekeeping force (the UN Force in Cyprus – UNFICYP) arrived on the island to police a 180-kilometer long "Green Line" separating Greek and Turkish Cypriot populations driven by ethnic mobilization into protected areas and communal redoubts. UNFICYP has remained in place to this day, at an estimated cumulative cost of over $3 billion.[20]

These events were decisive. As was the intention of their perpetrators, the atrocities committed by Greek Cypriot irregulars shattered the foundation of trust that was required to allow national institutions to function. The same kind of dynamic would be set to work by the Serbs and Croats of Yugoslavia years later, with comparable results. Reliance upon UN peacekeepers was both an admission that the island's problems were not resolvable in their own terms, and (as in Croatia during 1992-95) a panacea that made the ethnic separation provoked by violence appear to be tolerable. The Makarios government was discredited, and outside powers were quick to move into the emerging power vacuum. In the immediate aftermath of the communal violence of 1963-64, a Turkish military contingent was deployed in strategic positions on the north of the island, occupying the Nicosia-Kyrenia highway linking the capital to the northern coast. By 1967 Greek forces stationed on Cyprus had been expanded to over 10,000. In these threatening circumstances, consistent with a general pattern of post-colonial realignment in strategically sensitive areas and motivated by concern over the implications of the conflict for NATO, the United States stepped forward to take over the role of the U.K. as great power sponsor and crisis manager. In both 1964 and 1967 Turkey threatened invasion to restore order and protect its co-nationals, but was dissuaded by vigorous admonition from Washington.[21]

In 1968 intercommunal talks began, mediated by U.S. envoy Cyrus Vance with Rauf Denktaş representing the Turkish Cypriot community and Glavkos Clerides the Greek Cypriots. Denktaş and Clerides had grown up together in Nicosia as neighbors and schoolmates. Once risen to prominence as the legal voices of their respective ethnic constituencies, their personal relationship, and rivalry, would become an important part of the Cypriot puzzle. Negotiations arrived at a deadlock in 1971, but were resumed under UN auspices in 1972. Despite some will to compromise, a consensual middle ground proved to be elusive. Meanwhile, international events added new complications. The increasing intensity of cold war competition in the eastern Mediterranean made the U.S. distrustful of the nonaligned orientation and left-wing supporters of the Makarios regime — Henry Kissinger famously dubbed the Cypriot Archbishop "the Castro of the Mediterranean." The 1968 military coup in Athens, which placed power in the hands of an outspokenly anti-communist group of colonels, seemed to strengthen the Western posture in the region, but the colonels' lack of popular legitimacy and aggressive nationalism would soon become problems in their own right. In 1971, for the second time in a decade, the Turkish military seized control in Ankara. Though democratic institutions were eventually restored, Turkish elites felt constrained to reinforce their position by rebuilding domestic support. The government led by the social democrat Bülent Ecevit, which acceded to power in 1973, had a strong nationalist orientation and was particularly loath to give ground on the Cyprus question. These varied events created a volatile context that the Cyprus dilemma constantly threatened to set ablaze.

In November 1973 a student rebellion against the Greek junta was shattered by an army-led massacre of demonstrators in the heart of Athens. Simultaneously, Georgios Papadopoulos was ousted as leader of the ruling junta and replaced by Brigadier General Dimitrios Ioannides. Under domestic pressure, Ioannides turned to Grivas and his nationalist allies in Cyprus, hoping to restore the position of the junta through a dramatic gesture by attaching the island to Greece through a *coup de main*. On July 15, 1974, Greek National Guard and regular military contingents seized power in Cyprus, but failed in the attempt to abduct and murder Makarios, now viewed as an impediment to the agenda for *enosis*. Forewarned by allies at his sanctuary in the isolated Troodos Monastery, the Archbishop made a narrow escape, and was spirited away to London with British assistance.

In Makarios' absence the Cypriot presidency fell into the hands of former EOKA gunman Nikos Sampson, and intercommunal violence exploded. In reaction, and on the basis of what can be described as a legitimate desire to protect the Turkish Cypriot minority in a moment of extreme peril, on July 19 a Turkish expeditionary force set sail from Mercin. Once landed on Cyprus, Turkish forces seized a narrow stretch of the northern coast, but in the face of resistance from Cypriot National Guard and Greek army forces, they were not able to penetrate inland and secure control of Nicosia airport.[22] On July 22 an UN-sponsored cease-fire was imposed, and on July 24, after the Greek armed forces refused to obey Ioannides' desperate order for an all-out attack on Turkey, the junta collapsed in Athens. Power was temporarily placed in the hands of a coalition of civilian leaders directed by Konstantinos Karamanlis. Karamanlis was not responsible for the Greek provocation on Cyprus, and he was anxious to reverse the course of events. But the miserable failure of Ioannides' adventure had let the genie of communal mobilization out of the bottle and opened the door to a Turkish occupation of the northern part of the island.

Greece's military fiasco on Cyprus was followed by a diplomatic farce in Geneva. In a hastily organized forum on the shore of Lake Leman, Ankara presented demands for a Cypriot federation that would grant co-equal status to the Greek and Turkish Cypriot communities. The disorganized Greek government was not in a position to react effectively, and a distracted U.S. (with the administration of President Richard M. Nixon preoccupied by the Watergate crisis) chose not to force the issue.[23] After articulating its demands, and winning time for its forces to regroup, Ankara ordered a new offensive on Cyprus. On August 14 the Turkish "Peace Force" broke out of its beachhead on the northern coast to the east and west, eventually seizing control over nearly 40 percent of the island's territory. The advance culminated a process of ethnic cleansing that would leave about 230,000 Cypriots (including 180,000 Greek Cypriots) uprooted. In 1975, at a Vienna conference conducted under UN auspices, both sides agreed to a "voluntary" separation of populations, leaving the Turkish Cypriots assembled under Ankara's protection in the north, and the Greek Cypriots pressed below the Green Line in the south. The fate of the island was mirrored within Nicosia, which was also divided by a hastily thrown up wooden barrier into Greek and Turkish Cypriot zones.

Cyprus had been subjected to a de facto partition that would prove to be enduring. On February 11, 1975, a Turkish Federated State of Cyprus, with Denktaş as president, was declared into being. The name selected seemed to hold out the promise of reassociation with the Greek Cypriot republic in the south, but in 1983 Denktaş renamed his satrapy the Turkish Republic of Northern Cyprus (TRNC) and declared full independence. To date, the Turkish Republic is the only state in the world that has accorded the TRNC diplomatic recognition.

Christopher Hitchens has argued that the essence of the Cyprus tragedy from 1960 onward was "the exploitation of outside powers of internal differences that were genuine in themselves" with the purpose "to suborn the independence of the island."[24] Hitchen's thesis may be disputed, but there is little doubt that in the cold war context within which they unfolded Cypriot events were interpreted in view of an overriding Western interest in preserving the unity of NATO. For a time Washington sought to placate both sides, suborning Cyprus to a Western-oriented government in Athens that would block the emergence of an independent-minded, nonaligned, and left-leaning regime of the sort that Makarios seemed to aspire to, while simultaneously offering autonomy to a Turkish enclave in the north. The U.S.-sponsored Acheson Plan of the mid-1960s moved in this direction by proposing a division of the island between a Greek Cypriot republic in the south oriented toward Greece, and two Turkish Cypriot cantons defended by a Turkish military base in the north. In 1974, however, the United States had little choice but to bow to Ankara's military *fait accompli* in the hopes that ethnic partition might provide a new ground for stability. Between December 1975 and September 1978 the United States cut off military aid to Ankara in protest against the occupation, but, while the gesture had a viscerally negative impact upon U.S.-Turkish relations, it had no discernable effect upon Turkish policy. And, as Ankara has not failed to underline ever since, after 1974 the situation on the island was calm. The first Turkish incursion could be justified under the terms of the Treaty of Guarantee. The second offensive went beyond reasonable bounds in asserting control over more than a third of the island, but the Turkish Peace Force had done the work of the junkyard dog by imposing what appeared to be a sustainable status quo that did not affect strategic equilibriums in the Mediterranean.

The 1974 resolution rested upon a combination of *enosis* and *taksim* that provided some advantage to all sides. Athens' defeat on the island was humiliating, but Greece had emerged in a position to cultivate special relations with an ethnically homogenous Republic of Cyprus. Ankara had warded off the worst-case scenario of a successful Greek coup, reinforced its military position, and ensured that the Turkish Cypriot community would remain dependent upon Turkish sponsorship. The United States avoided a direct Greek-Turkish clash and removed the Cyprus imbroglio from its strategic agenda. Or so it hoped. In fact nothing had been permanently resolved, and the Cyprus question remained an open wound that would continue to poison efforts to craft an enduring Greek-Turkish rapprochement.

Greek-Turkish Relations after the Cold War.

The contours of the Cyprus problem changed remarkably little in the decades following the Turkish occupation. The TRNC controlled 37 percent of the island's territory and 18 percent of its population, almost uniquely of Turkish and Turkish Cypriot extraction, and was permanently occupied by approximately 35,000 soldiers of the Turkish 3rd Army. Turkey also maintained a dominant position within the TRNC's police force, militia, and secret services. Isolated internationally, the TRNC was for all intents and purposes a Turkish protectorate. To the south, across the Green Line patrolled by 1200 UNFICYP peacekeepers, lay the predominantly Greek Cypriot Republic of Cyprus, internationally recognized as the legitimate government of the island but with no effective authority inside the Turkish zone. The Republic of Cyprus flourished economically while the Turkish occupied areas stagnated — by the early 1990s average per capita income in the Republic of Cyprus was far higher than that of the Turkish zone, and also exceeded that of the Turkish Republic and of Greece itself.[25] The record of initiatives aimed at overcoming the impasse, pursued over the years by UN Secretary Generals, U.S. presidents, and multilateral negotiating forums, reads like an encyclopedia of diplomacy, but little of substance was achieved. The Cyprus problem, like the poor, seemed destined always to be with us.

The perception of stasis was misleading. During the cold war decades, Greek-Turkish competition was constrained by a number of domestic and international factors. Athens and Ankara were aware that they shared a common interest in helping to contain Soviet power, and both were dependent upon association with the Atlantic Alliance for basic security guarantees. Though forced to cater to nationalistic self-other images rooted in popular perception and prejudice, it was clear that a resort to force would not serve respective national interests. Greek-Turkish rivalry played out in the shadow of the superpowers and, like many other cold war conflicts with implications for the East-West strategic balance, was constrained by the exigencies of competitive bipolarity.

The end of the Cold War removed many of these constraints, and for a moment seemed to transform a chronic but contained rivalry into a potentially more volatile and dangerous one. The changed configuration of power in the "arc of crisis" along the southern flank of the Russian Federation complicated Turkey's strategic agenda, encouraging a more assertive foreign policy and stimulating Greek concern. In the new geopolitics of the post-Cold War, Turkey's relevance as a pro-Western strategic ally in the greater Middle East was enhanced, likewise exacerbating Greek fears. The strategic stakes were also heightened by the eastern Mediterranean's status as a potential terminal for east-west pipeline routes.[26] Balkan instability and international intervention raised the issue of strategic control in the region, viewed as the focus for "a multi-regional strategic calculus incorporating southeastern Europe, the Middle East, and the Caucasus."[27] Greece and Turkey lay at the center of this calculus, and their bilateral relationship was inevitably affected by it.

Greek-Turkish relations during the 1990s were also affected by tension between Turkey and Europe. Ankara concluded an EC Accession Agreement (the Ankara Agreement) as long ago as 1963, supplemented in 1972 by an Additional Protocol.[28] In 1987 it applied in due form for full membership, and on March 6, 1995, initialed a Customs Union agreement.[29] According to Ozlan Sanberk, Turkey's permanent representative to the EU, these gestures confirmed Turkey's "traditional goal which is to align itself with Europe," a precondition for modernization and democratization and "strategically necessary to the defense and security of the West."[30] With the Warsaw Pact in disarray, the strategic necessity was apparently less strongly felt by the European powers, and after 1989, despite the pedigree of its application and generally more evolved relationships with European institutions, Turkey was pushed to the back of the line for EC accession formed by the emerging post-communist states. In its July 1997 blueprint for enlargement entitled *Agenda 2000* the European Commission eliminated Turkey from its list of candidate members "for the foreseeable future," and the European Council's Luxembourg session on December 13, 1997, did not include Turkey in its list of candidate states.[31] The rejection was partly motivated by a pragmatic awareness of developmental and demographic imbalances — Turkey has a rapidly growing population and its GDP per capita is only about half the EU average. It was encouraged by a sincere concern for Ankara's less than adequate human rights record, and particularly the dirty war in progress in southeastern Anatolia against Abdullah Öcalan's Kurdish Workers Party (PKK). But it was bitterly felt in Turkey, where the EU decision reinforced the conviction that a line was being drawn between a European "Christians' Club" and the lands of the East, still perceived in Orientalist fashion as the domain of backwardness and cultural exotica.[32] Greece, as a consistent opponent of Turkish association with Europe that regularly used its veto within the EU to block cooperation, became an obvious target for resentment.

Turkey's differences with the EU, and consequent alienation from the West, gave impetus to a search for alternative cultural affiliations and diplomatic alignments. The quest was encouraged by a protracted domestic crisis, provoked by a series of emerging challenges to Turkey's traditional Kemalist consensus.[33] Kemal's original vision for the Turkish Republic included rejection of the Ottoman imperial tradition on behalf of a unitary Turkish national state, centralized political direction under the aegis of the progressive officer corps, strict secularism, a Listian philosophy of economic protectionism, and a pro-Western strategic orientation.[34] These sureties have not, and could not have, survived Turkey's confrontation with the challenges of modernization. The decision by Kemal's ruling Republican People's Party to surrender its monopoly of power after World War II partially dismantled the authoritarian foundations of the project by opening the political spectrum to a wider range of contending forces, though the armed forces were always on hand to crack down on egregious dissent. Turgut Özal's economic reforms of the 1980s struck a further blow by exposing the country to global market forces. The disappearance of the Soviet Union after 1991, and with it a centuries-old common border with an expansive Russia to the north, weakened another pillar of Kemalism by opening new areas of concern in the Caucasus and post-Soviet

Central Asia, and calling into question the necessity of a strictly pro-Western international orientation. The electoral victory of Necmettin Erbakan's Islamic Welfare Party in December 1995, and Erbakan's appointment as Prime Minister in January 1996, seemed to complete the assault by challenging the Kemalist commitment to secularism.

The "silent coup" that led to Erbakan's resignation under military pressure in June 1997 and the subsequent outlawing of the Islamic Welfare Party by the Turkish Constitutional Court represented a Kemalist reassertion of sorts.[35] In August 1998 new army chief Huseyin Kivrikoğlu left no doubt as to the armed forces intentions, denouncing the "dark forces of fundamentalism" and asserting that "those who seek to undermine the secular state will continue to face the Turkish armed forces as they did before."[36] Repression did little to address the underlying sources of popular affiliation with Islamic alternatives, however, and the intrusive role of the military only served to highlight yet again the gap between the Turkish political model and democratic norms as understood in the West.

These developments were accompanied by a new interest in Turkey's Ottoman past, regarded not as a model to emulate but rather as a neglected source of national identity and pride.[37] For centuries the Ottoman Turks were the ruling elite of a great power presiding over an autonomous geopolitical space, not supplicants speaking from a peripheral extension of the "real" Europe. The Kemalist assertion of a European vocation contradicted this tradition, but was not entirely successful in replacing it. The impact of the Balkan conflict, where the Bosnian Muslims and Kosovar Albanians were widely viewed as victims of campaigns of genocide that were tolerated if not surreptitiously encouraged by the West; the outcome of the Gulf War, where Turkey was perceived to have made important sacrifices on behalf of the allied coalition and to have been rewarded with the creation of a Kurdish autonomous area in northern Iraq capable of providing sanctuary for insurgents; and the EU's apparent hostility to Turkey's European aspirations all contributed to the crystallization of a sharper and less beholden Turkish national idea. These perspectives identified an alternative to Turkey's European orientation in the attempt to become "a regional center in the emerging Eurasian political reality and a bridge between Europe and the region to its east and southeast."[38]

Political and cultural friction was accompanied by enhanced strategic competition. The eastern Mediterranean's cold war status as the southern flank of the NATO-Warsaw Pact stand off was undermined by the collapse of the Soviet Union, but the stakes in the region were heightened rather than reduced as a result of new strategic alignments. Ironically, the importance of the Greek-Turkish relationship was enhanced at the same time that efforts to sustain it became more difficult. NATO's engagement in the Balkans as "the sheriff in Europe's wild southeast" further complicated the picture by placing the legitimacy of the Alliance itself at risk.[39] Athens looked on with concern as Turkey aligned itself with Israel, established diplomatic relations and special military arrangements with emerging post-Yugoslav states including Macedonia and Albania, took up the cause of the Bosnian Muslims against Serbia, and agreed to participate in Balkan peacekeeping missions. Concern with Turkey's superior military potential, combined with the perception of an ambitious Turkish Balkan policy inspired by the premises of neo-Ottomanism, created an enhanced perception of threat that led Greece toward a military build up and a stronger regional diplomatic posture.[40] These gestures were reciprocated by Ankara, constrained by popular opinion, including potent lobbies representing citizens of Bosnian and Albanian descent (about 10 percent of Turkey's population is of Balkan descent) to react to Balkan atrocities, and convinced of the need to counter real or imagined Greek provocations. The Aegean feud and the Greek-Turkish relationship thus became entangled with the Balkan conflict, relations between Turkey and the EU, energy politics in the Caspian basin, and a number of other issues specific to the post-cold war security environment.[41]

The most intractable issue remained Cyprus. In 1992, UN Secretary General Boutros Boutros Ghali launched a diplomatic initiative designated as the "Set of Ideas," intended to provide a comprehensive formula for moving beyond the post-1974 stalemate. These proposals, which corresponded to the spirit of the U.S.-sponsored Nimitz Plan of the 1970s and General Secretary Javier Perez de Cuéllar's Proximity Talks of the 1980s, recommended the creation of a Cypriot Republic with a single international personality and citizenship, but with broadly autonomous federal units in the north and south.[42]

The Set of Ideas suggested reducing the northern zone from 38 to 28 percent of the island's territory by returning to Greek Cypriot control the Varosha district of Famagusta, the northern citrus growing area of Morphou, and 34 other villages. The autonomous units were to receive equal powers, with safeguards to prevent impingement by federal authorities, whose responsibilities would be limited to foreign affairs, defense, federal juridical and policing matters, central banking, customs and immigration, posts and telecommunications, patents and trade marks, and health and environmental issues. Politically, the hope was to resurrect the principle of proportional representation, with a Greek Cypriot president and a Turkish Cypriot vice-president and a bicameral legislature with 50/50 percent representation in the upper house and 70/30 percent in the lower house.

The framework was to be accompanied by a series of confidence-building measures, including the transfer of Varosha to UN control and its gradual opening to commerce involving both communities, the reopening of Nicosia airport under the auspices of the UN and the International Civil Aviation Authority with freedom of access for both sides, and the relaxation of the Greek Cypriot embargo on the north. The President of the Republic of Cyprus Georgios Vassiliou accepted the Set of Ideas as a "basis for discussion," but in the end dialogue broke down around the core issues of sovereignty and restitution. President Denktaş demanded prior recognition of the TRNC as a condition for entering negotiations, formal equality between the autonomous areas including a rotating presidency, separate communal elections, strict equality of representation in all governmental institutions, and a rule of consensus for all decisions by the Council of Ministers. The Greek Cypriots wanted to elevate the "Three Freedoms" of movement, residence, and property rights to a more prominent position in the negotiations – principles that the Turkish Cypriots argued could eventually revive inter-communal violence. In February 1993, after edging out Vassiliou in a hotly contested election, the new president of the Republic of Cyprus Glavkos Clerides rejected the Set of Ideas as a basis for a settlement.

The United States picked up the torch in the wake of the UN's failure, presiding over the signature of a brief document at NATO's Madrid summit in July 1997, in which Greece and Turkey declared that they would respect "vital interests" in the Aegean and pledged to resolve disputes peacefully.[43] The gesture kick started UN-sponsored negotiations, which resumed, led by U.S. special envoy to Cyprus Richard Holbrooke, in the summer of 1997 at Troutbeck,

New York, and subsequently in Montreux, Switzerland.[44] These initiatives were quickly sidetracked, this time by Turkey's reaction to the release of the EU's Agenda 2000. The failure of the Set of Ideas, and subsequent U.S. proposals, left many convinced that international diplomacy on the Cyprus question had arrived at the end of the road.

Already in 1990 President Vassiliou had opened a door leading in another direction by filing a formal application to bring the Republic of Cyprus into the EU. Accession was a legitimate aspiration in view of the republic's economic achievements, but it was widely considered to be impossible without a settlement between north and south. Vassiliou's real intention was probably to win negotiating leverage, and to encourage the EU to become more active in facilitating the diplomatic process. In 1995, however, in part as a result of Greek pressure (Athens insisted upon accession negotiations as a precondition for supporting the EU-Turkey Customs Union), in part as a consequence of annoyance with Turkish Cypriot diplomatic intransigence, and in part due to a desire to discipline Ankara for its refusal to address European concern over human rights abuses and respect for democratic norms, the Republic of Cyprus was accepted as a candidate for accession by the EU Council of Ministers. In April 1998 negotiations on accession were formally opened. These negotiations were described by the EU as a possible catalyst for a permanent solution to the Cyprus question, but their immediate impact seemed to push in the opposite direction. Denktaş reacted with an uncompromising refusal to represent the TRNC in the talks, accompanied by a threat to support annexation of the north by Turkey in the event that EU membership should become a reality. In the course of 1998, Turkey and the TRNC proceeded to establish a joint economic area and put into place the institutional structures that would make annexation a possibility.

The friction provoked by the EU accession agenda was paralleled by military tensions. In 1994 Greece and the Republic of Cyprus announced a Unified Defense Doctrine intended to create a common defense area bringing the island inside the Greek national defensive umbrella. Under the terms of the agreement, Greece and the Republic of Cyprus conducted joint military exercises and opened a naval and air station, named "Andreas Papandreou" in honor of the recently deceased Greek premier, on the southwest coast near the tourist resort area of Paphos. When fully operational, the facility would allow Greek tactical aviation to extend its range over a significant section of Turkey's Mediterranean coast. As such, it was bitterly opposed by Ankara. On June 16, 1998, in the midst of a European summit in Cardiff, Wales with the Cyprus problem on the agenda, four Greek F-16 warplanes and two C-130 transports visited the base as part of a military exercise. The result was another flare up of Greek-Turkish tension.[45]

In 1996, the Republic of Cyprus announced the purchase of four systems of Russian-made S-300 (SA-10 in the NATO designation) surface-to-air missiles, each equipped with 12 missiles with a range of 160 kilometers.[46] The purchase, if brought to fruition, would have served several purposes. The missile systems would give a more credible defensive capacity to the Republic of Cyprus, which at present lacks an air force. They could also protect the Andreas Papandreou facility. Less tangibly, deployment would to some extent salve the frustration felt by Greek Cypriots at the lack of progress toward regularizing the status of the island. "The missile crisis," wrote Niels Kadritzke, was "rooted in the fears of men and women who feel themselves to have been abandoned by the entire world."[47] Turkey, however, condemned the move as an act of aggression that "poses a direct threat to Turkish security," and announced its intention to attack the sites should deployment commence.[48] Taken aback, the Clerides government offered to suspend the purchase in exchange for the revival of a 1979 agreement, never honored on the ground, calling for a demilitarization of the entire island. Not surprisingly, the offer was abruptly refused. The Turkish ultimatum made deployment a high-risk undertaking, but Clerides confronted considerable domestic pressure in support of the purchase. In the midst of the controversy the Cypriot Minister of Defense Iannakis Omirou publicly characterized the deployments as critical to Greek Cypriot security, and threatened to resign should they be delayed or cancelled. Twenty percent of the Greek Cypriot electorate backed a "Front of Refusal" committed to the reunification of the island under Greek hegemony and strongly supportive of deployment, and many moderate Greek Cypriots were convinced that the demilitarization of Cyprus would amount to the accreditation of forced partition.

Despite these pressures, in December 1998 Clerides backed away from the commitment to deploy. The retreat was linked to the suggestion that the Greek island of Crete could serve as an alternative venue — a suggestion that Ankara promptly labeled as unacceptable as well. Turkish intransigence, accompanied by military threats, had been sufficient to block the Greek Cypriot initiative, but at the price of reinforced hostility and new sensitivity to the undesirable consequences of an unfavorable military balance.

In the background of these disputes, several incidents threatened to push Greek-Turkish relations to the point of armed confrontation. In December 1995, a Turkish freighter ran aground on the small rocky islet of Imia (Kardak, in Turkish), in the Dodecanese group adjacent to the Bodrun Peninsula and the island of Kos. Greek vessels assisted in rescuing the crew, but in the process asserted sovereignty over the terrain. Turkey responded with counterclaims, by implication challenging Greek sovereignty over thousands of small Aegean islets in what would soon be designated as gray zones.[49] Blown out of all proportion by the respective national media, and adopted on both sides as a point of national honor, the incident came close to provoking open hostilities. Strong diplomatic pressure, including direct telephone calls to Ankara and Athens by U.S. President Clinton and NATO Secretary General Solana, was required to reverse the course of events, in a scenario that could be replayed in any number of other settings at almost any moment.[50] In August 1996 border incidents provoked by an organized attempt by Greek Cypriot demonstrators to force a symbolic breaching of the Green Line resulted in the deaths of two demonstrators — a warning that the status quo on the island could unexpectedly come under assault. The end of the Cold War and attendant reductions in East-West tension seemed to have done little to calm the waves of the Aegean dispute.

Earthquake Diplomacy.

Given the various issues that had kept Athens and Ankara at odds for decades, and the new strategic frictions associated with the post-cold war period, the Greek-Turkish rapprochement that set in from the late 1990s onward came as a surprise to many. Of course, voices for reconciliation had never been lacking, and the exigencies of modernization made many of the disputes around which Greek-Turkish rivalry revolves appear increasingly irrelevant. U.S. pressure for compromise was an important factor in encouraging new thinking, but hardly a new one. In retrospect, the Imia-Kardak incident may have served as a kind of catharsis by demonstrating how volatile and potentially destructive undiluted strategic rivalry had become.[51] Most fundamentally, however, momentum toward reconciliation was a product of independent strategic reevaluations motivated by changing perceptions of national interest.

In Greece, the election of Constantine Simitis to replace the recently decreased Andreas Papandreou during 1995 set the stage for a redefinition of priorities. Papandreou's burly populism rested upon a typically Balkan frustrated nationalism, often expressed in superficial anti-Americanism or anti-Turkish posturing. Simitis was more attuned to the Western and European vocation of modern Greece, and determined to make the sacrifices necessary to meet the criteria for joining the EU's unified currency zone. Eternal bickering with Turkey left Greece exposed in the face of an inherently more powerful neighbor, and imposed a burden of military expenditure that the country could ill-afford. Simitis seems to have concluded that engaging the Turks in a common European framework would in the long-term create a more propitious context for the pursuit of Greek national interests.

In line with these conclusions, Simitis began his tenure as prime minister in 1996 with proposals for the creation of a joint commission under EU auspices to ameliorate Greek-Turkish relations. Following the Imia-Kardak crisis, Simitis struck a novel tone by publicly thanking the United States for its successful mediation effort, rather than resorting to the more familiar expedient of complaining about purported pro-Turkish bias. One year later, Greece quietly backed away from its support for the deployment of Russian S-300s in the Republic of Cyprus. During NATO's air war against Yugoslavia Athens remained aligned with Ankara and loyal to alliance obligations despite the strong anti-war sentiments of the Greek public.[52] Resistance from the populist wing of Simitis' ruling party diluted the impact of some of these gestures in the short-term, but fresh winds were blowing.[53]

Ankara reciprocated Athens' interest in improved relations on the basis of a comparable redefinition of national interests and priorities. The electoral breakthrough of the Islamic-oriented Welfare Party, which won control of the mayor's office in six of Turkey's largest cities, including Istanbul and Ankara, in the municipal elections of March 1994, became the country's leading party in December 1995 elections with 21.4 percent of the vote, and in June 1996 entered the national government, came as a shock to the political establishment.

Widening economic disparities, chronic political instability, and the unresolved armed struggle against the PKK were creating an atmosphere of crisis that the Welfare Party was well positioned to exploit.[54] Growing disrespect for the political class was also a factor. The Welfare Party was able to enter the government June 1996 in alliance with Tansu Çiller's True Path Party in part because Çiller needed their support to ward off an impending corruption investigation. In November 1996 a high ranking police commander and member of parliament were killed in an automobile accident together with a notorious gangster involved in drug trafficking and arms transfers, giving rise to what would become known as the Susurluk (Yüksekova) affair, revealing endemic corruption reaching to the highest levels. The gradual expulsion of Erbakan and the Welfare Party between February and June 1997 temporarily suppressed the phenomenon of political Islam, but did little to restore public confidence, resolve a crisis of governance, or improve Turkey's democratic credentials. The most pressing issues on Ankara's domestic and international agendas, one might well conclude, had increasingly little to do with the logic of an outmoded, obsessive, and counterproductive rivalry with Greece.

After the conclusion of the Dayton Peace Accord, which partially ended Serbia's isolation and brought an end to violent assaults against the Muslims of Bosnia-Herzegovina, the Balkan policies of both Athens and Ankara also became more congruent. Greece gradually backed away from its unfortunate decision to contest the legitimacy of the Republic of Macedonia, regularized relations with Skopje, and resolved outstanding disputes with the unique exception of the republic's official name.[55] Athens continued to impose the use of the designation Former Yugoslav Republic of Macedonia (FYROM), on the grounds that the name Macedonia was part of the Hellenistic heritage and that its use by a foreign state implied territorial revindications against Greece, but over time the issue has declined in salience. As the Balkan conflict progressed. Turkey still provided rhetorical support for Turkish and Muslim communities, but shied away from the kind of intrusive regional role that Greece had originally feared. The costly rivalry over Aegean issues was also pushed to the sideline — only the most improbable worst-case scenarios, it was increasingly recognized, could produce a realistic Aegean threat. In Southeastern Europe both parties had common goals — support for international efforts to promote regional stability and insure that Balkan conflict would not become a source of tension in their bilateral relations. Informal contacts and encouragement from the Greek foreign ministry helped prepare the Serbian opposition to supplant Milošević after his defeat in September 2000 elections, a gesture that worked in the interests of the region as a whole.[56] Both Greece and Turkey expanded political, economic, and military assistance to a number of Balkan states, increased their level of investment in the region, and become active participants in regional peace operations. Their relationship in the Balkan region remained competitive, but was no longer antagonistic.

A first step toward actualizing a process of rapprochement was taken on July 8, 1997, when Turkish Foreign Minister İsmail Cem met with his Greek counterpart Theodoros Pangalos under the auspices of U.S. Secretary of State Madeleine Albright during a NATO summit in Madrid, and signed a joint declaration on fundamental principles for the conduct of bilateral relations. The two parties agreed to pursue good neighborly relations, respect each other's legitimate interests in the Aegean, and work to resolve disputes without resorting to threats of force.[57] Greece and Turkey went on to agree in 1997 to participate in the Southeast European Defense Ministerial process, leading to the establishment of a South-Eastern European brigade in 1998 with a Turkish general as its first commander and a Greek officer in charge of political-military activities. Reconciliatory gestures undertaken beneath the watchful eye of the U.S. big brother were nothing new, but this time the spirit of reconciliation seemed to rest upon a stronger foundation.

Rapprochement was pushed forward by cathartic events. The first, ironically, began with all the trappings of a major crisis. In early October 1998 Turkey moved to drive PKK leader Öcalan from his refuge in neighboring Syria by massing troops and equipment along the border. With the bulk of its forces deployed against Israel in the west, Damascus was badly exposed. Under the threat of a Turkish incursion, it agreed to Öcalan's immediate expulsion, and promised to cease all further support for the PKK. After being refused asylum by Russia, Greece, and Italy, Öcalan ended a brief international odyssey in Nairobi, Kenya, where on February 16, 1999, Turkish Special Forces took him into custody while under Greek escort. At the trial in which he was condemned to death (though the sentence was not been carried out), and from incarceration, Öcalan called upon his followers to turn away from armed struggle, and in April 2002 the PKK opted to reconstitute itself as the Congress for Freedom and Democracy in Kurdistan, and pledged to abjure clandestine activity on behalf of legal, political means.[58] The outcome was a singular success for the Turkish authorities, one that held out the overdue promise of a more constructive engagement with modern Turkey's ethnic and cultural diversity.

Ankara's belligerence in regard to Syria represented precisely the kind of coercive use of military power that Greece had always warned against, and Öcalan's capture in Kenya while under Greek protection was widely regarded as a national humiliation. Athens role during the Öcalan affair, however, was ambiguous. Rather than trumpet the PKK's cause as a means to provoke the Turks, it refused its leader asylum, and may even have been partly complicit in his capture. Foreign Minister Pangalos, notorious for his anti-Turkish rhetoric, was forced to resign in the wake of the affair and was replaced by Georgios Papandreou, son of the late prime minister but one of the most adamant proponents of dialogue with Ankara in the Greek political spectrum. In the end, the entire episode became a spur to communication. Shortly after Öcalan's detention Papandreou paid a state visit to Ankara, and in early July met his counterpart Cem in New York, where they pledged their governments to cooperate in the fight against terrorism. Henceforward joint work by Papandreou and Cem would be a driving force behind enhanced bilateral cooperation.

On July 17, 1999, a massive earthquake, measuring 7.4 on the Richter scale and centered near the Turkish industrial port of İzmit, within commuting distance of Istanbul on the Sea of Marmara, took nearly 20,000 lives and left 25,000 homeless. The event exposed widespread graft in the construction industry, and relief efforts were plagued by corruption, indifference, and political division (some state officials, for example, refused to accept humanitarian assistance from Islamic sources). Amid a sea of suffering, Greece's Special Disaster Unit stood out as one of the first and most effective rescue teams on the scene. On September 7 a lesser quake struck the Athens region, and the Turks did their best to reciprocate, offering generous assistance despite their own urgent domestic needs. Long-term assistance programs and substantial relief donations followed emergency efforts. Unstinting solidarity, graphically depicted by the respective national media, created an emotional climate supportive of the rapprochement that both governments sought to foster —

Papandreou spoke pointedly of the "new climate" of relations that cooperation in time of need had created.[59]

The tragic events of August and September gave rise to a flurry of negotiations, dubbed "earthquake diplomacy," that considerably improved the prospects for Greek-Turkish relations. In the 2 years that followed the earthquake summer of 1999, Athens and Ankara concluded a series of accords aimed at fighting organized crime and narcotics trafficking, preventing illegal migration, promoting tourism, protecting the environment, and enhancing cultural and economic cooperation. Both sides announced the intention to reduce defense spending and cut back on military procurement. In April 2001 an agreement was concluded to clear land mines placed along the Greek-Turkish frontier at the Evros River in Thrace (bringing both countries into compliance with the Ottawa Treaty banning the use of anti-personnel mines and removing the inconsistency of an internal NATO border defended by such means). Plans were made to conduct small national military exercises in the Aegean during the summer, and joint exercises, to be held on Greek and Turkish territory, were scheduled under the NATO umbrella. Numerous economic accords were concluded, including an agreement to cooperate in organizing transit of energy resources from the Caspian basin, reinforced by meetings between members of the business community. Between May 2000 and May 2001 trade, cooperative business ventures, and investment more than doubled. On the highest political level, the Greek prime minister was able to conduct a first ever-state visit to Ankara, and in the realm of popular diplomacy the incidence of citizen contacts, sporting contests, and cultural interaction increased dramatically. Perhaps most significantly, Greece agreed to lift its opposition to Turkish accession to the EU, with Papandreou stating unambiguously that; "Greece believes if Turkey is willing to submit to the rigor of the process of candidacy … then it should be accepted into the European Union."[60] Against this background, in December 1999 UN Secretary General Kofi Annan was able to launch a new round of proximity talks on the Cyprus question.

The results of earthquake diplomacy were impressive, but also discrete. In order to facilitate progress, Cem and Papandreou concentrated on soft issues where common ground was clearly identifiable. Almost none of the hard points of confrontation that had divided Greece and Turkey for decades, whether Aegean concerns, treatment of minorities, perceptions of strategic exposure, or the Cyprus conundrum, were substantively addressed. Both countries were required to deal with potent domestic lobbies that opposed concessions, including at least part of the powerful Turkish military hierarchy and the national-populist wing of the Greek political spectrum. Despite defense cut backs, and a major Turkish economic downturn during 2001, military expenditures remained high, and Turkey's military procurement program was a source of special Greek concern. Expanded military cooperation was real, but also limited. Greece and Turkey participated successfully in NATO's *Dynamic Mix* exercise conducted on Greek territory, but a follow up exercise on Turkish territory code-named *Destined Glory* had to be cut short when Greece withdrew its forces after Ankara insisted that the Hellenic Air Force could not over fly demilitarized Greek Aegean islands while entering Turkish air space. Earthquake diplomacy had dramatically affected the atmospherics of Greek-Turkish relations, but not necessarily, or at least not yet, the substance.

A Last Chance?

The major exception to improved Greek-Turkish relations remained the Cypriote stalemate. Over several decades, the concerned parties had learned to live with imposed division. From a Western perspective, a diplomatic resolution was considered desirable, but not essential so long as war was avoided and existing equilibriums within NATO and the eastern Mediterranean were maintained. Turkey and the TRNC consistently argued that enforced separation had helped the respective communities defend and preserve their identities — the situation was stable, and any attempt to impose reintegration risked reanimating inter-communal violence. Greece and the Greek Cypriots lamented partition, but their vision was increasingly turned outward, toward closer integration with Europe and prospects for economic development. The status quo offered benefits to all concerned, one reason why the post-1974 arrangements could endure for so long. By the late 1990s, however, trends had been set to work that inexorably undermined these arrangements. The status quo was becoming "unsustainable and irrelevant to any effort towards meaningful peace-building in Cyprus."[61]

The proximity talks launched under UN auspices by Kofi Annan in December 1999 sought to break the stalemate by developing an agenda for a bicommunal and bizonal federation that would maintain a façade of unity but concede considerable autonomy to separate Greek and Turkish zones. According the Annan's program Cyprus was to become a unitary state composed of two distinct federal entities with substantial prerogatives — a solution not dissimilar to that which the Dayton Accord proposed for Bosnia-Herzegovina. Despite some progress in addressing details of the plan, however, Turkish Cypriot President Denktaş could not be moved from his long-standing position that any negotiated settlement must be preceded by acknowledgement of the TRNC's sovereignty. After five rounds of talks, in November 2000 the Turkish Cypriot leader announced that the TRNC was pulling out unilaterally. His statement was issued in Ankara and with Turkish support, a discordant note amidst the symphony of reconciliation being conducted by foreign ministers Cem and Papandreou in the background.

Denktaş's decision to back away from the proximity talks reflected the conviction that reunification was dangerous and undesirable. From the Turkish Cypriot perspective, the concept of a bizonal and bicommunal federation had always been considered to be critically flawed. Any formula for unity that did not acknowledge the independence of the north, and guarantee sovereignty with limitations on movement, investment, and property restitution, was perceived to risk returning Turkish Cypriots to the status of an exposed minority living on the brink of a precipice. During the proximity talks, Denktaş insisted that the demand for recasting Cyprus as a confederation of fully sovereign states and nations was non-negotiable. There was method in the madness — intransigence blocked progress, and time was perceived to work against prospects for compromise. All diplomatic alternatives to partition rested upon the attempt to resurrect a common Cypriot identity as a foundation for reconciliation. On both sides of the island, however, that identity was at risk.[62] Association with the EU would inevitably draw Greek Cypriots closer to Greece and an enlarging Europe — Denktaş' description of the probable outcome as "enosis through the EU" was altogether plausible.[63] Within the TRNC, the continuing emigration of the indigenous Turkish Cypriot population, combined with a steady influx of immigrants from Anatolia, provided an enlarged popular base for projects to reduce the north to the status of a Turkish province. According to Alpay Durduran, head of the Turkish Cypriot opposition party Yeni Kibris (New Cyprus), over

40,000 Turkish Cypriots have left the island permanently since 1974. The 80,000 indigenous Turkish Cypriots who remain make up almost exactly half of the TRNC's population of 160,000 as recorded by the 1997 census.[64] The autochthonous population provides the political base for opposition to Denktaş and his pro-Turkish agenda. The opposition supports the UN concept of a bicommunal and bizonal federation as a prerequisite for association with the EU.[65] But it risks becoming a minority in its own land.

Ankara's strategic concerns were heightened by the EU's decision to initiate a process of accession for the Republic of Cyprus. The EU summit in Helsinki in December 1999 included the island as a candidate for membership and reiterated that the process would move forward on its own merits whether or not a negotiated solution to the division of the island had been achieved, on the sole condition that the Greek Cypriot side not be held responsible for the failure of negotiations. The process of accession was programmed to begin at the end of 2002, with 2004 as a target date for admission. In economic terms the Republic of Cyprus was an attractive candidate, but the EU's hand was to some extent forced by Greek threats to block the entire enlargement process should its Cypriot ally be left out. Turkey argued in response that the 1960 agreement on which the independence of Cyprus was founded precludes membership in any international organization of which both Greece and Turkey are not members, and vigorously opposed EU candidacy. In December 1996 Turkish Prime Minister Erbakan responded to an earlier version of the EU enlargement agenda by declaring that "the South of Cyprus cannot join the EU without the permission of Turkey: if it does so, the integration of the Turkish Republic of Northern Cyprus into Turkey will be carried out as quickly as possible."[66] During 1997 an Association Council between Turkey and the TRNC was created as a vehicle to facilitate such a step. Turkey's position on the question remained consistent despite its rapprochement with Greece. It evoked the possibility of war in the event that accession was affected, and left virtually no room for retreat.[67] Speaking before the European Council's Foreign Relations Committee on June 20, 2001, Deputy Prime Minister Mesut Yılmaz reiterated that Turkey would offer "no compromises" on the island of Cyprus, "never accept" the consignment of Turkish Cypriots to the status of a minority, and "never accept the EU membership of Cyprus in this condition."[68]

For EU representatives hostile to Turkish membership, Ankara's militancy might have been considered a blessing in disguise. An attempt to annex the TRNC would place Turkey's aspirations for accession into limbo for the foreseeable future.[69] Anything short of a negotiated outcome, however, would have dire consequences for Greek-Turkish relations, the people of Cyprus, and the Balkans as a whole. The EU's hope was that the accession agenda could serve as a catalyst for a negotiated solution, but it also had the potential to become a "time-bomb likely to wreck all chances of a settlement on the island."[70]

By walking out on the negotiations at the end of 2000, Denktaş sought to sabotage prospects for compromise and to concentrate upon confirming sovereignty under the protective arm of Ankara. In the short-term Turkey was supportive, in part because of the personal convictions of leaders such as Ecevit, in part because the government's options were constrained by nationalist opinion and the parliamentary role of nationalist parties, and in part because the all powerful Turkish National Security Council attached strategic value to military access to the island as a foundation for defense policy along the Mediterranean littoral and in southern Anatolia.[71] Confronting the imminent possibility of exclusion from Europe, however, voices in the Turkish media, business elite, and political class were quick to call attention to the extent that "the unresolved Cyprus problem stood in the way of Turkey's larger strategic interests in moving toward the West," and argued that in an issue of decisive national importance the Cyprus tail should not be "wagging the Turkish dog."[72] In fact the Turkish leadership was divided and of two minds. The Cyprus issue had brought to a head a long-standing dichotomy within elite perception, between partisans of resolute modernization, democratization, and a European orientation, and champions of more traditional values, a controlled society under the tutelage of the Kemalist military establishment, and a special geostrategic role for Turkey as Eurasian power prioritizing regional interests and strategic association with the United States.[73]

Under pressure from proponents of compromise, in January 2002 Denktaş agreed to attend a new round of negotiations, to be conducted on UN controlled territory in Nicosia under the direction of Kofi Annan's special advisor to Cyprus Alvaro de Soto. For Denktaş and Clerides, respectively aged 78 and 83, no further opportunity to resolve the Cyprus conundrum was likely to present itself. Described as "the last chance for Cyprus to reach a settlement" by the Foreign Minister of the TRNC, Tahsin Ertugruloğlu, the talks nonetheless progressed haltingly.[74] Initial negotiating positions were distressingly familiar. The Greek Cypriot government forwarded the concept of a bi-communal federal state with a constitution that accords the Turkish Cypriot minority substantial institutional representation and protections, including a bicameral legislature with the Turkish Cypriot community assigned 50 percent representation in the upper house, and procedures for substantive self-government for a Turkish Cypriot federal province. Security would be guaranteed by the demilitarization of the island, including the disbanding of the Cypriot National Guard, the withdrawal of foreign national military contingents, and the continued presence of a UN peacekeeping force. Turkish Cypriot counterproposals called for the creation of a confederation of separate, sovereign, and equal states, a lifting of the economic embargo against the north, and the continued presence of Turkish troops as a security guarantor. These alternatives were mutually exclusive, and without external pressure it seemed unlikely that the new round of negotiations would conclude any more positively than its predecessors.[75]

The target date for resolution of the problem was the December 12-13, 2002, EU summit in Copenhagen, where formal invitations for a first round of EU enlargement were to be issued. With negotiations between the Cypriote factions stalled, in part due to Denktaş's absence from the process while undergoing open heart surgery, Kofi Annan made a final effort to promote a settlement on November 12, 2002, issuing a 150-page document reconfirming a peace plan aimed at reuniting the island as a sovereign country with a single international personality and two equal "cantons" on the Swiss model in "indissoluble partnership." The proposal, which basically spelled out the terms of Annan's long-standing negotiating posture in greater detail, included provisions for a federal government consisting of a six-member Presidential Council with representation proportional to the population of the two sides, a 10-month rotating Presidency and Vice Presidency, a National Parliament with two chambers (a 48-seat Senate divided 50-50 between Greek and Turkish communities, and a 48-seat lower chamber with proportional representation), and a Supreme Court with three judges from each part of the country and three non-Cypriots.[76] Greek foreign minister Papandreou was quick to praise the proposal as the prelude to an "historic moment," but reactions from the Cypriot factions were tepid.[77] The Greek Cypriot community expressed concern with procedures for adjudicating property rights, and the status accorded to immigrants from Anatolia in the north, while Denktaş remained defiant of EU-determined time lines and insistent on the core issue of sovereignty.[78]

Ankara's position, still judged to be the critical factor in encouraging Turkish Cypriot compliance, was complicated by the resounding victory in parliamentary elections of November 3, 2002, with 34 percent of the popular vote and control over 363 seats in Turkey's 550 member parliament, of the Justice and Development Party (AKP) led by Recep Tayyip Erdoğan and Abdullah Gül. The AKP was the latest incarnation of the phenomenon of political Islam in contemporary Turkey. After the banning of its immediate predecessors, the Welfare and Justice parties, which had openly declared their Islamic orientation in defiance of constitutional provisions imposing secularism in the political arena, the AKP changed tactics by publicly downplaying an implied Islamic heritage and insisting upon its strictly secular character and respect for democratic institutions. In terms of domestic development, the AKP's victory offered a major opportunity — if Turkey could accept and co-opt a party of Islamic orientation within its secular state structure, and demonstrate "that democracy can function properly in a Muslim environment," it would be taking a large step toward political stabilization at home and the refurbishing of its credentials as a model for democratic development in the Islamic world as a hole.[79] As far as the Cyprus question was concerned, in line with its commitment to moderation, the AKP leadership took pains to assert continuity in foreign policy questions and placed public pressure upon Denktaş to come toward the UN agenda for a negotiated solution.[80]

In the end EU remonstrance, UN diplomacy, and encouragement from Ankara did not suffice to move the Turkish Cypriot leader away from the rejectionist posture that he has maintained over several decades. At Copenhagen in December 2002 the EU extended formal invitations to ten candidates for association, including the Republic of Cyprus, with a target date of 2004.[81] Accession for the Balkan states Romania and Bulgaria was also targeted for 2007. No breakthrough on the Cyprus question was achieved, however. Negotiations were continued subsequent to the deadline, but several months later Denktaş unambiguously rejected the Annan Plan in its current configuration.[82] The issue of the status of the TRNC against the background of the Republic of Cyprus's accession to the EU was thus put off yet again — the EU strategy of linking reunification and accession had apparently failed. Simultaneously, the EU refused Ankara's request for a firm date for opening negotiations on Turkey's own accession process, making due with a soft compromise that fixed December 2004 as a possible date for the opening of negotiations dependent on an evaluation of Turkey's progress in democratization, including a reduction of the military's role in the political process and improved human rights standards.[83] *The New York Times*, in line with U.S. policy strongly supportive of the Turkish accession agenda, lamented that the EU had "fumbled its chance to make an enormous contribution toward integrating Turkey into the West."[84] The new government in Ankara sought to put the best face on the decision, however, and reiterated its commitment to pursue Turkey's European vocation.

The unresolved Cyprus Question, and prospect that in 2004 the Republic of Cyprus may join the EU without having regularized its relations with the north, is a significant barrier to progress in Turkey's relations with Greece and the EU, and to stabilization in the entire southeastern European region.[85] One may argue that over time the issue has become more of an annoyance than a problem, that Greek-Turkish rapprochement makes the prospect of armed hostility over Cyprus highly unlikely, that the status quo which has endured for 38 years is not inherently unacceptable, and that even the worst case prospect of a Turkish annexation of the TRNC would not change the situation on the ground in a dramatic way. If Ankara is serious about blazing a trail to the EU, however, it will have no choice but to work toward some kind of negotiated outcome. Prolongation of the status quo, particularly in view of deeply entrenched European skepticism, will make Turkish accession nearly impossible.[86] Continued international pressure encouraging negotiations is therefore absolutely necessary. UN Secretary General Kofi Annan has done his best to facilitate a solution, but lacking a will to compromise on the part of the negotiating partners the UN's ability to force a settlement in limited. The U.S. has consistently urged a negotiated alternative, but has also been anxious to cultivate Turkey as a strategic ally and may not chose to bring decisive influence to bear if it feels that the problem can be contained at low cost. The EU has much to offer, but in order to make use of its leverage Brussels will have to make the prospect of Turkish accession more substantial than it has been willing to do to date. These are critical issues that will continue to demand careful attention. Despite failure to resolve the issue at the EU's Copenhagen summit, the complex and obscure Cypriot negotiations remain a key to the strategically vital effort to "set Turkey firmly on a European path," and build a stronger foundation for association between Europe and the Balkan region as a whole.[87]

Conclusion.

Despite their disagreements, Greece and Turkey weathered the storms of the Balkan conflicts of the 1990s without resorting to arms. Western observers repeatedly expressed the fear that Athens and Ankara might be drawn into the fighting against their will or best judgment, but in the end such concerns were overblown.[88] Greek-Turkish rivalry did not abate, but during the Yugoslav crisis, it culminated as a *guerre manqueé*.

Domestically, Greece has evolved toward a fully integrated member of the European family — progress that successful hosting of the 2004 Olympic Games could help to reinforce. A wave of populist demagoguery and nationalist extremism such as that stirred up by the Macedonian Question during the early 1990s appears increasingly archaic and unlikely to recur. In Turkey, a harsh economic downturn has substantially discredited virtually all established political parties and created an objective need for new direction. The AKP's sweeping victory at the polls in November 2002 represented a political earthquake parallel to the destructive 1999 tremors that proved such a spur to rapprochement with Greece. If the AKP can succeed in bringing the voice of Turkey's disinherited into the political process in a constructive way, revive popular confidence in the institutions of governance, and sustain its commitment to secularism and moderation, Turkey's long-term national interests will be well served.

At the dawn of the new millennium, Athens and Ankara launched into a process of rapprochement with the potential to produce considerable mutual benefit. If the dynamic of reconciliation can be sustained, both of the parties and the entire southeastern European sub-region will be winners. Expanding economic interaction will help to revive regional markets, Turkey's European aspirations will be forwarded at a realistic pace, the benefits of association with NATO and the EU will become more broadly accessible, democratization will be given new impetus, the Islamist factor, in regional politics and in Turkish domestic affairs, will be channeled in positive directions, and potential flash points and sources of conflict eliminated. Despite the progress of recent years, however, the corner has not yet been turned. Turkey continues to struggle with economic crisis and political instability, the national-populist faction of the Greek political spectrum is still a force to be reckoned with, strategic rivalry in the Aegean remains alive, and the Cyprus dilemma, if it is not managed intelligently, has the potential to upset quite a number of apple carts.

The Greek-Turkish relationship is an integral part of the Balkan security dilemma. As in Bosnia-Herzegovina and Kosovo, Western involvement will be a critical factor in determining whether the relationship continues to evolve in a positive direction. Unfortunately, that involvement cannot be taken for granted. NATO has been a sturdy deterrent to Greek-Turkish conflict in the past. Whether it will be able to accomplish that role in the future remains to be seen. The United States, when it has put its shoulder to the grindstone, has succeeded in managing regional conflict, but continued success will only be achieved at the price of sustained engagement. Institutional Europe remains a pole of attraction, but it must make the prospect of accession realistic if the promise of a Europe "whole and at peace" is to be extended to its troubled southeastern marches. There is still much at stake, and complacency is inappropriate. Athens and Ankara did not allow themselves to be drawn into the Balkan wars of the 1990s, but the Balkan subregion could yet be caught up in the Greek-Turkish imbroglio. In the contemporary Europe, as the Soviet diplomat Maxim Litvinov asserted during the crisis of the 1930s, peace remains indivisible.

ENDNOTES - CHAPTER 6

1. Oya Akgönenç, "A Precarious Peace in Bosnia-Herzegovina: The Dayton Accord and Its Prospect for Success," in R. Craig Nation, ed., *The Yugoslav Conflict and Its Implications for International Relations*, Ravenna: Longo Editore, 1998, pp. 61-70.

2. For example, Duygu Bazoglu Sezer, "Turkish Security Challenges in the 1990s," in Stephen J. Blank, ed., *Mediterranean Security Into the Coming Millennium*,

Carlisle Barracks: Strategic Studies Institute, 1999, p. 265, writes of "a strategy of the encirclement of Turkey by promoting an anti-Turkish coalition among Greece, Syria, and Armenia."

3. John Redmond and Roderick Pace, "European Security in the 1990s and Beyond: The Implications of the Accession of Cyprus and Malta to the European Union," *Contemporary Security Policy*, Vol. 17, No. 3, December 1996, p. 438. On this theme, see Stefano Bianchini, ed., *From the Adriatic to the Caucasus: The Dynamics of (De)Stabilization*, Ravenna: Longo Editore, 2001.

4. Amikan Nachmani, "The Remarkable Turkish-Israeli Tie," *Middle East Quarterly*, Vol. 5, No. 2, June 1998, pp. 19-29.

5. Henri J. Barkey and Graham E. Fuller, *Turkey's Kurdish Question*, Oxford: Rowman & Littlefield Publishers, Inc., 1998; and Michael M. Gunter, *The Kurds and the Future of Turkey*, New York: St. Martin's Press, 1997.

6. Henry Kissinger, *Years of Upheaval*, Boston: Little, Brown, 1982, pp. 147-151.

7. Marian Kent, ed., *The Great Powers and the End of the Ottoman Empire*, London: Frank Cass, 1984.

8. The story is told dispassionately by Michael Llewellyn Smith, *Ionian Vision: Greece in Asia Minor 1919-1922*, New York: St. Martin's Press, 1973.

9. The argument is presented from a Turkish perspective in Vamik D. Volkan and Norman Itzkowitz, *Turks and Greeks: Neighbors in Conflict*, Huntington: The Eothen Press, 1994.

10. Tozun Bahcheli, *Greek-Turkish Relations Since 1955*, Boulder: Westview Press, 1990, pp. 5-18.

11. Marcia Christoff Kurop, "Greece and Turkey: Can They Mend Fences?" *Foreign Affairs*, Vol. 77, No. 1, January/February 1998, p. 12.

12. Margarita Mathiopoulos, "Toward an Aegean Treaty: 2-4 for Turkey and Greece," *Mediterranean Quarterly*, Vol. 8, No. 3, Summer 1997, p. 116.

13. Niels Kadritzke, "Athenes et Ankara se disputent la mer Egée," *Le Monde diplomatique*, October 1996, pp. 14-15.

14. Frank Brenchley, "Aegean Conflict and the Law of the Sea," in Frank Brenchley and Edward Fursdon, *The Aegean and Cyprus, Conflict Studies No. 232*, London: Research Institute for the Study of Conflict and Terrorism, June 1990, pp. 1-8.

15. Balanced estimates appear in Hugh Poulton, *The Balkans: Minorities and States in Conflict*, London: Minority Rights Publications, 1997, pp. 173-192.

16. *Turkish Minority in Western Thrace: Briefing of the Commission on Security and Cooperation in Europe*, Washington, DC: Commission on Security and Cooperation in Europe, April 1996.

17. Nicole and Hugh Pope, *Turkey Unveiled: A History of Modern Turkey*, Woodstock, NY: The Overlook Press, 1998, pp. 115-116.

18. Joseph S. Joseph, *Cyprus--Ethnic Conflict and International Politics: From Independence to the Threshold of the European Union*, New York: St. Martin's Press, 1997, pp. 19-21.

19. Clement H. Dodd, *The Cyprus Imbroglio*, Cambridgeshire: The Eothen Press, 1998, pp. 22-23.

20. Farid Mirbagheri, *Cyprus and International Peacekeeping*, New York: Routledge, 1998.

21. In 1964 Turkish Prime Minister İsmet İnönü was warned against intervention by a harshly worded letter from U.S. President Lyndon Johnson. The "Johnson Letter" would become a source of great resentment among Turkish elites and with the public at large. In 1967, Turkish air strikes against Greek Cypriot forces attacking Turkish Cypriot villages in the north of the island motivated Washington to push for the evacuation of over 10,000 regular Greek troops from the island. See Bruce R. Kuniholm, "Turkey and the West Since World War II," in Vojtech Mastny and R. Craig Nation, eds., *Turkey Between East and West: New Challenges for a Rising Regional Power*, Boulder: Westview Press, 1996, pp. 54-55. See also Yiannis P. Roubatis, *Tangled Webs: The U.S. in Greece 1947-1967*, New York: Pella Publishing Company, Inc., 1987.

22. Georghios Serghis, *The Battle of Cyprus, July-August 1974: The Anatomy of the Tragedy*, Athens: Vlassi, 1996.

23. Henry Kissinger, *Years of Renewal*, New York: Simon & Schuster, 1999, p. 214, notes the impact of the Watergate scandal.

24. Christopher Hitchens, *Cyprus*, London: Quartet Books, 1984, p. 51.

25. Monteagle Sterns, *Entangled Allies: U.S. Policy toward Greece, Turkey and Cyprus*, New York: Council on Foreign Relations Press, 1992, pp. 110-111.

26. Friedemann Müller, *Machtpolitik am Kaspischen Meer*, Ebenhausen: Stiftung Wissenschaft und Politik, 1999, pp. 9-13. On the potential of the Caspian basin, see Ian Bremmer, "Oil Politics: America and the Riches of the Caspian Basin," *World*

Policy Journal, Vol. XV, No. 1, Spring 1998, pp. 27-35, and Rosemarie Forsythe, *The Politics of Oil Exploitation and Export in the Caspian Basin*, Oxford: Oxford University Press, 1996.

27. Elizabeth H. Prodromou, "Reintegrating Cyprus: The Need for a New Approach," *Survival*, Vol. 40, No. 3, Autumn 1998, p. 5.

28. These documents defined the framework for a permanent relationship and established the goal of a customs union. Article 28 of the Ankara Agreement specifically mentions the goal of full membership. For the texts, see *Official Journal of the EC*, December 29, 1964, and No. 293, December 27, 1972.

29. Heinz Kramer, *Die Europäische Gemeinschaft und die Türkei: Entwicklung, Probleme und Perspektiven einer schwierigen Partnerschaft*, Baden-Baden: Nomos, 1988; and Mahmut Bozkurt, *Die Beziehung der Türkei zur Europäische Union*, Frankfurt am Main: Peter Lang, 1995, provide complementary accounts of the evolution of the relationship.

30. Cited from Fotis Moustakis, "Turkey's Entry Into the EU: Asset or Liability?" *Contemporary Security*, Vol. 273, No. 1592, September 1998, p. 128.

31. European Commission, *Agenda 2000: For a Stronger and Wider Union*, Brussels, July 16, 1997.

32. Salahi R. Sonyel, "The European Union and the Cyprus Imbroglio," *Perceptions*, Vol. 3, No. 2, June-August 1998, pp. 73-83. For the rejection of the Turkish application on civilizational grounds, see Lionel Barber, "EU Group Rebuffs Turkish Entry Push," *The Financial Times*, March 5, 1997, p. 2.

33. Resat Kasaba, "Kemalist Certainties and Modern Ambiguities," in Sibel Bozdogan and Resat Kasaba, eds., *Rethinking Modernity and National Identity in Turkey*, Seattle: University of Washington Press, 1997, pp. 15-36.

34. In Turkey, Kemalism (*Atatürkçülük*) is defined by the "six arrows" of republicanism, populism, secularism, nationalism, étatism, and revolutionism. These principles were formalized in the early 1930s and incorporated into the Turkish Constitution of 1937. Udo Steinbach, *Die Türkei im 20. Jahrhundert: Schwieriger Partner Europas*, Bergisch Gladbach: Gustav Lübbe Verlag, 1996, pp. 139-144.

35. The term "silent coup" was coined by Turkish opposition leader Mesut Yılmaz. See Michael M. Gunter, "The Silent Coup: The Secularist-Islamist Struggle in Turkey," *Journal of South Asian and Middle Eastern Studies*, Vol. XXI, No. 3, Spring 1998, p. 11; and Ben Lombardi, "Turkey--The Return of the Reluctant Generals," *Political Science Quarterly*, Vol. 112, No. 2, 1997, pp. 191-215.

36. Amberin Zaman, "New Turk Army Chief Vows Pro-Secular Stand," *The Los Angeles Times*, August 31, 1998.

37. Kemal H. Karpat, "The Ottoman Role in Europe From the Perspective of 1994," in Mastny and Nation, *Turkey Between East and West*, pp. 1-44.

38. Heinz Kramer, *A Changing Turkey: The Challenge to Europe and the United States*, Washington, DC: The Brookings Institution Press, 2000, p. 183.

.39 In the words of a senior European diplomat cited in William Drozdiak, "NATO Role Grows as Threat of Force Calms Kosovo Crisis," *The Philadelphia Inquirer*, October 18, 1998, p. E4.

40. Elaborated in Peter Varraroussis, "Die griechische Diplomatie auf dem Balkan — Ruckkehr in die Geschichte?" *Südosteuropa*, Nos. 6-7, 1995, pp. 373-384. See also Ekavi Athanassopoulou, "Turkey and the Balkans: The View From Athens," *The International Spectator*, Vol. XXIX, No. 4, October-December 1994, pp. 55-64.

41. Strategic cooperation between Ankara and Tel Aviv, strongly supported by the United States, has become the subject of ongoing concern. It has been described in the Syrian press as "a destabilizing element that will provoke conflicts and bring back the climate of the 1950s in the Middle East, when the politics of alliances sparked conflicts and animated hostility towards the West in general and the United States in particular." Cited in Mouna Naim, "Vives critiques contre des manoeuvres israelo-turcs-americaines en Mediterranee," *Le Monde*, June 7, 1998, p. 3.

42. Dodd, *The Cyprus Imbroglio*, pp. 34-60, details these negotiations accurately, though from a consistently pro-Turkish perspective.

43. "Greek-Turkish Relations: The Madrid Joint Declaration," *Thesis*, Vol. 1, Summer 1997, pp. 44-45.

44. Evan Liaris, "A European Solution: Opportunity for Rapprochement in Cyprus," *Harvard International Review*, Vol. XX, No. 1, Winter 1997-98, pp. 38-41.

45. "Greek Fighters Land in Cyprus," *The Washington Times*, June 17, 1998, p. 17; and "Turkish F-16s Sent to Cyprus," *The Washington Post*, June 19, 1998, p. 33.

46. Michael R. Gordon, "Greek Cypriots to Get Missiles From Russians," *The New York Times*, April 29, 1998, pp. A1 and A3.

47. Niels Kadritzke, "Chypre, otage de l'affrontement entre Athénes et Ankara," *Le Monde diplomatique*, September 1998, p. 7.

48. Nuzhet Kandemir, "Turkey: Secure Bridge Over Troubled Waters," *The Washington Quarterly*, Vol. 8, No. 4, Fall 1997, p. 10.

49. Nazlan Ertan, "Turco-Greek Ties Hit Rocky Bottom," *Turkish Probe*, February 2, 1996, pp. 10-13.

50. Krateros Ioannou, "A Tale of Two Islets: The Imia Incident Between Greece and Turkey," *Thesis*, Vol. 1, Spring 1997, pp. 33-42.

51. Ekavi Athanassopoulou, "Blessing in Disguise? The Imia Crisis and Greek-Turkish Relations," *Mediterranean Politics*, Vol. 2, Winter 1997, pp. 76-101.

52. Turkey was intensively involved in Operation Allied Force and its aftermath. A squadron of Turkish F-16s stationed in Italy participated in the air campaign, during the final days of the campaign NATO made use of air bases in western Turkey to launch attacks, and a Turkish mechanized battalion moved into Kosovo with KFOR. Supply sorties were also flown out of Greece, but Athens refused the use of its territory to launch a ground invasion and was much more reticent about active involvement. Its willingness to defy public opinion and provide political support nonetheless made continued NATO engagement possible. Greece and Turkey cooperated as allies during the Kosovo operation.

53. Wes Jonassen, "Greece and Turkey: Still on the Rocks," *Middle East International*, June 27, 1997, p. 20.

54. Marvine Howe, *Turkey Today: A Nation Divided over Islam's Revival*, Boulder: Westview Press, 2000.

55. John Shea, *Macedonia and Greece: The Struggle to Define a New Balkan Nation*, Jefferson, NC: McFarland & Company, Inc., 1997.

56. Alexis Papahelas and Manuela Mirkos, "Il ruolo della Grecia nella caduta di Milošević," *Limes*, No. 5, 2000, pp. 69-72.

57. "Greek-Turkish Relations: The Madrid Joint Declaration."

58. Gaïdz Minassian, "Le PKK se saborde et devient le Kadek," *Le Monde*, April 17, 2002. The new party was quickly banned by the Turkish authorities.

59. "Turkish-Greek Earthquake Create a 'New Climate'," *Cyprus: Embassy Newsletter*, Washington, DC, September 1999, p. 1.

60. George Papandreou, "Greece Wants Turkey to Make the Grade," *International Herald Tribune*, December 10, 1999, p. 8.

61. Prodromou, "Reintegrating Cyprus," p. 8.

62. Thomas F. Farr, "Overcoming the Cyprus Tragedy: Let Cypriots Be Cypriots," *Mediterranean Quarterly*, Vol. 8, No. 4, Fall 1997, pp. 32-62.

63. Denktaş's observation is cited from Redmond and Pace, "European Security," p. 434.

64. Niels Kadritzke, "Rêve d'Europe dans le nord de l'île," *Le Monde diplomatique*, September 1998, p. 7. The reliability of Census data, and the implications of that data for the Cyprus Question, is a hotly disputed issue.

65. "Turkish Cypriots Want EU," *Turkish Daily News*, November 26, 2002.

66. Cited in Kramer, *A Changing Turkey*, p. 178.

67. See the remarks by Foreign Minister İsmail Cem in "Cem: Turkey Will Show Strong Reaction if Greek Cypriots Become EU Member," *Turkish Daily News*, June 28, 2001, p. 3.

68. "Yılmaz: No Concessions on Cyprus Issue," *Turkish Daily News*, June 21, 2001, p. 1.

69. Niels Kadritzke, "Ultimes tractations à Chypres," *Le Monde diplomatique*, April 2002, p. 23.

70. Dodd, *The Cyprus Imbroglio*, p. 107.

71. Mustafa Ergün Olgun, "Turkey's Tough Neighbourhood: Security Dimensions of the Cyprus Conflict," in Clement H. Dodd, ed., *Cyprus: The Need for New Perspectives*, Cambridgeshire: The Eothen Press, 1999, pp. 231-259.

72. Alfred H. Moses, "After 40 Years, A United Cyprus May Soon Be a Reality," *The International Herald Tribune*, April 4, 2002.

73. See Stephen Kinzer, *Crescent and Star: Turkey Between Two Worlds*, New York: Farrar, Straus and Giroux, 2001; and Heinz Kramer, "Die Türkei und der 11. September," *Südosteuropa Mitteilungen*, No. 4, 2001.

74. Cited by Hamza Hendawi, "Turkish Cypriot Minister Paints Bleak Picture," in *http://story.news.yahoo.com/news?tmpl=story&u=/ap/200…/islamic_terror_conference_cyprus*.

75. "Cyprus: Security Council Concerned About Lack of Progress in Peace Talks," *UN Wire*, April 6, 2002, cited from *http://unfoundation.org/unwire/current.asp*.

76. "UN Offers Hope for End of Division of Cyprus," *European Information Service*, Issue 234, November 18, 2002, cited from *www.lgib.gov.uk/nemws/story.html?newsld=506*; and Chris Alden, "EU Urges Cypriots to Reunite," *The Guardian*, November 12, 2002.

77. Cited from Helena Smith, "UN Sets Deadline for Cyprus Deal." *The Guardian*, November 12, 2002.

78. Kirsty Hughes, "Are Cypriots Ready for Reunification?" *The Guardian*, November 17, 2002.

79. Soli Ozel, "Islam Takes a Democratic Turn," *The New York Times*, November 5, 2002, p. A31.

80. "Pressure Building to Say 'Yes'," *Turkish Daily News*, November 26, 2002.

81. The candidates are Estonia, Latvia, Lithuania, Poland, the Czech Republic, Hungary, Slovakia, Slovenia, Malta, and Cyprus.

82. "Denktas: Changes Should be Made to a Great Extent to Accept Annan's Cyprus Plan," *turkishpress.com*, April 16, 2003, cited from *www.turkishpress.com/turkishpress/news.asp?ID=9402*.

83. Thomas Fuller, "Turkey Moves Closer to Entry Negotiations," *The International Herald Tribune*, December 14, 2002.

84. "Rebuffing Turkey," *The New York Times*, December 13, 2002, p. A32.

85. Ismail Cem, "A Common Vision for Cypriots," *The International Herald Tribune*, March 14, 2002.

86. Ziya Önis, "Greek-Turkish Relations and the European Union: A Critical Perspective," *Mediterranean Politics*, Vol. 6, No. 3, Autumn 2001, pp. 31-45; and Neil Nugent, "EU Enlargement and 'the Cyprus Problem'," *Journal of Common Market Studies*, Vol. 38, No. 1, March 2000, pp. 131-150.

87. Philip H. Gordon and Henri J. Barkley, "Two Countries and One Continent's Future," *The New York Times*, December 2, 2002.

88. War-fighting scenarios were nonetheless quite real. See Athanasios Platias, *Greek Deterrence Strategy*, Athens: Institute of International Relations, March 9, 2001.

CHAPTER 7

THE BALKANS BETWEEN WAR AND PEACE

The War of Yugoslav Succession.

The Kosovo conflict was the latest in a series of four wars occasioned by the purposeful destruction of the Yugoslav federation. Though waged sequentially and in different geographical areas (Slovenia, Croatia, Bosnia-Herzegovina, Serbia) they are best regarded as a single, protracted conflict with a consistent logic — the reallocation of territory and populations among the fragments of former Yugoslavia. Collusive bargaining among the leaders of Slovenia, Croatia, and Serbia, abetted by international support for the secessionist intentions of the western republics, set the stage for the deconstruction of the federation, but not all issues could be regulated peacefully. The *drôle de guerre* in Slovenia gave way to less tractable conflicts in Croatia and Bosnia-Herzegovina, Belgrade's attempt to seize control of a greater Serbia was checked, parties driven onto the defensive in the first phase of the fighting won time to rally their forces, ethnic mobilization created new patterns of confrontation, and open-ended warfare was the result.

The war of Yugoslav succession had a destructive impact throughout the region, but burdens were not distributed evenly. The Serbs, Croats, and Slovenes, who had combined to form the first Yugoslavia, emerged from the mayhem with independent states and reasonable prospects. The Slovenes broke away at low cost, and have been successful in consolidating a new regime and affiliating with institutional Europe.[1] Croatia's "thousand-year dream" of statehood was also secured, though the cost was considerably higher. The Serb revolt in Krajina and Slavonia was defeated, but the Croatian economy, ravaged by years of warfare and corrupt governance, has yet to recover. Though Serbia achieved independence, its aspiration to create a greater Serbia where "all Serbs would live in one state" was beaten back across the board. The expulsion of Serb minorities from the Krajina, Slavonia, and Kosovo, the surrender of hopes to absorb the Republika Srpska, the rise of a secessionist movement in Montenegro, the ruin occasioned by alliance bombing, and an enduring stigma of responsibility all bear witness to the extent of Belgrade's defeat. The smaller and more ethnically mixed republics, whose stability was most dependent upon the Yugoslav context, also paid a heavy toll. Bosnia-Herzegovina emerged from the Dayton process as a ward of the international community, plagued by swelling criminality, declining living standards, and poisoned intercommunal relations. Kosovo has been irretrievably polarized, and is likely to remain a de facto international protectorate for the foreseeable future. The Republic of Macedonia is a fragile polity with clouded prospects, challenged to integrate a disaffected Albanian population that could yet provide the spark for a new Balkan war. Outside the borders of former Yugoslavia, neighboring states such as Hungary, Romania, Bulgaria, Greece, Turkey, and Albania have also suffered as a result of the cumulative effect of international embargos, the collapse of regional markets, and the varied debilitating effects of protracted warfare.[2] Greek-Turkish relations have weathered the storms of the 1990s, but the rapprochement underway is still at risk against a background of continuing regional disorder. None of the Yugoslav successor states, with the partial exception of Slovenia, have achieved levels of well being, or prospects of integration with a greater Europe, comparable to those once enjoyed by the despised Socialist Federative Republic of Yugoslavia.

It is difficult to draw a definitive assessment of the war of Yugoslav succession, because it is not yet clear that it has come to an end. The peace accords in Bosnia-Herzegovina and Kosovo are precarious. The Albanian Question in the southern Balkans remains unresolved, and the region contains numerous other potential flash points where tensions could erupt at any moment. New security problems have spun off from a decade of warfare, including a proliferation of weak states with impoverished populations and corrupt governments, prone to exploitation by international criminal networks as staging areas for various trafficking operations. Most of all, no convincing framework for reassembling a viable regional order has been put in place. International engagement in the Balkan wars of the 1990s was tentative, reactive, and often short-sighted. Lack of commitment to seeing the job through has been exposed by chronic squabbling over responsibility, and more recently by calls for U.S. military disengagement. Without a larger vision for recasting regional order, and a sustained commitment on the part of the international community, the Balkans' progress from war to peace will remain reversible.

After Kosovo.

NATO's intervention in Kosovo imposed a kind of order upon the contested province, but did little to address the dilemmas of identity and development out of which the conflict between Serbs and Albanians had sprung. There was nonetheless a sense in which the Kosovo conflict could be regarded as a turning point. Yugoslavia's military defeat brought an end to a phase of Serbian national assertion that had been a basic source of regional instability. With Serbia neutralized, and the major conflicts of the past decade contained by the presence of international peacekeepers, prospects for enduring peace were considerably improved. The successor states of former Yugoslavia, after years of debilitating warfare, were increasingly constrained to abandon ethnic politics and visions of territorial aggrandizement, accept the necessity of good-neighborly relations, and face up to the demands of domestic reform. Solutions to regional dilemmas that looked beyond the construct of warfare have become realistic in a way that was not the case in the past. The Balkan region has not yet been tamed, but in the years since the Kosovo conflict it has witnessed a number of positive developments that hold out hope for a less tumultuous future.

1. NATO Comes to Kosovo.

The responsibility for administering Kosovo under UN Resolution No. 1244, which temporarily suspended Yugoslav authority in the province, was placed in the hands of a UN Mission in Kosovo (UNMIK) originally led by Special Representative of the UN Secretary General Bernard Kouchner, and a NATO-led Kosovo Force (KFOR) commanded by the German General Klaus Reinhardt charged with a peace support mission. KFOR quickly evolved into an extraordinarily complex command with over 40,000 troops representing 39 participating nations deployed in Kosovo, Macedonia, Albanian, and Greece. It was tasked with deterring further aggression on the part of Serbia, guaranteeing the personal security of the local population, demilitarizing the KLA, collaborating with UNMIK in an integrated peace building effort, and providing humanitarian assistance within the limits imposed by other responsibilities.[3] These are imposing tasks, and since its initial deployment KFOR has sustained relatively consistent force levels of around 38,000.[4]

327

As was the case with IFOR in Bosnia-Herzegovina, in the purely military domain essential tasks were accomplished with alacrity.[5] In the short-term, Serbian retaliation against KFOR was not really a threat, and after the fall of the Milošević regime in October 2000 the likelihood of any such action in defiance of NATO was virtually nonexistent. The integrity of the province was adequately insured by the deterrent effect of KFOR's simple presence. Cooperation with UNMIK was organized effectively, though interactions with the hundreds of nongovernmental relief organizations that were soon active in the province was predictably challenging. Humanitarian efforts, including assistance to refugee returns, reconstruction of infrastructure, and mine clearance, proceeded efficiently and were much appreciated. Despite its best efforts, however, KFOR was not able to prevent a new wave of intimidation, revenge killing, and ethnic cleansing targeting what remained of Kosovo's Serb and other minorities.[6] By the winter of 1999-2000, much of the remaining Serb community had withdrawn into the divided city of Mitrovica and adjacent territories north of the Ibar River, which became a focal point for ethnic tension, including occasional rioting.[7] The KLA was partially disarmed and formally disbanded, but the Kosovo Protection Corps, led by former JNA and KLA commander Agim Çeku, has provided a degree of organizational continuity. Çeku is on record stating that the Kosovar Albanians continue to maintain an underground military organization capable of acting when circumstances demand.[8] His organization has been implicated in cooperation with criminal networks that have made Kosovo a major transit point for drug trafficking.[9]

After the formal disbanding of the KLA, the radical wing of the Kosovar Albanian movement divided into two rival formations--the Democratic Party of Kosovo led by Hashim Thaçi, and the Alliance for the Future of Kosovo led by former KLA general Ramush Haradinaj. Armed with the prestige of victory, the KLA offshoots looked forward with confidence to Kosovo's first independent local elections on October 27, 2000. They did not count on the disillusioning effect of widespread corruption, racketeering, and inefficient local administration, as well, perhaps, on a backlash occasioned by the traumas of the war. Ibrahim Rugova's LDK, judged to be virtually defunct after Rugova's meetings with Milošević in Belgrade during the first phase of the allied bombing campaign, swept to victory with 58 percent of the vote, compared to 27 percent for the Democratic

Party and 8 percent for the Alliance.[10] Parliamentary elections in November 2001 affirmed this distribution of support, and on March 4, 2002, 114 days after the elections and following considerable factional strife, Kosovo's parliament confirmed a new government on the basis of a statute defining shared responsibilities with UNMIK (which was empowered to prorogue the parliament in case of disagreements).[11] Rugova was appointed President and Bajram Rexhepi from the Democratic Party Prime Minister. A ten-member cabinet was structured to reflect a power sharing arrangement, with four seats for the LDK, two each for Thaçi's Democratic Party and Haradinaj's Alliance, and one each for minority formations, the Serb coalition *Povratak* (Return) and a Muslim party.[12]

Once again, the civilian side of international administration in Kosovo has proven to be more problematic than the military side. The challenges of reconstruction, democratization, and development are inherently more difficult than those of peacekeeping.[13] Moreover, UNMIK administers Kosovo on the basis of a studied ambiguity — the presumption that the province is still part of something called Yugoslavia, or Serbia-Montenegro, awaiting a decision as to final status. Under present circumstances, this ambiguity can be sustained only so long as KFOR remains on call. The large majority of Kosovo Albanians (who must approve any decision on final status) support independence. Enthusiasm for attachment to a greater Albania is muted — the Republic of Albania is too troubled and politically distinct to be an attractive partner.[14] The idea of a greater Kosovo incorporating contiguous parts of Macedonia, Montenegro, and southern Serbia inhabited by Albanian majorities is doubtless more attractive, but can probably only be achieved at the cost of another war. Federative association with Serbia and Montenegro, including broad autonomy for Kosovo and perhaps some border adjustments to bring Serb majority areas in the north into Serbia proper, would be a win-win solution that the current leadership in Belgrade might be willing to accept, but is not likely to find favor in Priştina. Incompatible goals make compromise solutions unattainable and virtually condemn UNMIK to continue sustaining the ambiguous status quo.[15]

2. NATO Stays in Bosnia.
The role of SFOR and the High Commissioner in Bosnia-Herzegovina is equally troubled. After five years of international

supervision, there has of course been some progress in promoting reconstruction and reconciliation. External actors such as Serbia and Croatia no longer encourage confrontation. New political, juridical, and police authorities have been established, freedom of movement guaranteed, and some infrastructure repaired. The role of nationalist extremists in the political process has been constrained though not eliminated, the Bosnian Muslims have spurned the siren song of Islamic extremism, and pressure for partition arrangements has been dampened.[16] In view of such progress, SFOR has been able to draw down force levels, from approximately 60,000 in December 1995, to 32,000 in December 1996, to 22,000 in October 1999, and to 18,000 in the spring of 2002, with further reductions possible.

The question nonetheless must be posed whether international oversight can ever be terminated unless enduring problems, including the consolidation of national institutions, securing of public order, mine clearance, refugee return, and the capture of indicted war criminals, are more effectively addressed.[17] Ethnically based political parties remain influential within all three communities. The local economy has never recovered from the strains of war, and is burdened by high unemployment, endemic corruption, and an accumulated debt of over $3.2 billion. The International Crisis Group estimates that in every year since 1996 over 50,000 citizens have emigrated from Bosnia-Herzegovina, the majority youthful and well educated. Progress towards reconciliation between Bosnia's ethnic communities has been halting, and the prospect of a renewal of ethnic strife in the absence of an international peacekeeping force cannot be discounted.[18] The intrusive role of the High Commissioner, supported by the coercive potential of SFOR and the tutelage of an army of NGOs, has helped to smooth over some of the flaws in the Dayton process, but not allowed sufficient autonomy for the Bosnians to begin to manage their own affairs and to build the foundation of a self-sustaining peace.[19]

The case of the Republika Srpska is particularly revealing in this regard. In September 1996 Karadžić was forced to surrender the presidency to his wartime ally, Biljana Plavšić. Despite her abysmal record as a tribune of Serb nationalism, Plavšić was won over to cooperation with the West in opposition to the unrepentantly nationalist Momčilo Krajišnik, shifting the capital from the nationalist redoubt of Pale to Banja Luka and agreeing to work cooperatively with Bosnian national institutions. The Bosnian elections of November 1997, which gave a narrow victory to a coalition of parties opposed to the SDS organized by Plavšić and allowed the moderate Milorad Dodik to form a new government in the Republika Srpska, seemed like a triumph for SFOR and the High Commissioner. In September 1998 elections, however, Plavšić was roundly beaten for the presidency by the radical nationalist Nikola Poplašen, a self-styled Chetnik who enjoyed parading during the war with an unkempt beard and a knife in his belt. After several months of confrontation, in May 1999 High Commissioner Carlos Westendorp simply dismissed Poplašen despite the fact that he had come to office through an uncontested democratic election. Such harsh measures, criticized by some as the work of "a kind of protectorate that refuses to say its name," may be legitimate in view of the destructive nature of the political forces in question, but the need for administrative arbitrariness on the part of the occupying authorities to hold the line against extremism inevitably posed the question of what might happen in their absence.[20]

Without the reassurance provided by international peacekeepers, the eruption of local violence or republic-level conflict sparked by ethnic rivalry is well within the range of possibility. Precipitous or disorderly disengagement by the U.S. or the international community would therefore be a high-risk undertaking. Partition as an alternative to the Dayton bargain has always had its champions, but has never been supported by U.S. policy — partition arrangements would perhaps look too much like capitulation to be considered politically acceptable.[21] For the time being, it appears that the status quo can be sustained, and halting progress toward what might eventually become a self-sustaining peace maintained, only at the cost of an open-ended engagement by NATO or EU led peacekeepers.[22]

3. The KLA Comes to Preševo.

Despite the slow pace of progress, there are realistic prospects for an eventual disengagement of the international community from Bosnia-Herzegovina. The same cannot be said for Kosovo, where even the most optimistic assessments acknowledge that a robust peacekeeping force remains essential to preserving stability. KFOR helps to contain communal tension within Kosovo itself, but it is perhaps even more important as a mechanism for deterring the Albanian nationalist agenda, driven by a militant core of the former

KLA that has sought to use the province as a sanctuary for exporting insurrection.

In the spring of 2000, the Albanian uprising that the KLA had launched inside Kosovo in 1997 spread into southern Serbia's Preševo valley. The valley overlaps with the five kilometer-wide buffer area, or Ground Safety Zone, set up by KFOR after its occupation of Kosovo where Yugoslav Army and police forces were not allowed to penetrate. The region's population of over 70,000 is almost entirely Albanian, and the area is sometimes referred to as western Kosovo in Albanian nationalist discourse. The Preševo valley is an important line of north-south communication including the main road attaching Belgrade to Skopje. It also plays a significant role as a smuggling route. From January 2000 a shadowy so-called Liberation Army of Preševo, Bujanovac, and Medvedja (LAPBM), sustained by militants based across the border with Kosovo in the area controlled by the U.S.-led Multinational Brigade East, launched a campaign of intimidation against Serb police and local authorities in the Preševo valley. The policy of assassination, as in Kosovo in previous years, seems to have been aimed at provoking reprisals and encouraging international intervention as a foundation for establishing de facto Albanian control.

Whatever residual sympathy for the plight of the Kosovar Albanians might have been in play, Western chancelleries had no interest in further fragmentation in the southern Balkans. Fortuitously, the fall of Milošević in the autumn of 2000 provided an opportunity to address the problem without expanding KFOR's mandate, by negotiating with the new regime in Belgrade to permit Serbian police and security forces, under careful observation, to reenter the area. With Yugoslav forces carrying the bulk of responsibility, from the end of 2000 onward the Albanian insurgency in the Preševo valley was brought under control, culminating with a negotiated ceasefire on March 13, 2001. The irony of NATO appealing for Serbian assistance to reduce a KLA-led insurrection within little more than a year of the allied bombing campaign was striking, but not unfathomable. The change of regime in Belgrade had altered the dynamics of power in the region. During the Kosovo conflict, it was the capacity of Milošević's Belgrade to export disruption that lay at the center of Western concerns. In Preševo, the potential role of a post-Milošević Serbia as a factor for stability was brought to the fore.[23]

The battle for the Preševo valley was not sustained, but incidents in the area continue, and the demonstration of an unbroken will to fight on the part of a radical fringe of the former KLA is not encouraging. While UNMIK struggles to put Kosovo back on its feet, the unresolved Albanian national question constantly threatens to reverse whatever halting progress has been made.[24]

4. War Comes to Macedonia.

Instability in Kosovo inevitably affected the fragile relationship between Slavs and Albanians in neighboring Macedonia. Lacking a recent or reliable census, it is only possible to speculate concerning the precise balance of populations—the 1994 census placed the Albanian minority at about 23 percent of the population and the Slavic majority at 66 percent—442,000 Albanians against 1.3 million Slavs plus numerous other smaller minority communities including Turks, Serbs, Roma, and Vlachs. According to some Albanian estimates, however, the Albanian community now constitutes over 40 percent of the population, with a rate of increase that will make it a majority within a generation. In either case, Macedonian Albanians constitute a large and growing community, concentrated in northern and western districts, but also present in large numbers in major cities including Skopje, where about one-third of the 600,000 residents are Albanian.

Macedonia was the only Yugoslav republic to move toward independence without bloodshed. Its declaration of independence on September 8, 1991, came as a result of negotiations with Belgrade and was followed, on March 26, 1992, by a peaceful withdrawal of all Yugoslav armed forces based in the province. On January 8, 1992, the Titoist and Yugoslav loyalist Kiro Gligorov was elected president of the new Republic of Macedonia, an independent state for the first time in its long and troubled, though often illustrious, history.

The smooth transition to independence was deceptive. Macedonia was an impoverished, ethnically complex, and unstable state with difficult relations with most of its neighbors. Bulgaria became the first state to recognize Macedonian sovereignty, but it refused to acknowledge the existence of a distinct Macedonian identity or language—for a century and more Bulgarian nationalism has been constructed around the assertion that Slavic Macedonians are in fact Bulgarians cut off from their homeland by the foibles of history.[25] Recognition from the UN followed in April 1993, and from the

U.S. on 9 February 1994, but in deference to Greek protests, under the provisional title the Former Yugoslav Republic of Macedonia (FYROM). Skopje had been granted a right of self-determination, but not the right to choose its own name! Athens argued that the name Macedonia was part of the Hellenic heritage that could not be usurped by outsiders, and suggested that its use implied territorial demands against Greece's own Macedonian region. It further protested against the use of the Star of Vergina (a symbol associated with Alexander the Great) on the new Macedonian flag, the appearance of an image of the White Tower of Thessalonica on some Macedonian banknotes, and phrases in the Macedonian constitution implying a right to represent the interests of Macedonians resident outside the republic. On February 16, 1994, immediately following U.S. recognition, Greece initiated an economic embargo against its neighbor, closing the Greek consulate at Skopje, sealing the border, and preventing access to the port of Thessalonica. The notion that Macedonia was in some meaningful sense a threat to Greece was ludicrous, but the issue was whipped to fever pitch by demagogic politicians courting nationalist opinion, culminating with a huge anti-Skopje demonstration of over a million people in Thessalonica on March 31, 1994. In the spring of 1994 Serbia also mobilized troops along its border with Macedonia, sections of which are imprecisely delineated and contested.[26] In was against precisely this kind of threat that a small UNPROFOR contingent (renamed the UN Preventive Deployment or UNPREDEP in March 1995) was authorized to deploy in Macedonia in December 1992. Peacekeeping forces provided some reassurance to Skopje, but the 1,156 American and Scandinavian soldiers in place in the spring of 1994 were hardly an adequate deterrent.[27]

External pressure reinforced domestic instability. After independence, Skopje made a sincere but only partly successful effort to integrate the Albanian minority into a true multinational state. Albanian parties were brought into parliament and governing coalitions, but the Albanian minority remained subject to economic discrimination, and was underrepresented in the armed forces, police, and civil service. Although relations between Slavic and Albanian Macedonians were not traditionally embittered in the manner of relations between Serbs and Kosovar Albanians, interethnic tensions were a fact of life.[28] The Albanian Party for Democratic Prosperity (PDP) was constrained to become more demanding as popular agitation for change expanded, embracing demands for the creation of an Albanian language university in Tetovo, broader integration into national institutions, and a redrafting of the preamble to the Macedonian constitution that would give Albanians equal status as a constituent nationality. On October 3, 1995, Gligorov's motorcade was attacked by a car bomb while passing before the Hotel Bristol in the heart of Skopje. The chauffer was killed and the president, age 79, suffered serious wounds including the loss of an eye. Subsequent evidence has implicated the Serbian secret services in the attack, but at the time of the event it was speculated to be an act of Albanian terrorism.[29] Administrative elections in the autumn of 1996 saw large gains for the more extreme Albanian national parties in Tetovo and Gostivar, and by 1997 Macedonian Albanians were being drawn into the same web of intrigue that was bringing the KLA to life in Kosovo.

Meeting in Priština on July 22, 2000, representatives of the Albanian national movement made no secret of how they saw their struggle evolving. The program approved by the conference asserted that "a part of the nation still remains under the yoke of the oppressor in Serbia, Macedonia, and Montenegro . . . the Albanian peoples of Kosovo must orient themselves toward independence and form a state that will include all of the occupied territories where Albanians are in a majority."[30] After the autumn 2000 elections, with space for political work inside Kosovo constrained by the shifting popular mood and the heavy hands of KFOR and UNMIK, KLA leaders seem to have opted to look across the border. Once again Western observers were caught by surprise, and international mediators forced to run to catch up with a cycle of violence.[31] In the last months of 2000 several attacks against Macedonian policemen were reclaimed by an organization styling itself the National Liberation Army (NLA), rendered in Albanian with the same acronym (UÇK) used to designate the KLA.[32] Described by Duncan Perry as "an offshoot of the Kosovo Liberation Army" composed of several thousand "hardened warriors who learned their trade fighting Serbs in Kosovo," the NLA represented a Macedonian variant of the same Albanian nationalist movement that had already surfaced in Kosovo and the Preševo valley.[33]

In January 2001 a small group of NLA militants assaulted a police station in the village of Tanuševci, located near the border with Kosovo, adjacent to the Preševo valley, and about 20 miles north of Skopje. The action may not have been intended as the beginning of a military campaign—Tanuševci was a refuge on KLA smuggling routes, and the original violence could have been aimed at protecting traffickers from police interference.[34] On February 25, however, after national attention had been drawn to the site, up to 250 NLA fighters dressed in black seized control of the village. The Macedonian authorities cordoned off the town but did not venture to retake it. Soon fighting had expanded throughout the entire area.[35] In March the NLA upped the ante by launching an attack against Tetovo, Macedonia's second largest city with 170,000 residents, 75 percent of them Albanian (according to the census of 1994). The guerrillas, operating out of the imposing Šar Planina mountain range, moved into the surrounding hills, raised the Albanian flag on the Kale (an ancient Ottoman fortress on the outskirts of the city), and brought the city center under mortar fire. On March 26 Macedonian forces stormed the Albanian positions, only to find that their enemy had fled—or rather melted away into the hills without a trace.[36] A familiar pattern seemed to be emerging, with fighting escalating, thousands of refuges fleeing the war zones, government forces reliant upon heavy weapons and firepower incapable of pinning down and destroyed a more agile opponent, and the international community anguished over a situation with the potential to shatter regional stability.

Under siege, Skopje immediately closed its 140-kilometer border with Kosovo, and Foreign Minister Srjan Kerim flew to Brussels and called upon NATO to intensify border patrols. Officials criticized NATO for its inability to contain the NLA, and bridled under instructions to reign in their military response, but lacked confidence in the capacity of the small and poorly prepared Macedonian armed forces to master the problem without external assistance.[37] Reliable light infantry forces capable of taking positions by assault were sorely lacking. As an alternative, Skopje relied on air power, heavy weaponry, and rocket fire to attack occupied areas, affecting massive damage and often driving local residents into the arms of the NLA without achieving militarily significant effects. In April fighting spread to the northeastern town of Kumanovo, where water mains serving the civilian population were severed, and in June NLA fighters occupied the Albanian village of Aričinovo, ten kilometers from Skopje and adjacent to the country's only international airport and oil refinery. During May a government of national unity was pulled together in the capital, combining two Macedonian Slavic parties and two Albanian parties (the Social Democratic Alliance of Macedonia, IMRO-DPMNU, the PDP, and Arben Xhaferi's Democratic Party of Albanians), but it was weak and anything but united. The Albanian parties represented in the government supported national unity, but condemned disproportionate use of force against the insurrection and pushed a program for expanded Albanian rights that clashed with the priorities of the government. The NLA, represented by its self-styled leader and former KLA activist Ali Ahmeti, claimed to oppose secession and limited its demands to a series of reforms—changes in the preamble of the constitution recognizing Albanians as a "co-founding" ethnicity, designation of Albanian as an official language, sponsorship for the University of Tetovo, administrative autonomy in Albanian majority areas, and proportional representation in public administration.[38] The moderation of the agenda did not slow down the momentum of armed struggle. By June the Macedonian regime appeared to be on the verge of collapse.

Under these circumstances, the international community mobilized, belatedly but effectively, to head off the worst. During May, despite pledges to avoid all contacts with "terrorists," OSCE representative Robert Frowick coordinated a series of meetings between Macedonia's Albanian parties and the NLA in Kosovo with the goal of defining an arrangement that the Albanian community as a whole could accept.[39] Subsequently, the EU's new high representative for foreign and security policy, Javiar Solana, laid the groundwork for a diplomatic option during a series of shuttle missions. In June KFOR soldiers were brought into the theater to escort some 350 NLA fighters away from their threatening forward position at Aričinovo. Macedonian authorities were outraged, and rioting erupted in the capital protesting NATO's purported role as the NLA's protector, but Skopje had no real independent option.[40] During June and July former French Defense Minister François Leotard on behalf of the EU, Ambassador James Pardew on behalf of the United States, and special envoy Peter Feith on behalf of NATO hammered out the terms of a diplomatic settlement that was signed by the four parties constituting Macedonia's national unity government at the lake resort of Ohrid on August 13.[41]

The Ohrid Framework Agreement, like the Dayton Accord, gave something to all sides, but made no one happy. The NLA agreed to observe an armistice, surrender its weapons to international authorities, and disband as a forum for armed struggle. The voluntary handover of light arms subsequently organized by NATO as Operation ESSENTIAL HARVEST resulted in the collection of a grand total of 3,875 weapons—from an arsenal of hundreds of thousands believed to remain in stashes under the control of NLA militants. In exchange, the Macedonian authorities agreed to begin a process of institutional reform that would come toward the goal of greater autonomy for the Albanian minority by granting it the status of a constituent nation, introducing bilingualism, and forwarding proportional representation. Implementing these pledges in the face of domestic opposition did not promise to be easy, and it may be presumed that even if realized they will not correspond to the larger, long-term aspirations of the Albanian national movement.[42]

The Ohrid Agreement was imposed by international mediators and sustained by an international military presence. On September 26 an OSCE Monitoring Mission involving 125 monitors was chartered to observe compliance, to be accompanied by a German-led NATO protection force, with only 1,000 troops too small to intimidate, but sufficient to signal resolve, designated as Operation AMBER FOX.[43] Plans called for an EU force to succeed the NATO deployment, autonomous but drawing on NATO assets and attached to the NATO chain of command, a commitment described by French President Jacques Chirac as the "first reasonable but ambitious step toward a European defense policy."[44] Though its architects might prefer to ignore it, Ohrid transformed Macedonia into yet another Balkan protectorate—this time a protectorate lite.[45] The agreement has been praised as a new framework for Balkan conflict management—preemptive engagement by the international community, a viable compromise that offers positive incentives for all parties, and discrete monitoring that leaves the essential responsibility for post-conflict peace building in the hands of local actors. In its wake, Macedonia has had some success in attracting sorely needed international financial assistance.[46]

The fruits of the Ohrid Agreement arrived 1 year after its conclusion, when national elections brought a new ruling coalition to power. In these elections, Ljubčo Georgievski's IMRO, with its rhetorically nationalist orientation, was roundly defeated by the left-center Social Democratic League behind Branko Crvenkovski. Perhaps more surprisingly, the Albanian Democratic Party and its leader Arben Xhaferi, committed to an incongruous alliance with IMRO in the outgoing government, was bested by the new Albanian Democratic Union for Integration, led by none other than former NLA leader Ahmeti. The extent of the victories was impressive. In Macedonia's 120 seat parliament, the Social Democratic League was projected to control an absolute majority of 62 seats against 34 for IMRO, and Ahmeti's Democratic Union 17 seats against only 5 for the Democratic Party.[47] Though the Social Democrats were in a position to govern independently, the exigencies of implementing the Ohrid reforms made it imperative that they secure an agreement with a representative of the Albanian minority.

The outcome offers a precious opportunity to further an agenda for reconciliation. While accusations of corruption and collusion with the Slavic parties undermined Xhaferi, as the leader of Macedonia's Albanian insurrection Ahmeti accumulated tremendous popular support. In the year following the uprising, he has become an outspoken proponent of compromise solutions keyed to reform, which the Slavic majority would be well-advised to accept. On the other hand, suspicion within the Slavic community of the kind of Albanian militancy that the "terrorist" Ahmeti is perceived to have sponsored is deeply-rooted. Crvenkovski's success is in part a function of popular disillusionment with corrupt governance and clientelism—real problems that will, however, be extremely difficult to address. And Macedonian remains a fragile state with a poorly functioning economy and high unemployment. The NLA has been replaced by another shadowy guerrilla organization dubbed the Albanian National Army (*Armata Kombetare Shqiptare*) with an agenda for continuing armed struggle.[48] Disaffection among the Slavic majority, provoked by economic hardship but manifested as national intolerance, is likewise a wild card that will have to be carefully monitored. The elections leave the country at the very beginning of what will inevitably be a long and untidy process of economic recovery, state building, and ethnic reconciliation. If this process is to be brought to fruition it will "require, for the foreseeable future, a visible Western presence and generous support."[49]

5. Tudjman in Hell.

Croatia's reconquest of the Krajina during 1995 and subsequent absorption of eastern Slavonia was a triumph for Franjo Tudjman's narrow vision of Croatian state rights. Following these events, the "father of the nation" toured the country in a so-called peace train trumpeting Croatian virtue to popular acclaim, and his HDZ was reconfirmed in power in national elections. In June 1997 Tudjman himself easily won a third term as president. The victories culminated a phase of national mobilization, but also set the stage for change. By bringing the affront of occupation to an end, driving out the Serb population of the Krajina, and concluding the "Homeland War" (*Domovinski rat*) that had hitherto dominated the politics of independent Croatia, the events of 1995 allowed the Croatian electorate to devote more attention to real and present domestic difficulties.

Despite official triumphalism, all was not well. The quasi-authoritarian rule of Tudjman's HDZ had been accompanied by declining living standards, high unemployment lingering close to 25 percent, and insider privatization that placed the bulk of Croatia's economic assets in the hands of "a criminal elite sacking national resources."[50] Tudjman was used by the Western powers as an ally of convenience in the struggle with Milošević's Serbia, but never really respected, and his country had few reliable allies. Despite a virtual state monopoly of the mass media, and repressive policies toward political dissent, a more effective opposition was sure to emerge as the strictures of national mobilization declined.

Tudjman died of cancer on December 10, 1999, after more than a month in a coma, in the midst of a parliamentary election campaign. The seriousness of his condition had not been revealed, and news of his passing, sprung upon a population and political elite ill-prepared to receive it, necessitated early presidential elections and opened the door to regime change. On January 3, 2000, a six-party reformist coalition cruised to victory, winning 95 of 151 seats in the lower house of the Croatian parliament against only 46 for the HDZ and bringing Ivica Račan of the Social Democratic Party (heir to the Yugoslav League of Communists of Croatia) to office as Prime Minister.[51] One month later, Tudjman's former foreign minister Mate Granić carried only 22 percent of the vote in the first round of voting in the presidential contest. The 7 February runoff produced a new surprise when Stipe Mesić, representing the small Croatian Peoples' Party but familiar to the electorate due to his role as chair of the Federal Presidency during the agony of Yugoslavia at the beginning of the 1990s, prevailed over the favored Dragiša Budiša. The new leadership wasted no time in attacking the Tudjman legacy, arresting some of the more notoriously corrupt state officials, asserting a willingness to cooperate with the work of the ICTY, washing its hands of efforts to attach Herceg-Bosna to Croatia, and pledging sweeping administrative and economic reforms.

The voters' repudiation of Tudjman and the HDZ was a significant event that made possible a turn away from the archaic nationalism of the past decade toward more forward looking efforts to reattach Croatia to natural markets in the southeastern European subregion and realign with contemporary European standards of democracy and human rights. But the challenge of reform was made considerably more difficult by the legacy of war. Zagreb joined NATO's Partnership for Peace in May 2000, but it was clear that membership in the Alliance would be a long-term goal at best. The EU praised the new Croatia's potential as a leader in the post-conflict Balkans, but put off Croatian prospects for association. Economic performance continued to stagnate absent structural reforms that were sure to carry a high social price, and foreign aid and assistance remained modest. Friction within the ruling coalition slowed down the reform agenda, and popular dissatisfaction with lack of progress in improving living standards grew.[52] The HDZ has made modest gains in recent elections, and remains a factor in national politics, with an agenda that could set Croatia's realignment toward Europe reeling backward.[53]

A political cartoon appearing in the Croatian feuilleton *Feral Tribune* after Milošević's incarceration in The Hague shows a relaxed Franjo Tudjman sitting in Hell, pointing a mocking finger at his Serbian counterpart under lock and key, proclaiming the World War II slogan, *bolje grob nego rob* (better death than slavery). Though it is unlikely that Tudjman would ever have been dragged before an international tribunal, he was at least as complicit in the violent breakup of Yugoslavia and responsible for the degradation of his homeland as was Milošević. Discrediting the primitive nationalism of the HDZ and placing Croatia back on its feet economically are important prerequisites for reestablishing a stable regional order. Aiding in that task should be a priority for the West.

6. The Serbian Revolution.

The best news to emerge from the Balkans in the wake of the Kosovo conflict was unquestionably the fall of the Milošević regime. Perhaps deceived by conventional wisdom suggesting that his popular support had been strengthened by intransigence during the air campaign, Milošević himself made the decision to force through a constitutional amendment allowing him to stand in popular elections for the post of president of Yugoslavia, which had previously been appointed by parliament, in the autumn of 2000. The gesture was unnecessary — Milošević's term of office as Serbian president was scheduled to expire in July 2001, and some kind of arrangement allowing him to perpetuate power would eventually have been required, but there was no imminent pressure to act. In the presidential contest, to general astonishment, in a five-man race held on September 24, Milošević was defeated in the first round as opposition leader Vojislav Koštunica, representing a Democratic Opposition coalition, captured slightly more than 50 percent of the vote.

What followed was high drama. Back to the wall, Milošević refused to recognize the validity of the result. After some hesitation, the pro-regime Federal Elections Commission ruled that Koštunica had not crossed the 50 percent bar, and mandated a runoff election on October 8. The Democratic Opposition refused this ploy, declined to participate in a run off, and called for popular defiance. It succeeded in mobilizing a movement of contestation engaging a broad cross section of Serbian society, and culminating in a general strike. The high point of the mobilization arrived on October 5, with a nation-wide march on Belgrade that united hundreds of thousands of citizens in columns that swept aside police roadblocks and eventually stormed the federal parliament building.[54] On October 6 Milošević threw in the towel. Besieged in his residence in the elite Belgrade suburb of Dedinje, he formally accepted the results of the elections and recognized Koštunica as the democratically elected president of Yugoslavia. After 13 years of exercising power, the Serbian strongman who had masterminded the dissolution of Yugoslavia, presided over its war of succession, and emerged apparently unscathed from the NATO bombing campaign, had been swept away by crowds in the streets.

The reasons for Milošević's defeat are not difficult to identify. His electoral base had always been relatively narrow, built upon the support of pensioners in search of security, rural and southern Serbia, and economically troubled small and medium sized towns. Already in 1996 the *Zajedno* (Unity) coalition led by Zoran Djindjić and Vuk Drašković succeeded in winning an impressive victory in local elections, securing majorities in 14 of Serbia's largest cities and towns. Milošević refused to acknowledge the results, and 88 days of uninterrupted street demonstrations followed, concluding with the surrender of the authorities and validation of election outcomes, including recognition of Djindjić as elected mayor of Belgrade.[55] The Zajedno coalition could not stand the strains of victory, and by 1997 it had disbanded amidst partisan quarreling. Milošević's political weakness had been demonstrated nonetheless, and the sense of exposure may have encouraged him to maintain a hard-line stance during the Kosovo crisis. Serbia's defeat in Kosovo, coming on top of years of corrupt governance, economic decline, and international isolation, was the final straw. During his years in power Milošević had repeatedly mobilized the forces of order to defend himself against popular ire. At the decisive moment on October 5, there was no one left to fight for him — the army, led by General Nebojša Pavković, and the police forces, opted to defer to the mobilized populace. Serbia's revolution was disciplined, democratic, and essentially bloodless, an unambiguous manifestation of popular will.[56] In this it resembled many of the central European anti-communist uprisings of 1989, of which it is sometimes said to represent the culmination.[57]

The Serbian revolution concluded with parliamentary elections on December 23, 2000, where the Democratic Opposition of Serbia, now an 18-party coalition united behind Djindjić as its candidate for prime minister, carried two-thirds of the popular vote. With a democratic foundation in place, Serbia confronted the massive task of constructing what Koštunica called "a state without rivers of blood for borders, a good, efficient, democratic, European state, one that is free inside and free abroad, that is independent, with a normal economy, industry, banking system, social and health care, and media."[58] The task was not made easier by chronic political division. Djindjić as Prime Minister of Serbia and Koštunica as President of Yugoslavia, the two most important leaders in the new regime, were contrasting personalities whose agendas did not coincide. Dealing with the Milošević legacy quickly proved to be both a challenging and a dangerous occupation. The assassination of Djindjić on March 12, 2003, apparently at the hands of organized criminal figures integrated into the Milošević government the prime minister was seeking to neutralize, made the dangers clear, and provided a tragic example of the instability that continues to haunt Serbia's future.[59]

Serbia lies at the heart of the Balkans, and possesses a powerful state tradition and considerable economic assets. Its revival will be essential to any effort to restore regional stability. Not surprisingly, the Western powers embraced the Serbian revolution and moved expeditiously to bring an end to the quasi-isolation imposed upon the Milošević regime. In short order Yugoslavia was able to eliminate the sanctions maintained by the United States and EU, restore membership in the UN and the OSCE, and join the Stability Pact for Southeastern Europe, the European Bank for Reconstruction and Development, the International Monetary Fund, and the Council of Europe.

Belgrade was also able to come to an agreement concerning a new framework for relations with Montenegro. From assuming power in November 1997 onward Montenegrin president Milo Djukanović had pushed relentlessly for a referendum that would allow Montenegro to proclaim itself an independent state. In the aftermath of the Kosovo conflict, when support for Montenegro appeared to be a convenient way to keep the pressure on Milošević, Western chancelleries tended to stand in Djukanović's corner, though the agenda for separation was never unambiguously embraced. On November 2, 1999, Podgorica went so far as to introduce the Deutsche Mark as the official currency of Montenegro, creating the foundations of a state within a state. Secession would no doubt have worked in the interests of Djukanović and his entourage, suspect of reaping huge profits from the criminal trafficking for which Montenegro had become notorious.[60] The advantages of independence were less obvious to Montenegro's 650,000 impoverished citizens, and despite Podgorica's best efforts securing a clear majority for independence in a fairly conducted national referendum never seems to have been within reach. In national elections of April 22, 2001, touted as a referendum on independence, Djukanović's *Victory for Montenegro* coalition carried 42 percent of the vote and 35 seats in the national parliament, but was nearly overtaken by a *Together for Yugoslavia* opposition bloc that won 41 percent of the vote and 33 seats. On March 14, 2002, urged on by EU mediator Javier Solana, Koštunica and Djukanović met in Belgrade and agreed to disband the Federal Republic of Yugoslavia and create a new union provisionally entitled Serbia-Montenegro.[61] The issue of Montenegrin separatism was not definitively laid to rest—the arrangement included provisions for reviewing the status of the union after 3 years, including the possibility of a referendum on continued association.[62] Djukanović continues to assert that a majority of Montenegrins support independence, and invoke the possibility of "civil strife on a scale that could destabilize both Montenegro and its neighbors" should their desires be left unfulfilled indefinitely.[63] But the destabilizing gesture of unilateral secession has at least been headed off, allowing the government in Belgrade to concentrate its energies on domestic reform.[64]

Despite the priority attached to consolidating the Koštunica leadership, following the fall of Milošević Belgrade was immediately bombarded with demands on the part of the ICTY and the international community to surrender indicted war criminals, the most important of whom was now the deposed leader himself. These demands quickly became politically destabilizing. On April 1, 2001, after a daylong standoff at the Milošević residence, the former president was taken into custody by Yugoslav authorities. On June 28, 2001 (*Vidovdan!*), he was extradited to The Hague, and on June 29 became the first head of state ever to be arraigned before an international tribunal. Though supportive of cooperation with The Hague tribunal in general terms, Koštunica opposed the extradition as unconstitutional, and argued that only a domestic trial would allow Serbs to come to terms with the crimes of the past decade. Djindjić overrode his principled opposition on pragmatic grounds, yielding to a U.S. ultimatum asserting that if Milošević was not surrendered immediately contributions to the Internal Aid Donors' Conference scheduled for June 29 would not be forthcoming.[65] The Milošević trial opened in February 2002 to a good deal of fanfare, with the former tyrant unrepentantly denouncing the tribunal as a legal travesty and exercise in victors' justice.[66]

For a time, Milošević's perorations before the tribunal were the talk of Serbia. His condemnations of the ICTY as illegal and inspired by an anti-Serbian bias were widely shared and had considerable resonance. In the end, however, the game became stale. Out of power, Milošević had lost the aura of omnipotence that had made him so potent as a ruler. He was not a convincing representative of the Serbian national idea, which he had, in fact, repeatedly betrayed. The phase of national mobilization was now over, and the preoccupations of the Serbian people had moved on to managing the consequences of a decade of war and isolation. The Milošević trial in The Hague was of interest for what it revealed about the evolution of international law, but in some ways irrelevant to the course of Serbia's long march back to international respectability. Insistent demands from The Hague to surrender suspects and accept war guilt nonetheless had the potential to disrupt the fragile governing coalition, and there was unquestionably an element of truth in Koštunica's argument that only a domestic process, perhaps modeled upon South Africa's Truth and Justice Commission, could make a meaningful contribution to national reconciliation.

7. Europe and the Balkans.

On June 10, 1999, at the initiative of the European Union, more than 40 partner countries and nongovernmental organizations meeting in Cologne, Germany approved a founding document for the Stability Pact for South Eastern Europe.[67] The project was launched as a cooperative initiative under the general direction of Special Coordinator Bodo Hombach at Sarajevo on July 30, 1999. The idea for the Pact dated to 1998, but was lent impetus by the Kosovo conflict, which reinforced awareness of Europe's ineffective diplomacy in the region. The Stability Pact's founding document pledged support for all the countries of Southeastern Europe "in their efforts to foster peace, democracy, respect for human rights and economic prosperity in order to achieve stability in the whole region," and held out the promise of eventual integration with Euro-Atlantic institutions.[68] It was widely hailed as a belated effort to move away from reactive crisis response toward a comprehensive, long-term conflict prevention strategy capable of grappling with underlying sources of instability.

The Stability Pact is a framework agreement among partners committed to developing a common strategy for stability and growth, and a multilateral initiative in which governments, international organizations, financial institutions, and nongovernmental organizations pool their resources in a common cause. It works under the direction of the Special Coordinator and a small staff based in Brussels, through a Regional Table sub-divided into three Working Tables devoted to Democratization and Human Rights (Table 1), Economic Reconstruction (Table II), and Security Issues (Table III). During the 3 years of its existence the Regional Table has pursued a wide range of useful initiatives, but its most basic responsibility has been to promote economic recovery, operating on the basis of the recommendations of the World Bank's March 2000 strategy paper *The Road to Stability and Prosperity in South Eastern Europe.*[69] The program seeks to combine short-term efforts to address the lingering effects of war through humanitarian relief and reconstruction programs, with a long-term commitment to transformation including democratization, sustainable development, and nation building. It also aspires to set standards—donor contributions are conditioned by demands for structural reform on the part of recipient countries.

The Stability Pact is still a work in progress, but it is not too soon to conclude that its contributions to economic recovery have been disappointing. The amount of assistance generated by the Pact has simply been too small to roll back the development gap that increasingly divides the southeastern European subregion from neighboring areas in Central and Western Europe. Foreign direct investment and development assistance to the Balkan states through the entire decade of the 1990 only reached about one-half the per capita level that was provided to the more prosperous Visegrad countries of Central Europe. Since the creation of the Stability Pact, the scale of assistance has not dramatically changed.

Though non-European powers, including the United States, Canada, and Japan, have been associated with the Stability Pact since its inauguration, the EU has provided the bulk of funding for the initiative, which can be perceived as a part of a larger effort to address the Balkan regional dilemma by bringing Southeastern Europe in from the cold under the tutelage of the traditional European powers. The "Europeanization" of the Balkans, including "extending the cross-border monetary, trade, and investment arrangements that already operate within the EU across Europe's southeastern periphery," is often posed as a logical solution for a peripheral region that is nonetheless an integral part of Europe geographically and culturally.[70] In the United States, redefining the Balkan dilemma as a "European problem" sometimes becomes a prelude for arguments urging disengagement, but from a regional perspective there is no choice to be made.[71] The contemporary Balkans has already been subordinated to European and Euro-Atlantic direction. The only question that remains is how effective that direction will be in helping the region to emerge from its current degraded situation. Unfortunately, evolving U.S. priorities, the nature of the European integration process, and the international community's track record during a decade and more of Balkan conflict, warn against exaggerated expectations.

Following the collapse of European communist regimes in 1989, the EC was quick to offer the new democratic states of Central and Eastern Europe associated status, but cautious about opening its doors to new members. In December 1991, the first Association or Europe Agreements with post-communist states sought to promote commercial exchange and "political dialogue," but these agreements did not constitute a commitment to membership. The Copenhagen session of the European Council in June 1993 made eastern enlargement a practical possibility, but also conditioned eligibility upon the ability of an associated country "to assume the obligations of membership by satisfying the economic and political conditions required."[72] The conditions in question were stringent, and certainly well beyond the capacity of the states of Southeastern Europe. The European Commission sought to coordinate economic assistance to Central and Eastern Europe by launching the European Bank for Reconstruction and Development (EBRD) and Operation PHARE in November and December 1989. It also embraced the cause of democratization through projects in support of parliamentary reform, human rights monitoring, the development of an independent media, and the promotion of democratic trade unionism.[73] The majority of these programs were directed toward the Visegrad countries and the former Soviet Union rather than the Balkan states, however. It was not until 1997-98 that the European Council developed a project for Accession Partnerships, and the project disadvantaged the southeastern European area from the start. The attempt to draw up lists of "ins and pre-ins" among accession candidates upon which the EU's *Agenda 2000* was based excluded the Balkan region almost entirely.[74] By 2000 it had been discarded in favor of an approach basing eligibility upon bilateral discussions and individual merit. The Copenhagen summit of November 2002 confirmed accession for Slovenia and the Republic of Cyprus in 2004, tentatively looked forward to the possibility of accession for Romania and Bulgaria in 2007, and agreed to open accession talks with Turkey in December 2004 pending progress in a process of reform. The EU had belatedly extended its enlargement process to include the Balkans, but the core of the region constituted by the majority of Yugoslav successor states remained without prospects for accession in the near future.

There was some logic to the EU's reluctance. The chaos engendered by open-ended warfare and generally poor economic performance virtually precluded the majority of Balkan states from eligibility. The alternative to accession was positive association, but here, too, institutionalized Europe was slow to react to the special needs of a region in turmoil. After the failure of EC mediation in the first stage of the Yugoslav crisis, Europe ceased to play a dynamic role in regional conflict management, and, up to the 1995 Dayton Accord, it failed to produce any kind of uniform Balkan policy at all. In February 1996, chagrined by its effacement at Dayton, the EU's General Affairs Council initiated a Regional Approach in the Balkans, intended to supplement OSCE efforts under the Dayton Accord by offering financial and economic assistance and trade and cooperation agreements. It would await the watershed of the Kosovo crisis, however, before a more consistent approach took form. The Vienna European Council of December 1998 set the stage by calling for a common European strategy in the region, a call that would eventually be realized with the inauguration of the Stability Pact and its associated Stabilization and Association Process (SAP).

The SAP program was focused upon the negotiation of Stabilization and Association Agreements designed to grant contractual relations to the Balkan states heretofore left out of the European process altogether (Albania, Bosnia-Herzegovina, Croatia, Macedonia, and the Federal Republic of Yugoslavia as of 1999). Modeled on the Association (Europe) Agreements of the 1990s "but with a greater emphasis on regional cooperation, democratization, the development of civil society, and institution building," the Stabilization and Association Agreements and Process have become important levers of influence in European attempts to shape the Balkan regional environment.[75] Relations between the EU and individual Balkan states have remained considerably diverse nonetheless, and chronic instability continues to discourage deeper engagement and frustrate recovery. European priorities have also evolved, away from the humanitarian focus characteristic of the war years culminating with the Kosovo conflict, toward heightened concern for émigré flows and criminal trafficking—issues that are likely to dictate increased closure rather than inclusion. Conditioned, asymmetric association such as defined by the SAP program is a perfectly valid approach to integrating Balkan states into a larger European process that they are not yet ready to join as full partners, but it is not likely to bring the region the kind of benefits that are urgently needed if new bouts of instability are to be headed off. Europeanization is a valid and inevitable aspiration for the region, but it will not be a panacea for its many problems.

A variety of regionally based initiatives also seek to encourage closer coordination between the Balkan states themselves. Among these initiatives are the *Black Sea Economic Cooperation* (BSEC) whose 11 members include Albania, Bulgaria, Greece, Romania, and Turkey, the *Central European Initiative* (CEI) with 16 members including Albania, Bosnia-Herzegovina, Bulgaria, Croatia, Macedonia, Romania, and Slovenia; the *South East European Cooperative Initiative* (SECI) bringing together Albania, Bosnia-Herzegovina, Bulgaria, Croatia, Greece, Hungary, Moldova, Romania, Slovenia, and Turkey; and the *South East Europe Co-operation Process* (SEECP) including Albania, Bosnia-Herzegovina, Bulgaria, the Federal Republic of Yugoslavia, Greece, Macedonia, Romania, and Turkey, with Croatia as an observer.[76] These are clearly beneficial undertakings, complementary in nature, often coordinated with the work of the Stability Pact, and paralleled by a wide range of dynamic bilateral relationships. They are, however, condemned to work with severely limited resources.[77] Regional cooperation is also emerging in the military sector. In 1999, eight Balkan countries combined to establish a Multinational Peace Force South Eastern Europe which has evolved into a brigade sized force of 4,000 soldiers capable of participating in OSCE-mandated, NATO-led conflict prevention and peace support operations.[78] These various cooperative initiatives are mutually reinforcing and an important—indeed essential—complement to international efforts to build regional stability.

8. NATO and the Balkans.

NATO was created as a balancing alliance in response to the threat of a Soviet invasion of Western Europe. From its origins, however, the Alliance's commitment to collective defense was attached to the goal of building a security system within which the democracies of postwar Europe could learn to interact peacefully among themselves.[79] In the 1950s, Karl Deutsch spoke of the Alliance as a *security community* where war as a means of resolving disputes between states was becoming unthinkable.[80] And the benefits of security community did not lie in the military realm alone--the hard security guarantees provided by the Alliance encouraged a broader process of political, social, and economic integration that generated considerable collective benefits.[81] NATO has always had a dual character, as a defensive military alliance, but also as a political forum institutionalizing dialogue and cooperation.

The Alliance's post-cold war evolution has accentuated its character as a political agent. By redefining its mission and opening its doors to new members NATO has aspired, in the words of former Secretary General Javier Solana, to create "a new Alliance, far removed in purpose and structure from its Cold War ancestor," inspired by the premise of "cooperative security" and capable of serving as the centerpiece of an emerging European and Eurasian collective security regime.[82] From 1991 forward the Alliance has reduced and reconfigured its nuclear and conventional forces, transformed decisionmaking procedures to achieve greater transparency and balance, created the Euro-Atlantic Partnership Council and Partnership for Peace (PfP) process as means to engage the post-communist states of central and eastern Europe, actively pursued a process of enlargement, recast its security concept to encourage mutual security and out of area peace support missions, and institutionalized special relationships with the Russian Federation and Ukraine. Its self-proclaimed goal is no longer simply to deter aggression, but rather to help construct "a just and lasting peaceful order in Europe."[83]

Engagement in the Balkans has been an important test of these ambitious new commitments. The test has been successfully withstood, but not without problems. During the first years of the Balkan conflict, the NATO powers expressed a broad consensus in opposition to large-scale military involvement.[84] As the conflict expanded, it became more difficult to defend a policy of nonintervention — Europe's premier security forum could not stand aside indefinitely while a major European region was consumed by war without eventually sacrificing all credibility. Military engagement in the Bosnian conflict was belated but effective. Intervention in Kosovo was precipitous, and resulted in a war that probably did not need to be fought, but did create a context for bringing at least a trace of stability to the disputed province. In Macedonia the Alliance's role was more discrete, but no less essential. In addition to these ongoing peace support missions, and potentially more important in the long-term, the PfP and its Membership Action Plan have been enthusiastically embraced by a number of Balkan states, and Slovenia, Romania, and Bulgaria (together with Estonia, Latvia, Lithuania, and Slovakia in Central Europe) have been awarded full membership in the second round of enlargement. The Alliance also remains the single most important peace broker in the continuing rivalry between Greece and Turkey. Together with the EU, NATO has become a major point of orientation for the reform-oriented regimes of the new Southeastern Europe and an irreplaceable source of stability for the region as a whole.[85]

At the April 1999 Washington Summit, NATO launched a *South East Europe Initiative* (SEEI). The intention was to build on existing forms of cooperation and extend them to countries not yet engaged in the PfP process (Bosnia-Herzegovina, Croatia, and Yugoslavia during 1999), with the goal of promoting regional cooperation and long-term security and stability. In October 2000 a South East Europe Security Cooperation Steering Group was created to develop regional approaches to key security issues, and in May 2001, at the initiative of Romania, the SEEI presided over the drafting of a *South East Europe Common Assessment Paper on Regional Security Challenges and Opportunities* (SEECAP) agreed to by all southeastern European Foreign Ministers.[86] The SEECAP is an action-oriented document that identifies security challenges in the political, military, economic, social, and environmental realms and specifies cooperative mechanisms for addressing them. Under the aegis of SEEI, and on the basis the SEECAP recommendations, NATO has developed a demanding work agenda encouraging military modernization and security cooperation among regional partners. The Alliance's engagement in this process is a hopeful sign—but as yet no more than that. Peace building in the Balkans is a long-term project that will require a serious commitment on the part of all NATO allies, including the United States, for some time to come. Whether that commitment will be forthcoming, with the result that the benefits of a Deutschian security community will eventually be extended to all of the new democracies of Central, Eastern, and Southeastern Europe, remains to be seen.

* * * * * * * *

The Balkan region has arrived at the end of a decade-long cycle of violence. Though observers have become conditioned to expect the worst, recent years have seen a number of promising developments. The ouster of Milošević, and the political defeat of the HDZ, has made it possible to consign the war of Yugoslav succession to the past. All of the states of the region have democratically elected governments anxious to move forward by focusing on economic growth, regional cooperation, and closer relations with an enlarging Europe. The detritus of war, in the form of shattered infrastructure, ruined lives, and the poisoned spirits of alienated communities, nonetheless remains in place. Some of these problems are being addressed by NATO-led peace support missions in Bosnia-Herzegovina, Kosovo, and Macedonia. Progress toward Greek-Turkish rapprochement, also actively promoted in the NATO context, holds out great promise for the entire region. The international community has sustained a substantial commitment to peace building in the Balkans, and a host of international and regionally based initiatives are underway to promote development and understanding.[87]

Promising trends do not mean that the region has turned the corner. Progress toward democratic consolidation has been real, but it is reversible. The foundations for a self-sustaining peace in Bosnia-Herzegovina, Kosovo, and Macedonia have not yet been established. Poor economic performance, rampant criminality, and social disillusionment encouraging migration are serious dilemmas for the region as a whole. Changed priorities after the September 11, 2001, terrorist attacks against the United States have lowered the profile of the Balkan region in international affairs, and called international commitments that are vital to stability into question. If such trends are not reversed, and they will only be reversed as the result of renewed determination and purposeful action, a variant of the Eastern Question could be called back into life, with Southeastern Europe, excluded from the European mainstream, once again representing a chronic source of friction and violence.

Humanitarian Intervention and the Law of War.

The Balkan wars of the 1990s challenged the capacity of international law and institutions to address the problem of violence in the international system, in regard both to interstate conflict and cases of humanitarian abuse perpetrated by domestic authorities. The intensive media coverage extended to Balkan conflicts, the involvement of the international community in the conflict management effort, the high visibility of humanitarian violations, and the new field for activism apparently opened up by the end of cold war bipolarity combined to make the conflict a particularly fertile ground for efforts to expand the modern war convention.[88] The extent to which those efforts do or do not succeed will represent an important part of the legacy of the wars of Yugoslav succession.

Attempts to broaden the capacity of international instances to punish violations of legal or humanitarian norms rest upon a universalistic presumption—that in an increasingly interdependent international system common values must come to take precedence over the egoistic concerns of individual units. The goal is sometimes described as a shift from a "Westphalian" order, based upon the autonomy of nation-states in an anarchic system without effective supranational authority, toward an international society where at least some of the elements of domestic order pertain to the conduct of inter-state relations as well. International reactions to the wars of Yugoslav succession embodied this argument in at least three ways. First, Western interventions were justified in the name of a doctrine of *humanitarian intervention* asserting that, in cases of massive crimes against humanity, international instances and responsible national actors are obliged to respond, if need be, in defiance of the presumption of sovereignty.[89] Second, armed intervention and peace enforcement strategies were sanctioned as a legitimate use of force under the rubric of *humanitarian war*.[90] Third, the law of war was broadened to encompass a growing body of *international humanitarian law* that demands more intrusive monitoring of national behavior, including the convocation of tribunals to prosecute violators.[91]

In the wake of the bloodletting in Bosnia-Herzegovina, the relevance of a doctrine of humanitarian intervention was widely asserted. NATO's war in Kosovo was formally justified as a humanitarian war, where the intervening powers were presumed to resort to arms, not in respect of national interest, but in response to intolerable ethical violations. The ICTY has been in existence for nearly a decade and is mandated to impose legal accountability for humanitarian abuses. The Hague is now the site of history's first international prison, and home to the first head of state ever placed on trial by an international tribunal on criminal charges. Inspired and influenced by these initiatives, a permanent International Criminal Court (ICC) has been ratified by the UN, to take up its functions in The Hague during 2003.[92]

These are meaningful initiatives, but whether they will add up to a substantial extension of the international war convention remains unclear. Many of the states that were the most adamant champions of a doctrine of humanitarian intervention in the specific circumstances of the Yugoslav conflict have since cooled to the idea. War is not a humanitarian institution — the resort to arms may occasionally be just, or justifiable, but it is seldom humane. The ICTY is a contested institution, and the ICC lacks the support of many of the world's most significant national actors, including China, the Russian Federation, and the United States. As the Yugoslav wars of the 1990s fade into the past, the emotional reactions that galvanized opinion will begin to pale as well. Many of the conceptual and legal innovations that were applied during the Yugoslav conflict remain insufficiently institutionalized, and few rest upon a substantial international consensus.

NATO intervention during the war in Bosnia-Herzegovina was not formally sanctioned on the basis of a doctrine of humanitarian intervention. The use of force against the Serb faction (and occasional threats of a resort to force against the Croat and Muslim factions) came in response to violations of UN guidelines, and at UN request. In the Kosovo conflict, however, NATO intervention was not based upon any kind of convincing mandate from the UN or other relevant instance. Rather, a right to resort to force was asserted unilaterally by NATO Secretary General Javier Solana in a letter to the North Atlantic Council dated October 9, 1998, on the basis of an *interpretation* of UN Security Council Resolution No. 1999, which defined the situation in Kosovo as "a danger for peace and security in the region" and cited the imminent danger of "a humanitarian disaster." The circumstance of humanitarian necessity, according to Solana, provided NATO with "a legitimate basis for threatening the use of force, and, if necessary, a resort to force."[93] At the beginning of the bombing campaign, the notion would be elevated by British Prime Minister Tony Blair into an ethnical imperative to "act to save thousands of innocent men, women and children from humanitarian catastrophe," grandiloquently described as a "new internationalism where the brutal repression of whole ethnic groups would not be tolerated."[94] Blair's new internationalism implied a significant revision of classic just war theory, which demands right authority as a prerequisite for a resort to coercion. In cases of urgent humanitarian necessity, it was suggested, legal premises defining right authority, at least as they have been understood by the modern, or Westphalian tradition of International Law, could be overridden and responsible nations or international organizations self-empowered to fight in a just cause. As Blair put it in a speech before the Economic Club of Chicago on April 22, 1999, a "doctrine of international community" had "shifted the balance between human rights and state sovereignty."[95] For the neo-Kantian Jürgen Habermas, the war in Kosovo had encouraged "a leap away from classical international law understood as a law of states toward the cosmopolitan law of a society of world citizens."[96]

The doctrine of humanitarian intervention is compelling, but will not be convincing until several basic issues are resolved. The first is the issue of *institutionalization*. Ad hoc operations, such as that undertaken by NATO in Kosovo, do not rest upon a sound legal foundation. Article 2 paragraph 4 of the UN Charter forbids recourse to force by states with only two exceptions: (1) *Self-Defense* as referenced in Article 51 of the Charter (the same premise is mentioned in Article 5 of the North Atlantic Treaty); and (2) *Collective Security* measures under the auspices of the Security Council as defined in Chapter VII. NATO demonstrated its sensitivity to the issue during the Kosovo conflict by tying its actions to earlier UN Resolutions, but by any measure the campaign's legality was suspect.[97] In order to make a doctrine of humanitarian intervention more credible, international institutions and the collective security regime presided over by the UN will have to be considerably strengthened.[98] The UN Charter should ideally be rewritten to sanction such interventions, and consistent procedures for identifying violations developed. Likewise, in the spirit of consistent institutionalization, it would be best if some kind of formally constituted intervention force, such as that recommended by former UN Secretary General Boutros Boutros-Ghalli in his 1992 *Agenda for Peace*, could be placed at the disposition of the UN as an instrument of enforcement.[99] Such procedures would represent significant steps away from the Westphalian premise of state sovereignty toward more robust world governance. For that very reason, they are unlikely to be undertaken.

The issue of *standards* represents another dilemma. When do humanitarian violations create a situation of urgent necessity sufficient to justify a resort to arms? During the Balkan conflicts of the 1990s, decisions to intervene were often accompanied by a conscious exaggeration of the extent of abuses in order shape elite opinion and win public support. The use of the accusation of genocide has been particularly notable in this regard. Serbia's repression of the Kosovar Albanians was initiated on the basis of accusations of genocide in progress against the province's Serb minority.[100] During the run up to the outbreak of war in the spring of 1991 all three of Bosnia-Herzegovina's communal factions raised the charge of genocide against their rivals.[101] Croatian commentators accused Serb forces of perpetrating genocide during their 1991 campaigns in Croatia.[102] During the Bosnian conflict the Muslim community was repeatedly described as the victim of genocide.[103] In the winter of 1998-1999, when the victims of the fighting in progress in Kosovo numbered in the thousands, the charge was leveled against the Serbian authorities once again. As a result of the mass expulsion (but not necessarily systematic mass killing) of Kosovar Albanians during the war, it has found its way into the indictment against Milošević drawn up by the ICTY.[104] Unavoidably tied to the unprecedented crimes of the World War II holocaust, the term genocide provides a "high yield source of hatred," and is therefore, along with other charges directed against putative opponents, liable to abuse as an "indecent tool of propaganda."[105]

Determining when humanitarian abuses become liable to sanction will often demand an essentially subjective judgment based upon imperfect knowledge. In an age of instantaneous information, where public perception often is conditioned decisively by sensational media images and reporting, the risk that excessive emotionalism built upon compelling language may misconstrue events, and therefore create an irresistible momentum to "do something" before chains of causality are clear, is very real. Armed conflicts do not always produce unambiguous distinctions between victims and victimizers. Systematic monitoring by impartial observers and lucid adjudication of evidence are the only means to move beyond such uncertainty. At present, international instances are far from having the means, or the requisite moral authority, to accomplish such tasks reliably.

A doctrine of humanitarian intervention must also come to terms with the issue of *commitment*. Nations have traditionally crafted international policy on the basis of a discourse of interest. Though humanitarian concerns are not entirely foreign to this discourse, they are seldom at its essence. When interests are not deemed to be vital, a commitment of lives and treasure can seldom be sustained. During the war of Yugoslav succession, the uncertain commitment of the Western powers was repeatedly demonstrated. The West pursued a containment policy for 3 long years while over 200,000 Yugoslavs were cut down in wars and massacres. In Kosovo, NATO was willing to go to war on behalf of the Kosovar Albanians, but not to risk mass casualties.[106] The administration of George W. Bush came to office in January 2001 to a chorus of calls from influential supporters urging U.S. disengagement on the grounds that vital national interests were not at stake. The Balkan case makes clear that humanitarian motivation by itself will seldom provide the kind of sustained commitment that effective intervention demands.

The case for humanitarian intervention presumes that organized violence can be mobilized as an instrument of justice in complex regional contingencies within the confines of the test of proportionality. The very character of modern war calls this presumption into doubt.

Wesley Clark's account of Operation ALLIED FORCE is imbued with the conviction of fighting in a just cause, but his analysis leaves no doubt that in order to prevail in armed conflict belligerents must respect the laws of warfare and pursue victory uncompromisingly. In limited wars intended to provide "regional stability and humanitarian assistance," where there is arguably a substitute for victory, the result will often have more in common with imperial policing actions than classic armed conflict between peer competitors.[107] The difficulty of mobilizing and sustaining public support pushes inexorably toward a reliance upon air power in order to reduce or eliminate casualties among one's own forces, while maximizing damage to enemy infrastructure. In Kosovo, according to Michael Ignatieff, "the political leaders of NATO talked the language of ultimate commitment and practiced the warfare of minimum risk."[108] Reluctance to contemplate a ground incursion even in the face of truly massive humanitarian abuses, reliance upon medium altitude bombing with its unavoidable complement of collateral damage, attempts to assassinate the opposing leadership from the air, and attacks upon "dual use" infrastructure intended at least in part, in the spirit of Giulio Douhet, to break the enemy's will, were a consequence of that choice.[109] The structure of modern war, as defined by Clark, strains at the limits of the test of proportionality.[110] Moreover, according to Ignatieff, a zero casualties imperative imposed upon commanders by civilian authority "transforms the expectations that govern the morality of war."[111] The honor of the combatant—the ethical context that distinguishes warfare from crime—has always rested upon the assumption of reciprocal risk in service of a cause. If that contract is broken, Ignatieff insists, war becomes little more than a kind of chastisement.[112]

The capacity to wage war with minimum risk makes the

decision to resort to force easier to make. If not carefully monitored, such capacity may lead to precipitous and unconsidered actions, discourage the pursuit of diplomatic alternatives, and undermine the just war criterion of last resort. On the eve of Croatia's Operation STORM in the summer of 1995, confident of U.S. support, Tudjman used international negotiations as a pretext to buy time for last minute preparations. The Rambouillet negotiations have been portrayed as little more than a ploy intended to justify a resort to force. Such circumstances will recur should the presumption of a right to humanitarian intervention become imbedded in the operational code of the great powers. War without the risk of consequences likewise makes the temptation to use humanitarian pretexts harder to resist. The obvious danger is the transformation of an agenda based upon an assertion of universal human rights into a disguised form of hegemonism—Hedley Bull, for example, has noted the continuity between the theme of humanitarian intervention and the missionary and colonial traditions.[113] "The concept of humanitarian war," writes Danilo Zolo, "restores to states an indiscriminate *ius ad bellum*, voids the 'pacifistic' functions of international law, and discredits the cosmopolitan ideal of the universal citizen."[114] If these critiques are credited, the more widespread acknowledgement of a thesis of humanitarian war can be interpreted as a step backward for the international war convention.

The ICTY, created in May 1993 by the UN Security Council on the basis of Chapter I of the UN Charter, with a mandate retrospective to 1991, is the most ambitious dimension of efforts to use the Yugoslav wars as a context for expanding the oversight of the international community in regard to war and conflict. The wars in Bosnia-Herzegovina and Kosovo were the first armed conflicts in history fought in the presence of an international tribunal judged competent to judge crimes committed.

The effort to move judicial means toward the center of the war convention is a 20th century innovation. In the early modern centuries, the European traditions of pacifism and international law (Erasmus, Grotius, Crucé, the Duc de Sully, the Abbé Saint-Pierre, Penn, Vattel, Rousseau, Kant) emphasized interstate relations and political organization as the foundations of lasting peace.[115] The Versailles peacemakers' attempt to put the Kaiser, together with other German leaders (the surrender of 90 individuals was requested) on trial before an international tribunal with judges representing the United Kingdom, the United States, France, Italy, and Japan, was unprecedented. But Holland refused the Kaiser's extradition, Germany declined to surrender anyone, and in the end little came of the project. A more significant precedent was established at the end of the Second World War. The London Accord of August 6, 1945, created the Nuremberg Tribunal on behalf of the victorious nations of the war, and 1 year later an International Military Tribunal for the Far East was created in Tokyo. The Tokyo tribunal conducted two years of hearings before 11 judges designated by U.S. General Douglas MacArthur. All 28 of the accused that were placed before the court were convicted, and seven executed. The Nuremberg process began on November 25, 1945, with 22 accused placed before U.S., British, French, and Soviet judges. One year later it concluded with three not guilty verdicts, condemnations to prison terms of varied lengths, and ten death sentences that were carried out immediately.

Though it is often described as a continuation of the Nuremberg tradition, the ICTY rests upon a different set of premises. The Nuremberg Tribunal's charter specifically cited the "sovereign legislative power of the countries to which the German Reich unconditionally surrendered" as the basis for its authority. The ICTY is not a military tribunal, and Article 16 of its statute calls for action completely independent of any government.[116] A priority for the authorities at Nuremberg, noted in the opening address of Justice Robert H. Jackson citing "the privilege of opening the first trial in history for crimes against the peace of the world," though they also took account of war crimes (*jus in bello*) and crimes against humanity, was legal responsibility for instigating war (crimes against peace in the tradition of *jus ad bellum*).[117] The Hague Tribunal has focused almost exclusively upon crimes against humanity, and represents a conscious assault against state sovereignty on behalf of universal norms—though it should be noted that unlike the ICTY, the ICC includes the Nuremberg criterion of crimes against peace in its statute. Nuremberg and Tokyo did not establish ongoing traditions—after the processes were concluded the idea of an international criminal tribunal lay dormant until the 1990s.

The ICTY's legitimacy has been challenged on legal grounds (notably by Slobodan Milošević in the deposition at the outset of his trial).[118] Does the Security Council have the authority to appoint a court under Chapter VII of the Charter, and to remove juridical authority from sovereign states? These decisions, after lengthy review, were made by the ICTY itself, on its own behalf and in its own favor, in the Miroslav Tadić case.[119] The decisions may be contested, but they are substantial.

The issue of the Tribunal's autonomy is perhaps more troubling. The absence of any multilateral accord as a basis for the Tribunal (as opposed to the ICC) makes it a sort of subsidiary of the Security Council, which cannot be considered either impartial or universal. The same may be said of the Procurator General, who is directly appointed by the Security Council. Although Article 29 of the Tribunal's Statute obligates all state members of the UN to collaborate with its work, the real circle of collaborators has been quite narrow. Article 32 of the Statute specifies that revenues must derive from the UN's general operating funds, but already in 1993 a special fund for the ICTY was established on the basis of voluntary contributions. The Tribunal is in practice financially dependent upon a small number of Western powers led by the United States.

The Tribunal's procedures have also exposed it to the charges of bias and selective prosecution. Justice has been neither swift, sure, or equitable. Coercive detainment of indicted defendants was not initiated until the summer of 1997, and has proceeded irregularly and with numerous glitches. On July 10, 1997, British commandos in Prijedor approached Simo Drljača, a local police chief whose area of responsibility during 1992 included the Omarska, Keraterm, and Trnopolje prison camps, in mock Red Cross vehicles, a blatant violation of Red Cross neutrality. Drljača was killed in the resultant shoot out. On August 25, 1999, Momir Talić, former commander in chief of the armed forces of the Republika Srpska, was arrested on the basis of a secret warrant after he was baited to travel to Vienna as an invited guest of the OSCE. Irregular procedures such as these, inconsistency in enforcement of warrants, inability to bring in most wanted suspects including Karadžić and Mladić, and difficulties of prosecution lacking broad-based corroborative testimony, have cast considerable discredit upon the ICTY. In the nine years that it has been in existence, at a cost of over $400 million, 67 defendants have appeared before the court, 31 of whom have been tried. Eleven defendants are currently on trial, and approximately 30 indictees are still at large. The majority of indictees have been Serbs. The number of Croat and Bosnian Muslims on the list is considerably smaller, and only at the end of February 2003 were four Kosovar Albanians, all former members of the KLA, and the ABH Commander in

Srebrenica, Nasim Oric´, accused of perpetuating atrocities against Serb villages in Bosnia, made subject to indictment." At its current pace, the work of the Tribunal is likely to stretch over the better part of the next decade, at escalating cost, and with only the tip of the iceberg of abuses subjected to scrutiny. This is too slow, partial, and contested a result to represent a standard of justice, contribute meaningfully to reconciliation, or provide effective admonition to other world leaders contemplating aggression.[120]

There are clearly a large number of guilty parties in the dock at The Hague, who merit exemplary punishment. The premise of legal accountability in regards to the law of war is in principle admirable—if such accountability could be enforced reliably and fairly the international war convention would make a significant step forward. This will perhaps be the challenge confronting the ICC. The experience of the ICTY calls attention to how difficult the challenge is likely to be.

War in the Balkans: A Balance Sheet.

The wars of the 1990s were post-Yugoslav conflicts, born of the failure of the long cherished but now discredited South Slav idea. They were fought between communities with a history of antagonism, but also between peoples with a *lingua franca*, common history, and shared experience as fellow citizens. All were marked by the particular ruthlessness of civil war. None, with the possible exception of the Slovenian case, have been definitively resolved. Despite its many flaws, the Yugoslav federation offered a positive context for resolving the challenge of cultural diversity by sustaining a common space within which ethnic communities could coexist with reasonable guarantees of equity and balance. After a decade of warfare, no positive alternative has appeared to take its place. The chimera of the ethnically pure national state, still pursued by champions of partition arrangements in Bosnia, Kosovo, Macedonia, and elsewhere, cannot be the foundation for a sustainable political order in a culturally complex area such as former Yugoslavia. This is so even in the wake of the substantial social engineering affected by policies of ethnic cleansing over the last decade. If the process of anarchic fragmentation that has destroyed former Yugoslavia is ever to be reversed, some formula for reconciliation and re-association will have to be found.

The collapse of Yugoslavia has given rise to a complex mix of fragile new states and quasi-state entities. Slovenia, Croatia, and Serbia-Montenegro, the original founders of the Yugoslav federation, have considerable national potential. Ljubljana is well positioned to complete its association with institutional Europe. Belgrade and Zagreb, although they confront difficult economic circumstances that if unchecked could reanimate defensive nationalism, have the resources to follow the same path. Bosnia-Herzegovina, Kosovo, and Macedonia are international protectorates in all but name, and will likely remain so for some time. An independent Kosovo, or Montenegro, would have virtually no prospect for balanced development apart from reliance upon international assistance and criminal trafficking. Neighboring Albania is a virtual failed state, heavily dependent upon the support of the international community. In the contemporary Balkans the challenges of state and nation building are an integral part of post-conflict peace building that cannot be avoided.

The war of Yugoslav succession was also a Balkan war, waged over issues of identity and turf that have always been pronounced in a region marked by civilizational fault lines, weak states, and frustrated nationalism. The end of the cold war system, including the demise of the Yugoslav federation, the collapse of communist regimes in Albania, Romania, and Bulgaria, and the disappearance of the Soviet Union, shattered geopolitical equilibriums in all of Southeastern Europe. The wars of the 1990s reestablished regional balance in some cases, but generated new sources of conflict in others. The Macedonian and Albanian questions in the southern Balkans, in particular, are likely to remain sources of chronic instability. Other unresolved issues of identity and allegiance, including the fate of multistate nations such as the Serbs, Magyars, and Roma, could also become sources of tension. Recasting regional order has always been a prerequisite for effective conflict management. It is a challenge with which major regional actors, and the international community, are just beginning to come to grips.

The Yugoslav conflict posed world order concerns as well. It was one of the most protracted and destructive armed conflicts of the 1990s, and was in many ways a typical example of modern medium intensity warfare provoked by regional instability. Viewed as a case study, the Yugoslav model includes the disintegration of a failed state under the weight of economic dysfunction, a breakdown of domestic order exacerbated by ethnic tension and communal rivalry, armed conflict propelled by locally organized militias and paramilitary forces, war waged purposively against defenseless civilians with the aim of provoking terror and mass flight, the discrete involvement of major powers as sponsors for regional allies, and the frustrated attempts of the international community, often driven by sensational media coverage, to come to terms with the problem in an environment where vital interests and compelling motives were seldom in play.[121] The Balkan wars were post-cold war conflicts where the hand of the superpowers was not present to impose moderation—the fate of Yugoslavia bears witness to the potential for loss of control engendered by the end of bipolarity. It also poses the question of how medium intensity regional conflict will be managed in the future; by whom, with what means, and on behalf of what ends.

In this regard, three lessons emerge from an evaluation of international engagement in the Balkan conflict. First, there can be no such thing as partial or limited intervention. If the international community is unwilling, or unable, to stand aside and let regional conflicts run their course, it must be prepared to engage for the long haul. Interventions bring responsibility, place the reputations of the intervening parties at stake, and entail complex obligations to friends and allies that cannot be shirked, or frivolously abandoned, without cost. Second, in cases of incipient armed conflict where political means have been exhausted, decisive, preemptive military intervention followed by a serious commitment to peace operations should be the preferred option. Making such determinations, of course, is more easily said than done, but it is a mark of the kind of statecraft that should characterize international leadership. In retrospect it seems clear that unambiguous international admonitions backed by a credible threat of force could have blocked Slovenian and Croatian secession in 1991 and throttled the Serb project at its origins. At the time, however, the international community was not united, the consequences of inattention were not clear, and the path of least resistance—an ultimately futile containment policy—was preferred. Finally, peace operations in complex regional contingencies should if at all possible be multilateral, and ideally sanctioned under the aegis of the UN working through responsible regional organizations. The special military capabilities of the U.S. armed forces will make them a preferred, or in some cases essential component of many such contingencies. This imposes the responsibility of choosing areas for intervention carefully — on the basis of a hard-minded evaluation of national interest as well as humanitarian concerns. The United States should seek to avoid unilateral initiatives — its interests will be best served by coordination with allies and reliance upon established multilateral security forums such as NATO. The sacrifice of autonomy that such reliance entails will be tempered by the fact that few regional contingencies will pose imminent threats to vital national interests, and more than compensated by the wider range of perspectives brought to bear in decisionmaking and the force multiplier effect of coalition operations.

Changes in the international security environment following the terrorist attacks on New York and Washington of September 11, 2001, have impacted upon the Balkan region in contradictory ways. For America, the preoccupations with the former Yugoslavia evident during the 1990s have virtually disappeared. Well before September 11 spokespersons associated with the administration of President George W. Bush had articulated a desire to reduce or eliminate the U.S. military presence in the region, and though opinion within the administration remains divided, an agenda for disengagement is still on the table. The new responsibilities associated with the U.S.-led global War on Terrorism makes the burden of protracted peacekeeping responsibilities ever more difficult to bear. U.S. allies already provide 85 percent of the peacekeepers on the ground in Bosnia, Kosovo, and Macedonia, and that percentage is likely to rise along with the role of Europe as the leading force behind the conflict management effort. At the same time, the ramifications of the War on Terrorism have increased the strategic salience of the corridor linking the eastern Mediterranean, Black Sea, Caucasus, Caspian Sea, and Central Asia. As a partial result Romania and Bulgaria have been accepted a future NATO members, incentive to achieve some kind of compromise solution to the Cyprus problem has been increased, and the already considerable strategic weight of the centrally located Turkish Republic has grown even greater. The recent arrest of al-Qaeda operatives in Bosnia-Herzegovina, and discovery that Bosnia continues to serve as a transit point for international terror organizations, has called attention to the capacity of the region to generate new sources of instability.[122] When Bulgaria and Romania join NATO, the Euro-Atlantic community will have an even stronger motivation to ensure that the region does not once again become a theater of war. Under these circumstances, and given the heavy stake that the United States has accumulated after a decade of engagement, the national interest will best be served by a continued commitment to stand shoulder to shoulder with our allies in order to see current peace support operations through to a successful conclusion.[123]

After years of nearly unabated violence, the peoples of Southeastern Europe confront the monumental task of constructing peace. Military engagement remains an important part of that effort. In Bosnia, Kosovo, and Macedonia, some kind of international constabulary is essential to deter conflict and ensure the kind of safe and secure environment needed in order for peace building efforts to go forward. But there are no military solutions to the region's most pressing problems—these must be addressed in the political, economic, and cultural domains. What has been most sorely lacking, and what the international community can still help to provide, is the vision of a destination or end state—a regional framework capable of promoting development, encouraging reconciliation, and sustaining peace. The Stability Pact program, an expanding EU role, and the new dynamic of regional cooperation are helpful steps in this direction—but solutions will not burst upon the scene overnight. The gradual phasing out of international supervision, promotion of soft border regimes, flexible patterns of association within multinational polities such as Serbia, Bosnia-Herzegovina, and Macedonia that avoid harsh partition schemes, positive association with European institutions and the European idea, and expanded regional cooperation—all initiatives that international instances and local actors are aggressively forwarding—will need be part of the mix. If these goals can be identified, embraced, and effectively pursued, the likelihood that it will eventually be necessary to analyze a fifth Balkan war will be reduced.

ENDNOTES - CHAPTER 7

1. James Gow and Cathie Carmichael, *Slovenia and the Slovenes: A Small State and the New Europe*, Bloomington: Indiana University Press, 2000.

2. See, for example, Krassen Stanchev, "Impacts of Yugoslav War on Bulgaria," *Institute for Market Economics Newsletter*, Vol. 5, Nos. 3-4, March-April 1999, pp. 1-3, 16.

3. Klaus Reinhardt, "KFOR Peacekeeping in Kosovo," *Transatlantic Internationale Politik*, Vol. 2, No. 2, Summer 2001, pp. 47-51.

4. Bruce R. Nardulli, Walter L. Perry, Bruce Pirnie, John Gordon IV, John G. McGinn, *Disjointed War: Military Operations in Kosovo, 1999*, Santa Monica, CA: Rand, 2002, pp. 99-110.

5. Nikolaus Blome, "Als Kfor-Kommandeur hat man wenig zu kommandieren," *Die Welt*, June 19, 2000, p. 8.

6. "Après la guerre, le haro sur les Serbes," *Le Monde*, 11 January 2000. The victimization of Serb, Roma, and Turkish minorities during the months following the war is carefully documented in *The Human Rights Findings of the OSCE Kosovo Verification Mission, Part I, October 1998 to June 1999* and *Part II, June to October 1999*, Warsaw: OSCE Office for Democratic Institutions and Human Rights, 1999.

7. David Rohde, "Kosovo Seething," *Foreign Affairs*, Vol. 79, No. 3, May/June 2000, pp. 65-79.

8. Agence France Press, "Kosovo Albanians Threaten New War if Belgrade Troops Return," *Yugoslavia Today*, October 12, 2000.

9. Frank Cillufo and George Salmoiraghi, "And the Winner is . . . the Albanian Mafia," *The Washington Quarterly*, Vol. 22, No. 4, Autumn 1999, pp. 21-25.

10. "Pobeda Ibrahima Rugove nad Tacijem," *Republika*, No. 248, November 1-15, 2000, pp. 1-2.

11. OSCE statistics accorded Rugova's LDK 46 percent support versus 26 percent for Thaçi's Democratic Party in the November 2001 elections. See *www.osce.org/kosovo/elections*.

12. "Rugova zum Präsidenten Kosovos gewählt," *Neue Zürcher Zeitung*, March 5, 2002.

13. For an evaluation, see Eric Chevallier, "L'ONU au Kosovo: leçons de la première MINUK," *Strategic Institute of the European Union, Occasional Paper No. 35*, Paris: Strategic Institute of the European Union, May 2002.

14. Nils Andersson, "L'Albanie en quête de reconnaissance," *Le Monde diplomatique*, June 2002, pp. 20-21.

15. Alexandros Yannis, "Kosovo Under International Administration," *Survival*, Vol. 43, No. 2, Summer 2001, pp. 31-48.

16. "Promejene u Bosni i Hercegovini," *Republika*, No. 259, April 16-30, 2001,

pp. 1-4.

17. Demining is a relevant example of a "half-completed" task. According to the United Nations Mine Action Centre (UNMAC) there are over 30,000 mined areas in Bosnia-Herzegovina including over 750,000 mines, most of them running parallel to the present Zone of Separation. These mines disrupt agriculture and take an annual toll of lives. Most mine fields were laid in accordance with Yugoslav Peoples' Army doctrine, and therefore recorded and marked, making demining operations easier. The UNMAC and its Regional Mine Action Centers work in coordination with SFOR and the entities to accomplish the tasks of mine lifting and humanitarian demining, but years of effort will be necessary before the operation can be placed entirely into the hands of the entities.

18. Josip Crnoj, ""Dejton pet godina poslije--Sta je ostalo od nade?" *Republika*, No. 270-271, October 1-31, 2001, pp. 1-4.

19. David Chandler, *Bosnia: Faking Democracy After Dayton*, London: Pluto Press, 1999, and Džemal Sokolović and Florian Bieber, eds., *Reconstructing Multiethnic Societies: The Case of Bosnia-Herzegovina*, Aldershot: Ashgate, 2001.

20. Thomas Hofnung, *Désespoirs de paix: L'ex-Yougoslavie de Dayton à la chute de Milosevic*, Anglet: Atlantica, 2001, p. 85.

21. Thomas L. Friedman, "Not Happening," *The New York Times*, January 23, 2001, p. A27.

22. Trends in Bosnia-Herzegovina are tracked in Sumantra Bose, *Bosnia After Dayton: Nationalist Partition and International Intervention*, New York: Oxford University Press, 2002, and Elizabeth M. Cousens and Charles K. Cater, *Toward Peace in Bosnia: Implementing the Dayton Accords*, Boulder: Lynne Reiner, 2001.

23. Peter Finn, "Operation in Yugoslavia Highlights a New Alliance," *The Washington Post*, May 25, 2001, p. A24.

24. Justin L. C. Eldridge, "Kosovo: Land of Uncertainty," *European Security*, Vol. 10, No. 2, Summer 2001, pp. 34-66.

25. Voin Bozhinov and L. Panayatov, eds., *Macedonia: Documents and Materials*, Sofia: Bulgarian Academy of Sciences, 1979.

26. Alessandro Marzo Magno, "Macedonia: L'ultima atto?" in Alessandro Marzo Magno, ed., *La Guerra dei dieci anni. Jugoslavia 1991-2001: I fatti, i personaggi, le ragioni dei conflitti*, Milan: il Saggiatore, 2001, pp. 390-391.

27. Radoslava Stefanova, "Conflict Prevention in Europe: The Case of Macedonia," *The International Spectator*, Vol. 32, Nos. 3-4, July-December 1997, p.

113.

28. Aydin Babuna, "The Albanians of Kosovo and Macedonia: Ethnic Identity Superseding Religion," *Nationalities Papers*, Vol. 28, No. 1, March 2000, pp. 81-82. Friction between communities is vividly depicted in Milcho Manchevski's award winning film *Before the Rain*.

29. Nenad L. F. Stefanović and Perica Vučinić, "Attentat na Kiru Gligorova," *Vreme*, October 9, 1995, pp. 8-12.

30. Cited from *Programme du Mouvement populaire du Kosovo*, Priština, July 2000.

31. Up to 2000 Macedonia was widely held out as a positive example of the peaceful resolution of interethnic tensions. See the report *Macedonia: Prevention Can Work*, Washington, DC: U.S. Institute of Peace, March 27, 2000, and Alice Ackerman, *Making Peace Prevail: Preventing Violent Conflict in Macedonia*, Syracuse, NY: Syracuse University Press, 1999.

32. *Ushtria çlirimtare kombëtare* is the National Liberation Army, or NLA, and *Ushtria çlirimtare e Kosovës* is Kosovo Liberation Army, or KLA.

33. Duncan Perry, "Macedonia: Melting Pot or Meltdown?" *Current History*, Vol. 100, No. 649, November 2001, p. 362. Perry's assertion of the Kosovar origins of the NLA is challenged by Alex J. Bellamy, "The New Wolves at the Door: Conflict in Macedonia," *Civil Wars*, Vol. 5, No. 1, Spring 2002, pp. 117-144, who characterizes the KLA, LAKBM, and NLA as "loose networks of people with different motivations and aims" and emphasizes the need to differentiate between manifestations of the Albanian national movement in diverse local environments. Perry's interpretation is more widely accepted, and Bellamy himself goes on to note: "In many respects, however, the NLA is simply the KLA re-badged." *Ibid.*, pp. 129, 131.

34. Franz Gustincich, "Sui sentieri di una strana guerriglia," *Limes*, No. 2, 2001, pp. 37-50. On the criminal foundations of both KLA and NLA see Robert Hislope, "Organized Crime in a Disorganized State: How Corruption Contributed to Macedonia's Mini-War," *Problems of Post-Communism*, Vol. 49, No. 3, May/June 2002, pp. 33-41. On the origins of the armed conflict in Macedonia, International Crisis Group, "The Macedonian Question: Reform or Rebellion," *ICG Balkan Report No. 109*, April 5, 2001.

35. Jolyon Naegele, "The Tanusevci Story," *Radio Free Europe/Radio Liberty Balkan Report*, March 9, 2001.

36. Francesco Strazzari, "Il triangolo macedone," *Limes*, No. 2, 2001, p. 24, suggests that the absence of confrontation was the result of a behind the scenes

deal between the government and NLA leaders.

37. "Europska unija pozvala Makedoniju da ne proglašava ratno stanje," *Vjesnik-vanjska politika,* May 7, 2001, cited from *www.vjesnik.hr/html/2001/05/ 07Clanak-asp?r=van&c=l.*

38. P. H. Liotta and Cindy R. Jebb, "Macedonia: End of the Beginning or Beginning of the End?" *Parameters,* Vol. 32, No. 1, Spring 2002, p. 102.

39. William Drozdiak, "Secret Deal Threatens Macedonian Coalition," *The Washington Post,* May 25, 2001, p. A24.

40. During July, with fighting in progress around Tetovo, renewed protests against western appeasement of the rebels led to rioting and attacks against the U.S. Embassy and OSCE headquarters in Skopje. John Ward Anderson, "Macedonians Attack U.S. Embassy," *The Washington Post,* July 25, 2001, p. A16.

41. Text in Republic of Macedonia, Agency of Information, Framework Agreement, August 14, 2001, *www.sinf.gov.mk/PressRoomEN/2001/07/n1408.htm.*

42. Ulf Brunnbauer, "The Implementation of the Ohrid Agreement: Ethnic Macedonian Resentments, *Journal on Ethnopolitics and Minority Issues in Europe,* Issue 1, 2002, pp. 1-24.

43. "Nato, Macedonia Reach Accord," *Radio Free Europe, Radio Liberty (RFE/ RL),* September 30. 2001.

44. Laurent Zecchini, "Les Quinze prêts à assumer leur première opération militaire en Macédoine," *Le Monde,* March 18, 2002.

45. Alice Ackermann, "Macedonia in a Post-Peace Agreement Environment: A Role for Conflict Prevention and Reconciliation," *The International Spectator,* Vol. 37, No. 1, January-March 2002, pp. 73-82.

46. "Internationale Finanzhilfe für Mazedonien," *Neue Zürcher Zeitung,* March 13, 2002, reporting on the Donors' Conference in Brussels, organized by the EU and World Bank, where representatives of over 40 state pledged more than 300 million Euros of assistance.

47. "Die Opposition gewinnt die Wahlen in Mazedonien," *Neue Zürcher Zeitung,* September 17, 2002

48. H. Matoshi, "The Albanians' New Model Army," *IWPR Balkan Crisis Report no, 274,* August 24, 2001.

49. "Ein Neubeginn in Mazedonien?" *Neue Zürcher Zeitung,* September 17, 2002.

50. Emilio Cocco and Francesco Strazzari, "La Croazia si riscopre balcanica," *Limes*, No. 5, 2000, p. 77.

51. The opposition was a union of two coalitions. The first combined the two largest groupings, Račan's Social Democrats and the center-right Croatian Social Liberal Party led by Dragiša Budiša, and the second a "quartet" (*četvorka*) of four smaller parties including the Croatian People's Party of Stipe Mesić.

52. Marina Ottaway and Gideon Maltz, "Croatia's Second Transition and the International Community," *Current History*, Vol. 100, No. 649, pp. 375-380.

53. Mladen Schwartz, *Hrvatska nakon Tudjmana: Studija o nacionalnom usudu*, Zagred: Iuvenalis Samizdat, 2000, pp. 419-455.

54. Dragan Bujošević and Ivan Radovanović, 5. *Oktobar: Dvadeset četiri sata prevrata*, 2nd ed., Belgrade: Biblioteka PRESS dokumenti, 2000.

55. Robert Thomas, *The Politics of Serbia in the 1990s*, New York: Columbia University Press, 1999, pp. 285-318, and Mladen Lazić, ed., *'Ajmo, 'ajde, svi u šetnju!*, Belgrade: Medija Centar, 1997.

56. Vojislav Lalić, *Pad*, Belgrade: Zavet, 2001.

57. Damjan de Krnjević, "Serbia's Prudent Revolution," *Journal of Democracy*, Vol. 12, No. 3, 2001, p. 96.

58. Cited in *ibid.*, pp. 96-97.

59. "Gang Accused of Djindjic Killing," BBC News, March 13, 2003, in *http://newsvote.bbc.co.uk/mpapps/pagetools/print/news.bbc.co.uk/2/hi/Europe/2845381.stm*.

60. In June 2002 the anti-Mafia bureau of the prosecution office in the Italian port of Bari announced that Djukanović was under investigation in connection with a cigarette smuggling racket—a gesture that some interpreted as an attempt to undermine him politically in order to reverse the momentum of the movement for secession. Milka Tadic-Mijovic, "Montenegro: Djukanovic Threatened by Alleged Mafia Links," *Institute for War and Peace Reporting*, June 2002.

61. "Institutioneller Neuanfang in Belgrad," *Neue Zürcher Zeitung*, March 15, 2002.

62. See the text of the agreement in "Sporazum o principima," *Glas javnosti*, cited from *www.glas-javnosti.co.yu/danas/srpski/PO2031412.shtml*.

63. Milo Djukanovic, "Balkan Betrayal," *The Washington Post*, August 20, 2002, p. A13.

64. Nikola Ivanović, *Vlasti i država: Crna Gora i Srbija--Nastavak ili kraj fenomena balkanske destrukcije*, Belgrade: Pešić i Sinovi, 2002, especially pp. 277-284, usefully examines the potential for the issue to become a source of future problems, and suggests solutions.

65. "Verschärfte Koalitionskrise in Belgrad: Streit um Kooperation mit Den Haag," *Neue Zürcher Zeitung*, March 11, 2002.

66. Rémy Ourdan, "Milosevic se pose en victime d'un 'crime contre la vérite'," *Le Monde*, February 15, 2002. During the first phase of his trial Milošević was effective in pointing out numerous procedural irregularities and insufficiencies in the evidence presented. His defiant comportment was popular, and the televised proceedings became compulsory viewing throughout Yugoslavia.

67. Philip E. Auerswald and David P. Auerswald, eds., *The Kosovo Conflict: A Diplomatic History through Documents*, Cambridge: Kluwer Law International, 2000, pp. 1111-1123.

68. Cited from *The Stability Pact for South Eastern Europe*, Brussels: SCSP, July 2000, *www.stabilitypact.org*.

69. *The Road to Stability and Prosperity in South Eastern Europe: A Regional Strategy Paper*, The World Bank, Europe and Central Asian Region, March 1, 2000, available in *www.worldbank.org.ba/news/2000/pr-mar00-07.htm*.

70. Benn Steil and Susan Woodward, "A European 'New Deal' for the Balkans," *Foreign Affairs*, Vol. 78, No. 6, November/December 1999, p. 97.

71. This theme appears in the address by Greg Schulte, National Security Council Senior Director for Southeast Europe, "U.S. Strategy for the Balkans," presented at Georgetown University, Washington, DC, March 20, 2002. See also Richard Betts, "The Balkans: How to Get Out," *The National Interest*, No. 64, Summer 2001, pp. 53-65.

72. *Bulletin of the European Communities*, No. 6, 1993, p. 13.

73. Martin A. Smith and Graham Timmins, *Building a Bigger Europe: EU and NATO Enlargement in Comparative Perspective*, Aldershot: Ashgate, 2000, pp. 126-127.

74. Alan Mayhew, *Recreating Europe: The European Union's Policy towards Central and Eastern Europe*, Cambridge: Cambridge University Press, 1998, p. 392.

75. Dimitris Papadimitriou, "The EU's Strategy in the Post-Communist Balkans," *Journal of Southeast European and Black Sea Studies*, Vol. 1, No. 3, September 2001, p. 77.

76. BSEC promotes economic cooperation in the Black Sea area. N. Bülent Gültekin and Ayşe Mumcu, "Black Sea Economic Cooperation," in Vojtech Mastny and R. Craig Nation, eds., *Turkey Between East and West: New Challenges for a Rising Regional Power*, Boulder: Westview Press, 1997, pp. 179-202. The CEI is the successor to the Quadrangulare, founded in 1989 to broaden economic cooperation and political dialogue in Central Europe. *CEI Facing the Challenges and Opportunities of the New Europe, Ideas for a Programme: Policy Paper of the Forlì Conference 2-3 February 2001*, Forlì: Center for East Central European and Balkan Studies, 2001. The SECI is a self-help program that seeks to use the private sector to stimulate economic development. Richard Schifter, "Southeastern Europe in the Post-Milosevic Era: The Need to Lower the Barriers," *Mediterranean Quarterly*, Vol. 13, No. 2, Spring 2002, pp. 27-35. SEECP was launched on the initiative of Bulgaria in 1996 as a forum for regional cooperation with an emphasis upon confidence building, good neighborly relations, and stability. See its 2000 *Charter on Good-Neighborly Relations, Stability, Security and Cooperation in Southeastern Europe* at *www.stabilitypact.org/seecp/charter-02.htlm*.

77. See *Balkan Regional Profile: The Security Situation and Region-Building Evolution of South-Eastern Europe*, Sofia: Institute for Security and International Studies, 2002.

78. Balkan participants include Albania, Bulgaria, Croatia, Greece, Macedonia, Romania, Slovenia, and Turkey. Most countries have earmarked one battalion for the brigade except Macedonia and Albania, who have pledged a company each. An additional battalion has been made available by Italy should circumstances demand. "Southeast European Defence Ministers Promise Stronger Cooperation," *Balkan Times*, December 19, 2001, and "First Real Test for S.E. Brigade," cited from *www.greece.gr/POLITICS/South EastEurope/Sebrigade.stm*.

79. Sean Kay, *NATO and the Future of European Security*, Lanham, MD: Rowman & Littlefield, 1998, pp. 31-32.

80. Karl W. Deutsch, *Political Community and the North Atlantic Area*, Princeton: Princeton University Press, 1957; and John Gerald Ruggie, "Consolidating the European Pillar," *The Washington Quarterly*, Vol. 20, No. 1, Winter 1997, p. 109.

81. John Gerard Ruggie, *Winning the Peace: America and World Order in the New Era*, New York: Columbia University Press, 1996, p. 85.

82. Javier Solana, "A New Alliance for a New Era," *The Brown Journal of World Affairs*, Vol. IV, No. 2, Summer/Fall 1997, pp. 73, 75.

83. NATO Press Release NAC-S(99)65, "The Alliance's Strategic Concept," April 24, 1999.

84. Holger M. Mey, "Germany, NATO and the War in the Former Yugoslavia," *Comparative Strategy*, Vol. 12, No. 2, April-June 1993, pp. 239-245.

85. See Joyce P. Kaufman, *NATO and the Former Yugoslavia: Crisis, Conflict, and the Atlantic Alliance*, Lanham, MDF: Rowman & Littlefield Publishers, Inc., 2002.

86. *South East Europe Common Assessment Paper on Regional Security Challenges and Opportunities (SEECAP)*, Budapest, Hungary, May 2001, available at *www.nato.int/docu/comm/2001/0105-bdp/d010530b.htm*. Albania, Bulgaria, Croatia, Greece, Italy, Macedonia, Romania, Slovenia, Turkey, and the United States were charter members of the SEEI, later joined by Austria, Switzerland, and Yugoslavia.

87. Elizabeth Pond, "Balkan Dreams," *Transatlantic Internationale Politik*, Vol. 3, Fall 2002, pp. 67-70.

88. The war convention is defined here as the wide variety of ways, ranging from the formalities of international law through the evolving norms and conventions of international behavior, in which the international community attempts to constrain the inherent violence of the institution of war.

89. Robert L. Philllips and Duane L. Cady, *Humanitarian Intervention: Just War vs. Pacifism*, Lanham, MD: Rowman & Littlefield Publishers, Inc., 1996.

90. For the concept of humanitarian war, Adam Roberts, "Humanitarian War: Military Intervention and Human Rights," *International Affairs*, Vol. 69, No. 3, July 1993, pp. 429-449.

91. For the argument in classic form, see Hans Kelsen, *Peace through Law*, 2nd ed., New York: Garland Publishing, Inc., 1973. Paul R. Williams and Michael P. Scharf, *Peace With Justice: War Crimes and Accountability in the Former Yugoslavia*, Lanham, MD: Rowman & Littlefield Poublishers, Inc., 2002, apply the argument to the Yugoslav case.

92. Afsané Bassir Pour, "La Cour pénale internationale deviendra une réalité le 11 avril," *Le Monde*, April 4, 2002.

93. Cited in Bruno Simma, "Die NATO, die UN und militärische Gewaltanwendung: Rechtliche Aspekte," in Reinhard Merkel, ed., *Der Kosovo-Krieg und das Völkerrecht*, Frankfurt am Main: Edition Suhrkamp, 2000, p. 20.

94. See Stanley Henig, "Britain: To War for a Just Cause," in Anthony Weymouth and Stanley Henig, eds., *The Kosovo Crisis: The Last American War in Europe?*, London: Reuters, 2001, pp. 39-58. Blair's remarks appear on page 55.

95. Tony Blair, "Speech to the Economic Club of Chicago," April 22, 1999.

96. Jürgen Habermas, "Bestialität und Humanität: Ein Krieg an der Grenze zwischen Recht und Moral," *Die Zeit*, April 29, 1999, p. 4.

97. Robert Tomes, "Operation Allied Force and the Legal Basis for Humanitarian Intervention," *Parameters*, Vol. XXX, No. 1, Spring 2000, pp. 38-50, attempts to make the case for the legality of intervention using a *jus cogens* argument.

98. Hilaire McCoubrey, "Kosovo, NATO and International Law," *International Relations*, Vol. XIV, No. 5, August 1999, pp. 29-46.

99. Boutros Boutros-Ghali, *An Agenda for Peace: Preventive Diplomacy, Peacemaking and Peace-Keeping*, New York: United Nations, 1992.

100. The term genocide appears in the 1986 Memorandum of the Serbian Academy of Sciences, *Nacrt memoranduma Srpske Akademije Nauke u Beogradu*, Toronto: Srpske Narodne Odbrane, 1987, p. 12.

101. These factions (the HDZ, SDS, and SDA) were of course formally engaged in a coalition government prior to Bosnia's descent into war—a government ironically described in the critical Yugoslav press as the "coalition of genocide." "Koalicija genocida," *Borba*, May 27, 1991.

102. Dragan Ogurlić, *Svjedočanstva hrvatskog domovinskog rata '91/92: Dnevnik reportera*, Rijeka: Tiskara Rijeka, 1992, p. 167.

103. The relevance of the term in the Bosnian case is carefully analyzed in Steven L. Burg and Paul S. Shoup, *The War in Bosnia-Herzegovina: Ethnic Conflict and International Intervention*, Armonk, NY: M. E. Sharpe, 1999, pp. 181-185.

104. Milošević indictment cited from *www.guardian.co.yu/article/ o,2763,514441,00.htlm*.

105. Cédrick Allmang, *Les masques de guerre*, Paris: Stock, 1999, p. 47.

106. Tobias K. Vogel, " 'Preponderant Power': NATO and the New Balkans," *International Journal*, Vol. 55, No. 1, Winter 1999-2000, pp. 15-34.

107. Wesley K. Clark, *Waging Modern War: Bosnia, Kosovo, and the Future of Combat*, New York: Public Affairs, 2001, p. 419.

108. Michael Ignatieff, *Virtual War: Kosovo and Beyond*, New York: Metropolitan Books, 2000, p. 111.

109. Nat Hentoff, "Morality at 15,000 Feet," *The Washington Post*, June 19, 1999, p. A19.

110. See the argument in Raju G. C. Thomas, "NATO, the UN, and International Law," *Mediterranean Quarterly*, Vol. 10, No. 3, Summer 1999, pp. 25-50.

111. Ignatieff, *Virtual War*, p. 161.

112. On this "force protection" issue, see also Martin L. Cook, "Immaculate War: Constraints on Humanitarian Intervention," *Ethics and International Affairs*, Vol. 14, 2000, pp. 55-65.

113. Hedley Bull, "Human Rights and World Politics," in Ralph Pettman, ed., *Moral Claims in World Affairs*, London: Croom Helm, 1978, p. 81.

114. Danilo Zolo, *Chi dice umanità: Guerra, diritto e ordine globale*, Turin: Einaudi, 2000, p. 106.

115. Geoffrey Best, *Humanity in Warfare: The Modern History of the International Law of Armed Conflict*, London: Weidenfeld & Nicolson, 1980, p. 44, speaks of an "enlightenment consensus" in this regard.

116. Article 16.2 of the ITFY Statute reads: "The Prosecutor shall act independently as a separate organ of the International Tribunal. He or she shall not seek or receive instructions from any Government or any other source."

117. Cited from John Laughland, "This is Not Justice," *The Guardian*, February 16, 2002.

118. "Excerpts from Milosevic's Address to the Hague Tribunal," *The Guardian*, February 14, 2002.

119. Jolyon Naegele, "The Hague: Court's Legitimacy and Longevity Remains Uncertain," *Radio Free Europe/Radio Liberty (RFE/RL)*, February 15, 2002.

120. Jenny S. Martinez, "Troubles at the Tribunal," *The Washington Post*, July 3, 2001, p. A19.

121. For a comparable characterization of the phenomenon of "new wars" in the age of globalization, see Mary Kaldor, *New and Old Wars: Organized Violence in a Global Era*, Stanford: Stanford University Press, 1999, p. 5.

122. "Nato: Internationale Terrororganisationen in Bosnien," *Neue Zürcher Zeitung*, April 2, 2002.

123. This remains official U.S. policy, articulated to the allies by President George Bush during a visit to U.S. Camp Bondsteel in Kosovo during July 2001 with the phrase, "we came in together and we will leave together." Mike Allen,

"U.S. Role in Balkans 'Essential,' Bush Says," *The Washington Post*, July 25, 2001, pp. A14, A16. See also Steven Metz, *The American Army in the Balkans: Strategic Alternatives and Implications*, Carlisle Barracks: Strategic Studies Institute, January 2001, pp. 31-40.

ABOUT THE AUTHOR

R. CRAIG NATION has been Professor of Strategy and Director of Russian and Eurasian Studies at the U.S. Army War College in Carlisle, PA, since 1996. He specializes in security affairs with a special emphasis upon the European and Eurasian areas. He has taught History and International Relations at Duke University, the University of Southern California, Cornell University, and The Johns Hopkins University School of Advanced International Studies. Professor Nation earned his Ph.D. in Contemporary History from Duke University.

INDEX